Kentucky Treasure Trails

A Historical and Cultural Travel Guide

© Favorite Recipes® Press/Nashville EMS MCMLXXVIII
Post Office Box 77, Nashville, Tennessee 37202
Library of Congress Cataloging in Publication Data

Kentucky Extension Homemakers Association.
 Kentucky treasure trails.

 1. Kentucky--Description and travel--1951- --
Guide-books. I. Title.
F449.3.K46   917.69'04'4   77-28846
ISBN 0-87197-118-6

BOARD OF DIRECTORS 1977-78

OFFICERS:

President
Mrs. Samuel Whitt, Jr.

Vice President
Mrs. James Wallace

Secretary
Mrs. L. C. Yocum

Treasurer
Mrs. Prentice Burgan

Past President
Mrs. Mitchell Bertram

AREA PRESIDENTS:

Purchase
Mrs. Charles B. Jones

Pennyrile
Mrs. William T. Turner

Green River
Mrs. C. W. Scarbrough

Mammoth Cave
Mrs. Wendel Thomerson

Lake Cumberland
Mrs. Roy Garner

Lincoln Trail
Mrs. Sam Davis

Louisville
Mrs. Walter Wilson

Northern Kentucky
Mrs. Richard Gibeau

Fort Harrod
Mrs. Winston Williams

Bluegrass
Mrs. J. K. Powell

Licking River
Mrs. Robert Linville

Northeast
Mrs. J. B. Wright

Quicksand
Mrs. Earl Jury

Wilderness Trail
Mrs. Bonnie Whicker

EDUCATION CHAIRMEN:

Cultural Arts
Mrs. John L. Vickers

Issues & Concerns
Mrs. Harry Holt

Clothing & Textiles
Mrs. John Alexander

Family Life
Mrs. John C. Anggelis

Foods & Nutrition
Mrs. Wendell Roberts

Health
Mrs. Phillip McCandless

Housing & Home Furnishings
Mrs. William Eaton

Management
Mrs. Kenneth Barker

International
Mrs. Bobby Depew

Public Information
Mrs. James T. Brookshire

4-H
Mrs. H. L. Grannis, Jr.

National Extension Homemakers Council Publications Chairman
Mrs. James Rich

National Extension Homemakers Council Southern Regional Director
Mrs. Mitchell Bertram

Kentucky Association of Extension Home Economists
Mrs. William Forbes

Subscriptions (State & National)
Mrs. Mike Henderson

ADVISORS:

Assistant Director of Extension for Home Economics
Dr. Doris A. Tichenor

Program Specialist for Home Economics
Miss Martha Nall

AD HOC COMMITTEE:

Kentucky Treasure Trails
Mrs. Robert B. Foster, Chairman
Mrs. James Thornton
Mrs. Mitchell Bertram

ADVISOR:

Program Specialist for Home Economics
Helen H. Allen

DEDICATION

January, 1977

Dedicated to:

Thirty-one thousand Extension Homemakers —

Who have waited long for this dream of the Homemakers gift to Kentucky culture to materialize —

Who have had a treasured thought in mind and found that hands are strong when linked together and aimed in the same direction —

Who were far-visioned as they played their part with faith, toil, and patience —

Who love Kentucky, their land and their home, and hope to help familiarize each resident and visitor with the treasures in their state —

Who are the heirs of a rich heritage from Kentucky and feel that this book will help present and preserve historical and cultural attractions —

Who are aware that yesterday is gone and that all should be educated to facts reflected in these pages —

Who are willing workers to strengthen our organization and —

Who give credit to the foresightedness of the United States Department of Agriculture and Land Grant Universities in providing for our off-campus college training through the Cooperative Extension Service.

Mrs. Mary Virginia Foster
Kentucky Treasure Trails Chairman

FOREWORD

Kentucky Extension Homemakers Association, Inc. was founded in 1932 and at that time was called the Kentucky Federation of Homemakers. It began with only 29 counties in the state participating, but subsequently has grown to be the largest women's organization in Kentucky — now having a membership of 31,000 homemakers in 118 counties.

Since its inception 45 years ago, the central focus of the association has been to meet the changing needs of the people of the state. And as part of the Cooperative Extension Service, the association continues to fulfill its role as an informational and educational service of the College of Agriculture, University of Kentucky, directed toward "helping people to help themselves."

The impetus for this book, *Kentucky Treasure Trails,* came in 1972 when Epsy Johnson, cultural arts chairman of the National Homemakers Association, suggested that each state association make a record of all the areas of cultural, scenic and historical interest within its boundaries. And so, Kentucky's state cultural arts chairman, with guidance and help from the state advisor and local homemakers groups, compiled a booklet of Kentucky's treasure trails. The booklet, a precursor to this book, was used successfully by county homemaker groups and gained national recognition from the National Extension Homemakers Council.

Still the association members were not satisfied with the small booklet, and decided that a much more detailed book would be more useful. Under the guidance of the 1974-77 state cultural arts chairman, her committee and state advisor, and through the efforts of the area, county and club cultural arts chairmen, the Kentucky Homemakers uncovered even more "hidden treasures," gathered the data and compiled the information into this book. *Kentucky Treasure Trails* is a composite of the contributions of the more than 31,000 members in the state.

With the help of this book, you will be able to travel throughout Kentucky, finding a myriad of interesting and unique places. We invite you to enjoy the scenic and cultural interests first hand and then to share our beautiful state with the people outside our boundaries.

Great appreciation is extended to each and all who contributed to making this book a reality.

Mrs. Mitchell Bertram
President, 1974-1977
Kentucky Extension Homemakers
    Association, Inc.

Executive Mansion

Frankfort, Kentucky 40601

January, 1977

Mrs. Mitchell Bertram, President
Kentucky Extension Homemakers Association
Kenwood Court
Glasgow, Kentucky 42141

Dear Mrs. Bertram,

I would like to offer the Kentucky Extension Homemakers Association sincere congratulations for the dedicated work shown in the publication of Kentucky Treasure Trails. It is sure to become a welcome addition to libraries throughout the Commonwealth.

With a rural background and having been involved with Extension work I can certainly appreciate the worthy contribution that each member makes in each community. This book will give an interesting insight to these communities.

Governor Carroll joins me in extending heartiest congratulations.

Sincerely,

Charlann Carroll

Mrs. Julian M. Carroll

UNIVERSITY OF KENTUCKY | COOPERATIVE EXTENSION SERVICE

LEXINGTON, KENTUCKY 40506

COLLEGE OF AGRICULTURE

RESIDENT INSTRUCTION
AGRICULTURAL EXPERIMENT STATION
COOPERATIVE EXTENSION SERVICE

EXTENSION PROGRAMS

January, 1977

Mrs. Mitchell Bertram
Kentucky Extension Homemakers Association
Kenwood Court
Glasgow, Kentucky 42141

Dear Mrs. Bertram:

Kentucky has a rich and varied heritage of scenic areas, historic landmarks, and man-made features. Many of these are well-known and attract thousands of visitors each year. However, some of the state's most interesting spots are seldom seen and appreciated except by the people who live in the community where they are located.

This book, "Kentucky Treasure Trails," represents an attempt to list and describe selected points of interest in each of our state's one hundred and twenty counties. Homemakers in every county have provided information about their favorite places, enough to fill several books of this size. The editors have worked long and hard to select and condense the material so the book could be reasonably priced and small enough to be easily carried.

I want to commend all of the patient, wonderful people who have worked so hard to make "Kentucky Treasure Trails" a reality. And, I'd like to invite each reader of this book to share one of my family's favorite pastimes — travelling Kentucky's "Treasure Trails," learning and having fun as we explore the places listed.

Sincerely,

Doris A. Tichenor
Assistant Director
for Home Economics

DAT:kmy

The College of Agriculture is an Equal Opportunity Organization authorized to provide research, educational information and other services only to individuals and institutions that function without regard to race, color, sex or national origin

UNIVERSITY OF KENTUCKY, U.S. DEPARTMENT OF AGRICULTURE, AND KENTUCKY COUNTIES, COOPERATING

UNIVERSITY OF KENTUCKY | COOPERATIVE EXTENSION SERVICE

LEXINGTON, KENTUCKY 40506

OFFICE OF THE DEAN AND DIRECTOR

COLLEGE OF AGRICULTURE
RESIDENT INSTRUCTION
AGRICULTURAL EXPERIMENT STATION
COOPERATIVE EXTENSION SERVICE

January, 1977

Mrs. Mitchell Bertram, President
Kentucky Extension Homemakers Association
Kenwood Court
Glasgow, Kentucky 42141

Dear Mrs. Bertram:

The Kentucky Extension Homemakers Association is to be congratulated for preparing and publishing "Kentucky Treasure Trails."

Our Commonwealth has a rich heritage of historical sights, many that are not widely known. As years pass and people move, many of these historical treasures are forgotten and lost.

It is gratifying that the Homemaker Clubs, whose members are most knowledgeable of points of interest in their communities and counties, should undertake the publishing of this information.

Again, let me congratulate the more than 30,000 Kentucky Homemakers for making this significant contribution to all Kentuckians.

Very truly yours,

Charles E. Barnhart

bw

UNIVERSITY OF KENTUCKY, U.S. DEPARTMENT OF AGRICULTURE, AND KENTUCKY COUNTIES, COOPERATING

IN APPRECIATION

This state is filled with kindness, and with people who are led by dreams, people who share their knowledge, people who labor long with willing hands, and people who help enrich lives by doing good deeds.

Many people have watched "Kentucky Treasure Trails" materialize with pride. It is a treasured dream realized through toil and faith. And, for generations to come, we will be able to look back on what is dear and remember the most outstanding events and important places left to us by former Kentuckians. Also, we will recognize the contributions currently being made by modern-day Kentuckians to our cultural heritage.

Now as we enjoy the book, let us remember with gratitude some of the helping hands . . .

The County and Area Cultural Arts Chairmen and the Area Researchers — who travelled along the road searching out the important areas of cultural, historical, and natural beauty in each county. They compiled detailed descriptions and pictures, so that travellers would have a keen desire to see new marvels and scenic views, and so that readers at home could take "rocking-chair tours" through Kentucky.

Mable Bertram — who had a treasured thought in mind, envisioning "Kentucky Treasure Trails" in 1973 as she served as State Cultural Arts Chairman. She sowed the first tender seed, waited with patience and, with the help of *Marcy Stewart,* watched the first small "Kentucky Treasure Trails" grow and mature. It is said that "progress comes through intelligent use of experience," so, as Kentucky State President, Mrs. Bertram supported and encouraged the years of work on the present beautiful "Kentucky Treasure Trails."

Dr. Charles Talbert, Professor of History, University of Kentucky — who gave hours of his valuable time to review the manuscript from the perspective of Kentucky history. Through his generosity in this good deed we know that his is a life worthwhile through serving others. The Extension Homemakers wish him joy in his service.

Dorothy Henderson — who with courage coordinated material collected by the area research workers. As she wove her dreams into a pattern of hope, the manuscript slowly took shape — a product whose future looks bright.

LaVerne Speaks — who assumed the responsibility of helping type the original manuscript. Everyone was rewarded by the efficiency and dependability that she has displayed.

Marion Johnson, Extension Secretary — who typed the manuscript as it developed over a period of years from a small booklet into a travel guide. Miss Johnson worked patiently with the raw data as it was collected by county researchers and then as it was later embellished by area and state committees.

The Kentucky Department of Public Information — who generously gave their time and knowledge in editing the manuscript and in offering accurate information concerning the Commonwealth of Kentucky. Many photographs are included through their courtesy. Our appreciation is particularly extended to Mr. Charles Manning, Publications Editor, and to Ms. Mimi Lewis, Editorial Assistant.

Dr. Charles Barnhart, Dean of the College of Agriculture and Director of Extension — who lends his support to Extension Homemaker projects, who is alert to changes and to all that might be beneficial to Homemakers in Extension.

Dr. Doris Tichenor, Assistant Director of Extension for Home Economics — who stands tall in the Extension Service, leading with wisdom, encouragement, guidance, and support of Kentucky Extension Homemakers Association and especially "Kentucky Treasure Trails."

Kentucky Extension Homemakers Association Board of Directors — who over the past three years counseled and advised the direction of "Kentucky Treasure Trails," giving both monetary and spiritual support.

Helen Allen — who guided the development of "Kentucky Treasure Trails" as advisor, who encouraged the capable workers with consideration and thoughtfulness, and who was always available for service and information. As advisor, she watched and tended the growth of "Kentucky Treasure Trails." The Extension Homemakers will always be grateful to her and wish that fortune's bright smile will shine forever on her.

The Kentucky Historical Society — who generously granted permission to draw information from the Kentucky Historical Highway Marker Program, thus enriching the wealth of history available to readers of "Kentucky Treasure Trails."

The owners of private property — who allowed their property to be listed among the treasures of Kentucky's cultural heritage.

Others — who contributed in any way to "Kentucky Treasure Trails," we wish satisfaction in all ventures.

Mrs. Mary Virginia Foster
Kentucky Treasure Trails Chairman

INTRODUCTION

Kentucky's first trails were cut by prehistoric Indians. Through the centuries that followed, these trails were travelled and added to by their red-skinned descendants, by French and British trappers, and finally, in the 1700's by pioneer settlers dressed in buckskin clothing, carrying axes and long hunting rifles. These hardy explorers were seeking both adventure and a self-sufficient life in "Kah-ten-tah-teh," the Wyandot Indian word for "the land of tomorrow."

To colonists in Maryland, Pennsylvania and Virginia, Kentucky was simply "the land beyond the mountains." It was rumored to be a rich and fertile place, cut through by many rivers and streams, and abundant with game tracked by Indian hunters from many tribes.

Cumberland Gap, in the extreme southeastern corner of Kentucky, became one of the gateways to this land. It was discovered in April, 1750 when a Loyal Land Company scouting party led by Dr. Thomas Walker found and followed an ancient buffalo trail there.

Some of the early explorers and adventurers were Christopher Gist, James Harrod, Daniel Boone and John Finley. The first settlement in Kentucky was called Harrod's Town, and old Fort Harrod is one of the historic places you'll want to visit in Mercer County.

The famous trail that Daniel Boone blazed to the new land became known as the Wilderness Road. Now U.S. Highway 25E, it winds through the Cumberland Gap to the area south of the Kentucky River. Here Boone helped erect the second settlement, called Fort Boonesboro, in Madison County.

The Virginia government first established Kentucky as a county of Virginia. By 1780, the Virginia Assembly subdivided Kentucky County into three counties — Lincoln, Fayette and Jefferson. Statehood came to Kentucky on June 1, 1792, when it became the 15th state of the Union. Isaac Shelby, a Revolutionary War hero, was the first governor. The Commonwealth government was organized in Lexington and was moved to Frankfort the following year.

Kentucky, the oldest state west of the Allegheny Mountains, is often referred to as the Daughter of the East and Mother of the West, and also the link that binds the North and South.

Rich in natural resources — coal, forests, and fertile agricultural soil — Kentucky is also famous for Thoroughbred horses, tobacco, and whiskey, as well as her artists, writers, musicians and fine mountain craftsmen. It is a land of contrasts. Many of its counties seem to be separate little kingdoms — cross the county line and you often find a different vernacular, along with different loyalties, attitudes, and convictions as well as life styles unique to that area.

As you travel Kentucky's treasure trails from county to county, you'll find much that is unique and colorful in its history has been preserved.

Although your car rides smoothly over a modern mountain parkway and you meet today's Kentuckian attuned to an exciting world, you will still get a feeling for the past in your travels.

You'll sense this rich history in a beautifully restored old home, in a slave cabin untouched by the years, in the timeless forest of Lilly Cornett Woods, and in an ancient stone wall built to withstand the ravages of seasons countlessly repeated.

You'll find it at a sorghum-making festival, in a community craft shop, or at a sunlit outdoor fair full of the evidence of skills passed down unchanged from generation to generation.

You'll see it on Court Day in a county-seat as farmers come to mingle with their city cousins at a giant flea market, where a wood-burning stove, a horse print, and a fine old quilt are still sought-after treasures.

You'll recognize it by the old-time fiddle and dulcimer music often in the air, and by the gracious hospitality that is a part of every Kentuckian's proud heritage. You'll relive it in an outdoor drama that repeats with talented intensity a chapter of our state's history.

Welcome!

Mrs. Dorothy Henderson
Extension Homemaker Editor

KENTUCKY

This first brave stride into America . . .

Kentucky was one of the first and most influential settlements in the wilderness west of the original American Colonies, beginning an enterprising history that led the way to the pioneering of the vast and unknown western lands beyond the Mississippi River. In 1774, James Harrod had established the first white settlement here, and two years later, this territory west of Virginia across the Allegheny Mountains was made Kentucke County, Virginia. This first brave stride into America took place a little more than 165 years after Jamestown was founded on the Virginia coast. Considering this, it becomes apparent that the East Coast Colonists needed longer to settle these first few hundred miles into the Kentucky wilderness than the next wave of pioneers needed to cross and tame the United States Territory all the way to California. These first few hundred miles might seem such a small step, but it was actually one of the first and most important steps into America. Since then, Kentucky, along with the entire nation, has enjoyed the benefits accomplished by the people who opened up this land to the future.

By 1780, the Virginia General Assembly had divided the almost indefensable western reaches of the District of Kentucky into Fayette, Jefferson, and Lincoln Counties. Because Virginia was totally involved in defending its coast from British attacks, Kentucky was left virtually alone to defend itself against the brutal Indian attacks that killed 1500 settlers before 1790. Moreover, because it was not self-governing, the people were not allowed to attack their enemy first without permission from the Virginia government. The frustration arising from this situation gave way to the stirrings for statehood, and on June 1, 1792, Kentucky was admitted as the 15th state to the American Union.

By the time Kentucky became a state, it was comprised of nine counties. Historians have long realized that the county unit in Kentucky has always been the hub of existence for its residents. It was the force behind most of their social and economic advances, their important political struggles, as well as the center for the practical and convivial events of their everyday lives. Today, each Kentucky County is a historical unit in its own right, and each deserves to be examined and appreciated singly. Because of each county's spirited individuality, Kentucky as a whole, experiences a full and exciting history of both famous names and nameless brave citizens, thriving cities and forgotten settlements, as well as landmark events and tragic episodes. All Americans can be proud to point to Kentucky's history and say "This is an important part of my heritage, too, and I am glad it is being acknowledged and preserved."

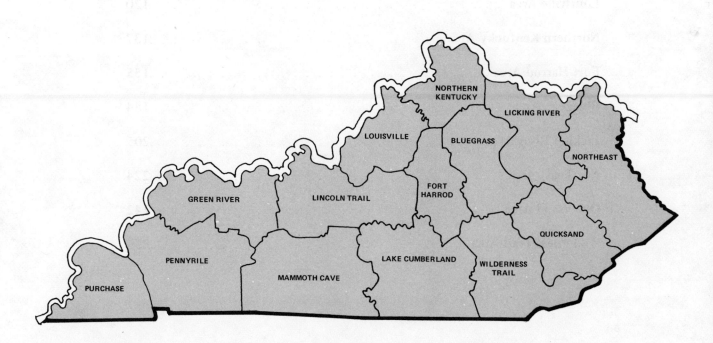

CONTENTS

Purchase Area

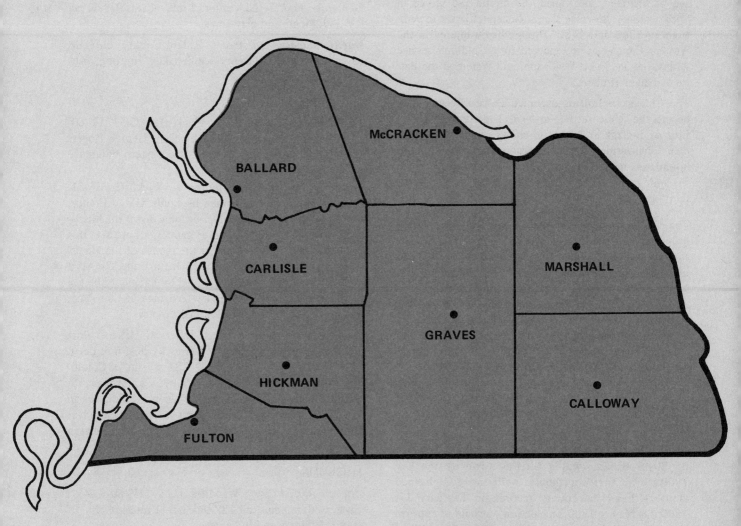

Ballard County

Ballard County was created in 1842, and was the ninety-third county to be established in Kentucky. It was named in honor of Captain Bland Ballard, an early Indian fighter who came to Kentucky in 1779 at the age of eighteen. He joined the militia and served in both Colonel Bowman's and General Clark's expeditions in 1780 and 1782. Though badly injured in the Western Campaign, he rendered future military service with Generals Scott, Wilkinson, and Wayne at the Battle of Fallen Timbers.

The Chickasaw Indians occupied Ballard County long before the white settlers arrived. The Ancient Buried City of Indians in Wickliffe, shows remains of an Indian civilization. The Mississippi and Ohio River boundaries made Ballard County a natural pathway for the Indians, as they used this route between villages for hunting and battlegrounds.

The first settlement in western Kentucky was established by General George Rogers Clark at Fort Jefferson, on the Mississippi River, one mile south of Wickliffe. The fort was erected in 1780 to protect the western boundary claims of the young United States. At this time, the area was still claimed by Virginia. The Indians laid seige to the fort within a few days after its establishment and reduced the settlers to starvation. General Clark came with provisions and reinforcements, but to no avail. The fort was soon abandoned for lack of men and supplies. During the Civil War, Fort Jefferson was occupied by Union forces under General Ulysses S. Grant. From this fort, the attack on Columbus was directed.

Blandville, the first county seat, also named in honor of Bland Ballard, was a thriving town by the late 1800's. The first courthouse, built in 1844, burned along with all the county records on February 17, 1880. On May 6, 1880, an election was held to approve the change of the county seat from Blandville to Wickliffe. Due to the continuous flooding of Mayfield Creek, most of the land was under water several months of the year, which prevented the residents of south Ballard County from getting to Blandville when

necessary. As a result, the southern part of Ballard County became Carlisle County in 1886.

PARKS, RECREATION, LAKES

La Center Park — La Center. 1 mi. N. off US-60 on KY-358. Picnic and play areas.

Wildlife Management Area — Ballard County, on Ohio River. Off US-60. Twenty scenic lakes. Hunting, fishing, and camping.

MARKERS

Fort Jefferson — 1 mi. S. of Wickliffe. US-51, US-60, US-62. Erected here in 1780 by Gen. George Rogers Clark to protect claim of U.S. to a western boundary on the Mississippi River.

Prince of the French Explorers — Wickliffe. US-51, US-60, US-62. Commissioned by Louis XIV of France, the Sieur Robert de LaSalle, sweeping down the Mississippi River with his flotilla of canoes, stopped at this point in 1682 in his quest for the mouth of the Mississippi, and an outlet for the French fur trade. On April 9, 1682, this river was proclaimed by LaSalle to be the northern watershed of the New Province of Louisiana, then a part of the French Colonial Empire.

Union Supply Base — Fort Jefferson. US-51. Fort Jefferson was one of the first Kentucky positions occupied by Union troops after the CSA seizure of Columbus in Sept. 1861. From this base, Gen. Ulysses S. Grant directed a demonstration against Columbus in Jan. 1862. One of 4 river ports in the area used as Union supply bases for operations in the western theater.

MUSEUMS

Ancient Buried City — Wickliffe. US-51, US-60, US-62. Excavated remains of 1,000-year old ancient city of mound builders and Indian relics.

OLD BUILDINGS

The Barlow Home — Barlow. US-60. Built 1903. Excellent condition. In the past, it was the Barlow Hotel.

Hinkle Lane Home — 1 mi. W. of Kevil. US-60. Built about 1840. Has a ballroom on second floor. One stairway went up from the bedrooms below to the front of the house, and was designated for use by the daughters of the family and their guests. The second stairway went up from the back porch to the boys' quarters. A solid partition separated the 2 areas.

The Lovelace Home — Lovelaceville. US-62. Constructed 1860-1862. In 1820, the town was named for Elias Lovelace, grandfather of Andrew Lovelace, Jr., builder of this house. Bricks were made on the site by slaves. The house was designed with a fireplace in every room. During the Civil War, CSA troops were fed by Mrs. Lovelace as they passed through. Accessible to the public.

Old Sullivan Home — About 5 mi. E. of Wickliffe. Off KY-286. Built about 1840 by slave labor. Now privately owned.

OTHER POINTS OF INTEREST

Big Tree — Jct. US-51, US-60. A truck driver from Poplar Bluff purchased a surrounding 50-ft. lot and the Big Tree, presumably to preserve this Big Tree. At 15 ft. in circumference, the Big Tree has a 150-ft. limb, the longest in this area.

Goose Haven — 1 mi. N. of Oscar. Off KY-405. Winter home of the Canadian Goose.

Westvaco at Wickliffe — Westvaco Corp.'s pulp and paper manufacturing complex on the Mississippi River at Wickliffe, is the largest industry in the 4-river counties in western Kentucky. Employs 450 persons, and produces 350 tons daily of fine, white paper for uncoated offset printing, envelope converting, and book publication markets. The facility represents the latest technology in pulp and paper manufacturing. An additional 250 tons of flash-dried market pulp is also produced daily at the plant. It has been in operation since 1970.

Fort Jefferson near Wickliffe.

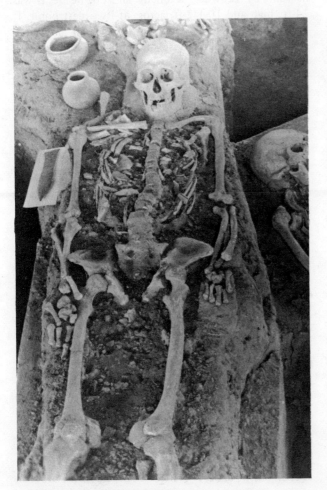

Ancient Buried City near Wickliffe.

Courthouse in Wickliffe.

17

Calloway County

Calloway County was the seventy-second county in order of formation in Kentucky; its land was carved from Hickman County in 1822. It was named in honor of Colonel Richard Calloway, who came to Kentucky with Daniel Boone in 1776. He was one of the founders of Boonesborough and in October 1779, was granted the first ferry franchise to cross the Kentucky River at Boonesborough. The ferry business in Kentucky is older than the state itself. In 1777, Colonel Calloway was appointed Colonel of the Militia, Justice of the Peace, and representative of Kentucky County in the General Assembly of Virginia. He was a true defender of the frontier, and was killed by Indians at Boonesborough in 1780.

In 1823, the first public building to be erected in the Jackson Purchase area was the courthouse in Wadesboro, which was the county seat of Calloway County from 1822-1842. It was a log building built for $100, and was used until a new courthouse was built in 1831. In 1843, Murray became the county seat of Calloway County and the original log building was moved to Murray State University Campus. It has been used as a residence for over a century.

Calloway County has long been an educational center of Western Kentucky with the establishment of Murray Institute before 1870. Later, it became Murray State College, and is now Murray State University.

FAIRS AND DRAMA

Calloway County Fair — Murray. KY-121. July.

Campus Lights, College Musical — Murray State University, Lovett Auditorium. Material presented is written and produced by students. Second week in February.

PARKS, RECREATION AND LAKES

Murray-Calloway County Park — Murray, N. 10th St. Original courthouse of Calloway County.

Governor's Cup Regatta — Kenlake State Resort Park. KY-94. Weekend preceding Memorial Day.

Watkins Cup Regatta — Kenlake State Resort Park. KY-94. Sailing. October.

MARKERS

Fort Heiman — Near state line. Due E. of Kentucky Lake, Fort Heiman Rd. KY-121. CSA fort erected in 1861. Federals occupied it in 1862. Seized by CSA Gen. Forrest in fall of 1864.

Gerard Furnace — Mt. Carmel Church. KY-121. Built in 1854 by Browder, Kennedy and Co. Inside, it was 24-ft. high and 10 1/2-ft. across at its widest point. It burned locally-made charcoal fuel. Its air blast machinery was powered by steam. In 34 weeks in 1857, it produced 1,595 tons of pig iron, mostly shipped by

Stubblefield home site in Murray.

18

steamboat on the Tennessee River. Did not operate after 1858.

MEMORIALS AND MUSEUMS

Confederate Monument – Murray, Courthouse Square. Honors Robert E. Lee.

Jesse Stuart Museum – Murray State University Library, Library Annex. Noted Kentucky author of *The Beatinest Boy,* 1953 and others.

Stubblefield Monument – Murray State University, N. 16th St. Nathan B. Stubblefield was born near here in 1860. He invented the radio at Murray in 1892.

CEMETERIES

Bowman Cemetery – Murray. KY-641. Grave of Nathan B. Stubblefield, inventor of radio.

OLD BUILDINGS

Hamlin House – W. of Murray. KY-280. Built about 1845 by Peter Hamlin of Virginia. Brick fired on grounds by slaves. Woodwork brought from Virginia.

Wrather Hall – Murray State University. First building on campus. Listed in National Register of Historic Places.

Town square in Murray.

OTHER POINTS OF INTEREST

The Jesse Stuart Room – Murray State University Library. This room is dedicated to the preservation and study of the life and works of Jesse Stuart, Kentucky's most versatile contemporary author. Almost all of the material in the collection has been presented to the University Library on a long-term loan by Mr. Stuart. The collection contains first American editions of all his works, American and British reprints, and translation of his works into Swedish, Danish, Spanish, and German. It contains the original manuscripts, typescripts, and galley proofs of almost all his books, as well as typescripts of many of his articles, short stories, and poems.

 # *Carlisle County*

Carlisle County is the sixteenth smallest county in the state and it was the last of the eight counties set up in the Jackson Purchase. Carved from Ballard County in May of 1886, it was the one hundred nineteenth county in order of formation in Kentucky. It was named for John Griffin Carlisle of Kenton County, who was prominent in public affairs of Kentucky, as well as the nation.

Bardwell, the county seat, is near the center of the county. It traces its beginning to the coming of the Illinois Central Railroad in the 1870's. The handsome colonial courthouse, the county's first and only courthouse, was built in 1887 and has recently been remodeled. Milburn, a small village of 150 residents, was one of Carlisle County's first communities.

Carlisle County is situated where Kentucky tapers off to its western point and borders on the Mississippi River. Hilly uplands and wide bottom lands make up its 196 square miles. Unlike its neighboring counties, Carlisle has no Mississippi River port of consequence, but in river-shipping days, it depended on the port in Columbus in Hickman County for its river trade. Carlisle County has an abundance of oxbow lakes and sloughs suitable for wildlife. Originally, the county was the hunting grounds for the Chickasaw Indians.

PARKS AND LAKES

Fish Lake — Burkley. Off KY-123. Fishing and campground sites.

Number 4 Lake — Burkley, past Fish Lake. KY-123. Fishing.

Indian Camp Lake — Burkley. Off KY-123. Fishing, open to public.

Veteran's Park — Near Cunningham. US-62.

MARKERS

Demonstration, 1862 — Bardwell. US-51, US-62. In Jan. 1862, Brig. Gen. Ulysses Grant sent 5,000 USA troops from Cairo, Illinois as a demonstration against the town of Columbus, then a CSA stronghold on the Mississippi River. Grant's forces combined forces with those led by Gen. J. S. McClernand from Ft. Jefferson, and marched through Bardwell to Milburn and back to Cairo. This march acquainted the USA forces with the area and "inspired hope" among many loyal Federal citizens.

OLD BUILDINGS

Elementary School — Milburn. Built 1869. Originally

Main Street in Milburn.

used as college for girls and was run by the Methodist Church. Now privately owned.

George Stone House — Milburn. KY-80. Oldest building in Milburn.

OTHER POINTS OF INTEREST

Adam's Trestle — W. of Bardwell. Off US-51. A man was buried standing up and facing west, with a rifle in one hand and a jug of whiskey in the other.

George Rogers Clark Trace — This trail runs through Carlisle County at Burkley, then to Wickliffe, Kentucky.

Clay Mines — Between Kirbyton and Milburn. W. off KY-307.

Courthouse in Bardwell.

Fulton County

Fulton County, formed in 1845, was the ninety-ninth county to be created in Kentucky. It was named in honor of Robert Fulton of Pennsylvania and New York, who perfected the steamboat. In 1819, James Mills received a military grant and settled in what was then called Mill's Point, but the name was changed to Hickman twenty years later.

Hickman, the county seat, is situated on a series of five bluffs overlooking the Mississippi River. This scenic view of the river was described by Mark Twain as the most beautiful sight along the river. At first, Hickman was a busy trade center because of the river traffic. Later, at the other end of the county, Fulton grew as the railroads developed its commercial opportunities.

Fulton County features an unusual area of land called the New Madrid Bend. The Bend is an isolated peninsula bound on three sides by the Mississippi River and on the south by Tennessee; it is completely cut off from Kentucky. Here, the Mississippi River makes its sharpest bend, and this is the only point where the river flows northward. The largest cottonwood tree east of the Mississippi River grows here, as well.

The early settlers of Fulton County arrived in covered wagons and flatboats. For years, wagons and horseback remained their only means of transportation until the stagecoach came into the area. Residents of Hickman depended on riverboats, also.

Cayce is a small community located between Hickman and Fulton. John Luther "Casey" Jones, the famous railroad man, lived here and received his nickname from the city. A monument now stands in Cayce dedicated to this historical figure.

FAIRS AND FESTIVALS

Fulton County Fair – Hickman. KY-94. July.

International Banana Festival – Fulton, Lake St. Authentic South American foods and international activities. August.

PARKS

Fulton City Park – Fulton. US-45 E. Bypass. Recreation area with tennis courts, ball park, picnic tables and playground.

Country-style living in the Old South.

Civil War battle in Hickman.

MARKERS

Civil War, Kentucky Invasion – Entering Hickman. KY-125. On Sept. 4, 1861, CSA troops invaded Hickman, ending the city's neutrality.

Yellow Fever Epidemic – Hickman Cemetery. KY-94. From Aug. to Nov. of 1878, there were 462 cases of this dread disease, and 150 deaths. Dr. Luke P. Blackburn, Governor of Kentucky, along with local and visiting doctors, rendered heroic services.

New Madrid Earthquake — Near Miller. KY-94. The greatest earthquake recorded in North America was centered in this area on Dec. 16, 1811 to Feb. 7, 1812. Earthquakes were felt at Louisville, 250 miles away, and tremors were felt at Boston, Detroit, and New Orleans. The 25,000-acre Reelfoot Lake was formed as a result of this earthquake. New Madrid, Missouri was destroyed.

Pioneer Spirit — Near Fulton, State Line Road, at Fulton-Graves County line. Nearby grave of Lucy Flournoy Roberts, believed to be the first woman of French Huguenot lineage to come to this area. Her husband and 25 dependents are also buried here. She was a descendant of one of the founders in this area.

Railroad Wrecked, 1862 — Jordan. KY-166, KY-239. Brig. Gen. Nathan B. Forrest's troops took Union City, Tennessee, then moved through here into Kentucky. They wrecked rails, bridges and trestles heading north to Moscow on Dec. 24-25, 1862. This prevented use of rails between Columbus, Kentucky and Jackson, Tennessee until after the war. Union forces had to ship supplies by river, which seriously delayed Gen. Grant's Vicksburg campaign.

MEMORIALS

Casey Jones Monument — Cayce. KY-94. Home of "Casey" Jones, famed railroad engineer. He received his nickname from the town of Cayce, Kentucky.

CEMETERIES

Hickman Cemetery — Hickman. KY-125. Yellow fever epidemic from Aug. to Nov. of 1878. There were 462 cases and 150 deaths.

OLD BUILDINGS

Carnegie Library — Hickman. KY-94. One of 4 original Carnegie structures left in the State.

Fulton County Courthouse — Hickman. Built in 1903 in grandiose style. Antique chiming clock operates on one of the towers, one of few of this type still in use.

Sowell Home — Near Hickman. KY-94. Beautiful country home built in 1890.

Wright House — Near Fulton, W. State Line Rd. Built in 1955 with the entrance, shutters, posts, gingerbread and inside louvres from Fulton's oldest home, built around 1865 by Dr. Gideon Paschall.

OTHER POINTS OF INTEREST

Cotton Gin and Cotton Fields — Hickman, KY-94. Last operating in Kentucky. Fulton County is the only county in Kentucky where cotton has typically been a major farm product, and is still produced today.

Largest Cottonwood Tree East of the Mississippi — New Madrid Bend. KY-94 into Tennessée. Take TN-22 to New Madrid Bend.

Hickman Ferry — Hickman, KY-94. Operates on the Mississippi River from Hickman, Kentucky to Missouri.

Hickman Harbor — Hickman. KY-94. Scenic spot along the Mississippi River.

New Madrid Bend — Hickman. Take KY-94 into Tennessee, then take TN-22 to the Bend. New Madrid Bend is an isolated peninsula bound on 3 sides by the Mississippi River, and at no point is it attached to the State of Kentucky.

Graves County

Graves County was formed in 1823, from part of the original Jackson Purchase Area of Hickman County. The seventy-fifth county in order of formation in Kentucky, it was named for the military hero and statesman, Major Benjamin Franklin Graves. Graves was a Virginian who came to Kentucky, served in the War of 1812 and was killed at the Battle of River Raisin. Graves County is also the birthplace of the late Senator and United States Vice President Alben Barkley.

Graves County's 560 square miles make it the eighth largest of Kentucky's 120 counties. It is also unique in its shape, as it is the only county in the state framed by four straight lines, forming a perfect rectangle.

Mayfield, the county seat, is noted for its large tobacco market, menswear manufacturing outlets, and for supplying ceramic clay worldwide.

FAIRS, FESTIVALS

Purchase District Fair — Mayfield. KY-121. July.

Marching Band Festival — Mayfield. KY-121. Memorial Football Stadium.

Mule Day — Mayfield, N. 17th St. February.

MARKERS

Camp Beauregard — SW of Mayfield. US-45. On a hill 1 mi. E. of this point stood Camp Beauregard, a training base for CSA troops from 6 states during 1861-1862. Severe epidemics caused high mortality rate here.

Two Successful Raids — Mayfield. US-45, KY-80, KY-116, KY-129. CSA Gen. Nathan B. Forrest, with his main body of cavalry, passed through Mayfield to and from a destructive raid on Paducah, March 25, 1864. Gen. Abraham Buford's division camped here. Kentucky regiments were given leave to visit homes to enlist recruits; all returned. Forrest sent Buford from Tennessee through here again on April 14 to capture horses.

MEMORIALS

Woolridge Monument — Mayfield, Lochridge St. Mayfield Cemetery.

Woolridge Monuments near Mayfield.

General Tire Company near Mayfield.

CEMETERIES

Beech Grove Cemetery — Near Tri-City, Swan Rd., at Presbyterian Church. 125-year old tombs.

Cuba Church of Christ Cemetery — Cuba. Harv Taylor, Civil War veteran, is buried here.

Morris Cemetery — Bell City. KY-97. Unusual crypt at roadside.

Pleasant Hill Cemetery — Water Valley. Off US-45, KY-94. Grave of Capt. David Dobbins, Revolutionary War Soldier.

Sims and Shelton Graveyard — Between Sedalia and Lynville. Off KY-381. Public cemetery. Slaves of families buried in one corner.

Wheeler Cemetery — Between Bell City and Boydsville, on Bell City-Boydsville Rd. Graves of Jetton and Wheeler, Civil War veterans.

OLD BUILDINGS

Birthplace of Alben W. Barkley — Wheel, S.W. of Lowes, 3 to 4 mi. off KY-849. Alben W. Barkley, U. S. Senator and Vice President was born near here, Nov. 24, 1877. Now privately owned.

OTHER POINTS OF INTEREST

Mid-Continent Baptist Bible College — Mayfield. Established 1949 in Hickman County. Moved to Mayfield in 1957 to a basement building bought from Christ Methodist Church. New campus now being built N. of Mayfield on US-45.

Ceramic Clay — 5 mi. N. of Mayfield. US-45. Ball clay is an important natural resource. Products are made from clay then shipped throughout U. S. and the world. Operation began in 1891.

Tobacco Market — Mayfield, N. 13th St. One of 2 markets in the world selling 3 types of tobacco: burley, air-cured and dark-fired.

Hickman County

Hickman County is one of the four Kentucky counties bordering on the Mississippi River. Originally, it comprised the entire Jackson Purchase area in Kentucky, a territory from which eight Kentucky counties have since been formed. It was the seventy-first county to be established in the State, and in 1821 was carved out of Caldwell and Livingston Counties. Hickman County was named in honor of Captain Paschal Hickman, a native Virginian who emigrated with his parents to Franklin County, Kentucky in 1785. Captain Hickman was one of the massacre victims of The Battle of River Raisin in the War of 1812.

Hickman County records date back to 1822. Major Andrew Jackson, later United States President, signed one of the first papers recorded in the County Clerk's office. The county seat at the time of formation was Columbus, Kentucky, and the first court was held there at the old blockhouse in 1802. In 1829, the county seat was moved to Clinton. A brick courthouse was built in 1832, and sessions were held in this courthouse until 1883, when the present courthouse building was erected.

FAIRS

Hickman County Fair — Clinton, 2 mi. N. of the Fairgrounds. US-51. August.

PARKS

Columbus-Belmont Battlefield State Park — Columbus. KY-58. Columbus was known during the Civil War as the "Gibralter of the West," as it was the key to the lower Mississippi River defense.

MARKERS

Clinton Seminary — Clinton, Courthouse lawn. This was the first high school in Kentucky west of Tennessee River, established in 1846. The frame structure burned in 1854. In 1850, Clinton Female Seminary was incorporated. Organized as Clinton Academy since charter made no mention of only women students. Professor G. W. Ray was early educational leader in Hickman County. Clinton was known as "the Athens of west Kentucky."

Columbus — Columbus. KY-58. First town in Kentucky to be moved entirely from one site to another. In 1927, after the most severe flood in its history, Columbus was moved from the banks of the Mississippi River to this bluff 200 feet above the river. The relocation was under the supervision of Marion Rust, National Red Cross representative.

"Gibraltar of the West" — Columbus. KY-58, KY-80, KY-123. Troops under Gen. Leonidas Polk fortified a strategic line of bluffs here, Sept. 3, 1861, marking the first CSA move into Kentucky. To prevent passage of Union gunboats, a huge chain was stretched across the Mississippi River. After Union success in Tennessee, CSA forces evacuated on March 2, 1862. Union troops moved in the next day and held their position throughout the war.

Iron Banks — Columbus. KY-58, KY-80, KY-123. So named by early French explorers. Columbus was proposed as the Nation's Capital after the War of 1812. The area was fortified by CSA forces during the Civil War.

MUSEUMS

Civil War Museum — Columbus-Belmont Battlefield State Park. A home which was turned into a CSA hospital is located in the park and is now used as a museum to house Civil War relics, as well as Indian relics found in this area.

Gibraltar of the West at Columbus.

Civil War museum in Columbus.

Marvin College in Clinton.

CEMETERIES

Columbus Cemetery – Columbus. KY-58.
Clinton Cemetery – Clinton. KY-58.

OLD BUILDINGS

Marvin College – Clinton. US-51. Alma Mater of U. S. Vice President Alben W. Barkley. A Methodist school, built 1884-1885, originally stood on this site. It operated until 1922 when it closed because of free public schools. Alben W. Barkley, later to become Congressman, Senator and U. S. Vice President, worked his way through school by doing janitorial work, giving rise to

the phrase, "Barkley swept here." One building remains. Now privately owned.

Courthouse – Clinton. When Hickman County was first established, court business was transacted in the private residence of William Tipton, near the Columbus Ferry landing, for more than 2 years. In Feb. 1822, the magistrates met and set up a permanent county organization. In 1829, the first courthouse, a log structure, was erected on the public square in Clinton. In 1832, a large brick building was constructed. A new brick building was built on the same site in 1884-1885 and still serves as the Hickman County courthouse.

Marshall County

Marshall County, the ninety-second county in order of formation in Kentucky, dates back to 1842. It was named in honor of John Marshall, United States Supreme Court Chief Justice, and "principal founder of the judicial review, and of the American system of constitutional law." The first settlement of Marshall County was established by James Stewart on Wade's Creek in 1818, soon after the Jackson Purchase territory was acquired from the Chickasaw Indians. The first church west of the Tennessee River in Kentucky was a Baptist congregation, started by the Rev. H. Darnall in 1819 on Soldier's Creek, in Marshall County.

Benton, the county seat, is located on The Purchase Parkway. Marshall County economy depended on agri-

culture until recently, when Kentucky and Barkley Dams were constructed. Referred to as the "heart of America's vacation wonderland," Marshall County offers any number of outdoor sports activities from spring to autumn.

FAIRS, FESTIVALS, DRAMAS

Arts Crafts – Hardin. US-641. August.

Benton Tater Day – Benton, Main St. Since 1843, only known event honoring the sweet potato. First Monday in April.

Big Singing Day Festival – Benton, at Courthouse. US-641. Since 1884. Fourth Sunday in May.

Kentucky Dam located near Gilbertsville.

Septemberfest — Gilbertsville. US-641. Kentucky Dam Village State Park. Annual square and round dancing festival. September.

Kenlake Amphitheater — Murray. KY-94. Dramas and musicals. June to September.

PARKS, RECREATION, LAKES, DAMS

Governor's Cup Regatta — Kenlake. Sailboats. May.

Kaintuck Territory — Benton. US-641. Complete 1880's town, featuring train and boat rides, a variety of shows, historical exhibits, and enactment of "Zebediah Jones."

Kenlake State Park — Aurora. US-68, KY-80.

Kentucky Dam — Gilbertsville. US-62, US-641. Spans the Tennessee River and is 208 ft. high and 8,422 ft. wide.

Kentucky Dam Village State Resort Park — Gilbertsville. US-641. Every kind of facility is available at this park.

Marshall County Fishing Derby — Kentucky Lake. Oldest continuous fishing derby in the U. S. Each week is a separate derby with weekly prizes. Grand prizes are awarded at the end of the derby.

MARKERS

Civil War Action — Benton. US-641. On March 23, 1864, two days before the Battle of Paducah, detached forces of CSA Gen. Nathan B. Forrest's Cavalry and Union forces, both searching for horses, met here by accident. Two skirmishes took place; 3 men were killed in the first, and 4 in the second.

OLD BUILDINGS

Luther Draffen's Home, "Oak Hill" — Calvert City, 26 Aspen St. Built 1860, by Potilla Calvert, for whom Calvert City was named. He gave land to a railroad company so that the railroad might run by his home. Also made provisions for food and shelter for early settlers. Calvert was one of the founders of Calvert City's First Baptist Church, and "Oak Hill" was the first building in Calvert City.

OTHER POINTS OF INTEREST

Hitching Post, or Old Country Store — Aurora. US-68. Reconstructed log house displaying gifts and souvenirs. Also old country store, wagon shed, blacksmith shop and moonshine still.

McCracken County

McCracken County received its name from Captain Virgil McCracken of Woodford County, who was killed at the River Raisin Massacre on January 22, 1813. Wilmington was selected as the first county seat in 1824, but it was moved to Paducah in 1832. Paducah, the sixth largest city in Kentucky, has the unique claim of being the only city in Kentucky named for an Indian Chief, Paduke. His tribe owned the land now known as "The Jackson Purchase" or "The Purchase."

Thirty-seven thousand acres of land in McCracken County were given to General George Rogers Clark from the State of Virginia in 1795. This territory was later purchased by General Clark's brother-in-law, George Woolfolk, so that General Clark could pay his debts. Years later, General Clark purchased the land back from Woolfolk for $5.00. In May of 1827 William Clark, the brother of General Clark, mapped out a town on this site which he called Paducah. Records show that an earlier settlement was built in 1821. The first house was made of round logs and built at the foot of what is now Broadway Street in Paducah.

During the Civil War, Paducah was taken by General Ulysses S. Grant. Fort Anderson was then built here and became the base from which Grant sent troops to conquer Fort Henry and Fort Donelson on the Tennessee and Cumberland Rivers in Tennessee. This was the beginning of Grant's famous Mississippi Valley campaign which split the Confederacy and led to its defeat.

Because it is located at the confluence of the Ohio and Tennessee Rivers, Paducah has an early history as a "steamboat city." These two rivers nourished Paducah and brought the city much prosperity, as well as some disaster. The railroad also played an important role in the prosperity of Paducah. The Illinois Central Railroad Shops, once located here, were the largest in the world.

FESTIVALS

Summer Festival — Paducah. All over town. Concert on riverfront at Broadway St. August.

PARKS AND RECREATION

Barkley Park — Paducah, foot of Madison St. Named for Alben W. Barkley, former McCracken County attorney and judge, member of Congress, Senate leader, and U. S. Vice President.

Bob Noble Park — Paducah, Park and Thompson Avenues. City's largest recreation park.

Land-Between-the-Lakes — US-641, US-62. 170,000 acres of outdoor recreation. A long, narrow peninsula between 2 large man-made lakes.

MARKERS

Fort Anderson — Paducah, 4th and Park Sts. Built in 1861 by Gen. Charles F. Smith. Union fortification manned by 5,000 troops at start of Grant's Mississippi Valley campaign.

MEMORIALS AND MUSEUMS

Alben W. Barkley Monument — Paducah, 28th and Jefferson Sts. Barkley was known as the "Veep."

Alben W. Barkley Museum — Paducah, 6th and Madison Sts.

Iron Horse Memorial — Paducah, end of 4th St. at Barkley Park. A Mikado-type steam locomotive, "The Big Steamer," is dedicated to Illinois Central men and women, past and present, and to the importance of the railroad to Paducah's history and commerce.

Chief Paduke Statue — Paducah, 19th and Jefferson Sts. Chief of the subtribe of Chickasaw Indians, for whom the city of Paducah is named.

Gen. Lloyd Tilghman Statue — Paducah, Fountain Ave., Long Park. Construction engineer on the first railroad into Paducah. He was a Civil War Capt. in the Kentucky Guards and fought in invasions of Columbus and Hickman. Captured in The Battle of Fort Henry and killed in the defense of Vicksburg, Mississippi.

Chief Paduke Statue in Paducah.

CEMETERIES

Oak Grove Cemetery — Paducah, 16th and Park. Grave of Irvin S. Cobb, journalist, humorist and author. The grave site is by a granite boulder in a grove of dogwood trees 500 feet inside of the main entrance. Before his death, he requested that his body be cremated.

Mount Kenton Cemetery — 5 mi. from downtown Paducah, near Lone Oak. US-45. Grave of Alben W. Barkley.

OLD BUILDINGS

The Angles — Paducah, 2722 Kentucky Ave. Built 1959. Home of former U. S. Vice President Alben W. Barkley. Greek design. Now privately owned.

Broadway United Methodist Church — Paducah's oldest institution. Organized in 1832 and built on present site in 1895.

Birthplace of Irvin S. Cobb — 321 S. 3rd St. Cobb was known as the "Duke of Paducah." Two-story frame house. Razed 1914. New Post Office being built on the site.

First Christian Church — Paducah, Alben Barkley Drive. Organized 1849. Moved to building of Swedish Colonial design in 1965.

First Baptist Church — Paducah. First located at 300 Broadway, then moved to 5th and Jefferson in 1860. Constituted 1840. Used as a military hospital for Union forces during the Civil War. New church dedicated in 1965.

First Presbyterian Church — Paducah, near Jefferson and 7th. Organized 1842. Present Oxford Gothic Structure dedicated in 1933.

Grace Episcopal Church — Paducah, on Broadway near 9th St. One of city's oldest landmarks. Founded 1838, and moved to first building, 1846. This building and the second building were made in Louisville and moved to Paducah by flatboat. Present building is of early Gothic design.

The Market House — Paducah, 2nd and Broadway. Built on land given to the city by Gen. William Clark, brother of George Rogers Clark. Formerly used as a market site for farmers. Occupied now by a museum, art guild and theater group.

St. Matthew's Lutheran Church — Paducah, 27th and Kentucky Ave. Organized November, 1856. Oldest Lutheran church in western Kentucky.

Tilghman Home — Paducah, Kentucky Ave. Gen. Lloyd Tilghman, soldier and railroad builder, lived in Paducah 1852-1861. Now privately owned.

OTHER POINTS OF INTEREST

The Atomic Energy Commission — 16 mi. W. of Paducah. Off US-60.

Flood Marks — Paducah, Jackson Foundry Building, near riverfront. Marks on this building show heights of major floods.

Ray Harm Wildlife Art Gallery — Paducah, Paducah Bank and Trust Company. Famous Kentucky artist and painter. Monday-Friday, 9 a.m. to 4 p.m.

Paducah Community College — Paducah, Alben Barkley Drive. The Matheson Learning Resource Center.

Paducah Marine Ways — Paducah, Kentucky Ave. Founded 1854. City's oldest industry still in operation.

Illinois Central Railroad Shops — Paducah, between 12th and 16th Sts. Twin stacks are 265 ft. tall.

Red Line Tour — Paducah. Follow the bright red line down the middle of the streets. This 12-mi. course passes almost 50 important stops.

Ride Round — Paducah. Unusual boat cruise that follows an 80-mi. loop on the Ohio, Tennessee, and Cumberland Rivers, Lake Kentucky, Lake Barkley, and on an inland canal.

The Riverfront — Owen's Island, across from the foot of Kentucky Ave. Historic events which occurred on the river front where the Tennessee River empties into the Ohio River include the landing of John Donelson's party in 1780, on their way to settle Fort Nashborough (Nashville, Tennessee); the landing of George Rogers Clark on his way to Kaskaskia and his conquest of the Illinois Territory; the landing of USA Gen. Ulysses Grant in Sept. 1861 to capture Paducah for the Union; the arrival of Clara Barton from Cairo, Illinois during the flood of 1884, to bring aid to flood victims in the first major flood disaster operation of the American Red Cross.

Walking Tour — Paducah. A 1 1/2-mi. tour around Paducah's historic downtown area and riverfront.

Courthouse in Paducah.

Paducah Community College.

Mural in the post office in Paducah.

Pennyrile Area

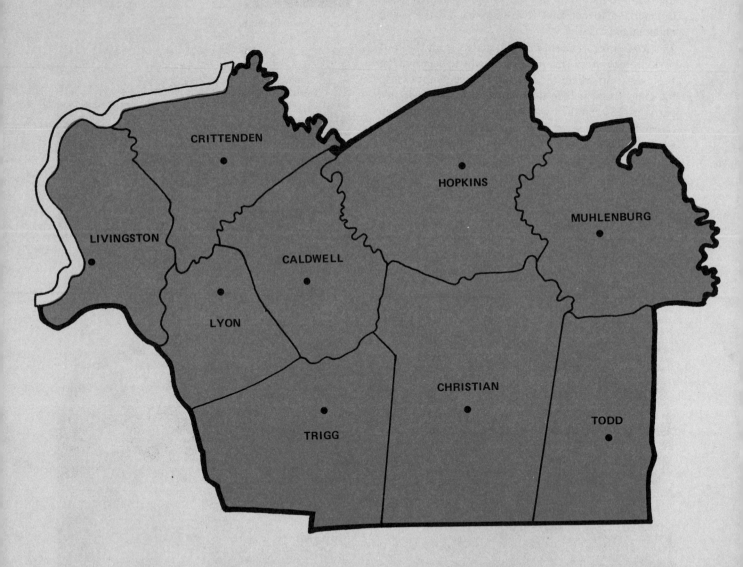

Caldwell County

Caldwell County was created in 1809 out of part of Livingston County. The fifty-first county in order of formation in Kentucky, it was named in honor of General John Caldwell. He was a native of Virginia, but moved to Kentucky in 1781. He was a great Indian fighter and served under General George Rogers Clark in the 1786 Indian expedition. In 1804, he was elected to serve as Lieutenant Governor of Kentucky under Governor Christopher Greenup.

The exact date that settlers came to Caldwell County is unknown, but there is a record of a settlement dating back to 1782. The first settlers of Caldwell County were Thomas Frazier and William Prince, who deeded the land to form Princeton, the county seat. When the town was first laid off, it was known by the name of Princetown, but the name was changed to Princeton on a motion by Thomas Frazier in 1818.

The county government was organized on May 1, 1809. A monument was erected in the Princeton Cemetery in honor of Thomas Prince, son of William Prince. The first courthouse was built in 1817 of crude logs and was only one room, 16 by 20 feet.

It has been said that "Tobacco is King" in Caldwell County, as it was the main crop in the county, even being raised by the earliest settlers. Princeton had two large tobacco factories, both of which were burned during a raid of the "Night Raiders" in 1906. The "Night Raiders" were farmers who, beginning in 1904, fought the tobacco trust. They burned, whipped and killed other farmers as well as salted and scraped tobacco plant beds. They were masked and travelled by night. Their efforts resulted in tobacco marketing co-ops, which guaranteed all farmers fair prices for their products.

Today, Princeton is one of the thriving cities of western Kentucky. Situated in the heart of Caldwell County, it is now known as the "Gateway to the Western Kentucky Lakelands" and is also called "The World's Friendliest City."

Caldwell County's farmland not only produces some of Kentucky's best tobacco, but corn, wheat and soybeans, as well. Beef cattle and hogs are other Caldwell County products.

FAIRS, FESTIVALS AND EXHIBITS

Black Patch Festival — Princeton, downtown. Tobacco is a part of Caldwell County history. Mid-September.

Antique Art Show and Sale — Princeton. KY-91. Caldwell County High School. June.

Art Exhibit — Princeton, 114 S. Harrison St. George Coon Library. All year.

Caldwell County 4-H Council Horse Show — Caldwell County Farm Bureau Fairgrounds. Has been held for 16 years. Annually in August.

PARKS

Big Spring Park — Princeton. KY-91.

MARKERS

"Trail of Tears" — Princeton, Big Springs Park. KY-91. Marks "Trail of Tears" followed by Cherokee Indians in their forced march from the Great Smoky Mts. to new Indian territory in Oklahoma in 1838. Big Springs Park was a campsite for the marchers.

Black Patch War — Princeton. US-62. The "Night Raiders" began fighting the non-cooperative farmers and businessmen on Dec. 1, 1906 until the end of 1908.

Big Spring Park near Princeton.

The Henry Home in Princeton.

Rock quarry mine near Princeton.

OLD BUILDINGS

Old Elkhorn Tavern — Princeton. KY-91. Built 1800's. Structure consisted of 4 rooms and basement with a spring that flowed through it without ever flooding. Wood for the floor was ripped by hand and fastened with pegs. A wagon train headed for the California Gold Rush was organized here. Tavern was also a stopping point for the Cherokee Indians on "Trail of Tears."

Col. "Ardsmore" Henry Home — Princeton, Hawthorne and E. Main Sts. Brick antebellum home with deed dating to 1847. Now privately owned.

Caldwell Courthouse — Princeton. Constructed 1939-1940. A bell purchased for a former courthouse in 1870 at the cost of $8.00 is still in use.

OTHER POINTS OF INTEREST

University of Kentucky Research Substation — Princeton. 1200-acre model farm. UK research and extension specialists study agriculture problems related to the western Kentucky area, as well as those of the entire state.

Christian County

Christian County was formed March 1, 1797 from part of Logan County. The county was named for Colonel William Christian of Jefferson County, who fought in the American Revolution. He was killed by Indians in a battle north of the Ohio River in 1786.

The northern part of the county was settled between 1790 and 1810, principally by people from the Piedmont region east of the Appalachian Mountains. This section of the county afforded freshwater, an abundance of wild game, and timber for building. South Christian, a flat, rich agricultural region, was settled by the Tidewater people of the East Coast between 1810 and 1830.

Records show that James Davis, John Montgomery, and Bartholomew Wood were the first settlers. The county seat was laid out in 1799 and called Elizabethtown, but was changed in 1804 to Hopkinsville in honor of General Samuel Hopkins, who served in the Revolutionary War and the War of 1812.

The county population is 69,000 with the city population of Hopkinsville at 25,000. There has been progressive improvement in the county with strong emphasis on education which has bolstered the prosperity of Christian County. Christian County is a large producer of bowling balls and wire magnets.

The city of Hopkinsville's nickname is "Pearl of the Pennyrile" because of its location in the Pennyrile region of southwestern Kentucky. Another familiar name for the city is "Hoptown" due to the friendly atmosphere found among its inhabitants.

FAIRS, FESTIVALS, DRAMAS, EXHIBITS

Rotary Radio Auction — Hopkinsville. April.

"Expo" — Hopkinsville Community College. Historical Pictorial Display and Quilt Show. Annual. March.

Western Kentucky State Fair — Hopkinsville. July-August.

Pennyrile Fine Arts Festival — Hopkinsville Community College. October.

Pennyrile Players — Hopkinsville Community College. During school term.

PARKS

Pennyrile Forest State Resort Park — Dawson Springs, Dawson Springs Rd. KY-109 off US-62. Lake, swimming and boating. Lodge and dining room.

MARKERS

Bethel College Baptist Institution — Hopkinsville, W. 16th St.

Church Hill Grange — 5 mi. S.W. of Hopkinsville, Cox Mill Rd. Built 1878. Only Grange Hall still standing in Kentucky.

Col. Nathan B. Forrest — Hopkinsville, N. Main, entrance to Riverside Cemetery. Col. N. B. Forrest quartered here in 1861-1862.

Genoa Home — Herndon. KY-345. Home of Winston J. Davis, Kentucky's first Commissioner of Agriculture.

Gen. James S. Jackson — Hopkinsville, N. Main, entrance to Riverside Cemetery. Grave of James Jackson killed at Perryville in 1862.

Hotel Latham — Hopkinsville, 7th and Virginia. (1895-1940). Tourist stop.

Peace Park — Hopkinsville, 9th and Campbell. Site of tobacco warehouse burned by "Night Riders" in 1907.

First Presbyterian Church — Hopkinsville, 9th and Liberty. Built 1849. Oldest building in Hopkinsville.

Birthplace of Adlai E. Stevenson — Hopkinsville, Junction KY-107 and KY-117. U. S. Vice President, 1893-1897.

"Trail of Tears" — Hopkinsville. KY-133. Forced Cherokee Indian movement to Oklahoma in 1837-1838.

MEMORIALS, MUSEUMS

Jefferson Davis Monument State Shrine — Hopkinsville. US-68. Birthplace of Jefferson Davis, President of the Confederate States of America, 1861-1865. The 351-ft. obelisk monument is the 4th highest in the U. S. Elevator to top for viewing.

Pennyrile Area Museum — Hopkinsville.

CEMETERIES

Pioneer Cemetery — Hopkinsville, 301 W. 13th St. Grave of Mrs. Amanda Leavy Morehead, wife of Gov. Charles S. Morehead. Gift of Bartholomew Wood, first settler. Grave sited dated 1812-1858.

Riverside Cemetery and Edgar Cayce Historical Marker — Hopkinsville, N. Main. Graves of Edgar Cayce, clairvoyant; John C. Latham, philanthropist; Post Wheeler, foreign diplomat; James S. Jackson, Union general.

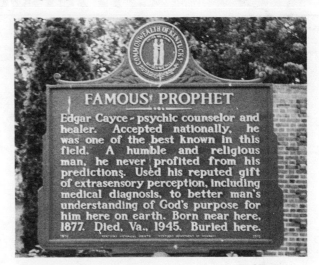

Riverside Cemetery in Hopkinsville.

Courthouse in Hopkinsville.

OLD BUILDINGS

Beverly Academy — S. of Hopkinsville. KY-107. Built 1889. Edgar Cayce attended school there. Academy no longer in use.

Blue Lantern Home — W. of Hopkinsville. US-68W. Built 1851-55. Two-story brick Gothic Revival.

Courthouse — Hopkinsville. Built 1869. Greek Revival. Site of famous "Night Riders" trail, 1911.

Crockett-Hickman-Winfree Home — Hopkinsville, corner 16th and Clay. Constructed 1834. Two-story brick Greek Revival.

Gordon Cayce Gifts and Antiques — Hopkinsville, S. Main. Constructed 1847-48. Former Dillard-Campbell-Green Home. Building used to house both Confederate and Union soldiers during Civil War.

Western State Hospital (Mental) — E. of Hopkinsville, US-68. Built 1850-1854; 1864-1867. Greek Revival.

Knight-Rogers Home — Hopkinsville, E. 7th. Built 1830's. Two-story, five levels, brick, Greek Revival.

Crittenden County

In April of 1842, Crittenden County became the ninety-first county to be created in the Commonwealth of Kentucky, and was carved from the eastern part of Livingston County. The name given to the new county was to honor John J. Crittenden, a United States Senator from Kentucky. Officers of other counties were commissioned to meet on April 1, 1842 at the home of James Cruce to institute the new county. They were also authorized to locate a county seat and to receive donations of land on which to locate the public buildings. The land was donated by Dr. John S. Gilliam; the land he had formerly bought from Samuel or Robert Woodsider for $2.00 per acre.

Marion became the county seat in 1844. It was first called Oxford, and later changed to Marion, after a French Huguenot, Frances Marion, the famous "Swamp Fox" of the Revolutionary War. In the early 1840's, Marion was a booming town with a strong economy based on the largest metallurgical fluorspar mine and plant in the United States. Now, 95% of the fluorspar used in this country is coming from abroad. A new fluorspar mine has opened recently in southwest Crittenden County.

The community of Ford's Ferry is across the Ohio River from the well-known robber's den, "Cave-In-Rock," on the Illinois shore. In the early nineteenth century, this cave was the headquarters of a vicious band of river pirates who terrorized flatboat travellers as they passed this great bend in the river.

Today, two important factors contribute to the success of Crittenden County: first, the millions of tons of high grade sandstone and limestone in the area, and secondly, the Ohio, Cumberland, and Tradewater Rivers on the county's boundaries.

PARKS

Cave-In-Rock State Park — KY-91. Across the Ohio River in Illinois.

County jail in Marion.

MARKERS

Centerville — On the Caldwell and Crittenden County line. US-641. In 1804, it was the county seat of the original Livingston County. The county seat was moved to Salem in 1809. A Presbyterian church was started here in 1797 by the Rev. Terah Templin. The U. S. Army used the earlier buildings as a supply depot on the "Trail of Tears," the Cherokee relocation march, 1834-1838. By Civil War days, little remained of the town. The only landmarks left today are foundations and earth depressions.

Courthouse Burned — Marion, Courthouse yard. US-60, US-641. The Marion courthouse was burned by guerrillas in Jan. 1865. The building was a total loss, and all of the county records were lost. The second courthouse burned in 1870.

Crittenden Furnace — 2 1/2 mi. N. of Dycusburg. Built in 1847 by Gideon D. Cobb. It is 9-ft. across and 30-ft. high. It was charcoal-fueled with steam-powered machinery. In 1855 it produced 1300 tons of iron. Named for the newly formed county, it was the last of several ironworks operated by the Cobb and Lyon families.

Hurricane Furnace — 2 mi. E. of Tolu. KY-387. Built in 1850 by Andrew Jackson, Jr. Also known as Jackson Furnace. Was rebuilt in 1856, 34-ft. high, with a maximum inner diameter of 10 ft. In 6 months in 1857, it produced 1200 tons of iron from ores of the Jackson Bank, 2 mi. S. Its soft iron was quite important to rolling mills. Operations ceased in early 1860's. This furnace was part of Kentucky's "Charcoal Era," in first half of the nineteenth century.

A Pioneer Route — Mattoon, 4 1/2 mi. N.E. of Marion. US-60, US-641. Marks the "Chickasaw Road," part of the Old Saline Trace used by Indians in pursuit of the vast herds of bison, deer and elk which came this way headed to the Salt Licks in Illinois. Flynn's Ferry began operating at the Ohio crossing of this trail in 1803, making it an important route of migration and commerce. Movement of Civil War troops was the last major use of this road.

CEMETERIES

Crooked Creek Missionary Baptist Church — 2 mi. N.W. of Marion. Organized 1835. Log church, the geographical center of Crittenden County. Ohio River Baptist Association organized here in Oct. 1883.

Maple Union Cemetery — Marion, E. side of KY-91N. Grave sites of 2 Crittenden County U. S. Senators, William J. Deboe and Ollie M. James. A large, marble shaft marks the James grave.

OLD BUILDINGS

The Cruce Home — Marion, Route 10, Princeton Rd. US-641S. Built in early 1800's, by Presley Cruce. The 3 front rooms are of logs. Accessible to the public.

The Dean Home — Marion, Old Ford's Ferry Rd. Constructed in 1826 by Alexander Dean. Now privately owned.

Dycus Home — Dycusburg, overlooking the Ohio River. Constructed in 1857 by Thephis Cooksey. Now privately owned but accessible to the public.

The Flanery Home — Marion, 317 W. Bellville St. Constructed in 1877 by John W. Blue, Sr. A fine example of Victorian architecture featuring lavish gingerbread trim and a steamboat Gothic front porch. Now privately owned, but accessible to the public.

Senator Ollie M. James House — Marion, 204 E. Depot St. Constructed early 1800. Was the home of the former U. S. Kentucky Senator Ollie M. James. Now privately owned.

Kykendall Home — Marion, 217 W. Bellville St. Constructed in 1868. Accessible to the public.

Nichols Home — Marion, 215 S. Moore St. Constructed by Ed Dowell. County sheriff at one time, he made the brick used to build the home in the back lot. Now privately owned.

Shewmaker Home — Marion, Old Ford's Ferry Rd. Constructed in 1888 by Peter Shewmaker. Now privately owned, but accessible to the public.

Tucker Home — Marion, 117 W. Bellville St. Constructed 1870 by Judge Thomas J. Nunn. Now privately owned, but accessible to the public.

The Flanery House in Marion.

The Hurst Home — Marion. KY-91. Constructed in 1833 by Granville Clement. Rock chimneys at each end of the house attract attention. Accessible to the public.

OTHER POINTS OF INTEREST

"The Holly" — Evidence of machinery and a shell of a building are all that remains of what was once the largest fluorspar producing mine in the country. "The Holly" now stands as a reminder of those days when the economy flourished along with the nation's fluorspar industry.

Prehistoric Mounds — Tolu. KY-387. Burial places of prehistoric mound builders. Some graves have yielded fluospar beads.

Crooked Creek Missionary Baptist Church near Marion.

Hopkins County

Hopkins County, the forty-ninth county created in Kentucky, was formed from the southern part of Henderson County. South Henderson County residents had long wanted a seat of government closer to their political affairs. State Senator Daniel Ashby was successful in bringing this about for his people, and Governor Christopher Greenup approved the act to create Hopkins County in 1806. The people named the new county after General Samuel Hopkins, cousin to both Zachary Taylor and Patrick Henry. Hopkins came to Kentucky in 1797 with the Transylvania Company after serving with distinction in the Revolutionary War, on General George Washington's staff.

Madisonville, the county seat, was incorporated in 1810, and named for President James Madison. The land was donated by Daniel McGary and Solomon Silkwood.

Dawson Springs, another Hopkins County community, was once a fashionable and famous health spa. Thousands of people came for the baths and mineral water, which was bottled and sold all over the United States.

Hopkins County covers 553 square miles of land that is rich in coal, oil, and gas. Coal was discovered in 1836, and people claim that Hopkins County mined the first coal in Kentucky.

FAIRS AND FESTIVALS

Hopkins County Fair — Madisonville, August.

Happy Goodman Family Homecoming and Gospel Sing — Madisonville, Life Temple Church. September.

Hopkins County Progress Homecoming — Madisonville. June.

Black Gold Festival — Madisonville. Takes note of America's number one energy resource, oil. July.

LAKES

Lake Beshear — S. of Dawson Springs. Off US-62 and Western Kentucky Parkway. Opened 1964. State-developed lake in Hopkins, Caldwell, and Christian Counties. Surface area about 857 acres in the Pennyrile State Forest.

MARKERS

Army of Six — Madisonville, High School Grounds. Commemorates incident in which a CSA commander with 6 men bluffed 300 Union troops and prevented the burning of local southern sympathizers' homes.

Steuben's Lick — At the village of Manitow. US-41A. A reminder of the Prussian general, Baron Von Steuben,

36

Hamby Well Building in Dawson Springs.

who came to the aid of Americans in the Revolutionary War. According to tradition, while Gen. Von Steuben visited the lick in 1787 inspecting land for military grants, he was slightly wounded in a skirmish with Indians.

OLD BUILDINGS

Hockersmith House — Madisonville, 218 S. Scott. Home of L. D. Hockersmith, a captain in Gen. John Hunt Morgan's CSA Cavalry. Hockersmith was captured by Federal troops during Morgan's Ohio Raid, July 20, 1863 and held with Morgan in the Ohio State Prison at Columbus. He helped dig the tunnel by which he and 5 others escaped with Morgan in Nov. 1863. This escape was one of the most daring of all times.

Maj. Maurice K. Gordon Home — Madisonville. Maj. Gordon coined the name "American Legion" in France when the organization was formed after World War I.

"Old Ship" — Madisonville, 304 Union St. Built in 1857 by Chittenden P. Lyon. This house has remained unchanged in its original Federal style for 118 years. Purchased in 1922 by Franklin Gardiner Bowmer and has remained in the Bowmer family since then.

Hamby Well Building — Dawson Springs, Main St. A national landmark.

OTHER POINTS OF INTEREST

Century of Coal Mining — Earlington. US-41A, KY-112. Earlington founded in 1870 by St. Bernard Coal Co. Named for John Baylis Earle, who discovered the No. 11 coal vein not far from this site in 1869. John Bond Atkinson, the president of St. Bernard Coal Co., planned free public schools, free public library,

the Loch Mary Reservoir, an arboretum, as well as home and church sites. In 1870, the L&N Railroad began coal shipments from this area.

The Dawson Springs — US-62 at Dawson Springs. Discovered in 1881 by W. S. Hamby. In its heyday in the early 20th century, this was one of the best known spas and health resorts in the south. Thousands of sick, lame and well persons came for the curative waters and to enjoy the social activities. Six firms bottled and shipped the chalybeate water all over the U. S. On Main St. in Dawson Springs is Hamby's Salts, Iron, and Lithia Well, one of the first mineral springs to be discovered, changing the course of history for the town.

Dawson Springs 4-H Camp — Dawson Springs, just off Western Kentucky Parkway. Camp used for state-wide 4-H Clubs.

Main Street in Dawson Springs.

"Old Ship" Home in Madisonville.

# *Livingston County*

In 1798 Livingston County became the twenty-ninth county to be established in Kentucky; its lands were taken from part of Christian County. It was named for Robert R. Livingston, a distinguished American from New York, and a signer of the Declaration of Independence. The first entry of lands in the office of the Virginia Military District was made in the name of William Brown, in the area at the mouth of the Cumberland River in Kentucky County, Virginia.

The first county seat was established at Eddyville in 1799, but was moved to Centerville by an act of the General Assembly in 1804, and then to Salem in 1809. In 1841, the Assembly ordered the courthouse moved again, this time to Smithland. The courthouse was built in 1842, is the ninth oldest courthouse in Kentucky and is still in use today. The county records have never been destroyed by fire or other misfortune, and the 1798-1865 records are on microfilm available for public reading. This courthouse was the scene of the last Kentucky hanging, which occured on April 19, 1935.

Smithland, situated on the bluffs overlooking the Ohio River at the mouth of the Cumberland River, is one of the most interesting and picturesque places in Kentucky. Its history dates back to 1804 when the town was first laid out. It was noted for many elegant homes, some of which are still standing. Southern planters and wealthy steamboat men brought their families to the town to spend the summer. Mississippi steamers discharged their passengers at Smithland to continue on up the Tennessee, Ohio, and Cumberland Rivers.

Fluorspar, a very scarce mineral, is still mined in the area of Carrsville. Today, with the construction of the Smithland Dam, and with Barkley and Kentucky Dams already complete, Smithland's river traffic increases. Livingston County is a well-known recreation area for vacationers who enjoy the water and all of its related activities.

LAKES AND DAMS

Barkley Dam — S.E. of Lake City, on the Cumberland River. Off KY-453, near Grand Rivers. S.E. of US-62, US-641. Completed 1966. A major U.S. Corps of Engineers project. Dam is 157-ft. high, 10,180-ft. wide and has a lock 800-ft. long.

Smithland Dam — Smithland, on the Ohio River. US-60E. Only dam in the world that has two 1,200-ft. locks. To be completed in 1980.

MARKERS

Jefferson's Sister — Smithland. Jct. US-60, KY-137. Lucy Jefferson Lewis monument and marker. She was the sister of Thomas Jefferson and is buried in the Birdsville Cemetery at Rocky Hill near Birdsville.

"Trail of Tears" — Smithland. KY-133. In 1829 the Cherokee Indians from Georgia and North Carolina were moved to Oklahoma. They were ill-clad, improperly nourished, and had no shelter. They died by the hundreds, many of pneumonia.

CEMETERIES

Carrsville Cemetery — Carrsville, overlooking the Ohio River. KY-135. Grave of Mary Lusk (1735-1803), the first person to be buried in Carrsville.

Mills Pioneer Cemetery — Salem, Pinckneyville Rd. KY-723. Monuments in memory of the Isaac Shelby family. He was the first Governor of Kentucky. The Shelby genealogy is engraved on the monuments.

Smithland Cemetery — Smithland. Overlooks confluence of the Ohio and Cumberland Rivers. The H. F. Given family mausoleum. The size of the vault doors would not admit modern-sized caskets. Cemetery has a white carved Italian marble monument erected to George W. Hagey, who died 1869. Many old tombs can be found in this cemetery. During the first year of the Civil War, Gen. Ulysses Grant built a gun emplacement within the cemetery to control river traffic to and from Nashville, Tennessee. Several mounds of this embankment still stand.

OLD BUILDINGS

Old Bush House — Smithland, Mill St. Built over 100 years ago by the Nomes of Italy. The house has 10 large rooms, as well as fireplaces with 1-ft. thick walls. There are 4 types of woodwork in the house, identical to the woodwork in Andrew Jackson's house, The Hermitage, in Nashville, Tennessee.

Old Coach House — Smithland. US-60. Built 1824. Red brick tavern which dates to stagecoach days. Known as the Alvis house. Same design as Old Kentucky Home in Bardstown. Legend holds that the old house was an inn and relay station. Some guests were Ford outlaws of the Cave-In-Rock. It is believed that Abraham Lincoln slept there. Now privately owned.

Conant House — Smithland. Overlooks the Cumberland and Ohio Rivers. Built in 1838 by Peter Haynes. Sold to Peter Conant in 1839. The Conants, unpopular with Smithland residents, were from the North, Republicans, and Union sympathizers. During the Civil War, the Union flag was flown from a large persimmon tree which stood near the house. Now privately owned.

St. Felix Hotel — Smithland, Front St. Overlooks the River. Built 1810. One of the most famous hotels on the river. Has been restored and remodeled. Grounds were an important Civil War base when taken by Union forces. Ten forts were built on hills overlooking the Ohio and Cumberland Rivers, and this hotel was used for storage and as a hospital.

Gower House — Smithland, Front St. Built circa 1780 by John Bell. Hotel and tavern known from Louisville to New Orleans. Walls are 15-in. thick and made of sturdy timber. Accommodated famous travellers such as Henry Clay, Lafayette, Aaron Burr, James K. Polk, Clara Barton, and Florence Nightingale. National Historic Landmark. Now privately owned.

Old House — Cedar Grove. One of the many historic homes found scattered all over Livingston County.

Old Indian Fort or Rock House — Salem. US-60. Built prior to 1800. It has 4 rooms in a row downstairs and once had 4 others upstairs. The original plaster of horse hair and mud still remains. The walls are 3-ft. thick. Now privately owned.

Old Salem Church — 3 mi. W. of Salem. US-60W. Established June 22, 1805 with 60 members, 7 of whom were slaves. Church still stands.

Lew Wallace Home — Smithland, Charlotte St. Gen. Lew Wallace built the home while he was stationed in Smithland during the Civil War. He later became famous for his novel, *Ben Hur.* Now privately owned.

John E. Wilson Storehouse — Smithland, College St. KY-453. Constructed in 1840, on Smithland Hill near a schoolhouse as a residence and office for Dr. Will

The John E. Wilson Storehouse in Smithland.

St. Felix Hotel in Smithland.

Saunders. Dr. Saunders converted it into a hospital for wounded Civil War soldiers. It is known as the Wilson House or Cumberland Marine Hospital.

OTHER POINTS OF INTEREST

Judge Elm Tree — Smithland, Front St. Across from the Gower House. This tree was used several times to hang wrongdoers. Legend holds that Henry Clay, the famous Senator, could be found here playing cards throughout the days of his frequent visits. Court was also held under its spreading branches.

Mantle Rock — Lola, on Ohio River. KY-133. The Cherokee Indians, during their "Trail of Tears" march fought for survival here. When they reached the Ohio River, it was frozen and had chunks of floating ice in midstream. They fell back seeking protection at Mantle Rock, but it was not enough. Hundreds died of pneumonia.

Salem Bell — Salem. US-60W. Only relic left of the old Salem courthouse, when Salem was the county seat from 1809-1842.

Lyon County

Lyon County was the one hundred second county in order of formation in Kentucky, and was formed from part of Caldwell County in 1854. It was named for Chittenden Lyon who came to the Lyon County area with his father, Matthew Lyon, in 1801. Matthew Lyon came to America from Ireland as an indentured servant in Vermont, and fought with the Ethan Allen Green Mountain Boys during the American Revolution. He married the daughter of Thomas Chittenden, the governor of Vermont, and was elected to Congress in 1797. As a leader in Thomas Jefferson's Republican Party, he was jailed and fined under the infamous Sedition Law for his criticism of President John Adams. When the election of 1800 was thrown into the House of Representatives, Lyon cast the deciding vote for Jefferson from his jail cell.

Matthew Lyon chose the site for his home, Eddyville, after visiting with his friend, Andrew Jackson at the Hermitage, who recommended the area to him. In the spring of 1801, he sailed with his family down the Ohio River and up the Cumberland River to Caldwell County, and founded Eddyville. In 1811-1812, he built the hulls of several war vessels for the U. S. Government. They were floated down the river from Eddyville to the ocean. This helped to build the iron and ship building industries in Eddyville.

Eddyville, named for the large eddies in the Cumberland River just above and below the town, was incorporated in 1810. It became the county seat in 1854, and was moved to its present location in 1957 when the Barkley Dam was built. Lyon County experienced major changes when the Tennessee Valley Authority built Kentucky and Barkley Dams and purchased the area between the rivers, now known as The Land-Between-the-Lakes. Recreation is now one of Lyon County's main industries, and there are numerous private and public campgrounds, as well as parks with boat launching areas.

FESTIVALS, EXHIBITS

Murray Art Guild — Land-Between-the-Lakes, Environmental Education Center. KY-453. Attracts approximately 200 exhibitors and 20,000 spectators. Annually in June.

Founder's Day Celebration — Eddyville. US-641, US-62. Celebrates relocation of county seat after flooding of old location when Barkley Dam was built. Gospel Sing, Founder's Day Queen, parade, booths, exhibits, dance. One full week in August; Grand Finale on last Saturday. Annually.

PARKS, RECREATION, LAKES, DAMS

Barkley Canal — KY-453. Connects Kentucky Lake and Lake Barkley near Grand Rivers. Northern gateway to the Land-Between-the-Lakes.

Barkley Dam — Near Grand Rivers. Off KY- 453. S.E. of US-62, US-641. A major U. S. Corps of Engineers Project, completed in 1966. 157-ft. high, 10,180-ft. wide, with locks 800-ft. long.

Lake Barkley — S. of Grand Rivers. KY-453. 2 1/2 mi. from Barkley Dam. Kentucky's second largest lake. Named for Alben W. Barkley, U. S. Vice President from 1949-1953. Connected with Kentucky Lake by a 1 3/4-mi. free flowing canal at the northern end of lake. Extends 118 mi. over a 1,000-mi. shoreline. Summer surface area is about 58,000 acres.

Eddy Creek Recreation Area — on Lake Barkley. 8 mi. S. of KY-93.

Kuttawa Harbor — Kuttawa. KY-295. 1 mi. S. of US-641. Open all year. Boat rental and supplies.

Land-Between-the-Lakes — Grand Rivers. KY-453. Giant TVA project between Barkley and Kentucky Lakes. Major national recreation area and conservation education center. Developed by the TVA on a 170,000-acre wooded peninsula. 5 to 10-mi. wide, and 40-mi. long.

MUSEUMS

Land-Between-the-Lakes Museum — Center Station. Off KY-453. Environmental Education Center.

Center Iron Furnace in Land-Between-the-Lakes area.

CEMETERIES

Old Eddyville Cemetery — Eddyville. W. of KY-93. The members of the Lyon family are buried here, the founders of Eddyville.

Old Kuttawa Cemetery — Eddyville, 1 mi. S. of US-62, US-641. KY-295. Governor Charles Anderson of Ohio and his wife Eliza are buried here. Their graves are enclosed in a crypt that is a replica of the bed they slept in all during their married life.

OLD BUILDINGS

Dr. George Huggans Home — W. of Old Eddyville, Kentucky State Penitentiary. KY-93. Built circa 1840, and now part of the Kentucky State Penitentiary property. Was the home of Dr. George F. Huggans, a physician in Old Eddyville in the middle 1800's. Huggans attested to the sanity of William Kelly, whose preoccupied obsession with his experimentation with a new steel-making process caused him to be called "Crazy Kelly" by fellow townpeople. Huggans supported Kelly's ideas.

Mineral Mound Home — 2 mi. S. of New Eddyville, on Lake Barkley. KY-93. Mineral Mound was the home of Willis B. Machen, who served in the U. S. Congress, and in the Congress of the CSA. He also helped to write the CSA Constitution. A die-hard rebel, Machen had the Confederate flag flown from his roof, and Union gunboats on their way to Ft. Donelson on the Cumberland River shelled his house. Machen was the grandfather of Zelda Sayre Fitzgerald, wife of American novelist F. Scott Fitzgerald. The house was destroyed by fire, but the original Mineral Mound tract now fronts Lake Barkley.

Kentucky State Penitentiary — W. of Old Eddyville. KY-93. The penitentiary, known as "The Castle on the Cumberland" built in 1883 from limestone quarried on the property of Gen. H. B. Lyon, CSA soldier and grandson of Matthew Lyon. Italian stone masons helped to construct the walls as well as the huge self-supporting arch in Cellhouse One. The electric chair, installed in 1911, when hanging as a means of execution came to an end in Kentucky, has been used in the execution of 166 men. The prison accommodated 1200 prisoners.

OTHER POINTS OF INTEREST

Center Iron Furnace — Land-Between-the-Lakes. KY-453. Ruins of historic iron furnace. Lyon County was the hub of the iron industry in the U. S. during the first half of the 18th century.

Environmental Education Center — N. end of Land-Between-the-Lakes. KY-453. Educational farm and Center Station, with films and displays. 5,000 acres for school and study groups. Open daily from 9 a.m.-5 p.m.

Kelly Kettle — Kuttawa. Off US-641. KY-295. Prized product of the Kentucky inventor's art, used in making sugar from cane. One of many kettles made in Lyon County by the Kelly ironworks.

Kelly Iron Furnace Office — W. of Eddyville. US-641. A relic of the mid-1850's. William Kelly developed a new pneumatic method of making steel.

Kuttawa Mineral Springs — Kuttawa, 1 mi. S. of US-62, US-641. Old Kuttawa was founded by Charles Anderson, former Governor of Ohio, who plotted and planned the town from its beginning in the 1870's. Governor Anderson dammed a stream to form a lake for a water system in operation before 1900. He laid out more than 100 acres in parks, and developed Kuttawa Mineral Springs, famous as a spa, and as the site of the huge camp meetings, which were held during the 1920's and 1930's.

Silo Overlook — Land-Between-the-Lakes. KY-453, or The Trace. Environmental Education Center. Overlooks Lake Barkley.

Muhlenburg County

In 1798, Muhlenberg County was the thirty-fourth county to be formed in Kentucky, and was carved from parts of Logan and Christian Counties. It gained its name from the Revolutionary War General John Peter Gabriel Muhlenberg, who fought at Monmouth, Germantown, Brandywine, Stony Point, and Yorktown. Although the General never visited this part of the State, the soldiers who had served under him named the county in honor of their commander.

The first five sessions of the quarterly court were held at the home of John Dennis, on the Greenville-Russellville Road in May 1799. The present Muhlenberg County Courthouse was erected in 1907. In the heart of the Western Coal Field, Muhlenberg County is one of the largest coal producing areas in the world. Moreover, its land and strip-mining operations are among the most advanced in the country.

There are three major communities in the county. Greenville is the county seat and was named in honor of General Nathaniel Green, who served with George Washington. Central City got its name from the Illinois Central Railroad and was a major coal center. Drakesboro is a small community once known as Ricedale, once an area of booming iron and steel production.

The county's population is 27,537 and its area is 482 square miles, of which a little less than half is farmland. Coal, gas and oil wells and limestone, sand and gravel quarrying are the chief sources of wealth.

FAIRS AND FESTIVALS

Arts and Crafts Fair — Greenville. Public arts and crafts fair sponsored by various women's clubs. November or late fall.

Homemaker's Arts and Craft Show — Various county locations. Held annually for the Homemakers to sell and display their handiwork. October.

Marching Band Festival — Central City. Local, state-wide and, often, out-of-state school bands participate in this important annual event.

Muhlenberg County Fair — Central City. The week of July Fourth.

Strawberry and Coal Festival — Greenville. In years past, it was held downtown. Now, streets around 3 sides of the courthouse are roped off for the festival. There are rides for young and old, display booths, prizes, etc. Held annually in June.

PARKS AND LAKES

Lake Malone State Park — 18 mi. S. of Greenville. Between US-431 and KY-81. This 826-acre lake offers swimming, boating, fishing, and water-skiing. A 374-acre park provides a beach, hiking trails, picnic shelters, playgrounds and camping facilities. Surrounding woodlands provide excellent hunting for deer and wild turkey. Park open all year.

Lake Malone Inn — 15 mi. S. of Greenville. Between US-431 and KY-81. A swimming pool and lake with white sand beaches are located just behind the lodge. Additional facilities include tennis courts, a miniature golf course, camping park, horse stable, boating and country store. Lake Malone Inn features 55 rooms, and suites with wood-burning fireplaces are available. Air-conditioned. Open all year.

Lake Venus — Bremen. KY-81. Provides special lakes for swimming and fishing, swimming pool, rides, amusements and an 18-hole miniature golf course. Group rates available.

MARKERS

General Peter Muhlenberg — Greenville, Courthouse yard. This gives a hint of the character of Gen. Peter Muhlenberg, for whom the county was named. His philosophy was, "A time to preach and a time to fight." An ordained minister, this colorful Lutheran preacher raised a regiment of Germans from Virginia's Shenandoah Valley to fight in the Revolutionary War. Many soldiers from this regiment became settlers in Muhlenberg County.

OLD BUILDINGS

B. L. Andrews House — Greenville, 109 S. Cherry St. Constructed 1855. Early owners were Green Eades, Mr.

Hess, Judge John C. Thompson, C. W. Townes, and the Martin Family. Mr. and Mrs. B. L. Andrews purchased the home, and at his death it was sold to Dr. and Mrs. Tom Maddox. Present owners enlarged front porch and replaced large white columns with wrought iron posts. Now privately owned.

M. C. Hay Home — Greenville, 111 S. Cherry St. Built circa 1850 by Dr. Frazier. Mr. Will Evans purchased it, then sold it to Mr. Hay, whose daughters owned it until their death. Two rooms have been added and the porch enlarged. Now privately owned.

Frank Hunter House — Greenville, 108 Hopkinsville St. Built early 1800's, by Frank B. Hancock. The ell was first built, then enlarged by the addition of a two-story front. Partially burned several times. Now privately owned.

Crawford Jonson House — Greenville, 301 E. Main Cross St. Erected by Judge Joseph Rickett. Big kitchen originally had a 16-ft. fireplace that burned 6-ft. logs. The rooms were built with wooden pegs, which still exist in the front rooms. Charles Wickliffe purchased the house, and enlarged it to 11 rooms then sold it to the Jonson family in 1892. The woodwork is solid black walnut and one of the fireplaces is handcarved. Now privately owned.

Old Greenville Seminary — Greenville, 137 N. Cherry St. Built 1851. Old red brick home was formerly academy for boys. Professor James K. Patterson taught here until the school was closed during the Civil War. Presently undergoing restoration.

George Short House — Greenville, 151 N. Main St. Constructed early 1840's by George Short, prominent tobacconist. He was very wealthy, and in love with Tabitha Brank. In hopes she would marry him, he sent to Cincinnati for carpenters and materials to be sent down the Ohio River on flatboats. The house was built but Tabitha refused to marry him. He remained a bachelor for the rest of his life. Now privately owned.

Lake Malone Lodge near Greenville.

Jonathan Short House — Greenville, 123 S. Cherry St. circa 1840. Jonathan Short built the house with materials shipped from Cincinnati. Has been improved and completely redecorated. Now privately owned.

Edward R. Weir House — Greenville, 206 S. Main St. Constructed 1839 by Richard Buynn and a slave, then was owned by Shelby Gene Stewart of Central City. Oldest house standing in Greenville today. Has large center hall, graceful stairway, and spacious bedrooms. Black walnut woodwork throughout. Flooring is wide, and the windows are tall and narrow. Plaster moldings and decorative rosettes in center ceiling. Mr. Weir and his bride rode horseback to Philadelphia to purchase the furniture and hardware, which was shipped by steamer to South Carrollton, then unloaded and hauled to Greenville.

Edward Yonts House — Greenville, 204 E. Main Cross St. Constructed in the 1870's, 5 rooms of hewn logs and brick. Mr. Yonts paid $1,000 for both house and lot, then remodeled the home. Now privately owned.

J. D. Yonts House — Greenville, 210 N. Main St. Constructed 1870's by J. D. Yonts. Now privately owned.

OTHER POINTS OF INTEREST

Airdrie Mine — Drakesboro. Banks of Green River. US-431. Remains of 1800's mine. Furnace and building still standing.

Big Shovel — Near Central City, off the Western Kentucky Parkway. One of the largest earth-moving coal shovels in the world. Owned by Peabody Coal Company. The shovel is 90 ft. taller than the Statue of Liberty, 45 ft. higher than Niagara Falls, and wider than an 8-lane highway. It creates power enough to serve a city of 15,000 and outreaches an average city block. The operator works more than 5 stories high in an air-conditioned cab. Shipment of machine components required over 300 railroad cars. Its big, 115-yard dipper uncovers almost twice its 18,000,000-pound weight in coal daily. This is enough coal to heat 7,500 average homes for one month, or 1,500 homes for an entire winter.

TVA Steam Power Plant (Paradise Steam Plant) — E. of Greenville. US-431. Built by the Tennessee Valley Authority on the west bank of the Green River, near Drakesboro in the Western Kentucky Coal Field. Location was selected to take advantage of unusually low costs of coal produced in nearby mining operations. Three giant cooling towers permit recycling of warm water from steam condensers in summer when river flows are low, to prevent "thermal pollution" effects of warm water discharge into the river. Each tower is 300 ft. in diameter at its base, and 437 ft. high. To control air pollution, this plant is equipped with large electrostatic precipitators to collect the fly ash produced when coal is burning, as well as a sulfur dioxide emissions limitation system, and chimneys 600 and 800 feet tall to dispense emissions high above the ground level. Operating at full load, this plant burns about 21,000 tons of coal a day, and requires up to 772,000 gallons of condenser cooling water per minute. This is the water that circulates through heat exchangers to condense steam from the turbines, in order to drive the generators. Three boilers produce a total of almost 18 million pounds of steam an hour, at temperatures of about 1,000 degrees and pressures up to 3,500 pounds per square inch. Guided tours.

Indian Knoll — E. of Greenville, across from the Paradise Steam Plant on the Green River. US-431. One of

Steam shovel located in Muhlenberg County.

the largest Indian mounds discovered in Kentucky. Approximately 50,000 relics and bones have been discovered.

Todd County

Todd County was formed on December 30, 1819, when settlers in Logan and Christian Counties asked the Kentucky Legislature to create a new county. For years, these settlers had found it almost impossible to reach their governmental and business centers. Colonel John Todd, a famous Indian fighter, was instrumental in the creation of this new county, the sixty-fourth to be created in Kentucky, and so the county was named for him.

Records show that early settlers arrived in the southern part of the county, west of what is now Guthrie, and built a fort similar to those in central Kentucky. Today, there is no trace of this fort, and no records of Indian attacks. In 1792, when Kentucky became a state, the first house was built in what is now Todd County by Justinian Cartwright. It was located 4 1/2-miles west of Elkton, on the trace which connected Hopkinsville and Russellville. In 1793, only four areas were settled between Russellville and Elkton.

Several localities were considered in deciding upon a county seat. Old Elkton had been established since

1818 on Elk Fork Creek, and was a central location. Newburg was proposed, too, because of its hotel and its central location between Hopkinsville and Russellville. The "New Elkton" site combined the advantages of the other two, with an added advantage of land having been donated by John Gray. Lewis Leavell of Trenton had extensive property holdings in his community, so he wanted the county seat to be established in Trenton. A bitter battle ensued, which nearly erupted into a duel. Elkton's central location, perhaps aided by Gray's influence and wealth, decided the designation of Elkton as the county seat in May of 1820.

Todd County's major industry is agriculture and its related businesses. Grain and dairy products are important aspects of Todd County economy, as well.

FESTIVALS

Annual Homecoming Day for Black People — Allensville. A traditional celebration, related to the emancipation of slaves, begun approximately 100 years ago by a small group of ex-slaves. It remains an impressive event which draws black people from all sections of the country. The high point of the week-long celebration is a picnic, a joint effort of 2 churches, whose members barbecue hogs, goats, and sheep in open pits. Annually in August.

MEMORIALS

Jefferson Davis Monument — Fairview, 10 mi. E. of Hopkinsville. US-68, KY-80. This 351-ft. obelisk is 4th highest monument in U.S., and was erected by the people of the South as a memorial. Completed and dedicated May 3, 1929. Birthplace of Jefferson Davis, U. S. Senator, Secretary of War under President Franklin Pierce, and then President of the CSA. Davis was born in Fairview on June 3, 1808, but visited his home only twice after leaving in 1811 with his family. In 1875, he visited his home, which was still intact, and addressed several thousand people gathered at the Christian County Fairgrounds. He returned again on March 10, 1886 to dedicate the Bethel Baptist Church, built on his home site. At that time, he presented an engraved communion chalice of silver which still exists.

OLD BUILDINGS

Todd County Courthouse — Elkton. US-68, KY-181. Second oldest courthouse in Kentucky.

Edwards Hall — Elkton, 2 Goebel Ave. Built in 1821 by Jesse Russell. It is made of brick fired on the place. Woodwork carved by one of Russell's slaves. Now privately owned.

Garth House — Trenton. Built 1890. Unusual feature is a water tower in the attic. Water ran into the tank from gutters, then excess water ran to a cistern in the basement. Water was then piped to the bathroom and kitchen. Now privately owned.

Northington Estate — Guthrie. Built 1867. Building began during the Civil War but before completion, slaves were freed. Former slaves, or freedmen, finished the house, using brick fired on the farm. Now privately owned.

Stagecoach Inn (Gray's Inn) — Guthrie. Jct. US-41, US-79. Built early 1800's, for Maj. John Gray under the supervision of Elga Covington. Famous patrons of the Inn include Andrew Jackson, Jenny Lind, and Jesse James. Now privately owned.

Old Sumpter Place — Elkton. KY-181. circa 1835. The original house (the bottom half) is made of brick. Of special interest is the upper portion, a later addition, which is divided into 2 parts. Originally, the boys had an outside stairway, while the girls side had an inside stairway with no adjoining doorway inside. Now privately owned.

Walton Manor — Allensville. KY-102. Built 1839. Original portion of the brick house was made by slave labor. Brick was made from dirt dug out of the basement. Each generation of the family has added a room or rooms. The last parlor of the home has not been redecorated since 1888. Now privately owned.

Walker House — Kirkmansville. Built early 1800's. Original structure made of walnut logs. Five generations of same family have lived here. Now privately owned.

OTHER POINTS OF INTEREST

The "Cliffs" — Clifty, northern part of Todd County. KY-181. Scenic spot for visitors, geologists, naturalists, hunters and picnickers. Cliffs rise 300-500 ft. and are 300-600 ft. wide. "Buzzards Ballyard" is sunning spot for flocks of buzzards. Popular also is Saltpeter Cave, 200-ft. wide and 50-ft. deep.

Green River Female Academy — Elkton. Organized 1835. Subscription school organized and built by a stock company. Now privately owned.

Meriweather Springs — Guthrie, at Tennessee state line, S.E. of Hopkinsville. US-41, US-79. Bubbling waters at 56 degrees Fahrenheit.

Jefferson Davis Monument in Fairview.

Presbyterian Girl's School at Elkton.

Trigg County

In 1820, 459 square miles of land were carved out of Christian County to form Trigg County, making it the sixty-sixth county to be established in Kentucky. The county was named for Colonel Stephen Trigg for his service in the American Revolution. He also established Trigg's Station on Cane Run, near Harrodsburg. Trigg was killed at the Battle of Blue Licks.

The first community, Cerulean, was settled as early as 1790 by Robert Goodwin and his two sons, Jesse and Samuel, all Carolinians. Cerulean became famous as a health spa due to the sky-blue medicinal water from Cerulean Springs. The resort was open to the public from 1817 until the hotel burned in 1925. It was a favorite vacation spot for hundreds of visitors who came to enjoy many social activities, as well as for those who came to take the waters.

In 1813, James Thompson was the first settler in the area of Cadiz. The land on which Cadiz was formed once belonged to Robert Baker, who was also an early settler. In December 1821, an act was passed by the General Assembly authorizing the citizens of Trigg County to vote on a place for the permanent seat of justice. At the March term of court in 1822, an election was held for the purpose of deciding the matter. George Street, Richard Dawson and Beman Fowler were appointed judges, with William Cannon as clerk. The towns competing for the seat were Cadiz, Boyd's Landing (now known as Canton), Warrington, and Center. The election was held in Cadiz on March 6, 1822, and Cadiz won by 91 votes.

Several interesting and educational attractions are located in Trigg County. One is the Historical Cadiz Railroad, completed in 1902, which runs ten miles from Cadiz to Gracey. The old homes in Trigg County also attract many visitors. Trigg County is on the Tennessee state line and is split roughly down the middle by Lake Barkley. The western part of this split forms the new Land-Between-the-Lakes National Recreation Area, 170,000, acres of wooded ridgeland.

Lake Barkley State Resort Park.

Boat Deck on Lake Barkley.

Fishermen from all over the country come to Kentucky to fish.

PARKS, RECREATION, LAKES

Boots Randolph Amateur-Celebrity Invitational Golf Tournament — Cadiz, Lake Barkley State Resort Park. US-68. October.

Lake Barkley State Resort Park — 7 mi. W. of Cadiz. US-68. Recreation, hiking, picnicking.

Land-Between-the-Lakes — Cadiz. "The Gateway" on KY-80. Southern part of the Land-Between-the-Lakes lies between Kentucky Lake and Barkley Lake. Recreation, camping, boating, picnicking.

MARKERS

European Colony — Golden Pond Community. KY-80, US-68. A colony of Germans built the first Catholic church in the county. The old parish cemetery is all that remains.

Center, Trigg, and Empire Furnaces — Cadiz. KY-453. "Follow the Trace," which indicates what was once the largest iron producing area in the nation.

Nathan Futrell — 6 mi. S. of Golden Pond. US-68. Grave site of Nathan Futrell, young hero of the American Revolution, who served as drummer boy at the age of 7.

OLD BUILDINGS

The Brick Inn or Canton Hotel — Canton, past Lake Barkley State Park. US-68. Stopping place for many famous people including Gen. Lafayette, President James K. Polk, and Jenny Lind. Ceased operating in 1930's, but still stands.

Jefferson House — Cadiz, Main St. Later known as Mrs. Malone's Boarding House. Remodeled in later years to accommodate offices and shops.

Mrs. Sidney McKinney's Home — Cadiz, behind Courthouse on Jefferson St. Built 1840's. Has been occupied by the same family for 107 years. Several members of the family served in Kentucky's early legislature.

"Rock House" — Cadiz, on Old Hopkinsville-Eddyville Rd. Built 1804, by Scotsman John McCaughan, the first public surveyor in Trigg County. The solid stone walls are 2-ft. thick, and the doors are low and wide. Massive fireplaces. Now privately owned.

Old Wooldridge Home — Cadiz. US-68. Built in 1830 by Dr. T. C. Wooldridge. Architectural features include a circular stairway, stoop entrance, dual windows which form doors, large open rooms, and at one time, there was a fish pond on the roof. Now privately owned.

47

Green River Area

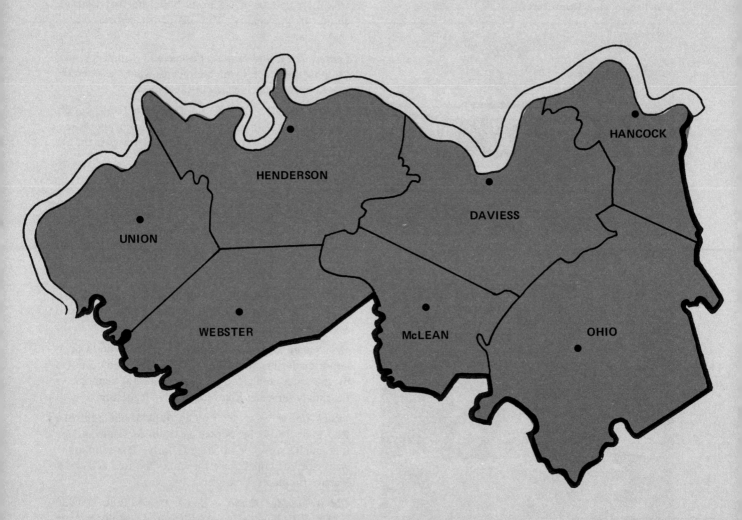

Daviess County

In 1780, the first white settlers came, via the Ohio River, to what is now the prosperous and progressive area known as Daviess County. In June of 1815, Daviess became the fifty-eighth county to be formed in Kentucky; its land taken from Ohio County. Early settlers included Joseph Blackford and William Smeathers (also known as Bill Smithers or Smothers.) Blackford came around 1780, established a hunting camp on Blackford Creek, and was later killed by Indians. Smeathers came in 1799 and built his cabin on a site near the river which is now St. Elizabeth Street in Owensboro. From this first dwelling, constructed by Smeathers, the first settlement began. It was called Yellow Banks, due to the deep yellow color of the river banks, caused by a high yellow clay content. Yellow Banks was selected as the county seat when the county was formed in 1815.

The county was named in honor of Colonel Joseph Hamilton Daviess, a distinguished lawyer and soldier. He was appointed U.S. Attorney for Kentucky, and was a prosecutor in Aaron Burr's treason case. Colonel Daviess was an extensive landowner, as well, having approximately thirty-thousand acres in what is now Daviess County. Colonel Daviess and his wife, Ann, made their home at "Cornland," a beautiful estate overlooking the Ohio River about two miles east of Yellow Banks. In the fall of 1811, Daviess joined the army of General Harrison, and died a hero's death at the Battle of Tippecanoe.

Yellow Banks was surveyed by Captain James W. Johnston, the first county surveyor, and a plat was approved by the commissioners, along with the change of its name to Rossboro, in honor of landowner David Ross. The main street was named for his daughter, Frederica. In 1817, an act of the legislature incorporated the town and changed the name to Owensborough (later changed to Owensboro) in honor of Colonel Abraham Owen, a native of Virginia who came to Kentucky in 1785, settling in Shelby County. Colonel Owen was a distinguished soldier and legislator and had been a member of the convention in 1799

which formed the state constitution. He, like Colonel Daviess, was killed in the Battle of Tippecanoe in the War of 1812.

FAIRS, FESTIVALS, DRAMAS

Daviess County Fair — Philpot. KY-54. August.

Festival of Arts — Owensboro. Visual and performing arts. November.

Owensboro Symphony Orchestra — Owensboro, Daviess County High School. US-231. Headquarters located at 18th and Daviess St. October to May.

Theater Workshop of Owensboro — Owensboro, 407 W. 5th St. Old Trinity Center.

PARKS AND RECREATION

Ben Hawes State Park — Owensboro. US-60 W. Golf course and other outdoor facilities.

Owensboro Nature Park — Owensboro, 20th and Daviess Sts. Many varieties of trees and shrubs, labeled for easy identification.

Regatta Week — Owensboro, Riverfront, Ohio River. National hydroplane competition featuring famous boats and drivers. Governor's Cup Race is climax of competition. July.

MARKERS

Buffalo Road — Owensboro, 1st and Frederica Sts. Buffalo herds opened first road in wilderness to present site of Owensboro. Bill Smothers, the pioneer settler of Yellow Banks, followed the trail from Rough Creek, near present day Hartford, to Ohio River. An old court record says the buffalo road was a "place of great resort for that kind of game."

First Coal by Rail — Owensboro. US-60 and KY-331. Robert Triplett built the first railway in Kentucky in 1826. Coal was moved from Bon Harbor hills to steamboats on the Ohio River. Triplett was the first to get coal substituted for wood as fuel on river boats below

Louisville. Coal was shipped south and sold by the barrel.

Birthplace of Governor Wendell H. Ford — Owensboro, 7th and Crittenden Sts. First home of Wendell H. Ford, Kentucky's 49th Governor, and first Owensboro native to become chief executive, 1971. Born Sept. 8, 1924; State Senator 1965; and U. S. Senator 1975.

Senator McCreery Home — Owensboro, 450 Griffith Ave. Homesite of Thomas Clay McCreery (1816-1890). One of Daviess County's most distinguished natives, an accomplished lawyer, orator, and farmer.

Madison's Land — 2 mi. E. of Sorgho. KY-54. James Madison, 4th President of the U. S., and wife, Dolly, owned 2,000 acres along Panther Creek. Land held by them until 1832-1834, when sold in parcels.

Panther Creek Battle — 7.5 mi. S. of Owensboro. US-431. On Sept. 19, 1862, CSA troops besieged Owensboro. Union troops at old Fairgrounds refused demand for surrender, and a skirmish followed. Union soldier swam Ohio River to summon help from Indiana Legion. CSA retreated to here. Indiana Home Guards crossed river and attacked next day. CSA retreated, 36 killed and 70 wounded. Union losses were 3 killed and 35 wounded.

Stirman's Folly — Owensboro. 519 Locust St. Built 1860 by Dr. William Doswell Stirman. This Victorian structure received its name because he spent a fortune building it. In 1915, Samuel R. Ewing, a civic leader and tobacco farmer, purchased and remodeled the house. He entertained Clara Barton, founder of the American Red Cross, at this house.

Uncle Tom Lived Here — Midway between Maceo and Lewisport. US-60E. Site of Riley family homeplace, owners of Josiah Henson, one of the characters on which Harriet Beecher Stowe based her 1825 novel, *Uncle Tom's Cabin.* Henson served as overseer of Amos Riley's farms, 1825-1829. On learning his owner planned to sell him down the river, he escaped to Canada, living there the rest of his life. He was invited to visit Mrs. Stowe in Andover, Massachusetts in 1849.

George Graham Vest — Owensboro, Courthouse yard. US-60. In 1852, he established Owensboro's second newspaper, *The Gazette,* with Robert S. Triplett, an Owensboro businessman. Vest was U. S. Senator from Missouri, 1879-1903. Author of world famous "Tribute to a Dog," a spontaneous oration in court in defense of a backwoodsman's dog, "Old Drum," which won the case for the client, and gained Vest world fame.

MEMORIALS AND MUSEUMS

Owensboro Area Museum — Owensboro, College Dr. and S. Griffith. Includes art gallery, planetarium, science and historic displays. Presently housed in Kentucky Wesleyan College's Peoples Hall. New building being built on college campus.

Owensboro Art Museum — Owensboro, 901 Frederica St. Formerly Old Carnegie Library.

Glenmore's Little Museum — Owensboro. US-60E. Only distillery open during prohibition, for medicinal production. Tours Monday-Friday.

CEMETERIES

Elmwood Cemetery — Owensboro, Old Hartford Rd. Grave of A. Kyle, CSA, who was taken prisoner at Shiloh.

St. Alphonsus Cemetery — St. Joseph. KY-56. Graves of Charles W. Thompson and Pierman Powell, Daviess County soldiers executed in Henderson, Kentucky on July 22, 1864 by Union firing squad.

St. Lawrence Cemetery — 2 mi. E. of Knottsville. Off KY-144. Earliest grave dated 1823. Oldest cemetery in county.

OLD BUILDINGS

Home of Thomas Clay — Owensboro. KY-405. Thomas Clay came here in 1812. It is uncertain when this home was built. Clay, a Revolutionary War captain, was a cousin of John Clay, father of the well-known statesman Henry Clay. He was an uncle of Cassius Marcellus Clay, famed Kentuckian of the Civil War era, and grandfather of U. S. Senator Thomas Clay McCreery.

First Baptist Church — Owensboro, 3rd and Lewis Sts. Oldest church in the city. Elder Reuben Cottrell began preaching in the courthouse in 1834. In May 1835, the First Baptist Church was organized with 8 white and 18 black members. First house of worship erected in 1840.

The Felty Husk House — Near Pup Creek. KY-1389. Possibly the oldest home still standing in Daviess County. Built circa 1805, by county's second settler, Felty Husk. Originally a 40-ft. by 20-ft. 2-story cabin of yellow poplar logs. Has since been weatherboarded and added on to several times. Some of the blown glass windowpanes remain intact.

Louisville and Nashville Depot — Owensboro, 1035 Frederica St. Built circa 1906 of brick with a tile roof. This historic landmark serves as a reminder of the

The Felty Husk House near Pup Creek.

bygone passenger railroad stations. Presently a restaurant.

Sen. Thomas C. McCreery's House — Owensboro. KY-405. Built circa 1840 by Sen. McCreery. He named it Beech Woods because of the surrounding beech trees. McCreery owned another home on Griffith Ave., in Owensboro, where the public library is located today.

John H. McFarland Home — Owensboro, 2731 Fairview Dr. McFarland was one of the most prominent farmers and tobacco growers in Daviess County.

John A. Medley House — Owensboro, 320 Maple Ave. Built 1848. It was situated on a farm of approximately 2,000 acres. Originally, the home faced Frederica St., while what is now Maple Ave. was the drive to the side of the house. The columns, added by Mr. Medley, were originally from a plantation in Mississippi.

The Morgan House — Owensboro, 2725 Frederica St. Built 1907. This Victorian home was once known as "the old haunted house."

The Morris House — Owensboro. 1 block off US-60E. Built circa 1890 by the Monarch family. The outer walls of this Victorian mansion are brick, and 17-in. thick. There are 4 full floors with 13-ft. ceilings. The house retains its original interior shutters throughout. Now privately owned.

Mount·Saint Joseph — Saint Joseph. KY-56. Was the first motherhouse of Catholic nuns in western Kentucky. It is also the oldest operating girls' academy in Daviess County, founded Aug. 14, 1874, by the Rev. Paul Joseph Volk.

St. Alphonsus Catholic Church — Saint Joseph. KY-56. First church was a log cabin built by the Rev. Walter Coombs in 1854, which burned in 1868. Rebuilt by The Rev. Paul Volk. The 150-year old cross in the vestibule of present building came from another church built by Father Volk.

St. Joseph Catholic Church — Owensboro, 4th and Clay Sts. Parish founded 1871 through efforts of German Catholics in the community. First building was erected at 9th and Sweeny Sts. After the church was destroyed by fire, a new one was built at present location. Beautiful stained glass windows were imported from Europe.

St. Lawrence Catholic Church — 2 mi. E. of Knottsville. Off KY-144. Considered the mother church of Daviess County. First records date to 1821. A log church was erected in 1831. A brick church was erected in 1839, but due to defective work, it was replaced in 1870.

Willow Hill — Thruston, on Jones Rd. Off KY-144.

Riverfront at Owensboro.

Built in 1821 of logs with hog hair and mud as mortar. The original logs can be seen in 2 rooms. The low ceilings, approximately 7-ft. high, allowed maximum comfort in heating. The bricks used in the fireplaces were made and fired on the site. Now privately owned.

Jeremiah Yewell House — Owensboro, off Fairview Dr. Built circa 1850, by Jeremiah Yewell, the first distiller of Oldham County. The structure was first designed to be a church, but as no pastor could be found, Yewell finished it as a home. Bricks were made and fired on the property. The solid brick walls are 13-in. thick. Each wall extends into the ground to form the foundation.

Locust Grove — Owensboro, 2731 Fairview Dr. Built by John H. McFarland, pioneer farmer and tobacconist. He purchased original 225 acres from George Mason of Virginia. Of simple early Kentucky architecture, the house is of 3-course common brick, rectangular-shaped with chimneys at either end. The ell-shaped extension on the north side was added in 1865. Now privately owned.

Juste Nicola Vairin House — Thruston. KY-405. Built circa 1842, by one of Napoleon Bonaparte's bodyguards who spent his last 30 years living with his 5 daughters in this historic home. Besides being a guard for Napoleon, Vairin also took part in the Battle of Waterloo. After settling in the U. S., he became a tobacco exporter in Daviess County.

Thacker and Thacker Law Offices — Owensboro, 209 W. 4th St. This mid-19th century townhouse is one of the city's oldest townhouses. Example of Federal architecture, the original front section was built for a doctor's office with living quarters above. It was renovated in 1970.

Col. Colin S. Throckmorton's House — Thruston. KY-144. Built circa 1793 of bricks made and fired on the site. First occupants of the home were believed to be the Mayos, grandparents of the Mayo brothers who founded the famous Mayo Clinic in New York. Col. Throckmorton, who died in 1878, was a resident of this home and an officer in the U. S. Army. At a much later date, Wendell Ford, now U. S. Senator, lived here when he was a boy. Now privately owned.

Old Trinity Centre — Owensboro, 407 W. 5th St. Built 1875. This building is the oldest example of Gothic architecture in western Kentucky. Served as Trinity Episcopal Church, oldest brick church building in Owensboro, until 1964. Now serves as community center.

OTHER POINTS OF INTEREST

Brescia College — Owensboro, 120 W. 7th St. Coed and liberal arts college. Largest speech and hearing therapy department in Tri-State area. Tours.

Dogwood and Azalea Trail — Owensboro, starting at Frederica St. and Griffith Ave., to Carter Rd. From Griffith, on all side streets to Ford Ave. Spring.

Kentucky Wesleyan College — Owensboro, 3000 Frederica St. United Methodist, coed, liberal arts college. Tours.

Sassafras Tree — Owensboro, 2100 Frederica St. This giant tree, first mentioned for its size in 1883, has been a landmark in Daviess County for years. Believed to be 250 to 300 years old, it measures over 100 ft. tall with a circumference of 16 ft. It is probably the largest of its kind in the world, and is registered with the American Forestry Association as largest in the U. S.

Juste Nicola Vairin House near Thurston.

Hancock County

Hancock County, bordering the scenic Ohio River, was created in 1829, from Daviess, Breckinridge, and Ohio Counties, and was the eighty-third county formed in Kentucky. It was named to honor John Hancock of Massachussetts, the first to sign the Declaration of Independence and President of the Congress at the time of the American Revolution.

Hawesville, the county seat, was once a busy boat-building center. It was here that the packets Gaxelle and Gertrude were built, as well as the Water Queen, the showboat with the longest record of service of any travelling on the inland waterways.

Hancock County is best known for its sorghum, and has the nickname of "The Sorghum Capitol of the World." Other cash crops include tobacco, soybeans and corn. Today, the county is a thriving industrial community. Murray Tile, now known as American Olean Tile Company, located in Lewisport in 1954. Since the early 1960's, Hancock County has become the home of Martin Marietta; West Cor Corporation; Western Kraft; National Southwire Aluminum; Kentucky Division of Southwire Aluminum; National Aluminum; and Big Rivers Electric Corporation.

FAIRS, FESTIVALS, AND EXHIBITS

Hancock County Arts and Crafts Exhibition — Hawesville, Hancock County High School. US-60. July-August.

Hancock Fair and Sorghum Festival — Hawesville. KY-1389. Sorghum-judging contest held on Saturday morning. Activities conclude with a parade through downtown Hawesville on Saturday afternoon. Second weekend in September.

PARKS

Vastwood Park — Hawesville. On KY-1847. County-owned park with lake for fishing, swimming and boating. Facilities are available for tennis, basketball, baseball, and picnicking. Playground equipment.

MEMORIALS

Heritage-of-the-Rivers — Hawesville, near approach to the Lincoln Trail. Memorial dedicated to Capt. James W. Cannon, one of the giants of inland river history. Capt. Cannon constructed, operated, and raced the Robert E. Lee, which defeated the Natchez in a race from New Orleans to St. Louis in July 1870.

War Memorial — Hawesville, Courthouse lawn. US-60. Erected in memory of Hancock Countians who died in World Wars I and II, the Korean War, and Vietnam.

CEMETERIES

Memory Garden Cemetery — Hawesville. US-60E. Mass grave of 36 victims of "Reindeer" Steamboat disaster of 1854. The steamboat blew up while pulling away from the dock at Cannelton, Indiana, across the river from Hawesville.

OLD BUILDINGS

Hancock County Courthouse — Hawesville. US-60. One of the 10 oldest courthouses in Kentucky. Now in the process of being remodeled, interior and exterior, to preserve its natural beauty. Across the street, construction of a Courthouse annex has begun.

Immaculate Conception Catholic Church — Hawesville, Water St. Built in 1862 of hand-hewn sandstone. Walls constructed of rock by slaves. Although not completed, walls were used in Civil War as protection from shell fire from the gunboat U.S.S. Springfield in July 1864. Increased membership and flood damage forced the congregation to build a new church in 1963. Efforts are now under way to restore the building to its original beauty.

Pate House — Lewisport. KY-334. Abraham Lincoln, 16th President of the U. S., won his first law case here in 1827. Charged by the Commonwealth of Kentucky with operating a ferry without a license, Lincoln pleaded his own case in a trial at the home of the presiding Justice of the Peace, Samuel Pate.

53

Courthouse in Hawesville.

Immaculate Conception Catholic Church in Hawesville.

The Pate House in Lewisport.

Lincoln Toll Bridge over the Ohio River.

Henderson County

In 1799, seven years after the admission of Kentucky into the Union, Henderson County was formed from a part of Christian County. It was the thirty-eighth county in order of formation in Kentucky. It was named in honor of Colonel Richard Henderson, a Virginian with the Transylvania Company, who purchased a large part of Kentucky from the Cherokee Indians. He also settled Boonesborough, but was unsuccessful in forming a permanent colony there.

At the time of its formation, Henderson County embraced all of the territory now included in Henderson, Hopkins, Union and Webster Counties. The county is noted for its rich and prosperous farmland, and agricultural crops of soybeans and corn. Henderson, the county seat, is situated on the Ohio River and was laid off by surveyors Samuel Hopkins and Thomas Allen. The city was also named for Richard Henderson.

FESTIVALS, FAIRS, AND EXHIBITS

Big River Arts and Crafts Festival — N. of Henderson, at John J. Audubon State Park. US-41. First Saturday and Sunday in October.

Henderson County Fair — Henderson. US-41. July.

Methodist Hospital Antique Show — Henderson, First Methodist Church, at corner of 3rd and Green Sts. September.

PARKS AND RECREATION

Audubon Mill Park — Henderson, at Audubon gristmill site. Original stones from gristmill ore used in entranceway.

John J. Audubon State Park and Museum — Henderson. US-41N. Named for John J. Audubon, Kentucky artist. Park contains 590 acres of woods and lake with a nature center and a bird sanctuary.

Ellis Race Track — Henderson. US-41N. Mid-July to Labor Day.

Flatboat Event — Annual flatboat race on Ohio River from Owensboro to Henderson, with boats competing from various cities. August.

Midwest Harness — Henderson. US-41N. June through October.

Sloughs Wildlife Management Area — Henderson, between Geneva and the Ohio River. 2,500 acres. State-regulated.

Transylvania Park — Henderson, 1st St. First municipal park west of the Alleghenies. The Transylvania Company provided for park in an ordinance signed by the proprietors on Aug. 9, 1797.

MARKERS

James Audubon — Henderson, 208 N. Main St. First National Bank is location of the log cabin home of John James Audubon.

Mother's Day — Henderson, School Yard. US-41, US-60. Mary Towles Sasseen Wilson in 1887 first observed Mother's Day. In 1893 she obtained national observance. Congress adopted 2nd Sunday of May as holiday in 1914.

OLD BUILDINGS

Henderson Family Home — Henderson. KY-54. Back of residence was built in 1792; front was built 1810. Family home of Col. Richard Henderson's brother.

Audubon State Park near Henderson.

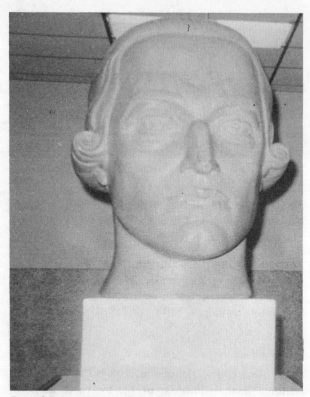

Bust of Colonel Richard Henderson.

Henderson Public Library — Henderson, 101 S. Main St. Built 1904. One of the oldest Carnegie buildings in the state.

Old First Christian Church — Henderson, Washington and Green Sts. Built 1854. Used as prison and hospital during Civil War.

Lazarus Powell Home — Henderson, 220 S. Elm. Built 1820. Residence of Lazarus Powell, 20th Governor of Kentucky.

St. Paul's Episcopal Church — Henderson, S. Green St. Built 1859.

Mary Towles Sasseen's Home — Henderson, 232 S. Main St. Built on property deeded to Walter Alves, whose daughter married Richard Henderson, nephew of Col. Richard Henderson. Later, the house was occupied by Mary Towles Sasseen, originator of Mother's Day.

MOTHERS DAY

HERE, MARY TOWLES SASSEEN WILSON IN 1887, FIRST OBSERVED MOTHERS DAY. STARTED WITH HER PUPILS. IN 1893, SHE OBTAINED NATIONAL OBSERVANCE. KY LEGISLATURE RECOGNIZED HER AS "ORIGINATOR OF IDEA." CONGRESS ADOPTED SECOND SUNDAY OF MAY AS HOLIDAY IN 1914.

KENTUCKY DEPARTMENT OF HIGHWAYS 191

Founder of Mother's Day lived here in Henderson.

McLean County

McLean County was established in 1854 out of parts of Daviess, Muhlenberg and Ohio Counties. It is situated on the Green River, which forms half of its eastern boundary, while the Pond River forms the county's western boundary. McLean was the one hundred third county to be formed in Kentucky. It was named in honor of Judge Alney McLean, who served Kentucky well as a circuit judge and state and U. S. Representative.

Calhoun is the county seat. It was first known as Vienna, or Fort Vienna, in 1788, when Solomon Rhoads built his fort here. In 1790, a party of trappers from Fort Vienna was attacked by Indians at the mouth of the Green River, and several men from the fort were killed. Today, a granite marker commemorates the site of Fort Vienna and indicates the hillside where the early settlers dug caves for refuge during the Indian attacks. The town was later renamed in honor of Judge John Calhoun, who was the first circuit Judge of old Fort Vienna, and who served as a U. S. Congressman from 1835-1839.

The treacherous Green River bisects the county in the center, and is the deepest river, for its width, in the world. There are many known places in the river where no one has found the bottom. Farming plays an important role in McLean County's economy, as well as the production of beef, cattle and hogs. There are 863 farms in McLean County covering 131,981 acres, which is an average of 152.9 acres per farm. The principal crops are corn, soybeans, wheat, and tobacco.

EXHIBITS

McLean County Arts and Crafts Show — Calhoun, McLean County High School. First weekend in May.

DAMS

Calhoun Lock and Dam — Calhoun, Green River. KY-256W. First locks built in 1837 on Rumsey side of the river. Present day locks completed 1956. River has 103 navigable miles.

MARKERS

Calhoun — Calhoun, at Courthouse. KY-81. Incorporated as Calhoun in 1852 and became the county seat in 1854. This is the boyhood home of builder and master of "My Old Kentucky Home," Senator John Rowan. The city is known as the "Capital of Green River."

Gen. Nathan B. Forrest's Cavalry Scouted Area — Calhoun, 2nd and Popular Sts. On reconnaissance searching for supplies, late in Nov. 1861, CSA Gen. Forrest's Cavalry scouted this area, as reported by the Union forces of Gen. T. L. Crittenden. Forrest moved on west, but returned Dec. 28, 1861. Forrest met and defeated Union scout force in Battle of Sacramento. CSA men escaped capture by Union troops sent from Calhoun.

McLean County Recruits Co. D — Calhoun. KY-250E. McLean county recruits Company D, 35th Regiment, Kentucky Volunteer Mounted Infantry. Charles (Frank) Prange, Capt. George W. Mosely, James T. Goode; Lieuts. Wm. A. Short, John H Taylor; Sgts. James R. Baughn, Western Mitchell, Joseph F. Baughn, Thomas A. Nalley, Allen H. Benton, James D. Nalley, Granville Brown, Charles F. Prange, Michael Conley, Malvin Presley, Cpl. Remos A. Cary, William L. Roads, Samuel A. Hudson, Mark L. T. Robertson, Hubbard V. Hicks, Lafayette Riley, George L. James, Alexander Stogner, John W. Little, James A. Taylor, Lucius L. Mitchell, and Wm. B. Taylor.

Rumsey — Rumsey. KY-81. Founded in 1834 and named for James Rumsey, steam navigation pioneer, at request of his nephew, Edward Rumsey, a U. S. Congressman from this area in 1837-1839. James Rumsey had the first boat successfully operated by steam to carry both freight and passengers on the Potomac River in 1786. The first steamboat on the Green River, *Lucy Wing,* was built here in 1846 by the Jones Brothers.

Surprise Attack Here — Sacramento. KY-81. CSA Cavalry from Hopkinsville under Col. Nathan B. Forrest surprised Union forces under Maj. Eli H. Murray on Dec. 28, 1861. Forrest sent dismounted men to attack both enemy flanks, and with the remaining mounted men, he bore down the road upon the Union center, which broke and fled. Forrest pursued for 4 miles and dispersed the USA troops, then returned to Hopkinsville.

MEMORIALS

Town Marker — Livermore. KY-136. Erected in 1837 as 100-year memorial.

City Hall Plaque — Livermore. KY-136. In memory of William Brown, who granted and dedicated the land from Elm St. to Popular St., including the Public Landing, to the town of Livermore for their public use.

Plaque of Fire Station — Livermore. KY-136. Dedicated in memory of all citizens of Livermore who have given their lives in the service of their county.

OLD BUILDINGS

First Post Office of Livermore — Livermore. KY-136. First Post Office. Mr. William Brown was appointed on May 15, 1838 the first Postmaster.

Griffis and Franklin House — Calhoun, 2nd and Popular Sts. Built 1850. Gen. Thomas L. Crittenden used this house as Civil War headquarters for Federal soldiers during the fall and winter of 1861. It also served as a hospital, selected because of its location on a hill overlooking the Green River. Colonial design. Seven different types of doors.

Mystery House — Calhoun. KY-256W. House built during World War II by a German man from New York. Purpose of the house was to be used as a retreat in case of invasion or bombing of New York. Constructed of Native field stones.

OTHER POINTS OF INTEREST

Corp. James Bethel Gresham Memorial Bridge — Rumsey. KY-81. Erected 1928, honoring the first American killed in action in World War I on Nov. 3, 1917 at the Battle of Sommerville. He enlisted in 1914 in Indiana and was with Pershing in Mexico in 1916. Sent overseas on June 14, 1917 with first American soldiers of AEF. Born in McLean County, Aug. 23, 1893, buried in France. Reinterred in Evansville, Indiana in 1921.

Livermore Bridge — Livermore. US-431S. Over the Green and Rough Rivers. Dedicated Nov. 13, 1940. When this structure was built, a unique contribution to history was made. Said to be the only river bridge in

the world to begin and end in the same county; also spans the Green and Rough Rivers while crossing Ohio County, a small point of which lies between the 2 rivers. This bridge is 1350-ft. long.

Livermore Bridge over the Green and Rough Rivers.

Calhoun Lock and Dam.

The Griffis and Franklin House in Calhoun.

Ohio County

Ohio County, the thirty-fifth county in order of formation in Kentucky, was formed in 1798 from part of Hardin County. It is the sixth largest area in Kentucky and received its name from the Ohio River, which forms the northern boundary line of the state. Counties formed from the original Ohio County territory include all of Daviess County in 1815, parts of Butler and Grayson Counties in 1810, Hancock County in 1829, and McLean County in 1854.

Ohio County and Hartford, the county seat, share one of Kentucky's proudest historical backgrounds. Few other parts of the Commonwealth can point to more important early landowners than those who first established claims to the acres on and around the Rough River.

Hartford was established as a fort in 1782 on a bluff overlooking the Rough River. It was the first fortified settlement in the lower Green River Valley, followed by Barnett's Station, two miles east, and Calhoun, in what is now McLean County, at "the lower falls of the Green." In 1799, the principal building in Hartford was the jail. The following year, Carl Wallace built a two-story log courthouse on top of the jail. Hartford, incorporated in 1808, was not officially mapped until 1816, and included an area of four acres donated to the county from a part of 4,000-acre Virginia land grant of Gabriel Madison for the public square of the county seat. Deer, also called harts, often crossed the Rough River below the bluff, and settlement was known as the "harts' ford," from which the name Hartford was derived.

FAIRS AND FESTIVALS

Arts and Crafts Show, Flea Market — Rosine. Third weekend in June.

Ohio County Arts and Crafts Show and Homemakers' Fair — Hartford. 100 W. Render St., at Wayland Alexander School.

Rosine Fall Festival — Rosine. First weekend in September.

Bill Monroe Bluegrass Music Festival — Rosine. Second weekend in September; lasts 4 days.

MARKERS

First Bridge — Just N. of Hartford city limits, at the Rough River. US-231. This is the site of the first covered bridge, built in 1823, and thought to be the first across the Rough River. When the original bridge decayed, it was replaced by another. Earlier river crossings were by ford or ferry. An iron bridge was constructed in its place in 1875, and removed 23 years later to Barnett's Creek. The present bridge was opened to traffic in 1934.

The Ohio County News — Hartford, in front of old newspaper building. US-231. This newspaper was formed by a merger in 1926, of the *Hartford Herald*, founded by John Barrett in 1875, and the *Hartford Republican*, established in 1888 by Col. Cicero Barnett. For 50 years "The Herald of a Noisy World" was the masthead of the *Hartford Herald*. McKowell Fogle and Wilburn Tinsley were the first coeditors of *The News*.

Early Surgery — Hartford, at the Green River Regional Library. US-231. The first known successful removal of an entire collarbone, performed in 1813 by Dr. Charles McCreery. The patient, a 14-year old boy, "made complete recovery with perfect use of his arm, living past middle age." Dr. McCreery was born in 1785, trained under Dr. John Goodlett of Bardstown, settled in Hartford about 1807, and was the area's first real doctor. He died in 1826.

MEMORIALS AND MUSEUMS

Ohio County Historical Society Museum — Hartford, Mulberry St. Open by appointment.

Memorial to Pendleton Vandiver — Rosine, Rosine Cemetery. Monument in shape of violin.

OLD BUILDINGS

Hartford Academy — Hartford, 200 block of Center St. Built 1835. Now privately owned by Kenneth Leach.

"Hillside" — Hartford, 403 E. Union St. Built 1861 by Dr. John E. Pendleton. Now privately owned.

Ohio County Library — Hartford, 413 Main St.

OTHER POINTS OF INTEREST

Cowden Company — Beaver Dam, Goshen Rd. Jeans manufacturer.

Cynthetex Corporation — Beaver Dam. US-231S. Manufactures unwoven fabrics.

Famous "Dundee" Goat — Dundee. KY-69. Listed in Ripley's Believe It or Not. A weather vane 75 ft. high, atop the Dundee Masonic Lodge Hall. One of 3 brought from London, England in 1904. The symbol of the Woodmen Lodge and erected originally on the Woodmen Lodge. This building including the "Dundee Goat" was sold to the Dundee Masonic Lodge.

Kimball Furniture Corporation — Fordsville. Manufactures furniture. Tours by appointment only.

Thomas Industries — Beaver Dam. US-231S. Lighting fixtures manufacturer.

Famous Dundee Goat in Dundee.

"Hillside" in Hartford.

Vandiver Memorial in Rosine.

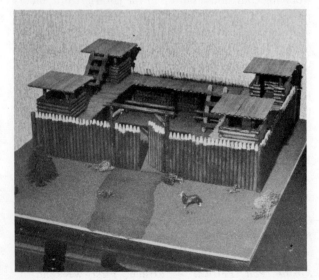

Fort Hartford replica in Hartford.

Union County

In May of 1811, Union County was the fifty-fifth Kentucky county to be created, and was formed from land taken from Henderson County. The origin of the naming of Union County is not clear. At the time the land was taken from Henderson County, there was no opposition to its establishment, because the people of Henderson County generally recognized that a new county was needed. It seems that, due to the unanimity on the subject, the county was named Union. It is also possible that the county was named to honor the American Union, as a large part of Union County land was a grant to General Daniel Morgan for his services in the American Revolution.

Today, it is hard to imagine that, at one time, only trails led through Union County. Turkey, sheep, cattle and hogs were driven to Uniontown and Caseyville, loaded onto ships and barges, and sent to market. Stagecoaches also served the area as a source of transportation.

Morganfield, the county seat, was laid out in August, 1811 on land donated by Presley O'Bannon, and was named for General David Morgan. Morgan Springs, where early settlers got their water, is located in Morganfield. In May of 1975, the city incorporated Morgan Springs into a beautiful fountain in the new City Plaza.

Today, in Union County, one can still find homes hewn from poplar trees, as well as homes built by slave labor. Some brick homes were built of bricks fired directly on the farms. Over half the county is rich farm land. While the county produces oil from deep wells today, their first oil well reached a depth of 900 feet, and was dug with wooden tools.

FAIRS, FESTIVALS AND DRAMAS

Union County Arts and Crafts Festival — Morganfield. First weekend in November.

Union County Community Playhouse — Morganfield. Two theatre productions per year.

Corn Festival — Morganfield. September.

Union County Fair — Sturgis. KY-109. July.

Trade Days Festival — Sturgis. KY-109. June.

PARKS AND RECREATION

Moffet's Lake — Morganfield. US-641. Camping, swimming, and picnicking facilities.

Henry-Higginson Wildlife Reservation — Morganfield. KY-56E.

MARKERS

Bell Mines — Sturgis. US-60, US-641. John Bell (1797-1869) of Tennessee owned coal mines 2 mi. S. of here. Congressman and Senator 1827-1859.

Camp Breckinridge — Morganfield. US-60. Named for John Breckinridge, first Kentuckian to be U.S. Vice President.

U. S. Treasurer Samuel Casey — Sturgis. Jct. KY-109, KY-130. Treasurer of U.S. from 1853-1859 under Presidents Pierce and Buchanan.

Civil War Action — Old Caseyville. KY-130. Every inhabitant of this pro-Southern town was taken prisoner by the crew of a Union Gunboat on July 26, 1862. All were released except 19 men who were taken to Evansville, Indiana as hostages to guarantee payment of $35,000 for damages done by CSA guerrillas.

CSA Gen. Forrest Reconnoitered Here — Morganfield. US-60, US-641. CSA General Nathan B. Forrest, on reconnaissance and foraging mission towards Ohio River, passed here with 300 men on way to Caseyville, where he found and took a large supply of hogs. After he left, USA took remaining hogs on way to Hopkinsville, but Forrest captured their horses, cattle, and more hogs when he returned to Hopkinsville.

Lincoln Spoke Here — Morganfield, Courthouse lawn. Site of Abraham Lincoln's only political speech in Kentucky, his native state.

Lewis Richards — E. of Boxville. KY-56, KY-983. Lewis Richards (1754-1846) was an early settler who served as a Sergeant with Gen. George Rogers Clark when he built first blockhouse at what is now Cincinnati. Continued in an attempt to save Kentuckians captured by British and Indians in 1779. Unable to overtake them, he destroyed the Indian villages at Chillicothe and Piqua. Richards was an Ohio volunteer at the Battle of Blue Licks in 1782.

Sturgis Coal — Sturgis. US-60. Steamboat Robert E. Lee won boat race against the Natchez in 1870. Nearby coal fields supplied fuel to power the steamboat. Greatest race in history began in New Orleans and ended in St. Louis. The Robert E. Lee won the championship of Mississippi River by 6 hours and 15 minutes. Both steamboat captains were Kentuckians.

OLD BUILDINGS

Baptist Girls' College Dormitory (McGill House) — Sturgis. Baptist College established in 1894.

Casey House — Sturgis, 6th St. between Main and Monroe. Oldest house in Sturgis.

Courthouse — Morganfield. Built 1873. First courthouse erected as county seat.

The Hugh's House — Morganfield, O'Bannon St. circa 1825.

St. Agnes Catholic Church — Uniontown. circa 1893.

OTHER POINTS OF INTEREST

Anvil Rock — 2 mi. N.W. of DeKoven. Stated in 1854 geological survey.

Coke Ovens — DeKoven, 3 mi. N. of Sturgis. US-60.

Duff's Cave — Caseyville, DeKoven Rd.

Hamilton Mine — Uniontown. Largest underground mining facility in the world.

Old City — Uniontown, 5 mi. N. of Sturgis. US-60. During 1800's had one of the world's largest distilleries.

Overland Coal Conveyor — Morganfield. US-60N. Longest continuous belt in the world.

Courthouse in Morganfield.

62

Webster County

Webster County, established in 1860 out of parts of Henderson, Hopkins, and Union Counties, was the one hundred ninth in order of the formation of Kentucky counties. The county was named in honor of Daniel Webster, one of the greatest of American orators, statesmen and lawyers. The early history of Webster County is not known extensively, but William Jenkins of Virginia is believed to have been the first settler. He was in charge of an arsenal at Yorktown, and received a land grant for his services in the Revolutionary War. Jenkins established a stagecoach inn at the site of present-day Dixon in 1794. This was the Halfway House which supposedly became a popular stopping place on the Natchez Trace.

The Green River forms most of the county's east boundary line, with the Tradewater River on the southwest. The county contains much rich soil, especially in the river bottom lands. Today, most agricultural activity is large scale commercial grain or livestock farming. Soybeans, corn and hogs are the leading agricultural commodities.

The history of no county would be complete without including at least one of its wild frontier-days tales. Webster County's most famous is probably that of the notorious Harp Brothers. Micajah, or "Big" Harp was slain here on July 22, 1806, and his head placed on a pole near a roadside tree as warning to outlaws. The initials "H.H." (meaning Harp's Head) were cut into the bark of the tree, and were legible for more than 60 years. Although there have been many accounts of the chase, Captain John Leeper and Moses Stigall are said to have been principals in the bloody capture of "Big" Harp.

The city of Dixon was incorporated as the county seat of Webster County on February 6, 1861. Named for Archibald Dixon, Lieutenant Governor of Kentucky from 1844 to 1848, the town of Dixon was laid out on land owned by Ambrose Mooney, who also gave the land for the courthouse. Dixon has streets named for Leeper and Stigall, the men who captured "Big" Harp, the outlaw.

During the Civil War, some CSA prisoners were confined in the log jail on the Courthouse square. They were stripped of their garments, clothed in odds and ends, and placed in the jail. They later escaped, and at the end of the war, the survivors of the group marched through Dixon on their way home and saw their uniforms on the home Guards. They forced these guards to carry logs from the log jail to the county jail where several CSA soldiers were still imprisoned. The prisoners were freed and the logs used to set the jail on fire. This is when many of the county records were destroyed.

FAIRS AND FESTIVALS

Webster County Arts and Crafts Show — Dixon, Main St. at Courthouse lawn. September.

Savage Days — Providence. Commemorates founding of Providence in 1820 by Richard Savage. Parade and beauty contest. August.

Show and Share Days — Dixon, Webster County High School. Annual craft show by Webster County Homemakers. November.

PARKS

Sebree Springs Park — Sebree. KY-370. Once the most famous summer resort in Kentucky, the mineral water was recommended by physicians for stomach, liver and kidney trouble. The city now operates the Sebree Springs Park, which includes a swimming pool.

MARKERS

Harp's Head — Dixon. US-41A. Marks where the head of "Big" Harp, notorious outlaw, was hung as warning to other outlaws.

MEMORIALS

War Memorial — Dixon, Courthouse lawn. Built in remembrance of 85 Webster County residents who died in World Wars I and II.

OLD BUILDINGS

Dixon Bank — Dixon, Main St. Organized 1895.

Rice House — Dixon, 400 S. Main St. Birthplace of poet Cale Young Rice, and his philanthropist wife, Leban Lacey Rice. Some outstanding titles of Rice and his wife are *Bridging the Years, Mrs. Wiggs of the Cabbage Patch, Winners and Losers,* and *Passionate Follies.*

OTHER POINTS OF INTEREST

Battle of Burnt Mill — Dixon, near Vanderburg. KY-630. First battle of Civil War to take place in Kentucky in 1861.

Shane Manufacturing, Inc. — US-41A. near Providence, and KY-56 near Sebree. Clothing manufacturers.

Courthouse in Dixon.

War Memorial in Dixon.

The Rice House in Dixon.

Mammoth Cave Area

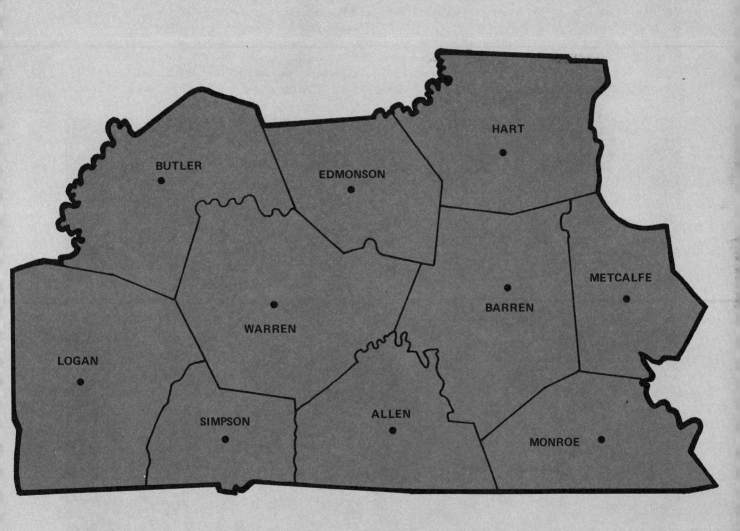

BUTLER

EDMONSON

HART

LOGAN

WARREN

BARREN

METCALFE

SIMPSON

ALLEN

MONROE

Allen County

On January 11, 1815, parts of Warren and Barren Counties were united by legislative enactment to form Allen County, the fifty-seventh county to be created in Kentucky. The county was named for Colonel John Allen, who was one of the many men killed at the Battle of the River Raisin in the War of 1812.

It is quite likely that white men visited the Allen County area more than twenty-five years before a permanent settlement was established. The famed Vir-

ginia Long Hunters camped in the Allen County area in 1775, it being the farthest point west they travelled before returning to their homes in Virginia. Most of the early settlers entered Allen County by way of the Wilderness Trail, one of the oldest roads in Kentucky, connecting Lexington and Nashville.

One of the earliest Allen County settlements was Gainesville, on the Old Trail, established in 1797. It is located north of Scottsville. Other settlements were

Old Stagecoach Inn near Scottsville.

Port Oliver, Motley, Allen Springs, Forrest Springs, Butlersville, Mt. Aerial, and New Roe.

For $200, John Brown sold 100 acres of land on Bays Creek to the appointed magistrates on which to build the county seat. The town site was laid off in lots, and the proceeds from these sales were the fund for building the courthouse. The county seat was named Scottsville after the fourth governor of Kentucky, Charles Scott. The big spring about two blocks from the public square in Scottsville, was the main factor in deciding the site of the county seat.

Life in Allen County today is as lively as it was in early pioneer days. Farming continues to be the principal business. The additional development of limestone and clay mining as well as oil production has been prosperous. The first oil wells were drilled in Allen County in 1913. The county was soon recognized as having the largest shallow oil field in the world. The resort trade is a new and growing business for the county.

FAIRS

Allen County Fair — Scottsville, at the Fairgrounds. US-31E. Sponsored by the Allen County Jaycees. An annual event.

CEMETERIES

Old Scottsville Cemetery — Scottsville, W. Maple St. Many tombstones are dated in the 1700's.

OLD BUILDINGS

Bethlehem Baptist Church — 3 mi. from Scottsville. US-31E. Oldest church in county. First called Upper Difficult.

City-County Building in Scottsville.

Big spring near public square in Scottsville.

Birthplace of Professor Lewis Harmon — KY-1533 on the Erwin Road. President of Bowling Green Business University. Now privately owned.

Tabernacle — Scottsville. KY-100, S.E. Built 1897. Still in use.

Old Walker House — Scottsville, Second and Maple. Built 1840. One of the oldest homes still standing in this area. Now privately owned.

OTHER POINTS OF INTEREST

Calvert Springs — Scottsville. KY-671. Spring water flows from crack in rock and supplies the city with 300,000 gallons of water daily. Water also comes from Barren River when needed.

Forrest Springs — Scottsville. Off US-31E. Old resort known for different types of mineral water within 30 yds. of each other. People from all over U.S. came here to benefit from the mineral baths.

Indian Mound — Scottsville. Between US-231 and KY-100. The mound is 40 ft. in circumference and 4 ft. high. Tribe of Indians is unknown. Large human bones have been exhumed — some of the bones measure 8 to 10 in. longer than the race of men thought to have inhabited this county.

Old Trail — Old Nashville Road. Early road connecting Nashville, Tennessee and Lexington, Kentucky. Mail carried in 1820 by horseback, later by stagecoach.

Oil Wells — Scottsville, on Bays Fork, West Fork, and Big Trammel Creek.

Barren County

Barren County lies in the Green River District. It was the thirty-seventh county in order of formation in Kentucky, and was formed in 1798 from Warren and Green Counties. Its name is derived from the "barrens," — vast, treeless plains or prairies, the name once given to the prairies common to southern Kentucky. Contrary to its name though, most of the "barren" land is fertile and highly productive. Tobacco is the principal crop, though grain is cultivated extensively, too. Much attention is devoted to raising livestock and dairy production. The economy in Barren County today is affected by the new Barren River Reservoir and State Resort Park, one of the finest in the state.

In 1880, Glasgow, the county seat, was a town of 1500. The origin of its name is uncertain. It was probably derived either from Glasgow, Scotland or Glasgow, Virginia. The first courthouse was a log structure, succeeded by five others over a period of years.

In 1880, the census reports showed Barren County was the fourth largest petroleum production section in the United States.

Caves, prehistoric remains, human bones, and old inscriptions upon trees are among the wonders and curiosities of the county.

FAIRS AND EXHIBITS

Arts and Craft Show — Cave City. Wax Museum, Mammoth Cave Rd. October.

Art Show, Exhibit and Sale — Glasgow, Columbia Ave. Held in St. Andrews Episcopal Church.

Barren County Fair — Glasgow. US-68W. Barren County Speedway. July or August.

Glasgow Garden Club Christmas Bazaar — Glasgow, S. Green St. Lera B. Mitchell Clubhouse. Variety of homemade gifts and Christmas decorations. Luncheon served. Second week in December.

PARKS

Barren River Lake State Park — Glasgow. US-31E. Resort Lodge, cottages, camping, nature trails, riding stables, fishing, boating, picnic area. Open all year.

MARKERS

Barren County — Glasgow, Courthouse yard. US-31E., US-68. County received its name from "the barrens" or prairies of this region. In Civil War Morgan's Raiders came through here on their first two raids. The invasion of Kentucky under Gen. Braxton Bragg also began in this area.

Bear Wallow — Glasgow. US-31E. at Hart County line. During the invasion of Kentucky by CSA, Gen. L. Polk's regiment moved through here in September of 1862 to attack USA troops at Munfordville.

Bell's Tavern — Park City. 2 blocks off US-31W. First tavern was erected by William Bell in 1830. Stagecoach stop for Mammoth Cave visitors. Burned in 1860. New tavern was never completed due to the outbreak of the Civil War. It still remains in its partially-finished state.

Christmas Mishap — Glasgow, Courthouse yard. US-31E., US-68. On December 24, 1862 the main section of Morgan's Raiders made camp south of here to celebrate Christmas. Capt. Quirk and scouting troops were also in the area, as well as a patrol of 2nd Michigan Cavalry. A slight skirmish resulted, but no Christmas celebration was held on either side.

Confederate Congressional Medal of Honor — Glasgow, Courthouse yard. US-31E., US-68. In 1862, CSA President Jefferson Davis was authorized to confer a Medal of Honor upon one enlisted man of each company for each victory. More Confederates from Barren County received this honor than any other county in Kentucky.

Preston H. Leslie Home — Glasgow, US-31E., US-68. Governor Preston Leslie was the 26th Governor of Kentucky. Leslie was noted for his sound judgment in state affairs, and for meeting the needs of a growing population and business.

General Joseph H. Lewis — Cave City. US-31W. Confederate Brig. Gen.; Commander of famous Orphan

Brigade in the Civil War. Buried in Glasgow Cemetery.

Long Hunter's Camp — Glasgow. US-31E., KY-90. Henry Skaggs and 2 hunter companions are thought to be the first white men in this area. Named "Long Hunters" due to the long period of time they spent away from their homes in the East. They were responsible for bringing many pioneers to this area.

Partisan Protected — KY-218 at Park. Civil War's first Kentucky Federal death. A Union Company slipped through the graveyard at night to arrest a Southern sympathizer, C. B. Hutcherson. The 10 poorly-equipped recruits from the CSA camp sent to guard him were attacked, resulting in the deafeated Union men with one dead — no CSA losses.

Settles Rifles — Glasgow. 5 mi. W. of US-31E. on KY-252. Now rare collector's items, the rifles produced by the Settles family here in Glasgow were prized by frontiersmen.

Trigg Fox Hounds — Glasgow. Plaque in Courthouse. Trigg Fox Hounds were developed in 1867 by Col. Haiden C. Trigg of Glasgow from a cross of the Bird Song (July), Maupin (Walker) and imported English Fox Hounds, to produce a superior strain. These hounds have become world famous and so popular that there is now a Trigg National Fox Hunters Association which holds a closed meeting annually.

Fort Williams — Glasgow, W. of Municipal cemetery and US-31E. bypass. Site of Civil War fort built in Spring of 1863. Attacked in October by Confederate John M. Hughs and his 25th Tennessee Infantry. A committee is presently formulating plans to rebuild the fort.

MUSEUMS

Biblical Museum — Cave City. KY-90, US-31W. House of past Biblical scenes from Genesis to Judgement.

Old Kentucky Museum — North Cave City. US-31W. Museum of Kentucky antiques.

Mammoth Cave Wax Museum — Cave City. KY-70, West interchange off I-65. Wax life-like figures of famous Americans, authentically costumed. Open all year.

Wildlife Museum — Cave City. KY-90, 1/2 mi. E. of Cave City exit to I-65. Unusual museum of wildlife in rustic cave grotto setting.

CEMETERIES

Crain Cemetery — Glasgow. One of the oldest cemeteries in the county. Located on Nathan Smith Farm.

Edwards Cemetery — Hiseville. One of the oldest cemeteries in the county. Located on Janie Edwards Farm.

Hardy Cemetery — Hiseville, Rock Springs Seymour Rd. Old cemetery located on Fred Watkins Farm.

Matthews Cemetery — Glasgow, in Morrison Park section. KY-63. Located on farm now owned by Marvin Matthews, between Tompkinsville and Burkesville Roads. Thought to be burial place of John Nelson Matthews and his wife, Elizabeth, who died in 1865 and 1868 respectively. The earliest marked stone in this cemetery is of infant son of Nancy (Peden) and Anderson Matthews who was born and died in 1846. There are many graves in this cemetery marked only by native stones, but with no names or dates.

Peden Cemetery — Glasgow, across Fallen Timber Creek. KY-63. Part of original plantation which Moses Peden settled about 1809. Brothers James, Benjamin and Francis came from Virginia, settled close by and died in 1819. The earliest burials in this cemetery date back to 1834 when 2 infants, grandsons of Moses Peden, died and were buried here. Also buried in this cemetery is a Revolutionary War soldier from Virginia, William Harris, Sr., who died in 1839. Several unmarked graves are in this cemetery.

Several old cedar trees are still growing in this cemetery. This part of the Peden plantation has never been out of the Peden family and is now owned by Rosie Lee Peden.

OLD BUILDINGS

Laurel Bluff and Mill Site (School House Site) — Temple Hill. KY-63. Named for an adjoining creek bluff that was always covered with laurel.

Marker on corner of square in Glasgow.

Saltpetre Cave near Temple Hill.

The Preston H. Leslie Home in Glasgow.

Old Richardson House or Spotswood House — Glasgow, N. Race St. Built by George Washington for his niece. A cave still connects with the house, and was used as a shelter from Indians. Home is now owned by the Coffmans, whose ancesters were relatives of George Rogers Clark. Two Confederate generals have lived there, William Thomas Martin and Joseph H. Lewis. Private property.

OTHER POINTS OF INTEREST

Huckleberry Hill — Cave City. KY-70W. and I-65. Adjacent to Mammoth Cave Wax Museum. Craft capital of the Cave Country.

"Old Trail" — Glasgow. US-31E. Early road connecting Nashville, Tennessee and Lexington, Kentucky. Mail carried on it by horseback in 1820's, later by stagecoach.

Old Ritter Mill Site and Temple Hill — Glasgow, 8 mi. E. near Temple Hill. KY-63. Mill began operating in 1820, sold to Fish Ritter in 1892, later to Tobe and John T. Boyter. In addition to being a wheat and corn grinding mill, it also served as a saw mill. This mill produced a flour called "White Dove." Original mill collapsed in April, 1974. Equipment from this mill is now at Wondering Woods, Cave City.

Saltpetre Cave — Temple Hill. KY-63. Saltpetre mined for powder during War of 1812. Tracks of wheelbarrows hauling the powder can still be seen.

Wondering Woods — Cave City, Exit I-65W., Jct. KY-70 and KY-255. "Where Yesterday Meets Today," at Tranquil Valley Village. Quaint buildings capture the spirit of the early 1900's. Chapel Garden Galleries and Harmony Tower with 70 ft. carillon bell tower.

Butler County

Butler County was organized January 18, 1810, from parts of Logan and Ohio Counties. The fifty-third county in order of formation, it is located in the southwestern part of the state. Butler County was named in honor of General Richard Butler of Pennsylvania, an officer in the Revolutionary War. He was slain by Indians in the ill-fated campaign by General Arthur St. Clair on the Wabash River in 1791. The northwestern part of the county is in the Western Coal Field of Kentucky and the southern part is in the Limestone area.

The Green River is the largest stream in the county and it flows through the county from south to north, almost equally dividing the population and wealth of the county.

Butler County was settled on the south side of the Green River by immigrants from Virginia and North

Carolina. The north side was settled by men with families from neighboring Kentucky counties. Many soldiers of the Revolutionary War also settled on the south side of the river.

Early leaders of county government were John Tyler, Jonathan Hobson, John J. Crittenden and John Breathitt, later Governor of Kentucky. There is still a log house in the county, the logs of which were cut and hewn by John Breathitt.

Soon after the organization of the court, the question came up as to the location of the county seat. Two places were nominated, one above the mouth of the Renfrow Creek, the other where Morgantown now stands, then known as Funkhouser Hill. Funkhouser Hill had the majority of votes and was selected as the county seat.

Eight miles south of Morgantown on a hill near the Little Muddy Church, stands the remains of a stockade built by the early settlers for their protection against the Indians. Near here also stood a house built by John Howard in the first part of the 19th century. The broad limestone chimney of this house was built by Thomas Metcalf, who later became Governor of Kentucky.

The limestone soil in the southwestern section of the county is especially adapted to growing fine tobacco. The greatest acreage of wheat in the county is grown here also. Bituminous coal is found in the west, north and some in the central parts of the county. This coal has proven to be almost as good as the best Pennsylvania coal. In 1900, coal mining was a very important industry in Butler County. Later, the high cost of transportation caused a large decline in the importance of Butler County coal mining.

Morgantown, the seat of justice for Butler County, was named in honor of a great hunter by the name of Morgan. Legends of his skill and accuracy are still told.

FAIRS AND EXHIBITS

Artists Show — Morgantown, Ohio St. Butler County Library. September.

Arts and Crafts Show — Morgantown, Ohio St. Butler County Library. November.

Butler County Fair — Morgantown. September.

MARKERS

Birthplace of Thomas Hines — Jct. US-231 and Woodbury Rd. Birthplace of "most dangerous man of Confederacy" in 1838. In November 1863, he led the escape of General John Hunt Morgan from a Federal prison in Ohio. Leader of northwest conspiracy in 1864.

Civil War Battle — Morgantown. KY-79, US-231.

Granville Allen — Morgantown, Logansport Rd. US-231, KY-79. First Union soldier killed in west Kentucky while skirmishing on the Big Hill with CSA scouting party Oct. 29, 1861. A stone monument erected in 1894. Union volunteers south of Green River risked danger for home and family.

Gunshop Site — Reedyville. KY-185. Site of gun shop operated by William Stephens, Sr. and two sons, English immigrants in 1855-1868.

MEMORIALS

Courthouse Monument — Morgantown. Monument dedicated to both Union and Confederate soldiers who fought in the Civil War. One of two such monuments in existence.

OLD BUILDINGS

Bethel Baptist Church — South Hill, between Morgantown and Rochester. KY-70. Only log church remaining in Butler County. Church organized in 1848; building erected 1871-72. One sill has been replaced, logs painted and floor recently sanded and varnished.

J. Guy Cook's Home — Morgantown, Warren Ave. First brick house built in Butler County. Bricks were made from soil near the house and garden area. House is the only one of its type in the city. Now privately owned by Cook family.

OTHER POINTS OF INTEREST

Rochester Dam — Green River was the main source of transportation for many years. Riverboats were the main way of getting food and materials in and out of the county.

Bethel Baptist Church in South Hill.

Rochester Dam on Green River.

Edmonson County

In 1825, Edmonson County was the seventy-ninth County in order of formation in the state. Hart, Warren and Grayson Counties contributed to its territory and it was named in honor of Captain John Edmonson, a Virginian who came to Kentucky in 1790 and settled in Fayette County. Captain Edmonson commanded a company of riflemen in Colonel John Allen's regiment and was killed in the disastrous Battle of the River Raisin in the War of 1812.

The Green River divides the county, flowing from east to west through the center, and, with its tributaries, offers excellent drainage. The land is rolling, rough and hilly in places. On the whole, the county is rather poor in regard to agriculture but is rich in natural wonders and mineral wealth. The county's coal deposits are considered inexhaustible, and the world-renowned Mammoth Cave is located in this area.

Brownsville, the seat of justice for Edmonson County,

is a small town with only a few hundred inhabitants. Noted for its quietness, old homes, shaded streets, and friendly people, the city is situated on the Green River near the center of the county. In 1828, the city was laid out and named for General Jacob Brown, Commanding General of the U. S. Army in the 1820's.

Mammoth Cave, one of the greatest natural wonders of the world, and the largest cave ever discovered or explored, is located in Edmonson County. Located a few miles from the Green River, the cave offers many breath-taking and magnificent attractions. Its historic value dates back to prehistoric man, to early settlers mining salt petre, and to its later use as a tuberculosis sanitarium. Several other caves can be found in the county, as well as many other natural wonders.

The construction of the Nolin River Dam and the impoundment of Nolin River Lake in northern Edmonson County now adds water sports and fishing to the county's recreation activities.

FAIRS

Edmonson County Fair — Brownsville. KY-70. September.

PARKS, RECREATION, LAKES, DAMS

Buzzard Cave — Brownsville. Up the river from Camp Joy.

Chalybeate Springs and Sulphur Springs — Chalybeate. Old spa with mineral springs.

Dismal Rock — Nolin River Dam. Large rock appears split off from cliff.

Green River — Central Edmonson County. Deepest little river in the world. River starts in Lincoln County and flows 360 miles west to the Ohio River near Henderson, Kentucky.

Indian Hill — Brownsville, off I-65 on KY-70. Unique elevation in Kentucky. One mile in circumference, it rises gradually and with great regularity on all sides except one which is nearly perpendicular, 100 ft. above the level of surrounding plain. On the summit of the hill is an indication of fortification and a number of mounds and burial sites. On the brow of the hill, a spring of water flows from a rock.

Mammoth Cave National Park — Brownsillve. KY-70, off I-65. One of the wonders of the world. Largest cave ever discovered or explored.

Nolin River Dam and Lake — North Central Edmonson County. Off I-65 and KY-728. 5,000 acres of water and beautiful shoreline. 20 mi. of remote woodlands.

Reservoir Hill — Brownsville. Hill overlooking Brownsville and the Green River Valley.

MARKERS

Battle of Brownsville — Brownsville. KY-259.

Naming of Brownsville — Brownsville. KY-259.

Naming of Edmonson County — Brownsville. KY-70. Courthouse lawn.

MUSEUM

Log Cabin Museum — Brownsville.

CEMETERIES

Hill View Cemetery — Brownsville on Dicky Mill Rd. Off KY-1827. Cemetery covered with moss and shells. Each year families return and replace the shells.

Old Guide Cemetery — Brownsville, Mammoth Cave National Park. KY-70, off I-65. Cemetery is located on a nature trail in park. Named in honor of Stephen Bishop, early guide and explorer in Mammoth Cave. Two graves contain tuberculosis patients who died in the cave during its use as a hospital in the 1840's.

OLD BUILDINGS

Dripping Springs Baptist Church — Park City. US-31W. Built 1831. The right side entrance was used by slaves to enter the balcony as they were not allowed below. The balcony has been removed, but the windows above the doors remain.

Edmonson County Courthouse — Brownsville. KY-70. Erected shortly after the Civil War by local volunteers. The building was built of native chestnut and bricks were made on the site of local clay. Recently renovated.

OTHER POINTS OF INTEREST

Iron Furnace — Brownsville. Off I-65. Historic and scenic.

Mammoth Cave National Park entrance near Brownsville.

Hill View Cemetery near Brownsville.

Hart County

Hart County dates back to 1819 as the sixty-first county to be formed in Kentucky. It was created from parts of Hardin and Green Counties, and named for Captain Nathaniel G. T. Hart, an early settler of Lexington, who also fought in the War of 1812.

Green River flows through the county from east to west, dividing it almost in half. The soil is very productive, and the county is one of the finest tobacco growing sections of the state. Farming is the main source of revenue along with livestock and dairy production, oil wells, numerous limestone quarries. Nolin Creek, which furnishes water power for a number of mills and factories, also aids the prosperity of Hart County. The railroad plays an important role in the history of Hart County as the Louisville and Nashville Railroad turnpike was the scene of many battles during the Civil War, with bridge-burning a constant hindrance to both the Confederate and the Union Armies.

Hart County abounds in caves, wonderful springs, holes in the ground and other natural attractions. In the level country, some six miles from Munfordville, a hole was discovered in the ground that created much excitement and interest. This bottomless pit is described as circular in shape, 60 or 70 feet in diameter, funnel-shaped for the first 25 feet from the surface, where it narrows down to 10 or 12 feet in diameter. The pit has never been explored below this point and a rock thrown into it can be heard to strike against the sides of the hole until the sound dies in the distance. This pit has been explored 275 feet without finding any bottom, and is popularly supposed to be the "short route to China."

Munfordville was laid out as the county seat by Richard J. Munford, donor of the land on which the present courthouse stands. The city is situated on a high hill overlooking the Green River. A very peculiar spring, situated about three miles from Munfordville near the banks of the Green River, has the regular ebb and flow of the ocean tides. About noon each day the water rises twelve or fifteen inches above its usual level, flows for a while over a mill dam erected below it, and then falls back to its original level.

FAIRS, DRAMAS

Hart County Fair — Munfordville. September.

Horse Cave Theater — Horse Cave, 107-109 Main St. Built 1911. Housed in the renovated Thomas Opera House. A professional repertory theater. Great plays are performed by members of Actors Equity Association. The lobby of the theater is a tobacco curing barn typical of the region's chief agricultural product.

MARKERS

Bacon Creek Bridge — Bonnieville. US-31W. Burned twice by John Hunt Morgan in 1860's.

Battle of Munfordville — Munfordville. US-31W. On Sept. 14-17, 1862, Mississippi Regiments of Gen. Bragg's army defeated Gen. Buell's Union forces. 50 were killed and 307 wounded. Confederates destroyed railroad bridge, the site of Fort Craig, and a monument to Col. R. A. Smith.

Glen Lily Home — Munfordville, Hammonsville Road. KY-569 off KY-357. Home of Confederate CSA Gen. Simon B. Buckner, Governor of Kentucky, 1887-91, and candidate for U. S. Vice President in 1896.

Last Recorded Indian Raid — 1/2 mile. N.E. of Legrande. KY-436. October 1792, ten Indians attacked travelers at Oven Spring. 3 killed, 2 captured. Settlers rescued captives. Records show no later raid in area.

On Washington's Guard — Hammonsville. KY-357. Burial site of Sgt. Joseph Timberlake, 1752-1841, member of Gen. George Washington's bodyguard. Cites Timberlake's outstanding qualities.

Site of Morgan's Induction — Woodsville. US-31W. October 27, 1861, Gen. Morgan and 84 of his men sworn in as second Cavalry Regiment, Kentucky Volunteers, CSA. Became "Morgan's Raiders."

Uncle Charlie Moran — Munfordville. KY-218. Centre College's famous coach of football and baseball.

CEMETERIES

Three Forks Cemetery — Hammonsville. KY-357.

OLD BUILDINGS

Dr. Lewis Barrett Home — Munfordville, 1st and Caldwell St. Built 1835. Plantation owner.

Civil War Nurses' Quarters — Munfordville, 3rd and Washington St. Built before Civil War. Formerly a school. Two rooms separated by 8-foot hall, one room for boys and one for girls.

Fort Craig Site — Munfordville. US-31W. Civil War earthen fort built by the Union Army on the south side of Green River in order to defend railroad bridge.

Frenchman's Knob — Bonnieville. Jct. US-31W. and KY-728. First settlement in Hart County. Scene of Indian ambush in 1788.

Richard De Grella Farm — Upton, KY-224. Natural waterfall is located on this farm as well as Indian graveyard and site where Indians ground corn. Now privately owned.

Richard Jones Munford Home — Munfordville, 1st and Washington Sts. Built in 1831 by Richard Jones Munford, founder of Munfordville. First house built in Hart County. Now privately owned.

Early Gunpowder Mill — KY-569. One of earliest industries begun before the county was formed. Thomas Gibson, its last operator, died in 1867.

Old Munfordville Inn — Munfordville, 1st and Washington St. Built in 1810 by Thomas Munford. General Andrew Jackson spent the night here on his way to inauguration.

Presbyterian Church — Munfordville, 3rd and Washington St. Built 1830. Used as hospital for Union Army during Civil War.

Rowletts Station — Munfordville. US-31W. In fall of 1861, Federals planned move into Tennessee by way of the Rowlett Station.

W. P. Savage Home — Munfordville. US-31W. Old National Turnpike. Winter headquarters of Gen. Mack Cash in 1862.

T. A. Smith House — Munfordville, Craddock and Washington St. Built 1836. Union Army headquarters in Civil War.

George T. Wood House — Munfordville, Caldwell St. Built in 1835 by George T. Wood, member of Kentucky Military Board during Civil War.

OTHER POINTS OF INTEREST

Horse Cave — Horse Cave. US-31W. Cave formerly used by Indians to hide stolen horses. Also Morgan's Raiders hid horses and supplies in cave.

Fort Willech and Fort Terrell — Munfordville. US-31W. Southside of Green River.

The Richard Jones Munford Home in Munfordville.

Old Munford Inn in Munfordville.

Presbyterian Church in Munfordville.

75

Logan County

Logan County is one of the early counties established in Kentucky. It was the thirteenth county in order of formation of the one hundred twenty counties of the Commonwealth of Kentucky. It was formed September 1, 1792, the year in which Kentucky became a state.

Benjamin Logan, for whom the county was named, was the founder of Logan's Station in Lincoln County. Born of Irish ancestry in Augusta County, Virginia, he and three slaves travelled with Daniel Boone to this area. Later, Logan served as a Representative to the Kentucky Legislature several times and was a member of the first two Constitutional Conventions in 1792 and 1799.

Russellville, the county seat, is situated in the center of the county. Logan County is sometimes referred to as one of the language isle counties of the Old South. This section was settled by Virginians and the language, culture and heritage of Logan County people are still that of Virginia.

Colonel William Russell, the person for whom the town of Russellville was named, was born in Culpepper County, Virginia on May 6, 1735. In 1756 he was captain of a company of rangers under General Braddock in the French and Indian War. Colonel Russell was given a grant of 2000 acres of land near Russellville, and the town was named for him.

At its present size, Logan remains the third-largest county in Kentucky. Its greatest length from north to south is approximately 29 miles. The southern half of the county is more level and rolling, and the better farming lands are situated south of Russellville and Auburn. Tobacco, corn and wheat have remained the chief farm products. The principal livestock that is raised is poultry, cattle, hogs and sheep. Industry came to Logan County in the period 1930 to 1962.

An interesting change took place in the political life of Logan County after the Civil War, because it became principally Democratic. Logan County wants to retain the best of the Old South and to welcome with open arms the best of a new and progressive day.

FAIRS AND FESTIVALS

Logan County Fair — Russellville. June.

Shakertown Revisited Festival — South Union. US-68. Between Auburn and Bowling Green. Honoring the Shaker Community. Arts, crafts, outdoor drama. Midsummer.

Tobacco Festival — Russellville. October.

MARKERS

Peter Cartwright Boyhood Home — Adairville. Renowned circuit-riding preacher of the Methodist Church, converted at Red River meeting house in 1800.

Confederacy State Convention — Russellville, City Square Park. US-68, US-431. Confederacy State Convention was held on Nov. 20, 1861. Confederate leaders from 64 counties seceded from the Union. The State was admitted as the 13th State in Confederate Union on December 10, 1861.

Dromgooles Station — Adairville. US-431. Fort built in 1788 by James Dromgooles. The name was changed in 1818 to Adairville.

Governors from Logan — Russellville, Courthouse yard. Seven Logan countians became governors in four states, Kentucky, Florida, Illinois and Texas.

Harrison's Mill — Adairville, between Adairville and Red River. KY-591. The historic marker is located in the Adairville park. The famous duel between Gen. Andrew Jackson and Charles Dickinson was fought near here in 1806.

John Littlejohn — Russellville, Town Square. Methodist circuit riding preacher, 1767-1832. Priceless journals preserved by Methodist church. Guardian of Declaration of Independence and other state papers in War of 1812.

MUSEUMS

Shakertown Museum — Auburn, S.W. of Bowling Green. US-68. Shaker architecture and furnishings. circa 1807-1822.

OLD BUILDINGS

Atkinson House — Russellville, 7th and Main St. Built in 1815 by Maj. Sherwood W. Atkinson, a Virginian. A unique feature in this house is the circular stairway on the north side of the house. Now privately owned.

Old Southern Bank of Kentucky — Russellville, 6th and Main St. Once the strongest bank in the state, and the first robbed by Jesse James. Constructed in 1810 as a home. Reconstructed and organized as a bank in 1850. Now known as Marcellite Hardy Memorial Museum, and houses historical documents and artifacts of the county. During the early days of the War Between the States, the president and cashier of the bank removed $1,000,000 from the vault and hid it in the surrounding hills until the danger of confiscation had passed. This bank was robbed by the James brothers and their gang in 1868, escaping with over $9,000. During the robbery Nimrod Long was shot in the head, slightly wounding him. The bullet furrowed his scalp and splattered against the wall covering the main vault. Bullet mark on wall is still visible.

Old Bibb Home — Russellville, 8th and Winter St. Maj. Bibb, a Revolutionary War officer, moved to Logan County in 1799. In 1829 he liberated 29 of his slaves and sent them to Liberia. His will provided for the liberation of the 70 remaining slaves. John Bibb, his son, developed Bibb lettuce.

Birthplace of Col. James Bowie — Russellville, Courthouse Square. Birthplace is on Terrapin Creek near the Simpson County line. Co-commander at the Alamo. Designed the Bowie knife.

Old Confederate Secession Convention Building — Russellville, 4th and Winter St. Clark Building. 116 delegates from 43 Kentucky counties met November 18-20, 1861, to form a Confederate Government for Kentucky and to elect state officials. House was built many years earlier by Mr. First, a cabinet maker from England. His name, corrupted to Forst, was later given to the Forst House Hotel, which for more than 100 years occupied the area where the Southern Deposit Bank now stands. Convention House is residence of Mrs. Wis Clark and may be visited on short notice to Mrs. Clark.

John J. Crittenden Home — Russellville, 9th and Main St. Crittenden came to Russellville in 1811 to study law under Judge George M. Bibb. Served three terms in the Kentucky House of Representatives, and in 1817 in the U. S. Senate. Later, he served as U. S. District Attorney, three more terms as U. S. Senator, as Governor of Kentucky, as Attorney General under President

Shakertown Museum in Auburn.

Fillmore. He was a member of the U. S. House of Representatives when he died in 1863.

Captain James Hunter Home (Samuel Caldwell House) — Russellville, 6th St. Built circa 1805. Samuel Caldwell, one of the earliest settlers, was Russellville's first merchant and the first Logan County Court Clerk. Because of his education and his excellent handwriting, his minutes in Order Book Number One, which are maintained in the present County Court Clerk's office, are beautiful to see as well as legible.

Captain John Lewis (Elmwood) — Dennis, between Russellville and Auburn. KY-68. Built circa 1811. Marker at grave in same section of county.

Presley Neville O'Bannon Home — Russellville, 9th and Main St. Built 1811. Lt. Presley N. O'Bannon, U. S. Navy, became a national hero when, during the war against Moorish pirates in the Mediterranean Sea, he captured Derna, Tripoli in 1805, freeing 180 American seamen that were being held for ransom, and the first American to plant the American flag on foreign soil. Shortly afterward, he moved to Russellville. Served four terms in the Kentucky House of Representatives, and one as State Senator.

Old Red River Meeting House — Schochoh, at the North Fork of Red River. US-431. The site of the early pioneer church, organized by "A Society of Presbyterians" in 1789. Here the great revival of 1800 was conducted by Rev. James McGready. The first camp meeting was held here. First grave dates back to 1798.

Roberts-Edwards Johnson Home — Russellville, end of Boxwood Drive. Built early 1800's. Used by Federal troops as hospital and major headquarters during the Civil War. Later it belonged to the Edwards family. Formerly known as "Oakhill." Renamed "Mockingbird Hill."

CONFEDERATE SOLDIERS 61 - 65

CAMP CALDWELL U.C.V. 139

Monument on square in Russellville.

Savage Home and Cave — Adairville. KY-591. Historic site; dwelling place of Palco Indians who lived there before the time of Christ. Historic house is reconstructed log stagecoach tavern once located on a Green River crossing.

Judge Wallace House — Russellville, 9th and Main St. In 1791 Judge William Wallace moved to Logan County and became the first jurist and the second judge of the Logan Circuit Court. In 1811 he built a two-room log house at what is now the S.E. corner of 9th and Main St. House was later used as a tavern. In 1822 Augustine Byrne incorporated the log structure and finished the home as it is seen today. Now privately owned.

OTHER POINTS OF INTEREST

Caldwell Saddle Factory — Russellville, 4th and Breathitt St. Built in the early 1800's by brothers, Andrew and David Caldwell, as a saddle and leather factory. Living quarters are in the rear of building. The twelve wide windows were designed so that two men at each window could work on the fine saddles made there. Still written in charcoal on a wall are the words, "Two years from today I will be free, 1828." Now privately owned.

Metcalfe County

Metcalfe County was organized in 1860, and was named for General Thomas Metcalfe, the tenth governor of Kentucky. It was formed from the surrounding counties of Adair, Monroe, Cumberland, Green, and Barren Counties; the largest portion from Barren County. The division came as a result of opposition to voting bonds for a railroad, making Metcalfe County the one hundred sixth county to be created in Kentucky. Early Metcalfe county settlers came from Virginia, Maryland and North Carolina, and are mostly of English and Scottish descent, as well as German and French.

The county is watered by tributaries of the Little Barren River, and has a diversity of soil. Agriculture has from the beginning been the main industry, with farming emphasis placed on corn, tobacco and dairy products. However, the sale of timber has been a lucrative source of income through the years.

Edmonton, the county seat, was named for its founder Edmund P. Rogers, a soldier of the Revolutionary War and a native of Virginia. The town was laid out in 1800, with the site being chosen, it is said, because of the spring located on the north side of the square. The old Rogers home stood on the western side of the town on the present site of the A. J. Thompson place.

The town's name was first spelled Edmundton, but gradually changed, and is the only town of that name in the United States.

Some of the other early settlements were Bridgeport, Antioch, Lafayette, Smith's Cross Roads and Randolph. The names have been changed to East Fork, Knob Lick, Center, Beaumont and Wisdom. All of

78

these settlements were thriving little villages with stores, water mills, blacksmith shops and various industries of the day.

PARKS

Sulphur Well Park — Sulphur Well. US-68.

MARKERS

Joseph A. Altsheler — Three Springs. KY-218. Newspaperman and author of 40 books on American history. Books reached peak of popularity about 1918. Died 1919.

Founder of Edmonton — 1/2 mi. W. of Edmonton. US-68. Edmund Rogers (1762-1843) was soldier in the American Revolution and was present at the surrender of Cornwallis in 1781. In 1783 he joined his cousin, George Rogers Clark, as a surveyor. Laid out Edmonton in 1800. Family burial is south of town.

William Henry Newman — Edmonton. US-68. Public square. Newman (1848-1918) was an associate of the great railroad builders. He was successor to Cornelius Vanderbilt as President of New York Central Railroad, 1901-1909. Merged 14 lines into New York Central system. Planned Twentieth Century Ltd., and Grand Central Terminal.

Savoyard — Savoyard. KY-314. Birthplace of Eugene W. Newman, whose pen name (Savoyard) was given to the town previously called Chicken Bristle. Newman, 1845-1923, was great political writer for several metropolitan newspapers.

Ed Porter Thompson — Center. KY-314. Born near Center (1834-1903.) Noted educator, mathematician, linquist and author. His *History of the Orphan Brigade* is valuable Civil War record.

CEMETERIES

Beauchamp Cemetery and Edmund Rogers Burial Ground — Edmonton, Dunham St., W. of Edmonton Baptist Church. Rogers and Beauchamps family intermarried, and are buried here in a private burial ground. Edmund Rogers, 1762-1843, laid out Edmunton in 1800.

OLD BUILDINGS, CHURCHES, HOMES

Mt. Mirah Church — Between Randolph and Summer Shade. KY-640. Cumberland Presbyterian Church. Established Mar. 18, 1848 while Metcalfe County was a part of Barren County. A wooden two-story building with the second floor used for Mason's meeting place. A new wooden church was erected about 1943. Members were both black and white and if any broke the rules, they were thrown out of church.

Dripping Springs Baptist Church — Edmonton, the Edmonton and Glasgow Rd. US-68 and KY-80. Oldest church in the county, constituted Feb. 3, 1798. Robert Stockton was the first pastor. The present brick building was erected in 1960.

Old Sulphur Well Springs — Sulphur Well. US-68. A relic of county resort hotel of 50 to 60 years ago.

Old Sulphur Well Springs in Sulphur Well.

Grave marker of E. P. Rogers in Edmonton.

Monroe County

Monroe County was established in 1820 as the sixty-fifth county to be created by the Kentucky Legislature. Carved out of Cumberland and Barren Counties, it lies in the southern tier of counties, bordering the Tennessee State line.

The county was named for James Monroe, the fifth President of the United States because at the time of its organization he had just been elected to his second term as President.

Tompkinsville, the county seat, was laid out in 1819, and is situated on Mill Creek, nine miles from the Cumberland River. As Monroe County was named for the President of the United States, the county seat was named for Daniel D. Tompkins, the Vice President. The city was laid out on lands belonging to Samuel Marrs, and according to records, the courthouse stands on the spot where his orchard stood.

Monroe County suffered severely during the Civil War, more severely than many of the surrounding counties, as it was an almost constant battlefield for opposing forces. Even after the war, guerrillas continued to rob and burn in Monroe County, especially around Tompkinsville.

A number of dates and names have been found carved on trees in Monroe County. One of the oldest, near Tompkinsville, reads "Dr. Boone, 1777." The carved names of Thomas Walker and Daniel Smith date from Feb. 25, 1780.

Even before settlers came, Monroe County was heavily timbered. Strong evidence of mineral wealth came with the discovery of zinc ore in 1856. Today, oil and gas wells contribute to the wealth of the county, and tobacco and grain are raised extensively. Timber is also of great importance, as well as various factory products.

FAIRS

Monroe County Fair — Tompkinsville. July.

PARKS, RECREATION

Old Mulkey Meeting House State Shrine — Tompkinsville. KY-1446. 30-acre park with picnic and playground facilities.

MARKERS

Famous Tree — Flippin, Indian Creek Church. KY-249. In 1894 a huge tulip poplar was felled 1 1/2 mi. So. of this site. Measured 11 ft. in diameter, 35 ft. in circumference. A four-foot log from it won first prize at the 1893-94 Columbian Exposition in Chicago. Main log was used to build the second Baptist church of Indian Creek.

Monroe County/Tompkinsville — Tompkinsville, courthouse yard. KY-63, KY-100. Of the 2957 in the U. S. it is the only county named for a President with county seat named for the contemporary Vice President. Named for James Monroe and Daniel Tompkins, whose terms covered 1817-1825.

Morgan's First Raid — Tompkinsville. KY-63, KY-100, KY-163. Morgan's Raiders came from Tennessee on first raid into Kentucky on July 9, 1862. Attacked USA force of 9th Pennsylvania Cavalry. Continued raids on 16 other towns before returning to Tennessee.

Courthouse at Tompkinsville.

CEMETERIES

Hannah Boone Grave — Tompkinsville, State Shrine. KY-1446. Old Mulkey Meeting House. Hannah Boone Pennington, sister of Daniel Boone, is buried in graveyard.

OLD BUILDINGS

The Old Brick House — Tompkinsville, East Fork Creek. KY-1366. First brick house in Monroe County; built in 1805. Original owner was William Howard who came to Monroe County in 1802 from North Carolina. A brick house was so rare then that it was referred to as "the brick house." Now privately owned.

Courthouse — Tompkinsville. The first courthouse was built in Samuel Marrs' orchard and was burned April 22, 1863 by the Confederate Army in reprisal for the Federal troops having burned Celina, Tennessee, 18 miles away. All records were destroyed. Monroe County was nearly devastated by roving bands of marauders during and after the Civil War. The courthouse was rebuilt, but burned in 1888 when the town was robbed and burned. Later in 1888, the present courthouse was constructed.

Mt. Vernon Free Church — Gamaliel. KY-100. Built in 1848 by free blacks. Only replacement of original building material is metal roof in place of wooden one. Logs held by wooden pegs, chinked with clay.

Old Mulkey Meeting House — Tompkinsville, Old Mulkey Rd. KY-1446. Erected 1798 or 1804 of round logs constructed in shape of a cross. Other interesting

The David Walden Home in Tompkinsville.

features include a crude pulpit, hewn log benches, the twelve corners in the building representing the Apostles, and the Trinity represented by three doors. Church members' names were copied with pokeberry ink.

David Walden Home — Tompkinsville, Route 3. Saltbox design log house built on the homeplace of the Walden family. Constructed 1974-1975, using all original logs, flooring, doors, and beams from the log house dating from 1830. The present home consists of two log pins connected by two halls, or dogtrots, and a shed extending on the back. Awarded a landmark certificate during Monroe County Sesquicentennial Celebration in 1970. Now privately owned.

Simpson County

Simpson County is one of the smallest counties in the state, having little more than 300 square miles, and dates its existence back to 1819. It was the sixty-third county to be created in Kentucky, and was formed from parts of Warren, Allen and Logan counties. It bears the name of Captain John Simpson, a statesman and soldier, and one of the many victims of the Battle of River Raisin Massacre in The War of 1812.

The county is drained by the Big Barren River, its tributaries, and the Red River. Though small in area, it is one of the most productive counties in the state.

Tobacco and corn are the main crops, but grain and grasses also produce large crops. Cattle, hog and calf production are also very important.

Franklin, the county seat, was an enterprising little city according to the 1880 census, and was named in honor of Benjamin Franklin, the eminent American philosopher and statesman. Three landowners competed to provide the site for the courthouse, but none of the sites had plentiful water. As a result, one of the owners dug a well, but found it dry. He secretly hauled water at night to fill the well and succeeded in selling his land for the new town. To his surprise, he had primed the well so that it furnished water for many years.

One of the interesting facts about Simpson County is its "nick in Kentucky-Tennessee state line." Most maps show a nick or jag in the Kentucky-Tennessee state line about midway in the southern boundary of Simpson County. Unofficial accounts showed this nick to be the result of Kentucky hospitality. Sanford Duncan, owner of extensive holdings west of the L & N Railroad, wanted no part of his land to be in Tennessee as he was intensely loyal to Kentucky. He requested that the surveyors include all his land in Kentucky, which was denied. When the surveyors reached his property at nightfall, they were invited to spend the night. During the evening the surveyors were taken to his well-stocked cellar, where he saw to it that they liberally sampled his supply of wines and cider. As a result, his original request was granted, and now the Kentucky-Tennessee state line follows Mr. Duncan's holdings, making the "jag" or "nick" in the otherwise straight boundary line.

FAIRS, EXHIBITS

Simpson County Fair — Franklin. July.

Tobacco Market — Franklin, 501 W. Madison St. Second largest air-cured tobacco market in the world. Auctions conducted from late November through January.

MARKERS

Beverly L. Clarke — Franklin, Main and Kentucky Sts., at N.E. corner of Courthouse lawn. He served in the Kentucky Legislature 1841-49 and was U. S. Minister to Guatemala 1857-60. Buried in the Frankfort Cemetery in 1868 by an act of State Legislature.

Forrest Foraged — Franklin, Gold City Rd. KY-265. Gen. N. B. Forrest's Confederate troops camped here Sept. 28, 1862, while guarding the left flank of Gen. Braxton Bragg as he moved north.

Hudspeth's Well — Franklin, Cedar St. and Public Square. Figured prominently in the location of Franklin as county seat.

Sue Mundy's Grave — Franklin. 2 blocks W. of Green-lawn Cemetery. US-31W. Calls attention to grave of the Confederate soldier, Marcellus Jerome Clarke, who was tried, convicted and hanged as "Sue Mundy," a CSA guerrilla.

Simpson County — Franklin, S. of Courthouse Square. Depicts founding of Simpson County, and county seat, Franklin.

Hudspeth's Well on city square in Franklin.

OLD BUILDINGS

Doctor Duncan House — Franklin, 301 N. Main St. Built before 1871 by Dr. George W. Duncan with steamboat Gothic-style ornamentation. Now contains four apartments.

Duncan Tavern & Linkumpinch — Franklin. US-31W. circa 1819. Recognized as old stagecoach inn owned by Sanford Duncan, where Sam Houston spent night before duel with Gen. W. A. White of Nashville. Duel fought at Linkumpinch dueling ground on Duncan farm.

Old Jail — Franklin, 206 N. College St., 1 block from square. circa 1884. Built with rough brown stones made in blockhouse construction. Walls are two feet thick.

Goodnight Memorial Library — Franklin, 1 block S. of Courthouse. US-31W. Completed 1937, later dedicated by Sen. Alben W. Barkley. 850-seat auditorium, and a meeting room used by community groups, and was recently enlarged for library facility. Library and memorial were made possible in the estate of Mrs. Ella Hoy Goodnight.

Octagon House — Franklin. US-31W. Built 1860 by Andrew Jackson Caldwell. Eight-sided, three-story brick house.

John B. Smith House — Hickory Flat, on Red River. KY-100. circa 1785. Log structure.

The Dr. Duncan House in Franklin.

OTHER POINTS OF INTEREST

Alexander Cave — Oak Ridge, N.E. corner of county. Off US-31W, on KY-1199. Mouth of cave large enough for horse to enter. Supposedly used as a hideout by Jesse James.

Hoy Cave — Franklin, exit on Morgantown Rd. to the West. US-31W. Entrance 1 1/2 mi. N. Underground passages 2 or 3 mi. in length.

Smokey Cave — Salmons, northern part of county. Off US-31W, on KY-1434. During the fall and winter seasons, a smoke-like fog rises from the cave resembling smoke from a chimney. Cave has signs of having been used by Indians. Presently designated as a shelter by the Civil Defense Emergency Unit.

Warren County

Warren County was created in 1796 from part of Logan County, and was named for General Joseph Warren, who fell at the Battle of Bunker Hill in the American Revolution. The twenty-fourth of Kentucky's Counties to be formed, it is situated in the southern part of the state. The Big Barren River, which has its source near the Cumberland, flows through the county and is navigable all the way to Bowling Green, Kentucky. The terrain of the county is undulating and well adapted to agriculture. The soil is rich and fertile, and tobacco, wheat and corn are raised in great abundance. Cattle production is also very successful.

McFadin Station, about twelve miles from the Bowling Green settlement, was known to pioneers as early as 1785 and it was a popular stopping place for travelers going over the Cumberland Trail to Nashville, Tennessee.

Two brothers, Robert and George Moore, came from Virginia about 1794 and built the first log cabin in the village. The dwelling was near a big spring which later furnished water to the settlers. The Moore brothers' cabin was surrounded by a large grove of beautiful trees. In the late afternoon the men of the village would gather there and roll wooden balls on the green, which gave rise to the name "Bowlinggreen," (old style). Bowling Green was incorporated March 6, 1798.

Now the county seat, Bowling Green is the fifth largest city in Kentucky and the most important city in the Green River country. It is one of the handsomest inland cities in Kentucky, showing a steady growth and increase in population. The center of the city features a beautiful park and fountain, which is a popular and attractive place to relax.

Many able men, past and present, figure in the history of Warren County and the liberal and extensive educational and religious privileges of Bowling Green make it one of the most inviting cities in Kentucky.

FAIRS

Warren County Fair — Bowling Green. July.

PARKS

Beech Bend Park — 3 mi. from Bowling Green, on Barren River. Beech Bend Rd. 1,000-acre Amusement Park. One of the largest campgrounds in the world.

Covington Woods Park — Bowling Green. US-31W, US-68. Gen. Elijah M. Covington of the Kentucky militia came here from North Carolina in 1795 to farm and survey. He acquired 23,000 acres in Warren, Logan, and Edmonson counties and became Warren County's first sheriff and surveyor. He helped to select the early site of Bowling Green and made the first survey of Mammoth Cave. This park is named for him and was purchased by the city in 1933.

Fort Webb Park — Bowling Green, Country Club Lane, off Beech Bend Rd. Constructed by Confederate and Union forces. Located at the head of the navigation system of the Barren and Green rivers. During Civil War, Bowling Green was an important stronghold with 2 railroads to Memphis and Nashville. Threats from Union forces caused CSA to abandon the town on Feb. 14, 1862.

Fountain Square Park — Downtown Bowling Green. Landmark on the original Moore tract. The Moores were founders of Bowling Green. Site of earliest courthouse. Fountain was erected in 1881.

Hobson Grove Park and Mansion (Riverview) — Bowling Green, W. end of Main St. US-31W, US-68. circa 1860. Home of Col. Atwood G. Hobson, lawyer, banker and Union officer. During Confederate occupation of Bowling Green in 1862, CSA Gen. Simon B.

Buckner saved the house at the request of his friend, USA Gen. W. E. Hobson, son of the owner. Used as munitions depot. After the war, Col. Hobson made this his home until his death in 1898. Among its most interesting features are the fresco paintings on the ceilings of the double parlor. Tours.

Reservoir Park — Bowling Green, Main and Park St. Site of Civil War fortification.

Riverside Park — Bowling Green. The land for this park was donated by Mr. James R. Hines several years ago. At one time it was the loading and unloading place for packets travelling the river from Evansville, Indiana to Bowling Green.

MARKERS

Civil War Occupations — Bowling Green, Fountain Square. CSA occupied city five months and fortified nine hills. When threatened by Union forces, CSA planned evacuation Feb. 14, 1862. City suffered CSA fires and Union bombardments during evacuation.

The Hershel Webb House in Bowling Green.

Confederate State Capitol of Kentucky — Bowling Green, Western Kentucky University Campus, US-68. Bowling Green named CSA Capitol, Nov. 20, 1862 at Russellville convention. George W. Johnson was first governor.

Home of Thomas Hines — US-31W. Bypass and Fairview Ave., at cemetery entrance. Termed "most dangerous man in Confederacy." With Morgan's Raider's when Gen. J. H. Morgan was captured July, 1863. Led escape from Federal prison in Ohio. Leader of northwest conspiracy in 1864. Buried Fairview Cemetery in 1898.

Long Hunters — KY-67, near entrance to bridge over Barren River. Denotes movement of Long Hunters exploring party along Barren River in 1775.

McFadin's Station — Bowling Green. E. of I-65. KY-234. circa 1785. First station in this area. Built by Andrew McFadin, who surveyed much land in this region.

MUSEUMS

The Kentucky Building — Bowling Green. Western Kentucky University Campus. US-68. Building dedicated to history of the Commonwealth of Kentucky, conceived by Dr. Henry Hardin Cherry, Western's first president. Two main portions: Kentucky Museum, in the left wing, contains thousands of artifacts; Kentucky Library, in the right wing, contains over 22,000 volumes dealing with Kentucky history, including collections of early church and social history, the Civil War, and the South Union Shakers. Tours.

The Maria Moore House in Bowling Green.

OLD BUILDINGS

Warren County Courthouse — Bowling Green, 10th and College Sts. Warren County established by legislature in 1796. Two earlier courthouses, the first log and the second brick (1812), were built in what is now Fountain Square. The present courthouse was erected in 1867-68. Architect, D. J. Williams.

Ironwood Home — Bowling Green, Old Richardsville Rd. circa 1855. Home of Joseph R. Underwood, lawyer and U.S. Senator (1835-43). Columns and serpentine balcony added by Robert Rodes, past owner.

Maria Moore House — Bowling Green, corner of 8th and State Sts. Oldest house in Bowling Green. Built in 1827 by Elizabeth Moore, the widow of George Moore, who with his brother Robert, founded Bowling Green. After the death of Elizabeth Moore, the house was occupied for many years by her daughter Maria, hence it became known as the Maria Moore House.

Old Union Baptist Church — Woodburn. U.S.-31 W, KY-240. Legislative act in 1795 gave rights to 200 acres of land for each settler in Green River country. This brought many Carolinians, among them two Baptist preachers, who started the Union Church in 1795. John Hightower, the first pastor, served until 1813. Other religious denominations also met in this meeting house. Services continued to be held here through the Civil War. Present building erected in 1866.

Hershel Webb House — Bowling Green, Richardsville Rd. Built in 1850 by U.S. Senator Joseph Underwood. Interesting features include solid walnut woodwork, 24-inch solid brick walls, 13-inch solid brick partitions and 13 to 14-foot ceilings. Brick was made on the farm. Now privately owned.

OTHER POINTS OF INTEREST

Cutler-Hammer, Inc. — Bowling Green, 2901 Industrial Dr. Manufactures electrical motor controls and accessories.

Firestone Textiles Co. — Bowling Green. U.S.-31 W. Manufactures tire fabric.

Master Division of Koerling Co. — Bowling Green, 2701 Industrial Dr. Manufactures kerosene-fired portable space heaters.

Western Kentucky University — Bowling Green. Campus includes 200 acres and more than 64 buildings. It is situated on a hill which was used as a Civil War fort. Trenches now used as pathways.

Lake Cumberland Area

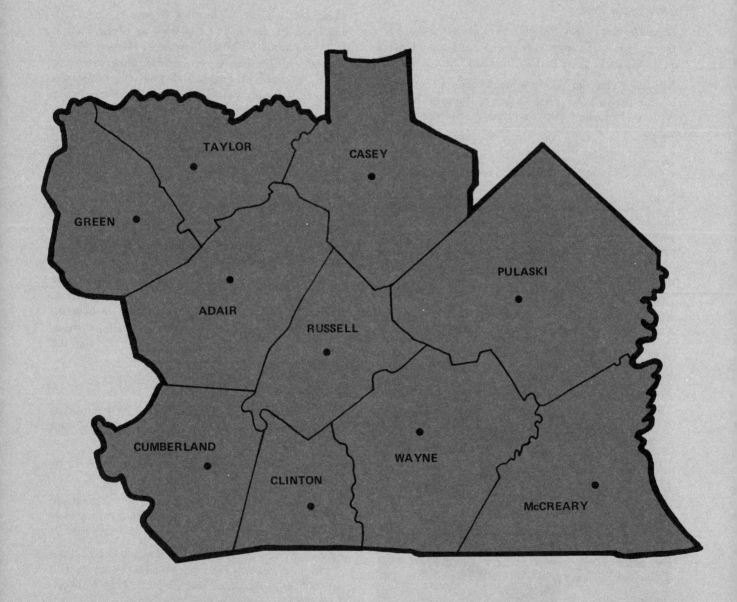

Adair County

Adair County is located in the Lake Cumberland district of Kentucky. The forty-fourth county in the order of formation in Kentucky, it was created in 1801. Adair County received its name from the famous General and Indian fighter, John Adair of Mercer County. He was commander of the Kentucky troops in The Battle of New Orleans in 1815, and Governor of Kentucky from 1820 to 1824.

On June 28, 1802, the court met to discuss a permanent seat of justice for the county. After much deliberation, the court ordered that the place commonly called the "public square" in the town of Columbia, be permanently set aside as the seat of justice. Many people have tried to learn when and why the name of "Columbia" was chosen, but no proven records have ever been found.

Adair County is mainly an agricultural county, but in recent years has gained economically from new industrial and recreation developments.

FAIRS AND FESTIVALS

Adair County Fair — Columbia, VFW Park. KY-206. Horse show, beauty pageant, exhibits and carnival. July.

Lindsey Wilson College Homecoming — Columbia. November.

MARKERS

Colonel Frank L. Wolford — Columbia, Courthouse yard. KY-55, KY-61, KY-80. A staunch champion of the Union, a true friend of the stricken South and defender of constitutional freedom. Born in Columbia in 1817, died 1895 and buried in the city cemetery. Veteran of the Mexican War. Leader of the famed First Kentucky Union Cavalry. Hero of many battles. Bold warrior, chivalrous foe. Renowned lawyer and orator. Member of the Legislature and Congress.

Confederate Raid — Columbia, Courthouse yard. KY-55, KY-61, KY-80. Gen. John Hunt Morgan's Cavalry, returning from their second Kentucky raid, were here on Dec. 31, 1862, took supplies, then went on to Tennessee. On the raid, Union's rail supply line wrecked and $2,000,000 worth of property was destroyed. Morgan came through here again after the 3-hour battle of Tebb's Bend, July 4, 1863. Continued raid into Indiana to northeast Ohio, where he was captured July 26th.

Courthouse Marker — Columbia, Courthouse yard. On June 28, 1802, court ordered this the permanent seat of justice on the public square. First courthouse was built in 1806. Unique architectural feature is the carved faces on the south columns. Placed on The National Register of Historic Places, 1974.

Jane Lampton Home — Columbia, opposite Courthouse yard. KY-55, KY-80. Girlhood home of Jane Lampton (1803-1891). Wife of John Marshall Clemens, and mother of Mark Twain (Samuel Clemens). Granddaughter of Col. William Casey, original Adair County settler.

Site of Casey Home — 3 mi. S.W. of Columbia. KY-80. Home of Col. William Casey, early Kentucky pioneer and great-grandfather of Samuel Clemens, better known as Mark Twain. Casey was born in Virginia and came to Kentucky in 1779. Built Casey Station on Dix River. In 1791, he moved to Russell Creek near here. He was a member of second Kentucky Constitutional Convention in 1799; a trustee of town of Columbia in 1802; and presidential elector in 1813. He died here in 1816. Casey County was named for him in 1806.

OLD BUILDINGS

Adair County Courthouse — Columbia, Public Square. Built 1885. Architectural example. Mid-Victorian brick with columned entrances on north and south. This is the fourth courthouse built since county was formed. Placed on National Register of Historic Places, 1974.

Baker House — Columbia, 520 Burkesville St. Built 1855. Originally the home of Judge Tyler Alexander, Circuit Judge and first president of the Bank of Columbia.

First Clerk's Office — Columbia, 307 Greensburg St. Built 1811-1812. Lower Right room was used as office by William Caldwell, first Adair County Clerk.

Garrett Conover House — Columbia, Burkesville Rd. Built March 28, 1800. Oldest log house in Adair County.

Creel Building — Columbia, 328 N. Public Square. Built 1816. Only original building still standing on square in Columbia. Originally housed a general store and later was a hotel. Home of Elijah Creel, prominent early businessman.

Samuel Feese House — Columbia, Old Greensburg Rd. Built 1865. Feese's mill on this property is one of the oldest mills in Kentucky.

John Field House — Columbia, 111 E. Fortune St. Built 1812. Originally owned by John Field, important early citizen. Right front room was used for girls' portion of Robertson Academy; later the home of John and Jane Clemens, parents of Samuel Clemens (Mark Twain.)

Dr. Nathan Gaither House — Columbia, 100 S. High St. Built 1812. Architectural example.

Hurt House — Columbia, Burkesville St. Built 1847. Originally owned by William Edward Frazier; later home of Judge Rollin Hurt, prominent lawyer and member of Kentucky Court of Appeals.

Old Jail — Columbia, 210 Greensburg St. Built 1858. Originally used as county jail. Now a funeral home.

Thomas Massie House — Columbia, Cane Valley. KY-55. The log house was built by Massie, the first settler of Cane Valley.

Page House — Columbia, 200 Campbellsville St. Built 1818. Originally the home of Elijah Creel, early businessman. Now a funeral home.

Pleasant View Baptist Church — Columbia, on Butler Creek. KY-531. Built 1884. This one-story log church is still used for church services today. Interior is primitive and still contains the wide handmade poplar benches.

Samuel Robertson House — Columbia, 209 E. Guardian St. Built 1812. Originally owned by Rev. Samuel B. Robertson, a Presbyterian minister and principal of the first school in Columbia, Robertson Academy.

Thomas Stotts House — Columbia, Burkesville Rd. Built 1824. Colonial house.

Daniel Trabune House — Columbia, Jamestown St. Built 1821 by Daniel Trabune, early prominent citizen.

William Trabune House — Columbia, Greensburg Rd. Built 1835. One of the finer old houses in Adair County.

Zion Baptist Church — Columbia, Glensfork Rd. Off KY-55. Built 1877. Church organized in 1802. Stands today as silent testimony to an earlier way of life, when the school and church occupied common grounds.

OTHER POINTS OF INTEREST

Diddle Tavern — Columbia, 104 Guthrie St. circa 1810. Brick section of building is considered oldest building in Columbia. Benjamin Lampton, master builder, worked with Diddle in building many houses in Columbia. Mr. Lampton was Mark Twain's grandfather.

Administration Building, Lindsey Wilson College — Columbia, 210 Lindsey Wilson Ave. Built 1904. The original 2-story brick structure, designed by architect Val P. Collins, included large chapel, instruction rooms, and a library. Opened as Lindsey Wilson Training School Jan. 1, 1904; became Lindsey Wilson College in 1923. This is the original building. Continues to be used as a major facility in the Junior College complex. College is now directed by the Methodist Church South.

Courthouse in Columbia.

Casey County

Casey County is situated on the border of three of Kentucky's traditional territorial divisions, the Green River Country, the Knobs Region, and the Pennyrile. It is also on the edge of the Cave Region and borders on the Bluegrass Region.

In 1806, Casey County was formed from part of Lincoln County to become the forty-sixth county in order of formation in Kentucky. It was named for Colonel William Casey, an early pioneer and great-grandfather of Samuel L. Clemens (Mark Twain). Colonel Casey was born in Virginia and came to Ken-

tucky in 1779. He built Casey's Station on the Dix River in 1791. He was a member of the second Kentucky Constitutional Convention in 1799.

Liberty, the county seat, is situated on the Green River. Liberty was named by veterans of the Revolutionary War who came to this section from Virginia in 1791.

FAIRS AND FESTIVALS

Casey County Trail Rides — sponsored by Casey County Saddle Club. Attended by horse enthusiasts

Apple Festival in Liberty.

The Richard Northcutt House in Liberty.

Winter Wonderland in Liberty.

from all parts of the state. Usually held on Sundays.

Apple Festival – Liberty, Casey County High School grounds, Liberty-Yosemite Road. KY-70. Festival features the world's largest apple pie. Listed in Guiness Book of Records as largest apple pie. Apples and cider for sale, arts and crafts, apple foods, country music and the sale of Casey-burgers (ground beef from Casey County stock). September.

MARKERS

Colonel Silas Adams – Liberty, Courtyard. US-127. Adams (1839-1896), was a spirited USA Civil War leader. Associated with well-known 1st Kentucky Cavalry from 1861-1864.

John Fry – Liberty Park, 1 mi. N. of Liberty. US-127. Fry was an early landowner in Casey County. Acquired land on Carpenter's Creek in 1780 on a Treasury Warrant for Service in American Revolution. Killed at Battle of Blue Licks in 1782 at age 28.

OLD BUILDINGS

Farmer Deposit Bank – Middleburg. Off KY-70. Built 1904. Oldest bank in county.

Richard Northcutt House – Liberty, Maple St. Built 1806. Home constructed of brick laid in Flemish bond. Bricks on outside of home were hauled from Danville, Kentucky on 2-wheeled ox carts, escorted by slaves. The home is constructed of a 3-brick thick wall. The inside bricks were fired on the farm. Inside walls are 20-in. thick. First Circuit Court was held in this house. Now privately owned.

Riffe Grist Mill Site – Middleburg. KY-198. Built 1825. Mill not in operation.

Water Grist Mill Site – Liberty. N. on US-127. Built 1833. Site of water-powered grist mill on Green River. Used also as a store and gathering place. Mill no longer in operation.

 # Clinton County

In 1835 Clinton County became Kentucky's eighty-fifth county in order of formation. Taken from parts of Wayne and Cumberland Counties, it was named after Governor DeWitt Clinton of New York, a U.S. Senator, Mayor of New York City and sponsor of the Erie Canal in 1816-1825.

Albany, the county seat, was named after the capital of New York. It is situated twelve miles south of Wolf Creek Dam and Cumberland Lake, and northwest of Dale Hollow. Albany was incorporated in 1838. Due to the location between Lake Cumberland and Dale Hollow Lake, it is quickly becoming a resort town. It was a Confederate outpost during the Civil War in a border region that was scourged by numerous bands of roving guerrillas. Federal troops took possession of the town early in 1863 and held it until the end of the war. Like so many Kentucky county seats, it suffered the loss of its courthouse when set fire by guerrillas in late 1864, and all the old county records were lost. One of the famous guerrillas in the area was Champ Ferguson, born in Albany in 1821.

FAIRS

Clinton County Fair and Horse Show – Albany Fairgrounds. 1/4 mi. off KY-738. July.

PARKS AND RECREATION

Dale Hollow Lake State Park – S.E. of Burkesville. KY-90 and KY-449.

Seventy-Six Falls – Albany. KY-734, E. of KY-90. Falls are 76-ft. high and flow into Lake Cumberland. Picnic area is located at roadside park near the falls. Indian Creek spills over a ledge through 76 different breaks.

Wolf River Recreation Area and Dock – Dale Hollow Lake. KY-738.

MARKERS

Civil War Terrorist – Albany, Courtyard. US-127. Champ Ferguson was born here in 1821. Guerrilla leader with Confederate leaning, but attacked supporters of both sides throughout Civil War in southern Kentucky and Tennessee. Over 100 murders ascribed to Ferguson alone. Hunted by both CSA and USA. Taken after end of war, convicted by U. S. Army Court in Nashville and hanged Oct. 20, 1865. Burial at home in White County, Tennessee.

Courthouse Burned — Albany, Courtyard. US-127. 22 Kentucky courthouses were burned during the Civil War, 19 in the last 15 months of war, 12 by Confederates, 8 by guerrillas and 2 by Union accidents. Courthouse at Albany was burned by guerrillas late in 1864 and all county records were destroyed.

Gen. Ed P. Warinner — Albany, Seventy-Six Falls Roadside Park. KY-734, E. of KY-90. Birthplace of late Gen. Ed P. Warinner whose ancestors settled here over 100 years ago. Served 16th district for 4 terms in state senate 1952-1959. In 1954 sponsored both Minimum Foundation Act (school support) and another to lower voting age to 18. In 1958 he promoted the veterans bonus legislation and public assistance program. He advocated the Bookmobile system.

OLD BUILDINGS

Hopkins Rural School — Albany, near Roadside Park. US-127. Old rural schoolhouse.

Jesse Noland House — Albany, Spring Creek Highway. KY-969S. Built 1822.

Water-Powered Grist Mill — Albany. US-127. Old Grist Mill is a relic of pioneer time. No longer in operation.

Courthouse at Albany.

Dale Hollow Lake near Burkesville.

Boating on lake in Clinton County.

Dale Hollow State Park near Burkesville.

91

Cumberland County

In 1798, Cumberland County was organized as the thirty-second county in order of formation in Kentucky. It received its name from the Cumberland River, which flows through it from one end to the other. The river got its name from the Cumberland Mountains that Dr. Thomas Walker, in 1750, named in honor of the Duke of Cumberland.

Cumberland County was taken from Green County. Later, between 1800 and 1860, parts of Clinton, Metcalfe, Monroe, Russell and Wayne Counties were taken from its original territory. The first known white men were here in 1769. Daniel Boone explored the area in 1771. Three Kentucky governors were born in Cumberland County.

Burkesville, the county seat, was laid out in 1798 on land owned by Samuel Burks. It was a vital river port for timber and farm produce during the steamboat era. Burkesville was incorporated in 1810, dating back to Colonial times. The present town site was recorded at the Virginia capital, Williamsburg, in 1776, and given the name Cumberland Crossing. Its name was changed some twenty years later to Burkesville, in honor of the man who gave the land on which the town was built.

FAIRS, FESTIVALS, DRAMAS

Cumberland County Fair — Burkesville, Veterans Park, Ferguson St. August.

Cumberland River Valley Arts and Crafts Guild — Burkesville. August.

"Miracle of Christmas" Drama — Burkesville, Veterans Park, Ferguson St. Week before Christmas.

Town and Country Music Hall — Burkesville, River St. Country, gospel and bluegrass music.

PARKS

Dale Hollow Lake State Park — Burkesville. On KY-90, KY-449.

MARKERS

Indian Battle — 3 mi. N. of Burkesville. The greatest recorded Indian battle in this area occurred here in 1790. A group of settlers fought with Indians camped at Little Renox Falls. The pioneers attacked the camp in an attempt to rescue a small white girl who had been kidnapped. The girl was saved. All the Indians were slain, but no white men were lost in this bloody encounter.

Melmont — 2 mi. N. of Burkesville. KY-704. Home of Brig. Gen. John Edward King (1757-1828). Acquired a land grant for service through Revolutionary War, attaining rank of Capt. in 1780. Born in Virginia and settled here in 1799. Outstanding military tactician in the War of 1812. Commended by Shelby for leadership in Battle of Thames in 1813. His gravestone here.

Old American Oil Well — 3 mi. N. of Burkesville. KY-61. Site of early American gusher that covered the Cumberland River with oil and created the spectacular "river of fire" in March 1829. Oil bottled from well was widely sold for medicinal use in U. S. and Europe under trade name of "American Oil." Claims of the superior qualities of this oil merited it the name of Old American Oil Well.

Courthouse in Burkesville.

Thomas Lincoln — Burkesville, Courthouse yard. KY-61, KY-90. Thomas Lincoln, father of Abraham Lincoln, made claim for land here in 1801. He was town constable in 1802-1804. He was married to Nancy Hanks in 1806. Thomas Lincoln was brought to Kentucky from Virginia as a child in 1782.

OLD BUILDINGS

Gen. John Edward King House (Joel Cheek Home) — Burkesville. KY-61N. Home of Cheek family, originators of Maxwell House coffee.

Obadiah Baker House — Burkesville, Little Renox community, Route 3. Built 1817-1820. He was a wealthy builder. The bricks used in building the house were made at the site by slave labor. His wife organized the first church in the community. Obadiah Baker was a Black soldier in the Civil War.

Shadrick Claywell Log Cabin — Burkesville, Veterans Park. Built 1800-1813. Reconstructed dogtrot log cabin.

OTHER POINTS OF INTEREST

Captain Jack McLain Grave — Alpine Hill, Burkesville. He was in Company J, First Kentucky Cavalry. Jack

McLain accidentally killed a good friend. In sorrow he took his own life, Sept. 21, 1866. Previously he had requested "When I die I want to be buried on top of that highest hill overlooking Burkesville, as that is as near heaven as I will ever get."

Green County

Green County was the sixteenth county in order of formation in Kentucky in 1792. Taken from parts of Lincoln and Nelson Counties, Green County was soon to become a thriving settlement. It was named for General Nathaniel Green from Rhode Island, a hero of the Revolutionary War.

Greensburg, the county seat, is located southwest of Campbellsville. Greensburg's courthouse building is the oldest in Kentucky and has been used as a courthouse for 135 years. The old bell atop the stone building, once used to call the courts, is still in place.

FAIRS, FESTIVALS, DRAMAS

Green County Fair — Greensburg, American Legion Park, on Legion Park Rd. June.

MARKERS

Lincoln's Mentor — 8 mi. N. of Greensburg. KY-61. Birthplace of Mentor Graham, the man given credit for having given Abraham Lincoln his higher education.

OLD BUILDINGS

Ben Will Penick House — Greensburg, at the corner of Depot and E. Columbia. Built 1840. Housed Greensburg Academy, a school for girls.

Clerk's Office — Greensburg, Public Square. Built 1804, by "Stone Hammer" Metcalfe, who later became the 10th Governor of Kentucky. Served as the home of Greensburg's only college, New Athens Academy, established 1805.

Courthouse — Greensburg, Public Square. Built 1800-1804. The oldest courthouse west of the Alleghenies. The second Green County courthouse was designed by "Stone Hammer" Metcalfe, who later became Governor of Kentucky. Restored 1973. Open to the public Tuesday-Saturday, 1 to 4 p.m.

Gen. E. H. Hobson House — Greensburg, Depot St. Built 1883. Hobson fought in the war with Mexico and organized the 13th Kentucky Voluntary Infantry in the Civil War. Hobson was the man who captured Gen. John Hunt Morgan, leader of Morgan's Raiders.

Jeremiah Abell House — Greensburg, N. Main St. Built 1796. Oldest log house in Kentucky. Restored 1972.

Montgomery's Mill — Greensburg, on Montgomery Mill Rd. 1 mi. off KY-88. Built 1795. Water-powered saw mill until 1930.

Mount Gilead Church — 10 mi. E. of Greensburg. Off KY-61. Built 1804 on site of camp used by the Long Hunters who came to Kentucky in 1769. Possibly the oldest church in the state.

Old Bank Building — Greensburg, Public Square. Built 1818. Houses doctor's office and beauty shop and now joined to Allen's Inn.

Old Vaughn Home or Allen's Inn — Greensburg, Public Square. circa 1806-1812. Early example of zoning as recorded in the deed, "Lot Number 23, Inn Lot." Operated by James Allen who entertained President Andrew Jackson, Sept. 26, 1832. President Jackson requested "cornmeal hoe-cakes and sorghum molasses for breakfast."

Pendleton House — Greensburg, E. Columbia Ave. Built 1845. Home of Ruehel Creel, President Lincoln's Consul to Mexico, 1863-1866. His son, Enrique Creel, in turn served as Ambassador from Mexico to the U. S., 1907-1909.

Shreve House — Greensburg, S. 2nd St. Built 1815. The first classical school ever taught in Green County was held here.

Simpson House — Greensburg, S. Main St. Built 1818. Birthplace of William Herndon, Abraham Lincoln's law partner, on Dec. 25, 1818.

Site of Jane Todd Crawford Home — 9 mi. S.E. of Greensburg. KY-61. Mrs. Crawford rode horseback from here to Danville where Dr. Ephraim McDowell removed a 23-pound ovarian tumor in a 30-minute operation without the benefit of an anesthetic. The first successful operation of its kind.

Courthouse in Greensburg.

Old courthouse in Green County.

The Jeremiah Abell House in Greensburg.

94

McCreary County

McCreary County, the last to be created and the youngest of Kentucky's one hundred twenty counties, was formed in 1912 from parts of Whitley, Wayne, and Pulaski Counties. It was named for Governor James B. McCreary (1838-1918) of Madison County. Governor McCreary was well known in the political world, serving as U. S. Congressman from 1885 to 1897 and from 1903 to 1909, as well as a delegate to the International Monetary Convention in Brussels in 1892. McCreary County is the only one in Kentucky without an incorporated town.

Whitley City, the county seat, is located nine miles south of Parkers Lake. When the county was first formed, Pine Knot was the temporary county seat, but was soon moved north to adjacent Whitley City. McCreary County is located in the scenic area of Daniel Boone National Forest. Eighty-five percent of the county is government-owned forest land, full of arches, streams, steep gorges, waterfalls, rough streams and woodlands.

PARKS

Buffalo Arch — Near Pickett State Park in Tennessee, off Parker Mountain Rd. Indians hid on this arch while hunting and killing wild buffalo.

Cumberland Falls — Cumberland Falls State Resort Park. KY-90, off US-25 and I-75. Called the "Niagara of the South." These falls are 150-ft. wide with a 68-ft. drop. A mysterious "moonbow" can be seen on nights of the full moon.

Cumberland Falls State Resort Park — Whitley County line. US-27, or I-75S.

Hollow Rock Arch — Off Parker Mountain Rd., near Bell Farm. KY-92. Natural arch formed from sandstone.

Koger Natural Arch — Near Yamacraw Rd. KY-92. One of the largest arches in the county, formed by wind erosion over many thousands of years.

Natural Arch — W. of Parkers Lake. KY-927. 3rd largest natural arch in Kentucky. Limestone arch and

trails. Scenic area open all year.

Timber Tunnel — Marshes Siding. US-27, KY-700. In 1899, Longsworth & Co. bought 1,485 acres of timberland in Wolf Creek Valley. A steam-powered mill was built on the creek as well as a 10-mi. tram road to Cumberland Fork. A 20-ft. tunnel was drilled through rock 80 ft. below. Mule-drawn tram cars moved products to the river, then by wagon to the railroad at Marshes Siding. Tunnel is still open.

Tombstone Junction Amusement Park — Parkers Lake, adjacent to Cumberland Falls. KY-90. Park features museum, locomotive rides and a replica of a western town. Country singing on Sundays, May to September.

Yahoo Falls — Whitley City. Marshes Siding. US-27 and KY-70E. Waterfall drops 121 ft. Limestone arch, scenic trails and overlooks can be seen along the trail to the falls.

MARKERS

Princess Cornblossom — Near Stearns. US-27. Burial site of the daughter of Chief Doublehead. Legend is that, as a young girl, she accompanied her father at the signing of the Treaty of Sycamore Shoals in 1775, transferring Cherokee lands between the Ohio and Cumberland Rivers to the Transylvania Society. The tribe then settled in a region south of the river. To protect the tribe's secret mine, she killed a renegade. She was married to Big Jake, a trader.

Robber's Roost Cave — 2 1/2 mi. W. of Strunk. US-27. Hideout of bandits, 1819-1822, who preyed on salt dealers returning to Beatty's salt mine along nearby trails. Legend is that Beatty, trying to outwit the bandits, sent a young Harmon girl to the salt market, but she was kidnapped. A friendly Cherokee Chief, Little Jake, son of Big Jake and Princess Cornblossom, rescued her and drove the outlaws out of the area.

OLD BUILDINGS

Beatty Oil Well — Between Stearns and Monticello. KY-92. Site of first commercial flowing oil well in

North America. Discovered 1819, while drilling for salt. Oil barreled for medicinal use and treatment of animals.

4-H Craft Center — Cumberland Falls. KY-90W. Log cabin filled with crafts made by 4-H youth and local craftsmen. First operation of its kind in U. S. Original log cabin was built in 1842 by John Abbott as part of a 200-acre land grant. Abbott and his Indian wife, Oocella, lived in this cabin until 1863. Cabin was used continuously as a home by 5 generations until rebuilt as a 4-H center.

Log Church House — Near Cooperative. Off KY-92 (unnumbered roads here). Built 1947 by free labor. Sunday School held each Sunday 10 a.m.

Stephen Mill and Water Mill — Pine Knot. Off KY-92. In existence since 1805. One of few remaining water mills used for grinding corn and wheat. Operated 1820-1950. Now private property.

Natural Arch near Parkers Lake.

Cumberland Falls in the state resort park.

Loading coal at Stearns Coal and Lumber Company.

Pulaski County

Pulaski County, the twenty-seventh county to be created in Kentucky, was formed in 1799 from Green and Lincoln Counties. It was named for Count Casimir Pulaski, a Polish patriot and soldier of liberty, who came to the United States when he learned of the colonies' fight for freedom. A Brigadier General in the Revolution, he gave his life to the American cause on October 11, 1779. Counties in seven states are named for him.

Somerset was established as the county seat in 1801, on 40 acres given by William Dodson. Its name is derived from Somersetshire, England. This site was picked because of a nearby spring; the path to it later became the town's most traveled street. The city was incorporated in 1888. The town clock was hauled by oxen from Stanford and placed in the courthouse steeple.

A new courthouse, or the Governmental Complex as it is now called, was built in 1975, replacing the oldest part of the original courthouse building. Kentucky's first raw silk was produced in Somerset in 1842 by Cyrenius Wait.

FAIRS AND FESTIVALS

Annual North-South Championship Boat Regatta — Lake Cumberland, at Pulaski County Park. KY-80W. June.

Pulaski County Fair — Somerset, Jaycee Fairground. KY-80. July-August.

PARKS

Bee Rock Park — Eastern edge of Pulaski County. KY-192. Nature hikes to the overlook and narrows of the Rockcastle River. Picnic and camping facilities.

Gen. Burnside State Park — Burnside. US-27. First named Point Isabel. Settled about 1800 by pioneers from the Carolinas and Virginia. During the Civil War in 1863, the Union Army set up a troop rendezvous and supply base here as a prelude to Gen. Ambrose E. Burnside's East Tennessee campaign. The area became known as Camp Burnside in official dispatches, and the name Burnside was retained after the war. Boating, camping, picnic area and golfing facilities.

Short Creek Park — Somerset. KY-80E. This creek is 200-ft. long, flowing only from the base of one cliff to the base of another. Gristmill still in operation on the site.

Zollicoffer Park — 1 mi. S. of Nancy. KY-235, KY-80W. Graves of 100 unknown CSA soldiers buried by Union soldiers. Also, monument where Felix K. Zollicoffer fell, mortally wounded, in the Battle of Logan's Crossroads, also known as the Fishing Creek Battle.

MARKERS

Battle of Dutton Hill — Somerset. KY-99N. Marker describes and points to the site of the Battle of Dutton Hill where CSA dead were buried in single grave. Site of the battle is visible from the road.

First Boy Scout Troop — Burnside. US-27S. Before Boy Scouts of America were officially organized in 1910, a troop of 15 boys had been formed here in the spring of 1908, by Myra Greeno Bass. Using the official scouting handbook of England, she guided them hiking and camping, as in scouting today. Known as Eagle Troop, with Horace Smith as the troop leader. Insignia was a red bandana around the neck. Reputedly, this was the first American Boy Scout Troop.

Boat Regatta at Lake Cumberland.

OLD BUILDINGS

Courthouse — Somerset, Fountain Square, Main St. and W. Mt. Vernon. Around 1802 a small log building was constructed for the first courthouse, then replaced in 1808 by a large brick building which served for 30 years, until it burned in 1838. A third was erected in 1839-1840 and burned in 1871, along with much of the town. The clerk's office was housed separately so none of the records were lost. The next courthouse was built in 1874. This was replaced as part of a modern Governmental Complex in 1975.

Flat Lick Baptist Church (Old Stone Church) — Somerset. E. on KY-461, off KY-80. Oldest standing church in Pulaski County. Organized Jan. 4, 1799.

Ruins of Brick House — Somerset. KY-80E. Brick home started by the Rev. John James from Virginia, for the girl he loved. House was never completed because she married another man.

Dr. John M. Perkins House — Somerset, 109 N. Main St. Built 1850. One of the oldest houses still standing, and still occupied. Morgan's Raiders stayed on the back porch one night.

George W. Sanders Log House — Somerset. US-27. Built 1836.

OTHER POINTS OF INTEREST

Old Town Spring — Somerset, off S. Vine St. This spring was a source of water in the 1800's. Area is being restored by C. K. Cundiff with a monument and shopping center.

Somerset Community College — Somerset. KY-80. University of Kentucky branch since 1965.

Stagecoach — Monticello, Monticello Garage. KY-90. Stagecoach traveled from Monticello to Burnside. Commemorates the first stagecoach to operate in Kentucky. Well-preserved stagecoach on display.

Russell County

Russell County was the eighty-first county to be formed in Kentucky. It was created in 1825 and was carved from Adair, Wayne and Cumberland Counties. It was named for Colonel William Russell of Fayette County, an Indian fighter who took part in the Battle of Tippecanoe, the Battle of Fallen Timbers, and succeeded General Harrison in command of the troops in that region.

Jamestown, incorporated in 1827, is the county seat and is located ten miles from Lake Cumberland State Resort Park. It was first known as Jacksonville, after General Andrew Jackson. However, when the Whigs came to power in 1836, they resented this tribute to their opponent and its name was changed to Jamestown in honor of James Wooldridge, who had donated 100 acres of land when the town was established.

Russell Springs, another prosperous town located in Russell County, was first known as Big Boiling Springs, then later as Kimble when a government post office was established there. This town was at one time considered a health resort, and many people came throughout the year to enjoy the spring water.

Creelsboro, an old Kentucky River town, was laid out in 1809 and named for pioneers Elijah and Eliza Creel. It was located on the banks of the Cumberland River, but lost a great deal of its importance when the river changed its course. All that remains standing today is the Creel Brother's house, constructed in the early 1800's. In 1920, Creelsboro was an oil boom town.

FESTIVALS AND FAIRS

Big Singing — Jamestown. Organized 1923, by local people interested in group singing. First singing held at Russell County Fairgrounds in 1927, then moved to Jamestown. Last Sunday in August.

Russell County Fair — Russell Springs Fairgrounds. US-127. Organized in early 1890's, continued through depression, closed briefly during World War II. July.

Lake Cumberland State Resort Park — S. of Jamestown. US-127. Became official park in 1951. The new lodge named Lure Lodge, completed in 1962, is situated on a high bluff overlooking the lake's shoreline. Open all year.

MARKERS

Chalybeate Spring Site — Russell Springs. US-127. Health resort long known as Big Boiling Springs. Operated before 1850 by family of Sam Patterson, among the earliest settlers. 12 log cabins called Long Row were built for guests who came here for amusement, pleasure, and to benefit from the medicinal iron and sulphur water. In 1898, a large hotel was built which burned in 1942. Spring has since been capped for use as a well.

Establishment of Jamestown — Jamestown, Court-house Square. Established 1827. Also site of Civil War skirmishes in 1861 and 1863.

OLD BUILDINGS

Bank of Creelsboro — Creelsboro. KY-619. One of the few remaining buildings in this old steamboat town.

Creel Brothers House — Creelsboro. KY-619. Built 1800. Oldest house in Creelsboro, later used as a tavern.

Rabon Drugstore — Creelsboro. KY-619. Built 1900. Used as drugstore, post office and later as farm implement company.

Farmer's Woolen Water Mill — Jamestown, 2 mi. S.W. on Greasy Creek. US-127. First turbine water wheel installed. In 1925, power was converted to a hydroelectric unit. Mill closed in 1949. Building still remains.

Irvin's Store — Creelsboro. KY-619. Built 1885. Has been operated since then by same family as a drugstore, general store, funeral home, post office and furniture store.

Reese-Woolen Mill — Jamestown. US-127. 1830-1840. Originally water-powered. Later converted to electricity. Original machinery now housed in a building erected in 1940.

Rockhouse Formation — Creelsboro. Off KY-1058. KY-379. Natural rock arch 60-ft. wide and 40-ft. high. Cumberland River flows nearby. Caves in which many artifacts have been discovered are located on top.

Outhouse — Creelsboro, Newton St. Built 1920. Only concrete reinforced outhouse in Kentucky.

Wolf Creek Dam.

99

Taylor County

Kentucky's one-hundredth county in order of formation, Taylor County was carved from Green County in 1848. It was named after President Zachary Taylor of Jefferson County, Kentucky. The adventurous Virginia Long Hunters came into the territory long before Campbellsville, the county seat, was first settled in 1800. Campbellsville was established by the legislature in 1817 and made the county seat at that time. It was named for Adam and Andrew Campbell, who along with their brothers came from Virginia to settle on their father's land grants.

FAIRS

Taylor County Fair — Taylor County Fairgrounds, KY-208E. First week in August.

PARKS, LAKES

Green River Lake — Campbellsville. KY-55S. Completed 1969. Dam is 141-ft. high and over 2,000-ft. long.

Green River Lake State Park — Campbellsville, KY-55S. Open all year.

Green River Wildlife Area — Campbellsville. KY-70. 14,000 acres. State-regulated hunting.

Stock Car Racing — Taylor County Fairgrounds, KY-208E. April.

MARKERS

Sanders Tavern Site — 6 mi. E. of Campbellsville. US-68. Built early 1800's. Well-known tavern-coach stop on the old turnpike. President Andrew Jackson was a guest at this tavern, which was torn down in the 1940's.

Tebb's Bend Battleground — Campbellsville, Green River Reservoir. KY-55S. Gen. John Hunt Morgan's Raiders encountered Federal forces in battle which took place here on July 4, 1863.

MEMORIALS

Adam Campbell Monument and Grave — Campbellsville, W. Main St. (Old Greensburg Road). Stone monument erected to the memory of Adam Campbell, who is given credit for founding Campbellsville in 1817.

Battle of Green River — Campbellsville. KY-55S. Battle occurred in 1863. Monument to Union victory over CSA Gen. John Hunt Morgan.

OLD BUILDINGS

Alfred F. Gowdy House — Campbellsville, Logan St. Large brick house erected 1843-1850 by Mr. Gowdy, first Taylor County Clerk. Original 2-story Greek Revival portico has been remodeled to contain a large porch. Now privately owned.

Barbee-Gaddie House — Campbellsville. KY-120N.W. Built in 1822 by Gen. Elias Barbee for his daughter. Large brick house in Georgian-Federal Style. Only 2 families have occupied this house, the Barbees and the Gaddies.

Bud Gowdy House — Campbellsville, 604 Lebanon Ave. Built 1860. Two-story brick house has a long front porch which runs the length of the house. House contains some unusual antique lamps and fine maple floors. Now privately owned.

Clay Hill — Campbellsville. KY-55N. Built in 1830's of Georgian-Federal Style. Also known as the James Sanders or Dr. White House. Placed on National Register of Historic Places. Now privately owned.

Cumberland Presbyterian Church — Campbellsville, Columbia Ave. Built 1889. Contained fine stained glass windows. Bricks were fired in kiln on land that is now part of Campbellsville College. First built as Baptist Church and is now being used as the Taylor County Library.

Durham Sanders House — Campbellsville, in Pleasant Hill area. US-68. Built in 1839 by Durham Sanders. Architecture focuses around a large central hallway. Now privately owned.

Emerald Hill — Campbellsville, Burdick Community. KY-55. Built during the Civil War. House contains much fine woodwork. Exterior features Greek Revival portico. Now privately owned.

Good Hope Baptist Church — Campbellsville. KY-527. Organized 1796. Present building erected in 1870 or 1880, with additions made in 1916-1919. Large cemetery adjoins the church.

Jacob Hiestand House — Campbellsville, Old Greensburg Rd. KY-210. Remains of stone house are located in a field.

James Cowherd House — Bengal. KY-323. circa 1800. Two-story brick and frame house. James Cowherd, Revolutionary War soldier, also helped build the old Green County Courthouse. Now privately owned.

John Chandler House — Campbellsville, between Greensburg and Hodgenville Rds. circa 1795-1800. Believed to be the oldest house in Taylor County. Stone walls are 26-in. thick. Now privately owned.

Joseph H. Chandler House — Campbellsville, 503 E. Main St. Built after the Civil War. House features a solid cherry spiral stairway. Now a funeral home.

Old County Clerk's Office — Campbellsville, Courthouse Square, Columbia Ave. Built 1866. Small one-story brick building used to house county clerk's office after the courthouse burned during the Civil War. Has since been restored.

Pleasant Union Church — Campbellsville. KY-210. Was first a log church. In 1850, a weather-boarded building was erected on land purchased from the Winston family specifically for a place of worship. Church still in regular use.

Clay Hill in Campbellsville.

Battle of Green River Memorial at Campbellsville.

Fruit of the Loom factory in Campbellsville.

Sublett House — Campbellsville, Old Columbia. circa 1848. Two-story log and frame house is of typical pioneer construction. Used as a Confederate hospital in Civil War. Was also used as a public inn and stagecoach stop for 64 years. Now privately owned.

Will Henry Cowherd House — Bengal. KY-323. circa 1848. Two story frame house also served as inn. Now privately owned.

OTHER POINTS OF INTEREST

Campbellsville College — Campbellsville, College St. Established 1906. Christian Church affiliate.

McMahan Furniture Co. — Campbellsville. 615 W. Main St. Manufactures cherry furniture. Tours, Monday-Saturday 7:30 a.m.-4 p.m.

Old Greensburg Road — The Cumberland Trace ran down this road. Travelers journeyed on it between Logan's Fort (Stanford) and Nashville, Tennessee (Fort Nashborough). Famous among the men who traveled this road were James Robertson, John Donelson, President Andrew Jackson and probably Aaron Burr and others.

101

Wayne County

In 1800, Wayne County was formed from parts of Pulaski and Cumberland Counties. The forty-third county in order of formation in Kentucky, Wayne County was named for General Anthony Wayne of Pennsylvania, sometimes known as "Mad Anthony". He was a Revolutionary War general and a famed Indian fighter.

Monticello, the county seat, is located east of Lake Cumberland, and was established in 1800. It was named for the home of Thomas Jefferson, who became the third President of the United States that same year. The name was suggested by Colonel Micah Taul, first Wayne County clerk. The town was laid out by surveyor Joshua Jones, another Revolutionary War veteran. The land was owned by William Beard.

PARKS, RECREATION, LAKES, DAMS

Beaver Creek Resort — Monticello. KY-92W. Open all year.

Conley Bottom Resort — Monticello. Lake Cumberland. KY-90. Campgrounds at the water's edge and recreation facilities. Commercial fishing dock and marina.

Mill Springs Park and Watermill — Mill Springs. KY-1275. Built in 1840 by a Scotsman, Mr. Arthur Rankin. In operation until 1950. Has second largest overshop water wheel in U. S. It was also a Civil War battle site. Near here on Jan. 19, 1862, 4,000 CSA troops were engaged in battle and were defeated by 12,000 Union troops. Gen. Felix Zollicoffer was killed in action here. This defeat was important, for it broke the CSA defense line and was the first in a series of events bringing Union control to Kentucky. Picnic facilities.

MARKERS

Joshua Jones — Monticello, S. Main St. Wayne Public Library. He was a native of Pennsylvania, appointed surveyor of public lands by Governor Isaac Shelby. Came to Kentucky in 1794 and surveyed Monticello

site in 1801. Owner of ironworks in Virginia. Built bloomery on Elk and Beaver Creeks in 1800. He was granted 1,000 acres in 1801 by the legislature to aid his ironworks in Kentucky in the manufacture of pig iron. Died here 1816.

Morgan's First Raid — Monticello, at National Guard Armory. KY-90. On his first Kentucky raid, CSA Gen. John H. Morgan, with 900 Cavalry, went as far north as Cynthiana. Returned via Paris, Winchester, Richmond and Somerset, then here on July 22, 1862. He then moved toward Livingston, Tennessee. Morgan was gone 24 days on this raid, traveled 1,000 miles, raided 17 towns, and destroyed USA supplies and arms along the way.

Near This Spot — Monticello, Main St. At courthouse, on Aug. 30, 1861, Elder W. A. "Uncle Billy" Cooper (1813-1909), pastor, scholar, statesman made his famous "plea for peace," and averted bloodshed between Wayne County home guards and the local states-rights guards.

MEMORIALS AND MUSEUMS

J. C. Burton Museum — Monticello. KY-90. Houses the last stagecoach which was operated from July 1, 1896 until 1915, from Burnside to Monticello. Started and operated by Charles Burton. The coaches made one trip a day, leaving Monticello at 6 a.m. and returning at 6 p.m. The fare was $1.50 per person and the coach could carry 18 passengers comfortably. It connected Monticello with the nearest railroad. The building is now being used as a gift and antique shop. Also has a collection of Indian artifacts and some Civil War relics.

Monticello's Doughboy — Monticello, center of Public Square. The Doughboy was dedicated in April 1923, as a memorial to the 23 Wayne Countians who gave their lives in World War I. Cast bronze, the monument details a hand grenade, a rifle, and other tools of battle common to World War I.

World War II and Korean War Monument — Monticello, Courthouse lawn. The first monument built in the

State of Kentucky by a Disabled American Veterans chapter, honoring World War II and Korean servicemen who sacrificed their lives for their country. The Bronze Plaque on the front of the Memorial bears their names.

OLD BUILDINGS

Horse Hollow Cabin (Or "Raccoon" John Smith Cabin) — Monticello, Michigan Ave. Built before 1814 by Elder "Raccoon" John Smith (1784-1868). In 1808, he was ordained as a Baptist preacher. In 1831, he organized the first Christian Church in Wayne County at Monticello. Cabin was moved from Horse Hollow and reconstructed in the churchyard of the First Christian Church. Elder Smith is buried at Lexington.

Lockett's Chapel — Methodist Church, N. of Monticello. KY-1275. Named in honor of a distinguished pioneer, William Lockett. He came to Wayne County about 1800 and built a church on this spot about 1802.

West-Metcalfe House — Mill Springs, Mill Springs Park. KY-1275. First brick house in area. Built 1800, by Capt. Isaac West, Revolutionary War soldier who came here about 1798 and received a land grant in 1799. He made the bricks himself. CSA Gen. Felix Zollicoffer had headquarters here in 1861. Used as hospital after Battle of Mill Springs in 1862. Confederate buried in family cemetery.

Mill Springs — Mill was originally run by Arthur Rankin, one of the family of famous Scottish millers. Originally operated by water running from natural springs through a long wooden race over a large home-made overshop water wheel. Changed to a roller system about 1884 when sold to R. L. Lanier and Dr. J. O. Jones. In 1906, B. E. Roberts & Sons purchased the mill and in 1912 installed the present steel overshop water wheel of 3-ft. breadth and 40-ft. diameter. It is now known as the largest overshot water wheel in the world. It has been restored and still grinds meal today.

Stagecoach at Hotel Ramsey in Monticello.

Old Mill at Mill Springs.

Mill Springs Watermill.

103

Lincoln Trail Area

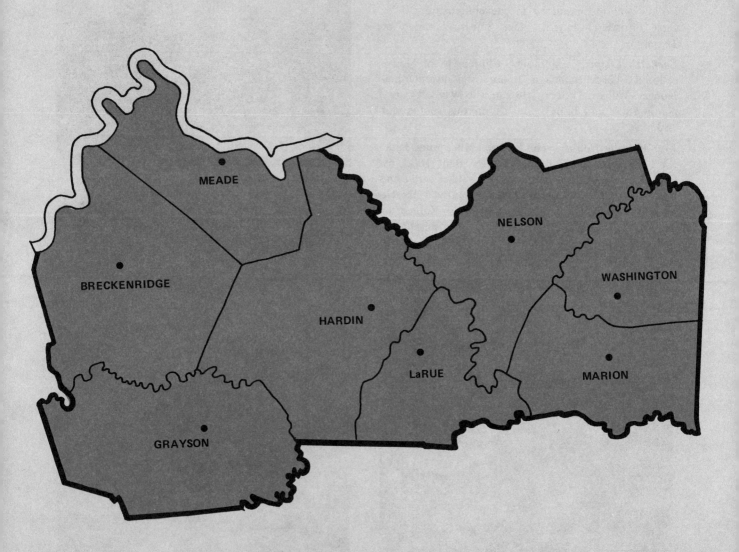

MEADE

NELSON

WASHINGTON

BRECKENRIDGE

HARDIN

LaRUE

MARION

GRAYSON

Breckenridge County

Breckinridge County was named in 1799 for John Breckinridge of Fayette County, a key figure in the writing of the Kentucky Constitution. John Breckinridge was a pioneer and founder of the Breckinridge family in Kentucky. The new county was carved from Hardin County, and was thirty-ninth in order of formation of the counties in the Commonwealth.

Captain William Hardin is known as the founder of Breckinridge County because he established Hardin's Fort, one of the first in the state. It was built in 1780 on the west side of the present town of Hardinsburg. Hardin was accompanied to this area by Christopher Bush, father of Sarah Bush Johnson, who was later to become the stepmother of President Abraham Lincoln. Captain Hardin was also active in politics and served in the Kentucky legislature.

Hardinsburg, the county seat, was laid out in town lots in 1782 and incorporated in 1800. It was named Hardinsburg on January 19, 1801.

In 1821, the state legislature established one of the first roads in Kentucky, running from Bowling Green to Cloverport. This road was built to open up commerce from the interior of the state to the Ohio River. From here, it was shipped to market in New Orleans.

FAIRS AND FESTIVALS

Breckinridge County Fair and Horse Show — E. of Hardinsburg, at the Fairgrounds. KY-1616. September.

Sacajawea Festival — Cloverport. US-60. The name Sacajawea was written into the priceless records of the Lewis and Clark Expedition to the Pacific Ocean, 1804-1806. Sacajawea, whose Indian name means Bird Woman, was of the Shoshone Tribe of Idaho. She had been captured by a roving band of Indians and was later sold to Toussaint Chaboneau, a French-Canadian trader, who had been employed as an interpreter by Lewis and Clark. But, she proved to be a better interpreter than Chaboneau. She saved the expedition by being able to converse with a tribe of Indians who sold the expeditioners much needed horses. Cloverport

honors this gentle Indian maiden for her contribution to American history with this annual festival. August.

PARKS AND LAKES

Riverside Park — Cloverport. US-60. Scenic view from the banks of the beautiful Ohio River.

Rough River Lake — Hardinsburg. KY-105, off KY-261. Formed by the Rough River Dam. Camping, boating, fishing, lodge.

MARKERS

Courthouse Burned — Hardinsburg, on Courthouse lawn. US-60. On Dec. 28, 1864, guerrillas set fire to the courthouse at Hardinsburg, but citizens were able to save the building and its records. CSA troops came in and allowed the public to keep arms for defense.

First Coal Oil — Coal oil was first produced here in 1851. Plant, built in 1857, was reputed to be first of its kind in the world. Mine was known for extensive veins of cannel coal. Coal was loaded here, then exported to England via New Orleans for gas manufacture.

Lincoln Crossing Ohio River — Cloverport. US-60. The Lincoln family crossed here on a log raft enroute to Indiana in 1816.

Official Naming of Breckinridge County — Hardinsburg, Courthouse lawn. Named for John Breckinridge, key figure in the writing of the first Kentucky Constitution. He served in Kentucky Legislature, the U.S. Senate, as Kentucky Attorney General, and U.S. Attorney General.

Shelter for Lincoln Family — Hardinsburg. KY-261. Lincoln family stayed in this cabin for 3 weeks enroute to Indiana in 1816.

Early Shipping Point — Cloverport. US-60. Cloverport, an important shipping point since Joe Houston came from Virginia, built a home, and started a trading and shipping business in 1798. Flatboats carried Kentucky tobacco and other goods for sale to New Orleans. Boats were sold for lumber, then the men would travel back over the Natchez Trace. Houston operated first ferry here in 1802, then as shipping increased, the steamboat came into use in 1820.

Tar Springs — Cloverport. 4 mi. S. of US-60. Fashionable health resort of 1840's which had the unique attraction of a 100-ft. cliff from which tar bubbled, while springs flowed from its base, each with a different type of mineral water. Indians knew of and used these curative waters. Wiley B. Rutledge, Justice of the U. S. Supreme Court 1943-1949, was born in 1894 at Tar Springs Resort.

MEMORIALS

Memorial on Courthouse Lawn — Hardinsburg, Courthouse lawn. Memorial in honor of Capt. William Hardin, founder of Hardin's Fort here on April 20, 1780.

OLD BUILDINGS

Holt House and Cemetery — Holt. KY-144. Twenty-two-room home and burial ground of Judge Joseph B. Holt, who presided at the trial of Lincoln's assassin,

Street Scene in Cloverport.

John Wilkes Booth. Now privately owned, but unoccupied.

OTHER POINTS OF INTEREST

Sand Knob — Rough River Dam. Off KY-79, KY-261, on KY-105. A peculiar rock formation 20-30 ft. wide, with almost perpendicular walls. The front is 110-ft. high and the back slopes to meet a ridge overlooking the Rough River Dam. On a clear day, it can be seen from almost 20 miles away.

Rolling Pastures and Woodlands.

106

Grayson County

Grayson County was established on January 25, 1810 and was the fifty-fourth county in order of formation in Kentucky. Its lands were taken from Hardin and Ohio Counties. It was named for Colonel William Grayson, a Virginia statesman, Revolutionary War soldier, and aide to General George Washington.

Leitchfield, the county seat, was named for Major David Leitch. The land on which the town is laid out was owned by Major Leitch of Leitch's Station in Campbell County, Kentucky. After his death, his widow married General James Taylor, executor of Major Leitch's will. The controversy over the location of the Grayson County seat was settled when General Taylor and his new wife offered to donate the land, only if the town would be called Leitchfield in honor of Major Leitch.

In 1781, George Washington traded his fine horse, Magnolia, plus $5001.00 to Colonel Richard Henry Lee for 5000 acres of land in Grayson County on the Rough River, adjacent to the land owned by Major Leitch. It is said that there is no other town in the world with the exact name of Leitchfield, as there are other towns with the same pronunciation, but not with the same spelling. Leitchfield was incorporated by an act of Legislature on February 5, 1866. Millerstown is the oldest city in Grayson County, having been settled before 1800.

In the western part of the county is Big Mouth Cave, located about one mile from a valley village called Pine Knob. This cave was the hiding place for Dock Brown and his clan of outlaws, infamous men who came to Pine Knob from Tennessee in the early 19th century to hide from the law. The county is hilly throughout, and perfect imprints of human and animal tracks much larger than those of modern-day humans and animals, have been found in the solid limestone rock located in many parts of the county.

FAIRS

Grayson County Fair — Leitchfield. KY-259 N. August.

PARKS AND LAKES

Nolin River Lake Resort — S. of Leitchfield. KY-259. Camping, water sports, fishing.

Rough River State Resort Park — Leitchfield. KY-105. Lodge, camping, water sports, fishing.

MARKERS

Grayson Springs — 3 mi. E. of Leitchfield. US-62. Site of famous spas and resorts that flourished 1830 to 1930, and were famous for the healing mineral waters. Also site of St. Augustine's, the first Roman Catholic Church in Grayson County, founded in 1815, by the great pioneer Kentucky missionary, Father Charles Nerinckx.

Green Mill — Falls of Rough. KY-79, KY-110. Land was bought in 1821 by Willis Green. Mill was built in 1823, and has been operated continuously by the Green family for over 140 years. It was part of a 6,000-acre timber farm complex supporting several family-owned industries. Farmers from 7 counties brought grain for milling into flour and cornmeal.

Courthouse square in Leitchfield.

Beehive Factory at Clarkson.

CEMETERIES

Brown Cemetery — Near Pine Knob, western Grayson County. Private family burial ground of Dock Brown, Grayson County's notorious outlaw of the early 1800's.

OLD BUILDINGS

St. Augustine Catholic Church — KY-88. Built 1815 by Father Nerinckx. Restored in 1852 over the grave of John D. Bellchase. A tablet in the wall of the church bears this inscription, "D.O.M. John D. Bellchase, Born in New Orleans, August 24, 1810. . . Died at Grayson Springs August 17, 1852."

Jack Thomas Home — Leitchfield, E. Main St. First brick house built in Leitchfield. Jack Thomas was the first County and Circuit Clerk of Grayson County.

OTHER POINTS OF INTEREST

Grayson County Courthouse — Downtown Leitchfield. Grayson County has erected 4 courthouses. The first, a log house, was burned by the Confederates on Dec. 24, 1864. The second burned in 1896, and only 3 record books were saved. The third courthouse was built about 1898, but it burned also on April 3, 1936, but all the records were saved.

Lashley Quads Birthplace — Near Leitchfield. KY-54. Three girls and one boy were born Feb. 23, 1941 in the frame house which stands nearby. The Carnation Milk Company was a sponsor for the quads, who stayed in a Louisville hospital several months, then came home to a new 13-room home with 2 baths and a nursery.

Hardin County

In 1792, the same year in which Kentucky became a state, territory was taken from Nelson County to create Hardin County, the fifteenth county to be established in Kentucky. In the fall and winter of 1779-1780, the first settlers were already staking their claims in the area that is now known as Hardin County. Captain Thomas Helm, Colonel Andrew Hynes, Samuel Haycraft, and Jacob Van Meter were among the first settlers, and each built his own fort and blockhouse. These stockades were constructed of split timbers and were deemed sufficient for defense against the Indian attacks. The sites were carefully selected, each on elevated ground with an excellent spring. One fort, which is now known as Elizabethtown, still gets much of its water from such a spring. The forts formed a triangle, each placed a mile apart from the others.

On the 17th day of June, 1781, eighteen people of Hynes Station, formed the Severns Valley Baptist Church. It was the first in Elizabethtown, and is now the oldest Baptist church in Kentucky.

In the early 1800's, Samuel Haycraft said, "Elizabethtown is as favorable a location for manufacturers as any other place in the state, and it only requires men of enterprise and some capital to make a start. A water course running through the town, abundant water and never-failing springs, and the inexhaustible forests of timber of the best kind, and our railroads and turnpike facilities makes it easy of access." These words have proven to be true for the people living in Elizabethtown today.

FAIRS, FESTIVALS, DRAMAS

By Way of the Valley — Freeman Lake Park. Located N. of US-31W. Outdoor drama. Early August.

Hardin County Fair — Elizabethtown Fairgrounds. Located S. of US-31W. June-July.

Annual Lincoln Heritage House Festival — Freeman Lake Park. Last Saturday in September.

PARKS, RECREATION, LAKES, DAMS

Elizabethtown Municipal Park — Elizabethtown, N. Miles St.

Freeman Lake Park — Elizabethtown. Located N. off US-31W. Picnic area and tables, two boat docks, 1 access ramp. Boats available to rent. Fishing. Year round, 7 a.m. until dark. Yacht races, April-November.

Hardin County Turkey Trot — Elizabethtown. November.

MARKERS

General Custer Here — Elizabethtown, Courthouse yard. US-31W, US-62. Cavalry and infantry battalions under Gen. George Custer assigned here, 1871-1873, to suppress Ku Klux Klan and carpetbaggers, and to break up illegal distilleries. He was then sent to Chicago to maintain order after the fire. Returning to Kentucky, he led an active social life. In 1873, he went to the Dakota Territory, with his service ending in July 1876 at "Custer's Last Stand."

Fort Sites — Elizabethtown, at cemetery. US-31W., US-62. Walls and terraces used to protect railroad. Civil War breastworks made by Gen. John Hunt Morgan's men. Also the location of one of four original forts settled by Col. Andrew Hynes in 1779-1780.

Lincoln-Haycraft Bridge — At bridge in Elizabethtown. S. on US-31W. Mill and raceway built in 1796.

Route of Lincoln's Pioneer Trail — Vine Grove, Main St. KY-144. Trail travelled by Lincoln family enroute to Indiana in 1816.

General Patton's Museum — Entrance to Fort Knox, Chaffee Ave. Building 4554 on Fayette Avenue.

CEMETERIES

Helm Cemetery — Elizabethtown. US-31W., Jct. with KY-447. This pioneer cemetery includes the graves of John LaRue Helm who served two incomplete terms as Governor of Kentucky, and his son, CSA Gen. Ben Hardin Helm, who fell at the Battle of Chickamauga on Sept. 20, 1863. Gen. Helm and Abraham Lincoln married half-sisters Emilie and Mary Todd, daughters of Robert S. Todd of Lexington.

Fort Knox Entrance.

OLD BUILDINGS

Gen. Ben Hardin Helm House — Elizabethtown. W. Dixie Ave. Located N. on US-31W. Home of former governor and state senator. This is also the area of one of the first forts in Elizabethtown, built 1779-1780 by Capt. Thomas Helm.

Lincoln Heritage House — On grounds of Freeman Lake Park. Located N. on US-31W. circa 1789. Originally a one-room cabin. There is a two-story addition, circa 1805, on which Thomas Lincoln did joiner's work for Hardin Thomas, an early pioneer.

Brown-Pusey House — Elizabethtown, 128 Main St. Once a stagecoach inn and community center. Restored and donated to community by two doctors, William and Robert Pusey. Memorial garden in the rear. Gen. Custer used house as his headquarters from 1871-1873. Now a historical library.

Severns Valley Baptist Church — Elizabethtown, W. Poplar St. The church, not the building, is the oldest church west of the Allegheny Mountains. Worship in this church began in 1781.

OTHER POINTS OF INTEREST

Elizabethtown Community College — Elizabethtown, College St. Off US-62W. Authorized 1960, founded in 1962, and began operation in 1964.

Embedded Cannonball — Elizabethtown, corner of Public Square. N. on US-31W. A cannonball, fired by CSA Gen. John Hunt Morgan, is now located in the

Courthouse in Elizabethtown.

brick wall next to Marshall's Jewelry Store on the square.

Fort Knox Military Reservation — Fort Knox, 35 mi. S. of Louisville, and 18 mi. N. of Elizabethtown. Located N. on US-31W. The U. S. Army Armor Center. Named for Maj. Gen. Henry Knox, Brig. Gen., Chief of Artillery, 1776-1782; Maj. Gen., Army Chief of Staff, 1785-1794.

U. S. Gold Depository — Fort Knox, Bullion Ave. Located N. on US-31W.

Hardin County Courthouse — Elizabethtown. First court was held 1793. Present courthouse built 1933, in the middle of the town square. Houses many interesting and historical documents.

 # LaRue County

LaRue County, the ninety-eighth county in order of formation in the Commonwealth, was established March 1, 1843 from the southeastern part of Hardin County, only after a debate over the selection of a name. An act to call it Helm County, to honor Speaker of the House John LaRue Helm, was amended by the Senate to honor Gabriel Slaughter, instead. As a compromise, it was called LaRue County for a family of early explorers and settlers in the area.

At the time LaRue County was formed, Hodgenville, which was established in 1818, became the county seat. It had been laid out by order of the Hardin

County Court on 27 acres of land owned by Robert Hodgen, tavern keeper and native of Pennsylvania. In 1886, the county seat had as many as 500 inhabitants and was considered quite an energetic business center. At that early date it had four churches, eight stores, a post office, two hotels, four doctors, seven lawyers, three blacksmith shops, a mill, a wagon and carriage shop and a tanyard. The large number of lawyers was due to the fact that Kentucky was having a great deal of trouble with land grants, which, incidentally, had caused the Lincoln family to lose the Sinking Spring farm a few years before.

LaRue County is predominately a farming community with considerable attention paid to raising stock. Rich in Lincoln lore, it is a great tourist attraction, as well.

FAIRS AND FESTIVALS

Annual Lincoln Day Celebration — Hodgenville. Activities throughout Hodgenville and LaRue County. February.

LaRue County Fair — Hodgenville. KY-210. July.

Lincoln Jamboree "Country Music Show" — Hodgenville. US-31E., KY-61. Country music, square dancing and a show every Saturday night.

MARKERS

Blab School (A, B, C School) — Athertonville. US-31E. Lincoln once wrote that while living on Knob Creek, he and his sister Sarah, were sent for short periods to A, B, C School, the first time taught by Zachariah Riney, and the second time by Caleb Hazle. These were schools and lasted only a few months. Free schools did not come to Kentucky until the 1830's.

1862 Civil War Invasion — Hodgenville, N. of Phillips Lane. KY-61. CSA troops under Gen. Braxton Bragg came through here in late Sept. 1862, planning to capture central Kentucky. Union forces under Gen. Joseph Wheeler were here, Sept. 23-27, scouting for the Union army, west along the Louisville road. There were many skirmishes with CSA until Oct. 4. On Oct. 8, CSA and Union forces met in Battle of Perryville, and CSA then retreated from state.

Courthouse Burned — Hodgenville, Courthouse yard. US-31E. Hodgenville courthouse burned by guerrillas Feb. 21, 1865. It had been used by Union soldiers as barracks. All county records were saved.

First Baptism in Kentucky — Hodgenville. South Fork Baptist Church. US-31E. Seven persons baptized in Nolin Creek in 1782 by the Rev. Benjamin Lynn, who founded the South Fork church, the second church in Kentucky. Church has assumed style of United, Separate, Regular and Missionary Baptists over the years. Once split by the slavery issue.

Indian Fighter Grave — Hodgenville, at South Fork Baptist Church. US-31E. John Walters (1770-1852), a Pennsylvanian, came to Phillip's Fort in 1780-1781. Commissioned as Lt., 2nd Regiment of Kentucky militia by Governor Isaac Shelby in 1792. He fought in local skirmishes in 1794, in the Battle of Brown's Run under Col. Patrick Brown, and in the War of 1812. Buried in South Fork Cemetery, 1/2 mi. W. of here.

Lincoln Knob Creek Farm — 6 mi. N.E. of Hodgenville. US-31E. Abraham Lincoln lived on this 228-acre farm from 1811-1816. He wrote in 1860, "My earliest recollection is of the Knob Creek place."

Lincoln's Playmate — Pleasant Grove Baptist Church. KY-84. In this church cemetery is the grave of Austin Gollaher (1806-1898). Lincoln, while President, once said, "I would rather see (him) than any man living." They were schoolmates when Lincoln's family lived in this area from 1813-1816. Gollaher is credited with rescuing Lincoln from flood waters of Knob Creek.

Phillip's Fort — Hodgenville, S. of Phillips Lane. KY-61. 1/2 mi. E. on North Fork of Nolin River is the site of the first settlement in LaRue County. It was built in 1780 by surveyor Phillip Phillips, and a company of settlers from Pennsylvania. Used as a refuge from Indians, it was abandoned and removed about 1786, when it became safe for settlers to build homes. Nearby, many pioneers lie in unmarked graves.

Pioneer Methodist — LaRue County. KY-210 at KY-462. In 1791, John Baird (1768-1846) became a Methodist circuit rider in Maryland. He emigrated to Kentucky in 1795 and preached his first sermon at Phillip Reed's house in Aug. 1796. This led to the organization of Level Woods Methodist Church. He is buried in the family cemetery near Level Woods Church, "An able expounder of the Word of God."

Lincoln Statue at Hodgenville.

Boyhood Home of Lincoln at Hodgenville.

Lincoln Memorial at Hodgenville.

MEMORIALS

Lincoln Memorial (Abraham Lincoln Birthplace) — Hodgenville. US-31E. and KY-61. National historic site. Original Lincoln birthplace cabin is enclosed in a granite memorial shrine on Sinking Spring Farm. Thomas Lincoln bought the 300-acre farm in Dec. 1808 for $200. Lincoln, his wife and infant daughter moved into a one-room cabin on this farm; later, Abraham Lincoln was born here. The 56 steps leading up to this granite shrine signify each year of President Lincoln's life.

Abraham Lincoln Statue — Hodgenville, Public Square. US-31E. Bronze statue erected in 1909 by Congress.

OLD BUILDINGS

Old Red Brick House — Athertonville. US-31E. Built 1833.

Old Stone House — Hodgenville. US-31E. Built 1791. Originally owned by Joseph Kirkpatrick, an early settler. Now privately owned.

Old Stone Springhouse — Hodgenville. US-31E. Built 1775. Located on the same farm as the Old Stone House and was used as a temporary dwelling until the Stone House was built. Later used as a school. Now privately owned.

OTHER POINTS OF INTEREST

Abraham Lincoln Birthplace — Hodgenville. US-31E. and KY-61. Various points of interest include a limestone spring which provided water for the Lincoln family; a 300-year old oak tree which marks one of the farm's boundary lines; an audiovisual program depicting Abe's boyhood travels; and the Nancy Lincoln Inn Gift Shop.

 # Marion County

Marion County is in the exact geographic center of Kentucky. It was first settled by Hardin Creek in 1779 by Colonels Charles and Edward Beaven. Surveyors James and Jacob Sandusky had explored the region in 1775, and built a blockhouse at Pleasant Run Spring. Marion County was part of Washington County until it became the eighty-fourth county to be created in Kentucky. It was named for General Francis Marion, the Revolutionary War hero from South Carolina who became known as the "Swamp Fox."

A famous Belgian priest, Father Charles Nerinckx, built one of the first Catholic missions in the area. This mission became the Motherhouse of the Sisters of Loretto in 1812, and also served as the first permanent school for girls in the west. Father Nerinckx escaped from Europe following the French Revolution, and for seven years lived with father Bedin, the first priest ever to be ordained in the United States. He then founded The Sisters of Loretto at the Foot of the Cross, the first American community of religious women founded without foreign affiliations.

Lebanon, the county seat, was incorporated in 1815. It was given its name because its cedar groves reminded the settlers of the Biblical "Cedars of Lebanon." A Presbyterian church built by Samuel and James McElray in 1789 became the nucleus of the future town. Recently, Lebanon was recognized by a Kentucky Chamber of Commerce award as the "most progressive of all small towns in the state." The first railroad in Marion County was built by the L & N Railroad Company in 1857. The depot building is believed to be among the first depots built in Kentucky.

Kentucky Country Ham Day and Flea Market — Lebanon, Main St. Features ham breakfasts on the town square; arts and crafts fair, parades, band festivals, and antique car show. September.

Marion County Fair — Lebanon, Fairgrounds Rd. July.

MARKERS

Battle at Lebanon — Lebanon. Railroad Station. US-68. Morgan's 2,400 Raiders marched to Ohio and were met by Col. C. S. Hanson's 380 Union soldiers on July 5, 1863. Hanson barricaded in the railroad station. The Raiders set fire to buildings, but rain prevented wide destruction. After 7 hours of battle, Union troops, almost encircled, surrendered.

Courthouse Burned — Lebanon, Courthouse yard. US-68. On July 5, 1863, the clerk's office at Lebanon was burned by Morgan's Raiders to destroy treason indictments against some of his men. All county records were destroyed.

Death of a Morgan — Lebanon. US-68. Lt. Thomas Morgan, 19, one of 4 Morgan brothers in Morgan's Raiders under John Hunt Morgan, was killed near here July 5, 1863 as he led an attack on Union forces in the depot at Lebanon. He died in the arms of his brother Calvin as the Union troops surrendered. He was reinterred in the Lexington Cemetery in 1868 where the Morgan family rests.

Sandusky Station — N.E. of Lebanon. KY-343, KY-1195. Pioneer surveyors Jacob and James Sandusky, who helped lay out Harrodstown in 1774, built a station around Pleasant Run Spring. The name is identified with this area.

CEMETERIES

Calvary Cemetery — Lebanon, at Calvary Church. KY-208. Union Soldiers burial site.

National Cemetery — Lebanon. KY-208. Established for burial of many Civil War soldiers, and in particular, Union Soldiers. Special monument for Cruso, a Spaniard who died in performance of duty. He fought with the Union forces serving in Russell Company, a Kentucky regiment.

Ryder Cemetery — E. of Lebanon. US-68. Grave site of Philip Walker, a Revolutionary War soldier.

OLD BUILDINGS

Dr. Irving Abell Birthplace — Lebanon, 223 W. Chandler.

Holy Cross Catholic Church — Loretto. KY-49, off US-150. Oldest Catholic Church west of the mountains. Built in 1785 and founded by Father Nerinckx.

Loretto Motherhouse — Loretto. KY-152. First religious order of women west of mountains. Museum, log cabin of Father Nerinckx, and chapel. Visitors welcome.

St. Mary's College — St. Mary's. KY-84, KY-327. Oldest Catholic college in Kentucky. Founded in 1821 by Father William Byrne. Now used as a seminary for training young men for the priesthood. Third oldest Catholic college in the nation.

"Myrtledene" — Lebanon. US-68. Built 1836. It was Gen. John Hunt Morgan's headquarters on his first visit to Lebanon in July 1862.

OTHER POINTS OF INTEREST

Star Hill Distillery — Lebanon. KY-52. Home of "Maker's Mark." Established 1954 by Mr. T. W. Samuels. Tours.

Holy Cross Catholic Church in Loretto.

Meade County

Meade County, the seventy-sixth county to be established in Kentucky, was formed from parts of Hardin and Breckinridge Counties by an act approved on December 17, 1823 by Governor John Adair. It was named for Captain James Meade of Woodford County, who volunteered his services to his country and rendered valuable aid in many engagements with the British and Indians. Captain Meade fought in the Battle of Tippecanoe and was one of the many Kentuckians massacred in the Battle of River Raisin in the War of 1812.

The first settlement of white men in Meade County was probably located at Wolf Creek. The date is not certain, but it was after June 1, 1785, when William Preston patented land at Wolf Creek. A fort was then built on a 1,000-acre tract of land, only to be abandoned later. The first corn grinding mill in the county was built by Jonathan Essery just below the mouth of Blue Spring Branch of Doe Run Creek. The exact date of this construction is not known, except that it took place some time prior to the admission of Kentucky as a state in 1792. The mill was later sold to Calvin Hurd and Jesse Brown, and enlarged in 1821. Abraham Lincoln's father, Thomas, is said to have worked as either a carpenter or stone mason on this construction. For 70 years the place operated as a flour mill, but later became a summer vacation spot for Owensboro and Louisville families. In 1927, it was expanded to include large dining facilities for which Doe Run Inn is now famous.

The city of Brandenburg, the county seat, is named for Solomon Brandenburg. He was the owner of a large tract of land purchased around 1804. Many of the historic buildings in Brandenburg, most of the antebellum era, were destroyed on April 3, 1974 by a tornado.

FAIRS AND EXHIBITS

Art Gallery — Brandenburg, on the grounds of Doe Run Inn. Off KY-448, Jct. KY-1638. A cabin, believed to be 200 years old, has been converted into an Art Gallery. Items for sale to the public. It is also the home of the Lincoln Trail Art Colony.

Meade County Fair — Brandenburg, Fairgrounds Rd., and KY-1692.

PARKS

Otter Creek Park — Brandenburg. KY-1638.

MARKERS

Audubon — Road through Otter Creek Park. 1 mi. off KY-1638. Artist, naturalist, and ornithologist John James Audubon often came through this county on sketching trips in 1820. Many sketches done in this area can be seen in *Birds of America,* his most famous work.

Morgan's Headquarters — Brandenburg. KY-228. Built 1832. This house, owned in 1863 by Col. Robert Buckner, was headquarters of CSA Gen. John H. Morgan, July 7-8, 1863, as Raiders crossed river on their way to Ohio in captured steamers. U. S. Gunboat Elk arrived and began shelling Raiders. CSA cannon returned fire, then the Elk left with ammunition gone. All CSA forces crossed river. Steamer Alice Dean burned. Hulk lies at bottom of river to the west.

Morgan On to Ohio — Brandenburg, Main St., at the river. On July 7, 1863 Morgan's CSA Raiders arrived here, captured 2 steamers and began crossing the river. They were fired upon, but Union forces fled under return fire. The Raiders made the crossing, and Morgan went on to N.E. Ohio, where he was captured on July 26. He was imprisoned at Columbus, Ohio, but escaped on Nov. 24 and returned to the South.

Muldraugh Hill — West Point. US-60N. On Dec. 28, 1862, CSA Gen. John Hunt Morgan burned 2 railroad trestles across this hill on the N. edge of what is now the Fort Knox Military Reservation. 800 prisoners were taken and paroled.

"Sue Mundy" Captured — 2 mi. E. at Breckinridge County line. US-60. In 1861, at age 17, Jerome Clarke,

called "Sue Mundy," joined the CSA. He was with Morgan's Raiders from 1862 until Morgan's death in 1864, and then became a notorious guerrilla. On March 12, 1865, Union soldiers captured him here with 2 other leaders of guerrilla bands. Clarke, then only 20, was executed 3 days later in Louisville, Kentucky.

CEMETERIES

Fontaine Cemetery — Brandenburg, on W. hill over-looking Ohio River, at Lawrence Ave. Burial sites of Elizabeth Brandenburg, wife of Solomon Brandenburg, and his mother, Hester.

Walker Cemetery — Brandenburg, behind Methodist Church. Burial place of Swan Brandenburg, second son of Solomon and Elizabeth Brandenburg.

OLD BUILDINGS

Brandenburg Methodist Church — Broadway. Constructed 1855. Federal soldiers were quartered in the church during Civil War.

Doe Run Inn — Brandenburg. Off KY-448, and Jct. KY-1638. Built 1821. Used as a gristmill for 70 years, then became summer vacation residence for Owensboro and Louisville families. Expanded in 1927 to include large dining facilities for which it is now famous. Land deeded and signed by Patrick Henry in 1786.

Dr. Robert's House — Ekron. Off KY-144. Built 1834 by slave labor. It has poplar beams running the full length of the house. Now privately owned.

Ben Wooly Shacklett House — Brandenburg, Stith Valley Rd., or "Jake's Grove." Off KY-560. Shacklett

Courthouse in Brandenburg.

was considered the best man in the county in his day. The 2-story part of the house has the original logs used when the house was built by a man named Jacky. It is over 150 years old. Farm is now privately owned.

St. Cloude Hotel — Brandenburg, W. side of Main St. Built 1838 by Isaac Malin and called Hotel Meade. Considered the finest hostelry between Louisville and Owensboro. Used as a barracks during the Civil War. In 1865, the name was changed to St. Cloude Hotel, and the building is still in use.

St. Martin of Tours Catholic Church — Brandenburg. Parish established Aug. 27, 1848. First church was a small frame building, and stood in graveyard where present outdoor altar now stands. Present church erected in 1894.

James Watts Home, "River Cliff" — Brandenburg, Lawrence St. Built prior to 1855, it is the former Buckner home that housed CSA Gen. John Hunt Morgan.

Nelson County

Nelson County was created from Jefferson County in 1785. It was named for Virginia Governor Thomas Nelson, and was the fourth county in order of formation in the new State of Kentucky.

Bardstown, the county seat, first known as Salem, was located on a tract of a 1,000-acre Revolutionary War Grant to David Baird of Pennsylvania. He never came to Kentucky himself, but his brother William came in

1784 to Salem. The settlement was later called Bairdtown, then Bardstown, and is the second oldest city in Kentucky. The town was incorporated in 1788 by an act of the Virginia legislature, although records show that settlements were established as early as 1775.

Cox's Creek, located nine miles north of Bardstown, was settled in 1775 by Colonel Isaac Cox, a Revolutionary War officer. It was first known as Cox's

Station, and was the first permanent fort in Nelson County.

The Bardstown area, rich in history and tradition, is now known as the heart of the distilling industry, as twelve well-known distilleries are located here.

FAIRS, FESTIVALS, DRAMAS

Annual Antique Flea Market — 3 mi. E. of Bardstown. US-62. Nelson County High School. April.

Stephen Foster Story — 1 mi. E. of Bardstown. US-150. Musical drama, singing, dancing. June-September.

PARKS, RECREATION

Bernheim Forest — Bardstown. KY-245. 10,000 acres of natural forest with arboretum, museum, and nature center.

Knob State Forest — Bardstown. US-62. Approximately 4,000 acres. Hunting in season.

My Old Kentucky Home State Park — 1 mi. E. of Bardstown. US-150, US-62. Park camping, recreation area.

MARKERS

Camp Charity — 10 mi. E. of Bardstown. US-62. Named by The Lexington Rifles commanded by John Hunt Morgan, who camped here September 1861, and were fed by friendly people who took no pay. With additional recruits, horses and supplies, they joined Confederates at Green River on September 30. The Rifles later developed into a CSA division well known as Morgan's Raiders.

Ferguson Chapel Site — W. of Jct. with KY-605. US-150. 3 mi. north is site of the first church in this area, and the second Methodist church in Kentucky. Built in 1792 by Joseph Ferguson. Original log structure was replaced by brick building in 1816, and by larger brick building in 1844. Old site abandoned in 1908. This church was the nucleus for the Salt River circuit.

Mile Stones, circa 1835 — Cox's Creek. US-31E., US-150. The Bardstown-Louisville Turnpike Company was chartered by the Kentucky Legislature in 1831, and the law required mile posts. Some were cut from stone and some cast in iron. They showed the distance to each end of the turnpike. 14 can still be seen along the east side of the present highway and are typical of the stone markers.

Courthouse in Bardstown.

Romantic 1825 Tragedy — Bloomfield Cemetery. US-62, KY-48. Jereboam Beauchamp and wife Anna buried here in the same coffin, by their request. To avenge her alleged seduction by Col. Solomon Sharp, Beauchamp murdered him at Sharp's Frankfort home in 1825. Beauchamp and Anna were held in Frankfort jail. She was released, then joined her husband in his cell, and refused to be separated even by force. On his execution day they attempted suicide by stabbing themselves. She was successful, but he lived to be hanged that day. First legal hanging in Kentucky in 1826. Edgar Allan Poe and many others have written of the tragedy, inspired by the Beauchamp's deep love and devotion.

MEMORIALS AND MUSEUMS

Barton Museum — Bardstown, Barton Road. US-31E., US-62, US-150. Museum of whiskey history.

John Fitch Monument — Bardstown, Courthouse Square. Inventor of steamboat in 1791. Fitch died in 1798, and is buried under the granite monument here.

Spalding Hall Civic Center — Bardstown, 5th and Flaget Sts. Built 1819. A replica of the steamboat on display. Formerly a prep school and college for boys and men; now a repository for memorabilia of local places and people. Sometimes local crafts are demonstrated and displayed. Open through tourist season.

CEMETERIES

Pioneer Cemetery — Bardstown, 5th and John Fitch Avenue. Old sarcophagi made of large, carved slab stones, making a safe above-ground burial ground for early pioneers. Records of all decipherable inscriptions on file in the archives of local historical society.

Old Presbyterian Cemetery — Bardstown. Notable family plots with stone walls around them.

OLD BUILDINGS

The Abbey of Our Lady of Gethsemane — Bardstown. US-31E., KY-247. First opened as elementary school for boys in 1805. Trappist monks made a second attempt to reestablish the foundation in 1848. Original monastery was founded in France in 1908. Guest house and chapel are occasionally open to public.

My Old Kentucky Home (Federal Hill) — Bardstown. US-150. circa 1800. Georgian-Colonial mansion. Home of Judge John Rowan, cousin of songwriter Stephen Foster. Foster's "My Old Kentucky Home" was written after a visit to Judge Rowan's home. Later became Kentucky's State Song. Back wing of home was built in 1795; the front was added in 1818. This home became renowned as a center of political and social activity during our early history.

Old Talbott Tavern — Bardstown, 107 W. Stephen Foster Avenue. Built 1779. Houses rare Indian portraits painted by Greenough in 1836. Oldest hotel west of Allegheny Mountains. Still in operation.

One-Room School House — Bardstown, S. 5th St. Restored from local cabins.

Pillory — Bardstown, W. Stephen Foster Ave., just off Court Square. Restored.

The Sisters of Charity of Nazareth — 3 mi. N. of Bardstown. US-31E. on Louisville Rd. Founded Dec. 1812 by Rev. John Baptist David. Purpose was to develop education west of Allegheny Mountains and to establish hospitals. Burial place of Rev. John Baptist David.

St. Joseph Cathedral — Bardstown, 310 W. Stephen Foster Ave. Completed 1810-1819. The first cathedral west of the Allegheny Mountains. Valuable paintings donated by Louis Philippe, later King of France, are on display. It is believed that Louis Philippe lived here during his exile from France. Old vestments and altar pieces displayed on request. Opened for viewing.

St. Thomas Catholic Church — 1/2 mi. S. of Bardstown. US-31E. Church and its settlement are known as the "cradle of the Catholic Church in Kentucky." In 1811, this site became the residence of Bishop Flaget, the first Bishop of Bardstown, and the Rev. John Baptist David, who worked so devotedly that he earned the title "Father of the clergy of the West."

Wickland — Bardstown. US-62. Erected in 1817 by Charles A. Wickliffe. Georgian-style mansion. Three floors of antique furnishings. Home of Governors Charles Wickliffe of Kentucky, Robert Wickliffe of Louisiana, and later for Governor J. C. W. Beckham of Kentucky.

OTHER POINTS OF INTEREST

Bloomfield — Bardstown. KY-48, KY-55. Incorporated in 1819 and founded by Dr. John Bemis who named the town in honor of his wife, the former Miss Bloom, and for Mr. Merrifield, who had married one of the Bemis daughters. Settlement was originally called Middlesburgh.

Botland — 6 mi. E. of Bardstown. US-150. First known as Bott's Stagecoach Stop. Part of the Wilderness Road leading to Louisville. Old building used by the travellers, and for changing horses is still there.

Chaplin — N.E. of Bardstown. US-62. Originally spelled Chapline. Named for Abraham Chapline, a member of Capt. James Harrod's party that reached what is now Harrodsburg in 1774.

Fairfield — High Grove and Bloomfield. KY-48. Settled by people from Cox's Station.

Information Center — Bardstown, Court Square. Cassettes for walking tours are available for a small rental fee. Brochures of points of interest in and about Bardstown and Nelson County. Maps and other aids for tourists. A tourmobile leaves the square each day at 9:30 a.m. and 1:30 p.m. for a guided tour of the area.

Nelsonville — Boston and New Haven. KY-52, KY-46. Named for Nelson Furnace, the location of the first iron smelting furnace in the knob section of the county. In operation until the early 1870's.

New Haven — 12 mi. S. of Bardstown. US-31E. Founded in 1820, incorporated in 1839. First known as Pottinger Landing.

Slave Block — Bardstown, Court Square.

Woodlawn — 6 mi. E. of Bardstown. KY-605. Founded 1887. Village and railroad stop named for its founder, Dr. Jonathan Clinton Wood. His wife, Ann Ferguson, was a relative of Joseph Ferguson, who brought Methodism into Nelson County in 1790. The first Methodist church at Woodlawn was known as Ferguson's Chapel.

Main Street in Bloomfield.

Washington County

Washington County was the first county formed in the new state of Kentucky. The bill to separate Washington County from Nelson County, Virginia, was prepared and introduced by Matthew Walton, Representative from Nelson County. This was seconded and passed by the Assembly of Kentucky meeting in Lexington on June 2, 1792. The first act established Kentucky as a state. The name of the county honors George Washington, then president of the new United States. A letter from Washington, thanking the citizens of the county for the honor, hung on the courthouse walls for many years.

In 1782, Captain Abraham Lincoln, grandfather of future President Abraham Lincoln, came to Washington County in hopes of acquiring large tracts of land. Before he could secure the deed to the land on which he had built, he was killed by Indians. Under Virginia law, his eldest son, Mordecai, inherited the estate and Thomas, the youngest son, received nothing. However, by 1806 Thomas had become a master carpenter and cabinet maker and married Nancy Hanks. The wedding was a sumptuous event, as her relatives were landed gentry in the area. Their son, Abraham, later became the President of the United States.

Churches came early to Washington County. Presbyterians were among the first, as before 1790, a group of Scotch-Irish Presbyterians settled along what was then known as Road Run, a small stream. They also established and served other churches in this area.

FAIRS

Washington County Fair — Springfield, High school grounds. Off KY-528. July.

PARKS

Lincoln Homestead State Shrine — Springfield. Off US-150, via KY-528 to KY-438. Park on land originally settled by Capt. Abraham Lincoln in 1782. Contains the Francis Berry house, replicas of Capt. Lincoln's homestead, a covered bridge, a blacksmith's shop and the Nancy Hanks Memorial. Recreation area.

MARKERS

Ben Hardin — 3 mi. S. of Springfield. KY-55. Ben Hardin (1784-1852), one of the noblest orators, lawyers and lawmakers in early Kentucky came to Springfield with his parents in 1788. In 1808, he settled at Bardstown where the career was launched that earned him the title of "last of a race of giants." Member of state legislature for 9 terms; U. S. Congressman for 5 terms; member of Kentucky Constitutional Convention, 1849. Before his death, he requested his children to bury him beside his parents.

John Hardin — 3 mi. E. of Springfield. US-150. John Hardin (1753-1792) was a soldier, Indian fighter and surveyor in Dunmore's War in 1774 and Revolutionary War. In 1792, he was foully murdered by the Indians while serving as U. S. Peace Envoy to the Indians in Ohio.

Jesse Head Homesite — Springfield, Main St., N. of Courthouse. US-150. On June 12, 1806, this man performed the marriage of Thomas Lincoln and Nancy Hanks, parents of future U. S. President Abraham Lincoln. Born in Maryland in 1768, Head "came a-preaching" to Kentucky in 1798. He was a cabinet maker and justice of the peace as well as a fearless preacher. He moved his carpentry shop to Harrodsburg in 1810, continued preaching and also started a newspaper.

CEMETERIES

Pleasant Grove Presbyterian Cemetery — Springfield. KY-55. Graves of Mitchell Thompson, cousin of Nancy Hanks, and of Mary Gregory Litsey, a close friend of Nancy Hanks.

Springfield Cemetery (Cemetery Hill) — Springfield, end of Walnut St. Established 1797. Several interesting old markers. Tombstones dating from late 1700's.

OLD BUILDINGS

Old Clerk Office — Springfield Courthouse, Main and Cross Sts. Original marriage bond of Thomas Lincoln and Nancy Hanks, dated June 10, 1806, as well as many other old records dating back to 1700's can be seen.

Washington County Courthouse — Springfield, Main and Cross Sts. Built 1814-1816. Oldest Kentucky courthouse still in use, and second oldest still standing in Kentucky. The first courthouse, built in 1794, was a small log building. The second, built of brick, was completed in 1797. Both were destroyed by fire. In 1814, Thomas Letcher was authorized to build a new one at the cost of $2,500. It was completed in 1816, and is still in use today.

Elmwood House — Springfield, Lebanon Hill. KY-55. Built 1851. Designed by foreign architect, Maj. Thomas Lewenski of Lexington. Solid brick exterior walls enriched by applied arches on vertical panels, and a pair of elliptical staircases rising from the great hall to the chamber rooms on second floor. Gen. Buell laid out maps before the Battle of Perryville in 1862 in the south parlor. Members of the Hugh McElroy Family were compelled to mark the water sources in the battle area. Now privately owned.

Mordecai Lincoln House — Springfield. KY-528. Built by Mordecai Lincoln, President Lincoln's uncle.

John Pope House — Springfield, corner of Walnut and High Sts. Built 1839. Home of only Washington County resident who voted for Lincoln in his race for the presidency.

Pleasant Grove Presbyterian Church — 6 mi. N. of Springfield. KY-55. Established Feb. 9, 1833. Building erected 1836, and is in an almost perfect state of preservation. Built on land donated by Stephen Cocke Browne.

Hubert Simms House (Elizabeth Madox Roberts House) — Springfield, 405 Walnut St. Home of James T. "Cotton" Noe, who was named poet laureate by joint resolution of the Kentucky General Assembly in 1926. Also home of Elizabeth Madox Roberts, who ranks with the finest novelists of this century. She conducted a private school in this house from 1900-1902. In 1921, she won the Fiske Prize for her poems, which were later published under the title *Under the Tree.* Her book *Green Meadows* portrays the life of people in early Kentucky. She has often been called the "poet of the Kentucky hills." Now privately owned.

St. Catharine — Springfield. US-150. Cradle and motherhouse of the first U. S. community of Dominican Sisters of St. Catharine of Siena, and of St. Cathar-

ine College, founded 1822. Originally a teaching institution for pioneer families, and a girls' academy until 1931 when it became a standard junior college. Original buildings burned 1904. Museum open daily.

St. Rose Priory and St. Thomas of Aquinas College — Springfield. KY-152. The great stone building with its octagon-shaped tower was designed in 1851 by William Kelly. Home of the first Dominican priory in U. S. Founded in 1806 by Fr. Fenevick from Maryland. Site of first Catholic college west of Alleghenies, 1807. Shortly after, a secular college, called St. Thomas, was established, 1809-28. Attended by Jefferson Davis from 1815-1816.

Matthew Walton's Office Building (House of History) — Springfield, 301 Walnut St. Built in 1803 by Gen. Matthew Walton, founder of Washington County. It is a log house with clapboard siding and is the oldest dwelling in Springfield. House had several illustrious owners, one of whom was David H. Spears, noted silversmith. From 1815 until his death, he fashioned beautiful silver items from coins brought by his customers.

OTHER POINTS OF INTEREST

Chaplin Covered Bridge — Sharpsville. KY-55, onto KY-458. Erected in 1853 by Cornelius Barnes.

Morresville Covered Bridge — 2 mi. N. of Springfield. KY-55.

Washington County Library — Springfield, Main St. A modern Williamsburg-design structure. Houses numerous modern and historical documents.

Courthouse in Springfield.

Louisville Area

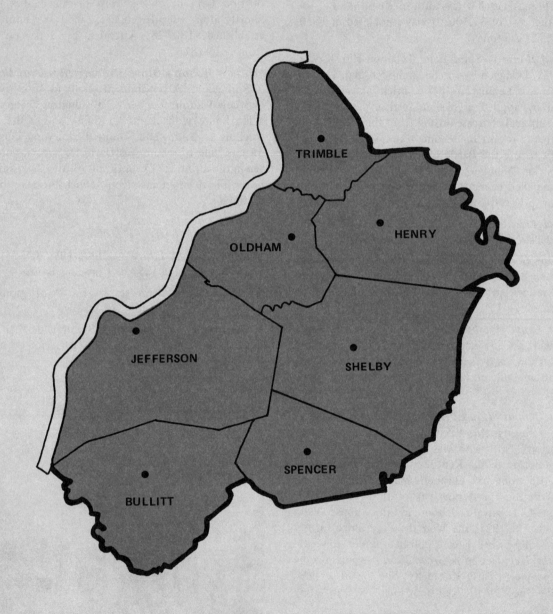

Bullitt County

Bullitt County was named for Alexander S. Bullitt of Shelby County, noted Indian fighter and statesman and Lieutenant Governor of Kentucky in 1800. Bullitt County was the twentieth county in order of formation in Kentucky. It was carved from parts of Jefferson and Logan counties in 1796.

The county was the center of the salt trade in pioneer days. Salt rock, also known as Bullitt's Lick, was discovered by Thomas Bullitt in 1773. Evidence shows that the salt licks were used by prehistoric animals as well as animals in pioneer days. The discovery of the salt lick led to Kentucky's first salt production. The area is surrounded by hills called "knobs," each with a breathtaking view.

Shepherdsville, the county seat, is located south of Louisville. The town was named for Peter Shepherd who settled here and registered the land under the Virginia Act of 1781. It is one of the oldest towns in Kentucky. Formerly known as Mud Garrison, it was located on the Wilderness Road from Fort Harrod to the Falls of the Ohio and became a garrison to protect the early saltmakers.

PARKS, LAKES, RECREATION

Bernheim Forest — 10 mi. W. of Bardstown, S.E. of I-65, KY-245. Renowned 10,000-acre forest park and sanctuary for plants and wildlife. Forest, fishing lakes, famous arboretum, nature center, museum, foot trails, picnic area. Open to the public.

Cedar Lakes — 10 mi. W. of Bardstown in Bernheim Forest. KY-245. Fishing, recreation area, hiking trails.

Louisville South K.O.A. — KY-44, off I-65 on Salt River. 348 trailer and tent sites. Indian artifacts may be found on the grounds.

MARKERS

Bullitt's Lick — 3 mi. N.W. of Shepherdsville. KY-44. Discovered in 1773 by Capt. Thomas Bullitt. Site of early commercial production of salt in Kentucky.

L & N Bridge in Civil War — Near Shepherdsville, at crossing of Salt River. KY-61. Bridge destroyed 3 times by CSA.

Mile Stones — US-31E., US-150. Along the early turnpikes, the law required mile posts to show the distance to each end of the turnpike. There are 14 of these typical stone markers along the east side of the present highway. This marker also indicates an early turnpike, The Bardstown-Louisville Turnpike.

Morgan — On To Ohio — KY-61 near the bridge crossing at Salt River. Reminders of raids of CSA Gen. John Hunt Morgan in his efforts to prevent USA movements into Tennessee and Virginia.

Salt River Furnace — Bardstown. Jct. Beech Grove Rd. and KY-61. Built 1832. Furnace stone stack stood 33 ft. in height. Charcoal fuel used to fire furnace. Produced 700 to 800 tons of iron castings annually.

Sherman Here — Lebanon. Jct. KY-434 at railroad crossing. USA Gen. William T. Sherman with 4,000 troops made headquarters here late in September, 1861 to secure Muldraugh's Hill against anticipated onrush of Confederates toward Louisville, and to rally Kentuckians to the Union cause. No major action occurred.

CEMETERIES

Mystery Cemetery — KY-245 near Jct. of KY-1604. Old graveyard discovered near here. Graves believed to be those of railroad workers struck down by the cholera epidemic around 1854, or burial ground for Civil War soldiers. Unmarked headstones.

OLD BUILDINGS

Crenshaw Home — 8 mi. E. of Shepherdsville. Early stone house attributed to Henry Crist, pioneer, salt maker, speculator and General in War of 1812.

John Dunn Home — 1 mi. N. of Shepherdsville, Blue Lick Rd. Built 1805. Brick house of unusual architecture. Brick was fired on the site.

Mud Garrison — N. bank of Salt River, 1 1/2 mi. above Bullitt's Lick Run. Built circa 1780. Unusual pioneer

Bullitt Central High School.

Homes in Shepherdville.

garrison used to house families of salt workers at Bullitt's Lick.

Paraquet Springs — Shepherdsville, N. bank of Salt River. Site of old hotel and mineral springs. Named after birds. Two buildings, sulphur wells close to Salt River, old grave site (The Lone Grave).

Pope Home — Shepherdsville, S. side of Salt River across from Dowdall's Station. Built in 1784. Fortified cabin at the Salt River ferry. Cabin is still standing and is now used as a dining room of the Maraman house.

Shanklin's — 3 mi. N. of Shepherdsville. KY-61. Pioneer settlement established 1785 as a fort against Indians. Original cabin still standing, and is used as dining room of Rhea house.

Yoe Home — 4 mi. S. of Shepherdsville. Built before 1800 by David Crable. Early pioneer home.

OTHER POINTS OF INTEREST

J. B. Beam Distilling Company — Clermont. KY-245. Manufacturer of whiskey and cordials. Tours available.

Belmont Iron Furnace — Belmont, E. of Kentucky Turnpike and S. of Belmont Rd. Founded in 1844. Iron furnace in operation during mid-1800's.

Kentucky Information Center — Kentucky Turnpike, Shepherdsville Interchange. Maps, directions, literature, travel specialists.

Henry County

Henry County was the thirty-first county to be formed in the state of Kentucky. Founded in 1798, it was named for Patrick Henry, Governor of Virginia and signer of many early Kentucky land grants. The land in the area was surveyed by Christopher Gist as early as 1750 and was purchased by men of means who secured patents from the state of Virginia.

New Castle, the county seat, was established in 1817, and is the state's third oldest incorporated town.

Farming is still the primary way of life in Henry County, as the limestone formation of the land is suitable to agriculture. The county is beginning to face an economical change as it assumes a more industrial role due to the establishment of many new manufacturing plants near Eminence and New Castle.

FAIRS AND FESTIVALS

Henry County Fair — Eminence. US-421. August.

Six-Mile Jamboree — Pleasureville. US-421. Country music show every Saturday night. All year.

MacGregor plant at Eminence.

Old Pollard Inn in Pleasureville.

LAKES, RECREATION

Lake Jericho and Lake Jericho Recreation Area — New Castle. KY-153, 1 mi. S. of I-75. 136-acre lake. Major camping area. Fishing, boating and picnic area.

MARKERS

Dutch Settlement — Pleasureville. US-421. Founded in 1780 by Dutch settlers. Site of first regular settlement in the county. Now private farms.

Old Pollard Inn — 2 mi. N.W. of Pleasureville. US-421. Built circa 1790. Gen. John H. Morgan and Capt. T. H. Hines, Confederate raiders, found shelter here December 1, 1863 after their Ohio prison escape.

CEMETERIES

Grave of Zach F. Smith — Eminence. Educator and historian who was born in 1827 in Henry County. He was state superintendent of public instruction and curator of Transylvania University for 50 years.

OLD BUILDINGS

Pollard House — Eminence. KY-22. Built 1790. Originally used as a tavern. James G. Blaine was a frequent guest while teaching at Western Military Academy in early 1850's. CSA Gen. John Hunt Morgan stopped here in 1863.

Pryor House — New Castle. US-421, KY-55. Built 1859. Originally the home of Judge W. S. Pryor, an ardent Confederate, who was made chief justice of Kentucky Court of Appeals in 1871. Now privately owned.

Thomas Smith House — New Castle. US-421, KY-55. Built 1818. Originally the home of Thomas Smith, prominent local farmer, landowner and businessman. He was one of the builders of the Louisville and Nashville Railroad from 1830-35. Now privately owned.

Western Military Academy — 9 mi. N.E. of New Castle. KY-202. Established 1850. Used as a federal recruitment station during Civil War. Now privately owned.

OTHER POINTS OF INTEREST

The Christmas Mail Town — Bethlehem, 8 mi. from Eminence. KY-22. People from all over U. S. send mail to be postmarked here.

Drennon Springs — 8 mi. N.E. of New Castle, on Drennon Creek. KY-202. Mineral springs discovered in 1773, site of former summer resort. A popular watering spot until late 1860's. Now private farm and woodland.

The Living Nativity — Bethlehem, S.E. of New Castle. Living tableau by townspeople. December 22-25.

Lockport — On Kentucky River. KY-389. Old river town with locks and dam.

Port Royal Hill Overlook — Port Royal. KY-193. Overlook of Kentucky River bottom land and hills of Owen County.

Living Nativity Scene in Bethlehem.

Jefferson County

Jefferson County was one of the original three counties carved from Kentucky County, Virginia in 1780. Jefferson County was named for Thomas Jefferson, who was at that time Governor of Virginia, an author of the Declaration of Independence, and later the third President of the United States. The "Falls of the Ohio River" was the first area to be mentioned in the history of Kentucky. The falls are a series of rapids which cause the Ohio River to drop twenty-six feet within one mile. This phenomenon of nature determined the history of Jefferson County and its county seat, Louisville.

In the summer of 1778, George Rogers Clark, along with 150 volunteer soldiers, moved down the Ohio River in flatboats. They landed on a small island covered with corn, now known as Corn Island which was located in the middle of the river above the "Falls of the Ohio." Here they established a permanent settlement until they found it to be unsuitable for year-round living.

Directly across from the island, Clark's volunteers could see flat, low land. It was formed with small hills rising to the south and east by a bend in the Ohio River. George Rogers Clark crossed the river from Corn Island and supervised the construction of Fort Nelson which was at the foot of present-day 12th Street. A city charter was signed May 1, 1780 by Thomas Jefferson, Governor of Virginia. The name Louisville was given the city in honor of Louis XVI of France, in gratitude for services rendered by France during the Revolutionary War.

Settlers continued to arrive, and by 1782, a larger and stronger Fort Nelson (Louisville) supplanted the 12th Street fort. After peace came in 1783, the number of settlers increased rapidly, and by 1800, Louisville was fast becoming a commercial city. Louisville has continued to grow, especially during the 1900's, and has become known as the metropolitan city of Kentucky, and one of the nation's leading river ports. It is now the largest city in Kentucky.

FAIRS, FESTIVALS, DRAMAS, EXHIBITS

Actors Theater — Louisville, 316 W. Main St. Established 1964. The state Theater of Kentucky. Tours by appointment. Spring and fall presentations.

Audubon Festival of the Dogwoods — Louisville, Audubon Park. Preston Highway, KY-61. Sponsored by Audubon Park Garden Club. April.

Bluegrass Music Festival of the United States — Louisville, River City Mall and Riverfront Plaza. Features top bluegrass musicians in the country. May.

Country Shindigs — Louisville, Convention Center, 525 W. Walnut St. July-October.

Derbytown Arts and Crafts Fair — Louisville, at various locations. Strictly Kentuckian arts and crafts, demonstrations, entertainment, food.

Heritage Weekends — Louisville, Riverfront Plaza. Heritage groups stage weekend activities and festivals throughout summer. Features ethnic food, costumes, dancing, music and crafts.

Kentucky Derby Festival — Louisville. State's greatest spectacular. Features Pegasus Parade, Coronation Ball, Steamboat race, balloon and bicycle races. Last week in April.

Kentucky Derby — Louisville, Churchill Downs, 700 Central Ave. Most prestigious Thoroughbred horse race in America. Only race in the world run over the same track in the same place each year since its beginning, May 17, 1875. First Saturday in May.

Macauley Theater — Louisville, 315 W. Broadway. Refurbished theater opened in 1972. Host to major musical organizations and legitimate theater.

Kentucky Opera Association — Louisville, Macauley Theater. Presents at least 4 operas each season. September-March.

Kentucky State Fair — Louisville, Kentucky Fair and Exposition Center, off Crittenden Drive. I-65, I-264. Features World's Championship Horse Show. August.

Louisville Ballet Company — Louisville Memorial Auditorium. Semiprofessional company. Programs October-April.

Louisville Orchestra — Louisville, Macauley Theater. Since 1937 it has been a major force in the city's cultural life. Concerts September-May.

Oktoberfest — Louisville, 300 block of Story Ave. in Butchertown. German entertainment and food. October.

Shakespeare in Central Park — Louisville, 1400 S. 4th St. Open air theater. July-August.

St. James Court Outdoor Art Show — Louisville, St. James and Belgravia Court. Exhibits, sales, entertainment. First Weedend in October.

Tour of Homes and Gardens — Louisville. Sponsored by the Garden Club of Kentucky. May.

Youth Art Festival — Louisville. First National Bank Community Center. March.

PARKS, RECREATION

Cherokee Park — Louisville, off Eastern Parkway. 409 acres. Recreation area. First of three parks based on 1887 plan.

Iroquois Park — Louisville, off Southern Parkway. 781 acres. Recreation area. 720-ft. lookout gives view of surrounding area. Third of three parks in 1887 original plan.

Shawnee Park — Louisville, off Western Parkway, on Ohio River. 181 acres. Recreation area. Second of three parks based on original 1887 plan.

Memorial Forest — Fairdale. Off I-65, between KY-1065, KY-1020. Forest acres, picnic area, recreation area.

Otter Creek Park — Fort Knox. KY-1638. Camping, picnic, recreation areas. Once used as hunting ground by Indians.

E. P. "Tom Sawyer" State Park — Louisville, 3000 Freys Hill Rd., off Westport Rd. Recreation area, picnicking. Dedicated to the late Jefferson County judge.

Zoological Gardens — Louisville, 1100 Trevilian Way. Zoo features over 600 animals in natural settings. Open daily except Mondays.

MARKERS

Abraham Lincoln, Grandfather of President Lincoln — Eastwood. US-60, US-460. Killed by Indians here in 1786.

Artist of Confederacy — Louisville, Cave Hill Cemetery. US-60, US-460. Nicola Marschall designed the Stars and Bars, the official flag of the CSA, and gray uniform of the Confederate Army here March, 1861. Died in Louisville in 1917.

Discovery of the Ohio River — Louisville Municipal Bridge. US-31E. In 1669 Robert LaSalle travelled this river, seeking a water route to China and Japan.

Falls of Ohio — Louisville, 26th and Northwestern Parkway. Marker reads "Fall Line of Ohio River, formed by outcrop of coniferous limestone 22 ft. thick." Falls now expose coral reef with visible fossils over 350 million years old. George Rogers Clark Northwest Expedition started in this area.

Floyd's Station — Louisville, Breckinridge Lane at Hillsboro Ave. This pioneer fort was begun in 1779 and is one of five on Beargrass Creek. Three of these forts were owned by Col. John Floyd, who made his headquarters at Floyd's Station. From these forts of defense and refuge, war was carried on against the British and the Indians in Ohio.

Isaac Hite's Home — Anchorage, 12215 Lucas Lane. This log house was on the plantation, Cave Spring, owned by Isaac Hite, an early surveyor. Hite came to Kentucky in 1773 with Capt. Thomas Bullitt's party, which was the first to survey Jefferson County and the land on which Louisville now stands.

Jefferson County — Louisville, Courthouse yard. Describes origin of county. One of three original counties formed when Kentucky County, Virginia was divided in 1780. Included 19 present-day counties and parts of 11 others.

Lewis and Clark Expedition — Louisville, at the park, 7th and Main Sts. This exploration of the Northwest Territory was the first undertaken by the U. S. Government. Lewis began voyage at Pittsburgh, Pennsylvania and descended the Ohio River to The Falls at Louisville where he met Clark.

Long Run Massacre — Eastwood. US-60, US-460. Indians killed 60 or more pioneers here in 1781.

Lyndon — Lyndon. KY-146. Named in 1871 by an early settler, Alvin Wood. Kentucky Military Institute moved here in 1896. Points of interest include Central State Hospital, founded on site of Issac Hite's home, and Oxmoor, home of Alexander Scott Bullitt, who helped draft first Kentucky State Constitution. Presented by Lyndon Homemakers Club.

Mansfield — Jeffersontown. Watterson Trail. KY-155. Home of "Marse Henry" Watterson (1840-1921), the famed editor of the Louisville *Courier-Journal*. The color and force of his writing brought the newspaper to preeminence in the South.

Soldier's Retreat — E. of St. Matthews. US-60, US-460. Birthplace in 1805 of Robert Anderson, who, as commander of Fort Sumter in April 1861, was the first Union hero of the Civil War.

Trainer and Jockey — Jeffersontown, Town Square. Roscoe Goose (1891-1971) rode the 1913 Derby winner, Donerail, which paid biggest odds in Derby history. One of first 10 men named to Kentucky Athletic Hall of Fame.

MEMORIALS AND MUSEUMS

Brennan House Museum — Louisville, 631 S. 5th St. Built 1868. Italiante in style. Tours.

Castleman Statue — Louisville, Cherokee Rd. and Cherokee Parkway. Erected in 1913 in honor of Gen. John B. Castleman, founder of the Saddle Horse Breeders Association.

Confederate Monument — Louisville, 2301 S. 3rd St. Tapering granite shaft was erected in honor of Confederate soldiers in 1895.

Filson Club Museum — Louisville, 118 W. Breckinridge St. Established 1884. Famous historical society museum contains pioneer and Indian relics, portraits, maps. Library contains 32,000 books. Club also has authentic example of one of Daniel Boone's famous beech tree inscriptions "Killed a Bar."

Fort Nelson Monument — Louisville, corner of N. 7th and W. Main Sts. A slab of Georgia granite commemorates Fort Nelson. Built in 1782 by George Rogers Clark as a military base and refuge for Louisville's first settlers.

Hillerich and Bradsby Company — Louisville, Finzer St. Home of famous "Louisville Slugger" bat. Items displayed reflect history and growth of baseball, including bats used by famous sluggers.

Kentucky Derby Museum — Louisville, 700 Central Ave. Records of all Derby winners, flags, trophies. Free guided tours during summer months.

Kentucky Railroad Museum — Louisville, River Rd., W. of Zorn Ave. I-71. Exhibits of old steam engines, railroads, cars and trolleys.

Museum of Science and Natural History — Louisville, 727 Main St. 15,000 articles on display including minerals, fossils, mounted animals, Daniel Boone's gun, and an Egyptian mummy.

Louisville Ballet Company.

Rauch Memorial Planetarium — Louisville, 2301 S. 3rd St. Named in honor of Rabbi Joseph Rauch, civic and religious leader. Lectures and films on wonders of outer space.

J. B. Speed Art Museum — Louisville, 2035 S. 3rd St. Founded 1925. Contains modern and historic art of all periods, especially medieval and Renaissance. Kentucky's oldest art museum. Also on display is bronze sculpture of horse and horseman attributed to Leonardo da Vinci.

CEMETERIES

Cave Hill Cemetery — Louisville, 701 Baxter. Graves of George Rogers Clark and Nicola Marschall, designer of CSA flag and uniform. Cemetery entrance has Renaissance-style tower. Built in 1887. 291 acres of lakes, trees, and rare shrubs.

Zachary Taylor National Cemetery — Louisville, 4701 Brownsboro Rd. Monument marking the grave of Zachary Taylor, 12th President of the U. S. Also graves of Mrs. Zachary Taylor and thousands of World War II Veterans.

OLD BUILDINGS

Cathedral of the Assumption — Louisville, 443 S. 5th St. Completed 1852. Gothic-Revival style with four-faced clock and 287-ft. spire.

Christ Church Cathedral — Louisville, 421 S. 2nd St. Built 1822. Oldest church in the city. Jefferson Davis married Zachary Taylor's daughter here in 1835. Church has been Episcopal Cathedral since 1894.

Thomas Edison's Butchertown House — Louisville, 729 E. Washington. Edison lived here for one year.

Farmington — Louisville, 3033 Bardstown Rd. Built in 1810 by Judge John Speed. Designed by Thomas Jefferson, and its original deed bears the name of Patrick Henry. Tours.

Hughes Presbyterian Home — Louisville, 1402 St. James Ct. Built 1895. Mansion among finest built in the early period. Tours by appointment.

Locust Grove — Louisville, 561 Blankenbaker Ln. Built 1790. Georgian architecture. Mansion was last home of George Rogers Clark. Located on grounds are a log cabin, slave quarters and smokehouse. Tours.

Jefferson County Courthouse — Louisville, 531 W. Jefferson St. Built in 1835-1842 by Gideon Shryock as City Hall and Courthouse. Completed in 1858-1859. Greek Revival design. Statues in courthouse are of Henry Clay, Thomas Jefferson, and Louis XVI of France. Designed to be used as the statehouse should state capitol ever be moved to Louisville.

Long Run Baptist Church — Louisville, Long Run Rd., off Shelbyville Rd. Built 1844. Shell of church on land claimed by Abraham Lincoln's grandfather.

Louisville City Hall — Louisville, 633 W. Jefferson St. Built 1873. French Renaissance design.

Old Bank of Louisville — Louisville, 320 W. Main St. Built in 1837 by Gideon Shryock. Greek Revival Design.

Zachary Taylor House — Louisville, Brownsboro Rd. and Blankenbaker Ln. Built 1785. Southern Colonial farm home of Zachary Taylor, "Old Rough and Ready," 12th President of the U. S.

OTHER POINTS OF INTEREST

American Printing House for the Blind — Louisville, 1839 Frankfort Ave. World's largest Braille publisher. Established 1878.

Farmington in Louisville.

Churchill Downs in Louisville.

Belle of Louisville — Louisville, 4th St. and River Road at Carrie Gaulbert Cox Park. One of two sternwheel steamboats still plying the Ohio River. Music by authentic steam-powered calliope. Public excursions from Memorial Day through Labor Day.

Brown and Williamson Tobacco Corporation — Louisville, 1600 W. Hill St. One of the nation's largest producers of tobacco products. Tours.

Cabbage Patch Settlement — Louisville, 6th St., S. of Magnolia. Historical charitable institution made famous in Alice Hegan Rice's book, *Mrs. Wiggs of the Cabbage Patch.*

Churchill Downs — Louisville, 700 Central Ave. at S. 4th St. Established 1874. America's most historic and famous Thoroughbred racing track. First Derby held in May, 1875. Guided tours.

Coast Guard Station — Louisville, 600 Federal Place. Founded in 1881 as lifeboat station. Nation's only inland Coast Guard station.

Courier-Journal and Louisville Times — Louisville, 525 W. Broadway. Founded 1826. One of America's foremost newspapers. Tours by appointment.

First National Bank — Louisville, 101 S. 5th St. At 512 ft., this is the tallest building in Kentucky. 40 stories. Tours by appointment.

Founder's Square — Louisville, 501 Walnut. Site of tourist and visitors information center. Pavilion building completed 1970 with unusual design. Roof suspended among six sweeping concrete arches.

General Electric Company (Appliance Park) — Louisville, Newburg and Old Shepherdsville Roads. World's largest manufacturer of home appliances. Tours of Monogram Hall.

Horse Farms — Louisville area has 8 important Thoroughbred farms and over 12 saddle horse farms. 5 Thoroughbred farms are along US-42, northeast of Louisville. Now privately owned. Tours with permission only.

Jefferson Community College — Louisville, 109 E. Broadway. Built 1909. Gothic design. Formerly Presbyterian Seminary. Largest community college of University of Kentucky since 1964.

Louisville Public Library — Louisville, 301 York St. Established 1871. Beaux Arts design wing built 1906-1908. Present wing built in 1969. Houses the Junior Art Gallery.

McAlpine Dam — Louisville, 26th and Northwestern Parkway. When the Portland Canal was dug as a bypass from the Falls of the Ohio, a giant "Z" was formed, giving shape to the dam that was built later for proper navigation and flood control.

Old Pumping Station — Louisville, River Road at Zorn Ave. Built between 1858 and 1860. The Louisville Water Company's old pumping station and water tower have been listed as National Historic Landmarks. Cited as finest example of the symbolic and monumental style of 19th Century industrial architecture. Famous for its statuary of 9 mythological goddesses and the figure of an Indian hunter.

Old Steamboat Landing Area — Louisville, 4th and River Rd. Wharf area. Steamboats landed here, then passengers had to travel by land to circumvent Falls of the Ohio.

Simmons Bible College — Louisville, 1811 Dumesnil. Founded 1879. Elijah P. Marrs, an ex-slave, was first director. Served as Black University 1931-1951. Now used as theology training center.

Southern Baptist Theological Seminary — Louisville, 2825 Lexington Rd. Founded 1859. Largest in eastern U. S. Museum on campus, as well as archives of Evangelist Billy Graham.

Union Station — Louisville, 1000 W. Broadway. Completed 1893. Cathedral-like structure was railway center when railroads were at their peak.

University of Louisville — Louisville, 2301 S. 3rd St. Chartered 1798. Oldest municipal university in the nation.

Steamboat the "Belle of Louisville."

Waterfront Plaza in Louisville.

Locust Grove near Louisville.

Oldham County

Oldham County, the seventy-fourth county to be formed in Kentucky was created in the year 1823 from Jefferson, Shelby and Henry Counties.

The county was named for Colonel William Oldham of Jefferson County, a native Virginian and Revolutionary War officer. Oldham commanded a Kentucky militia regiment in the bloody St. Clair Indian Campaign in 1794 on the Wabash River, and was one of the 800 soldiers killed.

Oldham County is divided into three main historical areas — Pewee Valley, Westport, and LaGrange, the county seat. Although Oldham County is one of the smallest counties in Kentucky, it claims to be one of the prettiest and fastest growing. The county is steeped in history due to its access to the Ohio River. The early settlers founded a trading center in Westport, located in a beautiful valley next to the Ohio River. The trading center became a settlement around 1800 and served as the county seat for a period of time before being moved to LaGrange. The old Westport courthouse is now used by the Methodist church for services. A number of homes built before the Civil War can still be seen in this quaint little town, which is still known for its river activities.

Pewee Valley was first established as Smith's Station, and named for Thomas Smith, president of Kentucky's first railroad, chartered in 1830. Smith convinced several friends and relatives to build their homes in this peaceful area. Soon the town's people began to look for a new name for the growing community. Legend related that the name was chosen at Professor Noble Butler's home, Tuliphurst. A group of citizens visiting at Tuliphurst saw a small Pewee bird; hence the name Pewee Valley. Pewee Valley has a certain peaceful charm of its own, which is enhanced by the community's efforts to preserve the historical houses and the quaint village square. It is best described in the Annie Fellows Johnston books *The Little Colonel* and *Floydboro Valley*. Based on real people of Pewee Valley, the books were published in 14 languages and are now out of print and considered collectors items.

In 1934 Shirley Temple brought *The Little Colonel* to life on film.

LaGrange, the county seat, was named for the home of Marquis de Lafayette in commemoration of his services to America in the Revolution. Lafayette was a well-known hero at that period of time and was also a visitor to Kentucky in 1825.

FAIRS, FESTIVALS, DRAMAS

Oldham County Fair — LaGrange, Fairgrounds. KY-146. August.

Oldham County Day — LaGrange, Courthouse Square. Parade, items for sale and trade. Third Saturday in July.

Annual Fish Fry — Westport, Town Square. KY-524. Second Saturday in June, and Saturday after Labor Day.

PARKS

Westport Park and Boat Dock — Westport. Recreation area.

MARKERS

Funk Seminary Site — LaGrange. KY-53, KY-146. In 1841 William Funk bequeathed $10,000 to establish a seminary, then the Masonic University of Kentucky. Building burned in 1911.

Independence Day 1863 — 9 mi. S. of Campbellsville Bypass on old KY-55. On July 4, 1863 Morgan's Raiders demanded surrender of 200 Michigan Infantry under Col. O. H. Moore. Moore replied that the 4th of July was no day to entertain such a proposition and repulsed 8 CSA assaults in a 3-hour battle.

MEMORIALS

Duncan Memorial Chapel — Floydsburg, Floydsburg Road near Crestwood. Early English-Gothic style. Constructed of native stone gathered from old fences around the countryside. The stained glass windows above the altar are of the medallion type. One of the windows was selected by the research department of the Rockefeller Foundation to be exhibited at the 1937 Paris Exposition. Under the window on the altar is a carving representing the Last Supper by Leonardo da Vinci. The remains of Mr. and Mrs. Duncan are buried in the Chancel of the chapel.

CEMETERIES

Confederate Cemetery — Pewee Valley, Maple Ave. Established in 1902. Marked by a granite obelisk to honor 313 soldiers who died while residents of the Kentucky Confederate Home. Only commonwealth-owned Confederate cemetery.

Mt. Tabor Cemetery — Crestwood. KY-22. Grave of David M. Griffith (1875-1948). Motion picture director and outstanding figure in the development of the movie industry. Famous films include *Birth of a Nation.* Memorial placed by Screen Actors Guild to mark his grave.

Valley of Rest Cemetery — LaGrange, 1st St. Grave of Rob Morris, founder of the Order of the Eastern Star. Marked by marble shaft.

OLD BUILDINGS

Barrickman Place — Westport. Built 1836. Runaway slaves were hidden in the secret compartment beneath the house to await transportation across the Ohio River to freedom.

The Beeches — Pewee Valley, Central Ave. circa 1900. Home of Mrs. Annie Johnston, author of the "Little Colonel" stories for children. Designed and developed by early residents. Estate surrounded by "Pewee Valley fence." Diamond-shaped pieces can be seen on posts. Originally the home of Mrs. Henry Lawton, widow of Gen. Lawton, who reportedly killed Geronimo.

Edgewood — Pewee Valley, Central Ave. Built 1860. Originally the home of Walter N. Haldeman, founder of the *Louisville Courier-Journal* and *Louisville Times.*

The D. W. Griffith House — LaGrange, 4th and Madison Sts. Built by motion picture producer D. W. Griffith. A pioneer in the motion picture industry, he invented more camera techniques and lighting effects than any other producer. LaGrange was Griffith's hometown.

Foster Johnson House — Floydsburg. Built 1790. Log house now covered with clapboard. At one time, it was the town hall of Floydsburg.

Kittery or Maple Grove — Brownsboro, Glenarm Rd. Built 1809. Architectural example; originally owned by Isaac C. Smith.

The Locusts — Pewee Valley, LaGrange Rd. E. Built 1800. Fictional home of the grandfather of the "Little Colonel" in books written by Mrs. Annie Fellows Johnston. West wing of house was built as a fortress.

Rob Morris Home — LaGrange, 110 Washington St. circa 1850. Founder of the Order of the Eastern Star, lecturer, writer of many books and poems. President of Masonic College 1861-1865. Tours.

The Old Tavern — Westport. One of the town's oldest structures. It was once used as a tavern and hotel.

Frances Snowden Home — Goshen. Off US-42. Built circa 1795. Front of home is the original house. Architectural example. Presently serves as Harmony Landing Country Club.

Traveler's Rest, or "Bit of Heaven" — Prospect. Off US-42. Built 1800's. Inn had an elaborate stone entrance. Built with a brick sentry house that guarded the Indian crossing point of the grassy flats area. Also used as a meeting house. Old gunpowder mill still located on grounds.

Trigg — Between Skylight and Goshen. circa 1793. Originally 2 log houses with a dogtrot between. Later covered with clapboard.

Tuliphurst — Pewee Valley, LaGrange Rd. W. Built 1855. One of the first houses in Pewee Valley.

OTHER POINTS OF INTEREST

Correctional Institution for Women — Pewee Valley, Ash Ave.

Kentucky State Reformatory — LaGrange. KY-146.

The Beeches in Pewee Valley.

Shelby County

Shelby County was the third county to be formed after Kentucky became a state in 1792. Its territory was taken from Jefferson County. The first settlement in Shelby County was Painted Stone, a fort built by Squire Boone. This county was named for Isaac Shelby, of Lincoln County, an officer in all operations on the frontier, and later in the American Revolution. He was later to become Kentucky's first and fifth governor. While governor, he also commanded part of General Harrison's army in the War of 1812.

Shelbyville, also named for Governor Shelby, is the county seat. Its land was donated by William Shannon. Shelby County has a history rich in tales of Indian fighting and pioneer lore. Present-day Shelby County is the leading dairy county in Kentucky.

FAIRS, FESTIVALS, DRAMAS, EXHIBITS

Beef-N-Boards Dinner Theater — Simpsonville, Veechdale Rd., between I-64 and US-60. Broadway plays all year. Performance is preceded by buffet dining. Reservations necessary.

Dogwood Festival — Shelbyville. Tours of Shelbyville's pink and white dogwood trees. Music, arts and crafts displays. April.

June Dairy Month — Shelbyville. June.

Shelby County Fair and Horse Show — Shelbyville, Fairgrounds. US-60. August.

PARKS AND LAKES

Guist Creek Lake — Shelbyville. Off US-60. Camping, fishing, boating.

Park I, Park II, Park III — Shelbyville, Main St. at Fountain Square. These three parks were formed from land donated by William Shannon. Fountain was built 1895. Methodist church courtyard.

Lake Shelby — 2 mi. N. of Shelbyville, on Clear Creek, off Burks Branch Rd. 100 acres. Fishing, boating, boat dock and small recreation area.

MARKERS

General Joseph Winlock — Dr. John Knight — KY-55, 2 1/2 mi. S. of I-64. Commemorates Winlock (1758-1831) soldier and statesman; and Knight (1748-1838) first physician to practice in Shelby County.

Hemp in Kentucky — 3 1/2 mi. E. of Shelbyville. Jct. US-60 and KY-714. First crop grown in 1775. From 1840-1846 Kentucky produced the largest amount in the U. S. and Shelby was one of the chief producing counties.

Jeptha's Knob — Clay Village. US-60, US-460. A cryptovolcanic structure that never reached the volcanic stage.

Pioneer Station — 2 mi. N. of Shelbyville. Squire Boone's Station, or Painted Stone, 1/2 mi. W. on Clear Creek. KY-55. Founded in 1779 by Squire Boone and others. Boone painted his name and the date on a creek stone, hence the name Painted Stone. For more than a year, this was the only refuge on the road between Harrodsburg and Louisville.

Shelbyville Fountain — Shelbyville, Public Square. US-60. Erected in May, 1895 to commemorate the loss of horses when "Black Dave" Martin's Civil War guerrillas attacked a stockade located there in 1864.

Tick Creek Massacre — 6 mi. E. of Shelbyville, near Tyler Station. US-60. 3 mi. N. of here, Bland Ballard and family were massacred by Indians at Ballard's cabin on Tick Creek in October, 1788.

The Armstrong Hotel — Shelbyville, corner of 7th and Main. US-60. Established in 1859 by George A. Armstrong. Had wide reputation for its good food and lodgings. Scene of 1864 slaying of guerrilla leader Ed Terrill and Brig. Gen. Henry H. Dernhardt in 1937. Hotel destroyed by fire in 1944.

Whitney M. Young, Jr. — Simpsonville. US-60W. Commemorates Young, (1921-1971) a civil rights leader who was born here. As Director of the National Urban

League, he helped thousands find employment. Originally buried in Lexington.

MEMORIALS, MUSEUMS

Carnegie Library — Shelbyville, Washington St. Built 1903. A Kentucky room is being furnished with books, articles and other state memorabilia.

Wakefield-Scearce Galleries (Science Hill Inn) — Shelbyville, 525 Washington St. Off I-64. Founded in 1825 by Mrs. Julia Tevis. Operated as a girls' school for 114 years. School closed in 1939. Purchased by Mr. Mark Scearce. Show rooms feature many beautiful English furniture, silver and china imports. Food is served in the Georgian Room, which was the main dining room of the school and in the Red Lion Room, which has an Old English atmosphere.

CEMETERIES

Benjamin Logan Cemetery — Shelbyville, Brunerstown Rd. Graves of pioneer Benjamin Logan (1743-1802) and Col. James Knox, famous Kentucky "Long Hunter."

OLD BUILDINGS

Benjamin Logan House — Shelbyville, Brunerstown Rd.

Chatham Station — Shelbyville, 220 N. 7th St. KY-55N. Built 1895. Originally L & N Railroad Station. Teddy Roosevelt and Harry Truman campaigned at this station. Jesse James' brother, Frank, stopped at the station in 1921. This Victorian Station was bought by Dr. Donald Chatham and now houses antiques, crafts, and gifts.

Lee's Log Cabin — Shelbyville, 515 Ashland Ave. Built 1804 in Nelson County. Taken apart and rebuilt by the Purcell Lees in 1957, using original materials throughout. Cabin has ash floors, black walnut pegged doors and rock used in the massive chimney and fireplace. Over 300 pioneer articles are displayed throughout the cabin. Tours by appointment.

The Old Blockhouse — Shelbyville, Main St. Replica of blockhouse erected 1858 by the townspeople to defend themselves against bands of guerrillas.

Old Mill Shop — Shelbyville, 115 N. 7th St. Antiques and reproductions.

Old Stone Inn — Simpsonville, 7 mi. W. of Shelbyville. US-60. Completed in 1827 by Fleming P. Rogers on the first Virginia land grant. Built by slave labor. Second oldest residence in Shelby County. Stone for

building was quarried on the farm. Stones were stacked with no mortar used. Originally used as a resting station for stagecoaches and called Stone Tavern. Meals served at the inn.

Shannon Place — S. of Shelbyville, Old Taylorsville Rd. circa 1820-1828. Originally the home of Samuel Shannon, II, nephew of William Shannon, who donated the land on which Shelbyville is built. Architectural example.

Shelby County Courthouse — Shelbyville. Main St.

Shelby County Jail — Shelbyville, Washington St. Built in 1891 of stone slabs. Unique in design.

Spring House — Shelbyville, 820 Henry Clay Blvd.

Governor A. O. Stanley Birthplace — Shelbyville, 3rd and Washington Sts. Built early 1800's. Gray brick house. Stanley was Governor of Kentucky 1915-1919. Now privately owned.

Stockdale — 5 mi. from Shelbyville. KY-55. Home of Charles Stuart Todd and Letitia Shelby Todd, daughter of Governor Isaac Shelby. Built on land Shelby gave to his daughter. House was a copy of the old Governor's Mansion at Frankfort.

Squire Boone Fort — KY-55, 2 mi. off US-60. Site of first settlement in Shelby County.

OTHER POINTS OF INTEREST

Whitney M. Young, Jr. Residential Manpower Center — 7 mi. W. of Shelbyville, Lincoln Campus in Simpsonville. US-60. Campus, former site of famed Lincoln Institute, was outstanding school of black resident students from 1911-1966. Named in honor of Dr. Young, National Director of Urban League from 1961-1971. Tours by appointment.

Chatham Station in Shelbyville.

Wakefield-Scearce Galleries in Shelbyville.

Science Hill Inn in Shelbyville.

Courthouse in Shelbyville.

Spencer County

In January of 1824, the thirty-second General Assembly established Spencer County from Shelby, Nelson and Bullitt Counties, thus creating Kentucky's seventy-seventh county. The county was named for Captain Spear Spencer, a valiant Indian fighter who lost his life at The Battle of Tippecanoe. In December 1824, the General Assembly made Taylorsville the official county seat, and in 1829 the town was incorporated.

Taylorsville was founded in 1799 on the land of Richard Taylor, proprietor of a gristmill, and owner of a large tract of land at the mouth of Brashears Creek on the Salt River. About sixty acres of land were taken from the Taylor tract for the Shelby County Courthouse on a motion by Taylor himself.

Belgrade and Spencerville were names formerly used for the town, before Taylorsville became the official county seat.

FAIRS, FESTIVALS

May Day Festival — Taylorsville, grounds of Spencer County High School. KY-44. Booths, rides, band concert, 4-H Fashion Revue. Usually held 1st week of May.

Spencer County Fair — Taylorsville, grounds of Spencer County High School. Carnival, agricultural, homemaking and youth exhibits, horse show, beauty contest, dog show, Old-Fashioned Day, Homemakers' Bazaar, beef and dairy show. Usually held during first full week of August.

MARKERS

County Named — Taylorsville, Courthouse Yard. KY-44, KY-55. Established 1824. Describes the career of Capt. Spear Spencer in the Indian campaigns.

Guerrilla Quantrill — 5 mi. S. of Taylorsville. KY-55. William Quantrill, alias Capt. Clarke, 4th Missouri Cavalry was captured here May 10, 1865, ending four months of Central Kentucky guerrilla raids. Surrounded in Wakefield's barn by Capt. Terrill's 30 Kentuckians. Quantrill tried to escape but was mortally

Main Street in Taylorsville.

wounded and was moved to Louisville Military Prison Hospital. He died June 6th, ending a career as a notorious outlaw and guerrilla for the confederacy.

CEMETERIES

Family Burial Grounds of Jacob Yoder — 2 mi. N. of Taylorsville. Yoder Station on Knox Brown farm. Inscribed iron tablet over grave of Jacob Yoder dates back to Revolutionary War era. Surrounded stone fences.

OLD BUILDINGS

Bourne-Anderson House — Taylorsville. KY-55. Built 1815. Premises once had a distillery. Nominated for the National Register of Historic Places.

Courthouse — Taylorsville. KY-44. Burned by guerrillas in June 1856. Guerrillas captured by Federal scouts and also saved courthouse records.

Dyke House — Rivals. Built 1780's or 1790's. Old rock house.

Halloway Home — 1 1/2 mi. W. of Taylorsville. KY-44. circa 1820. Colonial home. Many antiques.

McClain House — Taylorsville. KY-55N. Built 1836 with brick made on premises. Present-day kitchen is former slave quarters. Listed in National Register of Historic Places.

Rusk House — Taylorsville. KY-1251, Jct. KY-1060. circa 1800. Rock walls 16 in. thick.

Spear House — Taylorsville, Back St. Built circa 1790. Oldest house in city. Once served as a tavern for travelers to Taylorsville. House faced the river at that time. Now privately owned.

Spencer House — Taylorsville, Main St. Built 1837. In 1860's Isaiah Yocum operated this as hotel for traveling "drummers." Yocum also operated a buggy to take travelers from hotel to train station and back. Served as a tavern for 95 years. Now a funeral home and private residence.

"Vaucluse" Home — 2 mi. N. of Taylorsville. Home of Jacob Yoder who took the first flatboat with a load of cargo down the Mississippi River to New Orleans. House was built by slave labor from bricks made on the farm. Now privately owned.

OTHER POINTS OF INTEREST

Beam's Distillery — Wakefield.

High Grove Lookout — Between Bardstown and Mt. Washington, 1/2 mi. from High Grove. US-31E. Road stop overlooking several hundred acres of Salt River bottom land being used for agriculture.

Salt River Dam and Reservoir — 4 mi. S. of Taylorsville. KY-44. Future site of dam, reservoir, recreational facility and park scheduled for completion in 1978.

Scenic Overlook — 8 mi. E. of Taylorsville, Briar Ridge. KY-248. Hills along the river in this area have wonderful view.

Trimble County

Trimble County was the eighty-sixth county in order of formation in Kentucky and was formed in 1836 from parts of Gallatin, Oldham and Henry Counties. It was named in honor of Judge Robert Trimble of Bourbon County, the Chief Justice of the Kentucky Court of Appeals and later as Justice of the Supreme Court.

Milton, a small community established by the Virginia Legislature in 1789, is located on the Ohio River and is one of the oldest towns in Kentucky. In early pioneer days it was considered an important river port. It was made the county seat of Trimble County in 1836.

Near the center of the county on a ridge by a large pond, Richard Ball built a log cabin in 1805. He was the first settler of this settlement which became the village of Bedford, so named in honor of Bedford, Virginia. In 1837 Bedford became the county seat of Trimble County and still is today.

Trimble County was witness to two of the most dramatic events in the history of early Kentucky. First, the flow of immigrants into Kentucky on flatboats to settle along the Ohio River and second, the flight of slaves through the "underground railway" to freedom in the territory in the North.

FAIRS

Trimble County Fair — Bedford. US-42. Carnival, farm and homemaker exhibits, fish-fry. Schedule determined yearly.

MARKERS

"Petticoat Abolitionist" — Milton. US-421, KY-1255. New England schoolteacher, Delia Webster, used the Preston Mansion as a refuge for fugitive slaves on their way north.

CEMETERIES

Corn Creek Baptist Church Cemetery — Bedford, on Old Bedford Rd. Off US-421. Among the oldest burial sites in the county. Burial site of the Parker family, one of the founders of this area. An old slave cemetery is located over the break of the hill.

OLD BUILDINGS

Corn Creek Church — Bedford. Off US-421. Second oldest church in state that remains in the original building.

County Jail — Bedford, downtown. Off US-42. Antiquated county jail of stone construction dating to 1837. Among those housed were Delia Webster, the "Petticoat Abolitionist."

Pierce Brothers House — Milton, Old Bedford-Sulphur Rd. circa 1860-1865. Architectural example.

Old Preston Place — Milton, on Peck's Pike. circa 1850's. 350-acre farm which originally was 2,300-acre plantation owned in 1840's by Col. Preston. Slave cabins still exist. Delia Webster, famed "Petticoat Abolitionist", used this home and an Ohio River cave

on the farm to aid the cause of slaves seeking freedom. It is claimed that Little Eva of *Uncle Tom's Cabin* fame stayed here after she fled the Bluegrass section on the way across the Ohio River to freedom.

Richwood Plantation — Milton, Carrollton Rd. or River Rd. Built 1803. An exquisite French-Colonial antebellum home. Originally the George Fearn place. Slave cabins still exist. One room of the home is called the McKinley Room in honor of President McKinley who visited there. Now a summer riding academy for girls. Private home with 22 rooms filled with antiques.

Rock Post Office — On the private farm of Daniel Wright. 1/2 mi. off US-421. Large rock topped by a hanging boulder full of holes. Used as Post Office by soldiers to communicate with families during Civil War. Trimble County was a border county between the North and South and loyalties were divided. Had soldiers used regular means of communication, they might have been discovered.

OTHER POINTS OF INTEREST

Bedford Spring — Bedford. Off US-42. Popular resort in the 1800's. Burned February, 1967.

Lookout Point — Milton, on Milton Hill. Off US-421. Offers panoramic view of the Ohio River and bridge, the surrounding countryside, and neighboring Madison, Indiana.

Remains of Old Richwood Distillery — Milton, on Milton-Carrollton Rd., on the Ohio River. Whiskey made there widely known for its good, clear taste which is attributed to the pure water.

Wise's Landing — Bedford. Off US-42. Busy trading post where boats and travelers stopped and Trimble County settlers bought supplies.

Jail behind courthouse in Bedford.

Main Street in Bedford.

Northern Kentucky Area

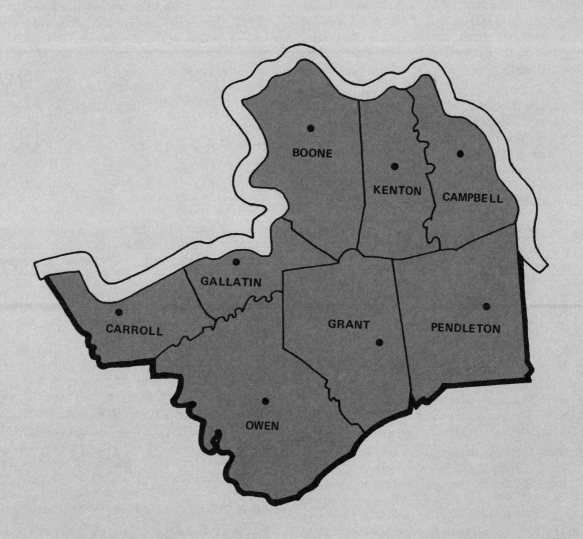

BOONE

KENTON

CAMPBELL

GALLATIN

CARROLL

GRANT

PENDLETON

OWEN

Boone County

Boone County was formed in 1798 from part of Campbell County and named in honor of the well-known explorer, Daniel Boone, who traversed this region in 1767. The thirtieth county to be established in Kentucky, it has an average length of twenty miles and an average width of fifteen miles. The Ohio River flows along the north and west for approximately forty miles, providing plenty of productive river bottom land.

The city of Burlington is the county seat. The first courthouse, built in 1817, had a brick floor and columns. Remodeled later, it was finally torn down and the present courthouse built in 1899. The major population center in Boone County is the city of Florence, settled in 1813 and incorporated in 1830. Its original name was simply Crossroads, then Connersville, after a leading citizen of the growing town. In 1830, Connersville applied for a first class post office and was told that it must change its name because there was already a Connersville, Kentucky. The citizens held an election and sixteen votes were cast for the name Florence, which was the first name of Mrs. Conners.

In 1783, Tanner's Station, now called Petersburg, became the first settlement in Boone County. The Reverend John Tanner, a Baptist minister, built the first blockhouse and the town began on 2,000 acres owned by Tanner and John Taylor. Tanner's 9-year old son was captured by Shawnee Indians and held until grown. He later became a valued interpreter for the United States in dealing with the Indians.

Mrs. Mary Inglis was the first white woman to set foot on Boone County soil. She was with a group of pioneers; including her two sons and her sister-in-law, when they were captured by the Shawnee Indians in 1756 in Virginia. She became separated from the others in Portsmouth, Ohio, and brought to Big Bone Lick in this area. Here, she was compelled to make salt, given few liberties, and was adopted by the Chief. A courageous and resourceful pioneer, she escaped in late fall with another woman, and reached home after 40 days. She died in 1813 at the age of 83.

The bones of the largest known Ice Age mammals were discovered in 1729 in what is now Big Bone Lick State Park. It is one of the great fossil sites in the United States, and has been a tourist attraction since the early days of the Nineteenth Century. Discovered by Captain Charles de Longueil, a Frenchman from Canada, Big Bone was a salt lick for prehistoric animals. They sank into the mud, which then hardened, and preserved their bones for thousands of years.

FAIRS

Boone County Fair — Burlington. KY-18. August.

PARKS

Big Bone Lick State Park — Florence. KY-338. Site of important fossil find, the largest graveyard of Ice Age mammals ever found. Park contains a museum displaying the skeletons of these prehistoric animals. The parks also feature camping, picnic areas, playgrounds, and fishing.

River Ridge Park — Burlington. KY-18.

MARKERS

Maj. John P. Gaines — KY-338, 2 1/2 mi. W. of I-65. Home site of John Pollard Gaines (1795-1857), Kentucky statesman and soldier. Fought in War of 1812. State legislator 1825-1836. Maj. in First Kentucky Cavalry and aide-de-camp to Gen. Winfield Scott in the Mexican War. Elected U. S. Congressman 1847-1849, while prisoner of war. He was appointed Governor of Oregon Territory in 1850-1853 by President Zachary Taylor, who was a comrade-in-arms in Mexico.

CEMETERIES

Richwood Cemetery — S. of Florence, Richwood Rd. KY-338. Two marble slabs in memory of Col. Abner Gaines' grandchildren, who died of yellow fever while on a voyage rounding South America, and were buried at sea. Their father, John Pollard Gaines, was on his way to take up duties as Governor of Oregon Territory.

In spite of the tragedy, he proceeded on, but never returned to Kentucky.

OLD BUILDINGS

April Hill Farm — Burlington, 248 East Bend Rd. Built in 1790 by Robert Johnson, an early settler. The two-story house is made of walnut logs, clapboard and stones.

Baptist Church — Bullittsville, Bullittsville Church Rd. Organized 1794, as the first church in Boone County. Present building built in 1819.

Boone County Courthouse — Burlington, at the corner of Burlington and Jefferson. KY-18. Built 1899.

Burlington Methodist Church — Burlington, N. Jefferson St. Built 1837. Brick building, remodeled in 1922-1923. Also called Sally Campbell Memorial Methodist Church.

Robert Chambers House — Burlington. Built 1832-1836 by Robert Chambers. Now privately owned by John Caldwell.

James Dinsmore House — Burlington, E. Bottoms Rd. Off KY-18. Home of authoress Elsie Dinsmore, who wrote *Rebecca of Sunnybrook Farm.*

Benjamin Piatt Fowler Home — Union. US-42. Built 1814. Architectural example. Now privately owned.

Abner Gaines House, The Haunted House — Walton. US-25. Built in 1791 by Col. Abner Gaines, an early pioneer. Historic mansion has 20 rooms, 3 stairways, a secret room, an underground tunnel, and 10 carved mantels. One outstanding feature is the home's curly maple stairway. Col. Gaines used the house as an inn or tavern, as well as for a stagecoach station. It was noted for its lavish style of entertainment, frequent festivities, murders, and ghost stories. House was bought in 1937 by John Gault.

Hopeful Lutheran Church — Florence, 214 Hopeful Rd. In 1805 a group of settlers came from Virginia to Boone County and in 1807 organized and built the first Lutheran Church west of the Alleghenies.

Cave Johnson House — Hebron. Built 1796. Home of Cave Johnson, an early Boone County clerk, sheriff, and colonel in county militia. Pin oaks on lot are original. Now privately owned.

Orchard Hill Farm — Burlington, 210 Rodgers Lane. Built in 1817 by W. A. Delph. One-story brick residence.

Jacob Piatt Home, or Piatt's Landing — Petersburg Highway. Built 1805. A 14-room house that served the pioneer flatboat trade after the Revolutionary War.

Richwood Presbyterian Church — Florence, Richwood Rd. KY-338. Founded 1934. Original structure. Marker indicates that its founder and benefactor was Joseph Cabell Harrison, first cousin to President William Henry Harrison. Part of his land on Hick's Pike is presently owned by his great-great-niece, Mrs. Mary Ella Bedinger Logan. He and another cousin, John Breckinridge, edited the first religious paper in Kentucky, "The Western Luminary."

Courthouse in Burlington.

Big Bone Lick State Park.

139

Campbell County

Campbell County was the nineteenth Kentucky county in order of creation and was formed in 1794. Segments of land were taken from Harrison, Scott and Mason Counties to form the new county which was named for Colonel John Campbell of Jefferson County. Colonel Campbell at one time held a Virginia land grant of 4,000 acres adjoining the city of Louisville. He also participated in the first Kentucky Constitutional Convention. This county covers 149 square miles at the confluence of the Ohio and Licking Rivers, was the site of Leitch's Station, established in 1753-1794 by Major David Leitch. Another pioneer station, Newport Barracks, was built in 1804 and was used in the War of 1812 as an army post and military prison.

Alexandria is the county seat and was incorporated in 1834. Alexandria has a handsome old courthouse, built in 1842, which houses some of the oldest records in northern Kentucky.

Newport, the second largest city in northern Kentucky, is located across the Ohio River from Cincinnati. In early years, it competed with Cincinnati for river commerce, and even dominated it for a time, because it had control of the Licking River. Newport was plotted on February 14, 1792, by Hubbard Taylor, as agent for his father, James Taylor, the Elder, of Virginia. It was named in honor of Captain Lord Christopher Newport, who was in charge of the first ships that came over to old Jamestown in 1607. Hubbard Taylor's brother, Gen. James Taylor, added more property to the site in 1795. President Zachary Taylor was a cousin of these men.

The city of Fort Thomas was organized originally in 1867 and was called the District of Highlands. When one hundred twelve acres of prime land was set aside in 1887, the army post of Fort Thomas was built and served in three wars as an important installation. It is now the site of a Veteran's Administration Hospital. As the area around the fort became more populated, the District of Highlands was, in 1914, incorporated into the present city of Fort Thomas.

Other cities in Campbell County of historic and scenic interest include Bellevue, Dayton, and Southgate. Highland Heights is where Northern Kentucky University is located.

A scenic road in eastern Campbell County along the Ohio River, KY-8, is called the Mary Inglis Highway, as a tribute to the first white woman in Kentucky. Captured by Indians in Virginia in 1756, she was taken to Ohio, then brought to the Big Bone Lick in Boone County, Kentucky. She later escaped and made her way through the Kentucky wilderness to her Virginia home.

FAIRS AND EXHIBITS

Campbell County Fair — Alexandria. Fair is over 100 years old, and has been held at the same site since 1856, except during the Civil War. Labor Day weekend.

Christmas Exhibit — Highland Heights. Northern Kentucky University, Regents Hall. US-27. Campbell County Homemakers Association. Annual event in November.

PARKS

A. J. Jolly County Park — S. of Newport. US-27. Camping, fishing, golf, recreational areas.

Newport Barracks, Gen. James Taylor Park — Newport, foot of Columbia St., through floodwall gates, at the confluence of the Licking and Ohio Rivers. Newport Military Barracks were used from 1803-1887 as protection against Indians. Because of flooding, the barracks were moved to the Highlands.

MARKERS

Battle of Highlands Site — Fort Thomas, Newman Ave., bounded by Highland and Grand Avenues. Site of battle fought by the Cherokees against the Shawnee and Miami Indians in 1749.

Samuel Woodfill School and Marker — Fort Thomas, 1025 Alexandria Pike. US-27. Attractive brick grade school commemorates exploits of Samuel Woodfill, Maj. in U. S. Army, and much-decorated hero of World War I.

OLD BUILDINGS

Campbell Lodge — Cold Spring, 150 Skyline Dr. Built 1869-1879. During the early 1900's this was the home of artist Henry F. Farny. Now a Boy's Home.

Cherry Field — Alexandria, 21 E. Main St. Built 1811-1813. Home of Richard Tarvin Baker, where Mark Twain, famous American author, was a frequent guest. Now privately owned by William Zinn.

Flag Spring Baptist Church — Flag Spring, Smith Rd., S. of Mentor. KY-10. Built 1833. Early county church.

"Limestone" — Alexandria, Steffen Rd. Off US-27. Built 1874. Originally owned by John Steffen. Example of the type of native fieldstone used for houses built by German settlers in this area.

2 Mid-Victorian Mansions — Dayton, Fairview and Dayton Avenues, and 320 Fairview Ave. On crest of hill overlooking Ohio River and Cincinnati. Over 100 years old, the two 25-room homes, constructed of brick made on the place, are believed to have been built by Gen. James Taylor, founder of Newport, for each of his two daughters. Both feature hand-carved woodwork and mirrors from floor to ceiling, as well as doors in unexpected places that open on narrow passages leading to other unexpected places. At one time, a tunnel connected the 2 homes, but has since been closed off.

General James Taylor House in Newport.

General Taylor Memorial in Newport.

Mt. Pleasant — Fort Thomas, 1810 N. Fort Thomas Ave. Built 1830. Home of the Taliaferro family since Methodists held services here in early 1830's.

Mount Vernon School — Fort Thomas, Highland and Newman Avenues. Built 1850. Second school built in Fort Thomas, and the only school in central Fort Thomas until late 1800's. A neat white cottage that now serves as Highland Hills Baptist Church office is adjacent to it. The first school in Fort Thomas was Mt. Pleasant School. It was built in 1832, a log cabin, in what is now the vicinity of Holly Lane and N. Fort Thomas Ave.

Newport Courthouse — Newport, 4th and York Sts. Built 1884. Victorian architectural example.

Samuel Shaw House — Fort Thomas, Audubon Place. Built 1859. Federal-style 3-story brick house. Architect and builder, Patrick Henry Wilson. Now owned by Christ Church.

Richard Southgate House — Newport, 24 E. 3rd St. Built in 1814-1821 for Col. Wright Southgate by British prisoners of War of 1812 confined in Newport. The 20-room brick mansion has a winding staircase and lookout with 4 small windows. Abraham Lincoln visited Richard Southgate here about 1856. John Taliaferro Thompson, inventor of the Thompson submachine gun, was born here in 1860. Now owned by Knights of Columbus.

Gen. James Taylor House, "Bellevue" — Newport, 335 E. 3rd St. Built 1837 by Gen. Taylor, who fought in the War of 1812, and was taken prisoner at the surrender of Detroit. Born in Virginia in 1769, and married Keturah Moss Leitch. Lost all but 4 of 11 children in their infancy. Died in 1848 and was buried in Evergreen Cemetery, Southgate. Home was left to his son, Col. James Taylor. The Marquis de LaFayette was once a guest in this house. Now occupied by Vonderhar-Stetter-Betz Funeral Home, Inc.

OTHER POINTS OF INTEREST

Boone's World Clock, a 60-Day Marvel — Highland Heights, Northern Kentucky University Library. Massive 8-ft. clock with planetarium. Built in 1911. In operation over 60 years. One of a kind.

Fort Thomas Stone-Water Tower — Tower Place and S. Fort Thomas Avenue. Elaborate stone structure at entrance to old military reserve. Completed in 1892, and built to supply water to the fort. Plaque on the tower states Fort Thomas was named for Gen. George Henry Thomas (1816-1870), West Point graduate. Another plaque, erected in 1900, commemorates the 28 men of the 6th Infantry Regiment from this area killed in the Spanish-American War.

Grant's Lick — Grant's Lick. Off US-27. circa 1790. Remains of a salt water well used for the manufacture of salt by Samuel Bryant, Charles Morgan, and John Grant. Mary Boone Bryan, sister of Daniel Boone, is buried at Grant's Lick.

Gubser's Mill — California, Wesley Chapel and California Crossroads. Old sawmill built by John Gubser

Gubser's Mill at Wesley Chapel and California Crossroads.

more than 100 years ago. Has been in continous operation since.

Northern Kentucky University — Highland Heights. Louis B. Nunn Drive and Alexandria Pike. US-27.

Shaler Battery — Southgate, Evergreen Cemetery. S. of Newport, Alexandria Pike. Portion of network of batteries to protect Licking Valley during Civil War.

Carroll County

In 1776, the area now known as Carroll County was still a part of Kentucke County, Virginia. As the frontier grew in population, Kentucky County was divided into smaller counties. Two, Carroll and Gallatin Counties, were united as one and called Gallatin County, with Port William as the county seat. Then in 1838, Carroll County was again separated from Gallatin County, to become the eighty seventh Kentucky County created. It was named to honor Charles Carroll, a colonial Marylander and signer of The Declaration of Independence. Port William remained the county seat, but was renamed Carrollton.

Situated on the Ohio River, the town of Port William was a well-known river port and was founded in 1794. A meeting of trustees took place at the home of Richard Masterson to lay out lots and establish the town. Many well-known names, including Craig, Masterson, Butler, and Ogburn were among the first settlers of the Port William, or Carrollton, area.

Named All-Kentucky City in 1973, Carrollton boasts of an interesting Victorian courthouse, built in 1884. Next to the courthouse is the old Carroll County jail, a picturesque example of an early prison. The area that now comprises Carroll County was originally an Indian hunting ground. Indian tribes lived in Kentucky for centuries before the white man crossed the Cumberland Gap, and their burial mounds are now among the common features of Carroll County.

FAIRS AND FESTIVALS

Carroll County Fair — Carrollton. July-August.

Tobacco Festival — Carrollton. Parade, musical entertainment, carnival, flea market, art exhibits. September.

PARKS

Gen. Butler State Resort Park — Carrollton. US-227, off US-42, I-71. The park's 809 acres include a modern lodge, dining room, cottages, camping lake, picnic area. Recreational facilities include swimming, hiking, trails, horseback riding, boating, and fishing.

MUSEUMS

Butler Mansion Museum — Carrollton. US-227 of US-42, I-71. Contains many period antique pieces and personal articles belonging to this famous Carroll County resident. Gen. "Pearce" Butler was a Revolutionary Soldier and member of a prominent family originally from Ireland and Pennsylvania. He moved to Kentucky in 1776, and in 1784, settled in the area of Port William. He claimed a large tract of land, now known as the Gen. Butler State Resort Park.

OLD BUILDINGS

Carrollton Courthouse and County Jail — Carrollton. US-42. Built 1884. Early Victorian style.

Grass Hills Home — Carrollton, on Sanders Rd. Off I-71. Built 1823 by Lewis Sanders. Log house still has the original wooden floors and fireplaces. The Sanders family brought the first purebred cattle to the Ohio Valley.

Richard Masterson House — Carrollton, E. across from M & T Chemical Co. US-42. Built in 1790 by slave labor. Oldest 2-story brick house between Pittsburg, Pennsylvania and Louisville. Masterson was one of the early founders of Port William and helped establish the Methodist Church in Kentucky.

Riverview — Carrollton. US-42. Built in 1805 by Benjamin Craig, II. He was one of the early settler families. This beautiful home overlooks the Ohio River. It was the scene of a double suicide of 2 lovers in 1886.

Schuerman House — Carrollton, 4th and Sycamore Sts. Off US-42. Built 1880's Example of Victorian architecture. Home is currently being restored and furnished in period antiques by its owners.

Gen. William O. Butler Home — Carrollton, Highland Ave. US-42. Built 1800's. Example of Georgian architecture, and practically unchanged since its construction. Gen. Butler was the son of Gen. "Pearce" Butler.

Bridge over Kentucky River.

General William O. Butler Home in Carrollton.

He was graduated from Transylvania University and served as a soldier in the War of 1812. He received the rank of Major at age 22 due to his valor in battle. Also served as aide to Gen. Andrew Jackson but resigned in 1817 to return to Carrollton to practice law. He became a Representative to the State Legislature, was Democratic candidate for Governor, and in 1884, was named Chief Commander of the U. S. forces in the Mexican War. Because of his success in this position, he was nominated for Vice President on the ticket with Gen. Lewis Cass of Michigan, but lost to Taylor and Fillmore in 1851. He returned to Carrollton and served the county the rest of his days as poet, lawyer, and gentleman citizen.

Rio Vista Mansion — Carrollton, Highland Ave. and 11th St. Built in 1918 by G. G. Wood, a hardware dealer. Brick and wood on the inside were imported from Germany and France. Mansion was built at the nostalgic end of the "Innocent Age" of the U. S., as a tribute to the past in Carrollton.

OTHER POINTS OF INTEREST

Tobacco Market — Carrollton. Buildings of many private tobacco companies scattered throughout the city. This is the third largest tobacco market in Kentucky.

Carrollton Furniture Factory — Carrollton, building on S. 4th St. Off US-42. Manufactured fine furniture in the 19th Century and, during the Cleveland administration, furnished a bedroom in the White House.

The Town of Ghent — E. of Carrollton. US-42. This old town is known for its wide streets and fine old houses. Named by Henry Clay, who often travelled through here to Vevay, Indiana directly across the river, to buy the famous wines of the area. Clay often stayed overnight in Ghent. The town was also home of

Carroll County Jail in Carrollton.

James Tandy Ellis, a well-known lecturer and poet of the late 19th century. The streets of Ghent are lined with beautiful old river homes and a ferryboat still makes daily trips across the Ohio River from Ghent to Vevay.

 # *Gallatin County*

In 1798, six years after Kentucky became a state, Gallatin County was formed from parts of Shelby and Franklin Counties, becoming the thirty-third county to be created in Kentucky. The original boundaries of the county included what is now Carroll County, as well as parts of Trimble and Owen Counties. The county was named after Albert Gallatin, who was born in Switzerland and was a prominent Congressman at the time the county was formed. Later, Gallatin served as Secretary of the Treasury under Presidents Thomas Jefferson and James Madison. Albert Gallatin was also an authority on North American Indians.

Warsaw, the county seat, was known as Fredericksburg from 1804-1831. In 1804, Henry Hates, along with Henry Ellis and Colonel Robert Johnson, laid out the town of Fredericksburg on Johnson's land on the Ohio River. Johnson named the town after his native city in Virginia. In 1831, it was learned that there was an older town in Kentucky known as Frederickstown, so the name was changed to Warsaw by enactment of the Legislature. Captain Blair Summons suggested the name, having recently read *Thaddeus of Warsaw*, a romantic novel based on the life of Tadeusz Koscinsko,

a Polish patriot who designed the fortifications at West Point and aided the cause of the Revolution along with Count Pulaski.

Warsaw remains a picturesque town along the Ohio River, retaining the atmosphere of the steamboat era. The main economic factor in Gallatin County is agriculture. The rich, fertile lands along the river valleys are used for thriving nurseries, rows and rows of seedlings, young shrubs, and evergreens.

LAKES AND DAMS

Water Festival of Regional Outboard Motor Powerboat Association — Warsaw, on Ohio River. August.

Craig's Creek Lake — Warsaw. US-42. 1,000-acre lake with boating, fishing, and other water sports.

Markland Locks and Dam — Warsaw, on the Ohio River. US-42. Dam in 1,416-ft. wide, with 2 locks and 12 gates, each 42-ft. high. Public recreation facilities with observation and boat launching platforms.

MARKERS

Great River Tragedy of Steamboat Days — US-42, US-127. At midnight, on Dec. 4, 1869, two large passenger steamboats collided 2 miles above Warsaw. Barrels of kerosene carried on deck of one of the steamers ignited, enveloping both boats in flames and killing 162 people.

CEMETERIES

Old Indian Graveyard — 1 mi. S. of Warsaw. KY-35. Stone-age cemetery. Rich in artifacts.

OLD BUILDINGS

Gallatin County Courthouse — Warsaw. Built 1838. Handsome colonial building.

Lucy Dupuy Montz Home (Adams House) — Warsaw, 457 High St. Dr. Lucy Ann Dupuy Montz, D.D.S. (1842-1922), was the first woman to practice dentistry in Kentucky. She was graduated from the Cincinnati College of Dental Surgery in 1889, then registered to practice dentistry in Warsaw in June 1893. House was later purchased by Mrs. Kate McDannell Riley, a local

artist, whose paintings are found in many Warsaw homes today.

Old Stone Abutments at Eagle Creek — Sparta, KY-35. Remains of old abutments mark site of old covered bridge over Eagle Creek.

Yates House — Warsaw, 357 High St. circa 1861-1865. Birthplace of Illinois Governor Richard Yates (1815-1873), who also was a U. S. Congressman and Senator. He was the son of Henry Yates, one of the original founders of Warsaw, then called Fredericksburg.

OTHER POINTS OF INTEREST

Indian Mounds — 6 1/2 mi. E. of Warsaw. US-127. On banks of Ohio River. This area is rich in prehistoric Indian artifacts. Village site and burial field about 100 yards away.

Warsaw Furniture Factory — Warsaw. US-42. Built in 1901 by O. A. Bogardus. Manufactures and exports beautiful cherry and pecan wood furniture.

Lucy Dupuy Montz House in Warsaw.

Grant County

Grant County, one of the larger of Kentucky's counties, was created from Pendleton County in 1820 to become the sixty-seventh county to be formed in Kentucky. It was named for two brothers who came from North Carolina in 1779 and established Grant's Station in Fayette County. John Grant developed a saltworks on the Licking River, while Samuel Grant was killed by Indians in Indiana in 1794. The county's 250-square mile area is ninety percent farmland, and has tributaries of the Licking and Kentucky Rivers within its boundaries.

Williamstown is the county seat, and boasts of a number of fine old homes. Its handsome courthouse is the third on the site of one and one-half acres of land donated by William Arnold, a Revolutionary War soldier. In gratitude, the city was named Williamstown in his honor.

Perhaps the earliest settlement in Grant County was Campbell's Station, founded sometime before 1792 and located near a mineral spring close to the present city of Dry Ridge.

Several miles north of Crittenden, another Grant County community, is the site of one of the last Indian massacres in Kentucky. It occurred in 1805 when a party of Indians burned a homestead after scalping the parents and children. All died except the mother, who escaped to the home of neighbors and eventually recovered.

FAIRS AND FESTIVALS

Dry Ridge Court Days — Dry Ridge. US-25. Parade, musical entertainment, and dancing. Annually in August.

Grant County Fair — Crittenden. July.

Marigold Festival — Williamstown. US-25. Features dancing, flea market, parade, and musical entertainment. September and October.

PARKS AND RECREATION

Boltz Lake — Dry Ridge. Off KY-467. Fishing and boating.

Buffalo Trace — Williamstown. KY- 22.

Bullock Pen Lake — Crittenden. KY-1548. Fishing and boating.

Corinth Lake — Corinth. US-25. Fishing and boating.

Curtis Gates Lloyd Wildlife Management and Recreation Area — Crittenden. US-25. Fish and wildlife reserve with 300 acres of virgin timber. Features nature hike trails, trapshoot and archery ranges.

Eagle Creek Recreation Area — Western portion of Grant County. Recreation area includes fishing, swimming, and golfing facilities.

Grant County Park — Crittenden. US-25. Picnic area, hiking trails, and ball park.

Williamson Lake — Williamstown. Off KY-22. Fishing, boating, and water skiing.

MARKERS

Williamstown Raid — Williamstown. In 1864, CSA forces, hoping to seize sums of Federal money rumored to have been in the city's banks, raided Williamstown. Finding the money had been removed, they raided a Union firearms store.

A Civil War Reprisal — Williamstown. US-25. Three CSA soldiers were brought from Lexington and executed in reprisal for guerrilla slayings of 2 Union sympathizers.

OLD BUILDINGS

Bank of Williamstown — Williamstown. US-25. Established 1880. Oldest bank in Grant County.

Carter House — Williamstown, N. Main St. Date unknown. Oldest house in town. Now privately owned.

First Educational Academy — Corinth. KY-330. Established 1878.

Glass House — Williamstown, S. Main St. Date unknown. Best example of Victorian architecture in the county. Now privately owned.

Grant County Courthouse and Library — Williamstown. US-25. Built 1937, replacing an earlier brick building dating to 1856. It is the third courthouse on the site donated by William Arnold, a Revolutionary War soldier for whom the town is named.

Grant County Deposit Bank — Williamstown. US-25. Established 1882.

Henderson House — Crittenden. US-25. Marquis Lafayette stayed here. Now privately owned.

Old Home Tour — Williamstown. US-25. Held in the Spring.

Rouse House — Crittenden. US-25, KY-491. circa 1800. Reportedly, Lafayette was entertained here. Now privately owned.

Sherman Tavern, or Old Drover's House — Sherman. US-25. circa 1812. Drivers of cattle, hogs, and turkeys stayed overnight here enroute to Cincinnati, Ohio stockyards and packing houses. Fifty men slept in one large room. Lafayette stopped here overnight.

William Littell House — Williamstown, off N. Main St. circa 1812. First State Legislator from Grant County. Now privately owned.

OTHER POINTS OF INTEREST

American Telegraph and Telephone Company — Williamstown. Off KY-22. One of 4 underground communication systems linking telephone and telegraph lines across the U. S.

Sherman Tavern in Sherman.

Courthouse in Williamstown.

Dry Ridge main street.

Kenton County

Kenton County was named in honor of one of the greatest of the early frontiersmen, Simon Kenton. The nintieth Kentucky county to be created, Kenton County was organized in 1804 when the western section of Campbell County was partitioned. The county is bound on the north by the Ohio River and on the east by the Licking River. The land on the Kenton County side of the Licking River, where it empties into the Ohio River, is known as "The Point" and stood out as a landmark for early travellers moving up and down the Ohio River.

Christopher Gist and his men from the Ohio Land Company were the first white men to set foot on Kenton County soil, landing at "The Point" in 1751. Gist was followed by many noted pioneers, including Daniel Boone, Simon Kenton, and George Rogers Clark, who used it as a gathering place for his men several times as they rallied to fight the Indians.

Covington, the third largest city in Kentucky, is located across the river from Cincinnati, Ohio. Chartered in 1815, it became a trading center as settlers headed down the Ohio River and through Kentucky. Covington was named for General Leonard Covington, a hero in the War of 1812. Its Riverside District has been listed on the National Register of Historic Places. The District consists of over four square blocks which contain forty buildings dating from 1815 to 1920, and is the original Covington. It is believed that John Roebling, who designed the Suspension Bridge across the Ohio River from Covington to Cincinnati, and the Brooklyn Bridge in New York, lived in this historical area while the bridge was being built. A stone tunnel on the property where the Carneal House stands served as the last stop on the Underground Railroad during the Civil War, adding to the history of this area.

Independence, located southeast of Covington, serves as the Kenton County seat. Its handsome courthouse was built in 1840. The county seat was so named to celebrate the independence of Kenton County. Other cities in the county include Erlanger, Fort Mitchell, and Fort Wright, named for the commanders in charge of fortifications during the Civil War, as well as Elsmere, Edgewood, and Taylor Mill.

FAIRS AND EXHIBITS

Art Exhibits — Covington. Kenton County Library, 5th and Scott Sts. Also at the Old Kenton County Library (Carnegie), 1028 Scott St.

Christmas Exhibit — Covington. Location varies. Sponsored by the Kenton County Extension Homemakers Association. November.

Kenton County Fair — Independence. August.

PARKS

Devou Park — Covington. W. of I-75. This 550-acre park overlooks the scenic Ohio River. Civil War earthworks and museum are located in the part. Also features an old trolley named "Kentucky."

George Rogers Clark Park — Covington, Riverside Dr. and Garrard St. Bronze markers designate site of Thomas Kennedy House and Inn built in 1791. In 1780-1782 George Rogers Clark led 2 excursions from this park area. The first was against the Indians during the Northwest Expedition. The second was to avenge the Battle of Blue Licks, the last battle of the American Revolution in Kentucky. After his second excursion, the Indians in Kentucky were never again able to mount a strong fight for the land. In Nov. 1782 the Kentucky Long Knives leveled Indian towns and broke their will to resist.

MUSEUMS

Behringer-Crawford Museum of Natural History — Covington, Devou Park. W. of I-75. Early pioneer articles, natural science and historical exhibits. Open Easter through Thanksgiving.

Vent Haven Museum — Fort Mitchell, 33 W. Maple Ave. Haven for 400 ventriloquist dummies bequeathed to William Shakespeare Berger. Reputedly the largest, most complete ventriloquist museum in the U. S.

Cathedral Basilica of the Assumption in Covington.

CEMETERIES

Garden of Hope — Covington, on Edgecliff Rd. Off I-75, Jefferson Ave. Exit. Replica of Christ's Tomb and Holy Land landmarks. Plants, trees and flowers were brought directly from Bethlehem. A stone from the River Jordan, and a rock from the Garden of Gethsemane can be seen. Guided tours, admission free.

Linden Grove Cemetery — Covington, Holman St. from 13th to 15th Sts. Graves of William Goebel, assassinated Governor of Kentucky, as well as those of John G. Carlisle and the Thomas Kennedy family. Oldest readable headstone dated 1819. Cemetery in use prior to that date.

OLD BUILDINGS

Baker-Hunt Home and Foundation — Covington, 620 Greenup St. Build 1830. Twenty-two room mansion. Former home of John W. Baker family, who made it headquarters for a foundation for classes in art, music, and crafts.

Beechwood House — Ft. Mitchell, Buttermilk Pike. Built 1839. Home of Thomas Buckner, early leading citizen.

Carlisle Home — Covington, 1533 Garrard St. Built 1859. John G. Carlisle became State Senator in 1865, elected Congressman in 1877, and appointed Secretary of the Treasury under President Grover Cleveland in 1893.

Carneal-Southgate House — Covington, 405 E. 2nd St. Built 1815. First brick house in Covington. Transitional Georgian architecture with Palladian influence. Lafayette was house guest in 1825 when the house was owned by the Southgate family. A stone tunnel on the property was the last stop of the Underground Railroad during the Civil War.

Cathedral Basilica of the Assumption — Covington, 12th and Madison. Built 1901. Gothic cathedral, styled after Notre Dame Cathedral in Paris, France. Features the largest stained glass window in the U. S. Famous murals from Covington's own artist, Frank Duveneck,

149

grace the chapel while Italian mosaics and hand-carved altars beautify the church.

Daniel Carter Beard House — Covington, 322 E. 3rd St. Boyhood home of the founder of the Boy Scouts of America.

Dry Creek Baptist Church — Ft. Mitchell, 15 Buttermilk Pike. Built 1856. Originally housed a church that was founded in 1800. Now privately owned.

Duveneck Home — Covington, 1226 Greenup St. Built 1845. Boyhood home of Kentucky's distinguished 19th century artist, Frank Duveneck. His sarcophagus is in Mother of God Cemetery, Covington.

Elmwood Hall — Ludlow, 244 Forest Ave. circa 1818-1820. Home of Thomas D. Carneal.

First United Methodist Church — Covington, 5th and Greenup Sts. Built 1866-1867. Gothic brick building.

Grant House — Covington, 518-520 Greenup St. circa 1845-1860. Occupied by Jesse Grant, father of President Ulysses S. Grant.

Historic District — Covington. Extends from Ohio River to 4th St., and from Licking River west to the alley between Garrard St. and Greenup Sts.

James M. Bullock House — Covington, 528 Greenup St. Built in 1839 of ship timbers. During the Civil War, the house was used as a private school attended by Gen. Ulysses Grant's son, Frederick, while he was staying with his grandparents.

Jonathon Hearne House — Covington, 500 Garrard St. Built 1874. Late Victorian architecture with Italiante and Romanesque elements. Jonathan David Hearne was a prominent banker and businessman.

Kenton County Courthouse — Independence. KY-17. Built 1840. Refurnished 1975. Architectural example.

Lovall Home — Covington, 327 Riverside Dr. Built 1855. Patterned after an Italian provincial town house.

LaSallette Academy — Covington, 7th and Greenup Sts. Girls' School, opened in 1856 by the Sisters of Charity of Nazareth when Covington was a small river town. First academy in the Catholic Diocese of Covington. Still in operation.

Masonic Hall — Covington, 4th and Scott. Built 1865. Three-story brick building. Now commercially owned.

Monte Cassino Chapel — Ft. Mitchell, on Turkeyfoot Rd. Off I-75. On campus of Thomas More College. Built in 1878 by Brother Albert Soltes of the Benedictine Order for a private workshop. Interior measures 6-ft x 9-ft., probably the smallest church in the world.

Mother of God Church — Covington, 119 W. 6th St. Built 1870. "Mutter Gottes Kirche." German Catholic Church built in Italian Renaissance design. 200-ft. towers, stained glass windows, and murals. Organ built 1876 by Koehnken and Grimm. One of only 2 left in the world. Organ is considered a masterpiece; acoustics are superb.

Suspension Bridge connecting Covington with Cincinnati.

Duveneck Home in Covington.

Old Williams Place — Independence, 198 Maher Rd. Built 1847. Original owner, James M. Williams.

Schleuter Home — Ft. Mitchell, 317 Buttermilk Pike. Built 1858. Two-story brick house. Original owner, John F. Schleuter.

Shinkle Row House — Covington, E. 2nd St., between Garrard and Greenup Sts. Built 1800's. Row of 3-story houses with divided walls built in Old English tradition. Popular town houses of 19th century.

Somerset Hall — Ludlow, Penner and Closson Court. Built 1835. Second house built in Ludlow, and was first named "Lygeis."

Timberlake — Erlanger, 108 Stevenson Rd. Built 1826. Home of William Thornton Timberlake.

OTHER POINTS OF INTEREST

Suspension Bridge — Covington, Kentucky to Cincinnati, Ohio. US-25, US-42. Erected 1867. Designed by John Roebling. At time of construction, this bridge was the longest suspension bridge in the world, and the first to cross the Ohio River.

Thomas More College — Ft. Mitchell, Turkeyfoot Rd. I-75. Private Catholic, co-ed college. 1400 students. Campus built 1968, and dedicated by President Lyndon B. Johnson. College was founded in 1921 by the Catholic Diocese of Covington, and was originally named Villa Madonna College.

Mouth of Licking River at Covington.

Owen County

Owen County is located on the Kentucky River, nestled in the hills of the outer Bluegrass area. The county was formed in 1819, from parts of Scott, Franklin, and Gallatin Counties. Owen County, the sixty-second to be created in Kentucky, was named for Colonel Abraham Owen of Shelby County, who settled in Kentucky and was later killed at the Battle of Tippecanoe. The county's beauty and quiet rural atmosphere offer a perfect blending of the past with the present.

Owenton, the county seat, is in the heart of Owen County. Monterey, one of Owen County's most scenic sections, is located on the Kentucky River and was settled in 1820. Numerous Indian mounds, as well as evidence of ancient changes in the course of the Kentucky River, make this area of interest to archeologists and geologists. A long beach at the river's edge, and the natural beauty of the area make this a desirable place for fishing and camping.

New Liberty, the first town settled in Owen County, is still a prosperous and lovely place with numerous historic homes and churches.

FAIRS

Owen County Fair and Horse Show — Owenton. July.

RECREATION, LAKES

Eagle Valley Recreation Center — KY-227.

Elmer Davis Lake — Owenton. KY-22, US-127.

Kleber Wildlife and Recreation Area — KY-368. 1200 acres.

Twin Eagle Wildlife and Recreation Area — KY-355. Along the Kentucky River.

MARKERS

Old New Liberty — New Liberty. KY-227. Settled before 1800. Incorporated 1827. Owen County was formed in 1819. Site of county's first church, formed 1801.

OLD BUILDINGS

Alexander House — New Liberty, Mosley Rd. CSA Gen. John Hunt Morgan and aide stopped here in Nov. 1863, after escaping from a Union prison in Columbus, Ohio.

Berryman House — Owenton, Blanton St. circa 1835-1840. Built by Thomas Alexander Berryman, pioneer lawyer. Has been used for girls school, dormitory, buggy manufacturing. Now privately owned.

Ford House — Owenton, Main St. Built 1870. Home of Robert Carrick Ford, prominent Owen County resident.

Glenwood Hall — Perry Park, near Perry Landing on Kentucky River. Impressive two-story frame house with corner pilasters.

Highfield House — Owenton, N. Adams St. Built 1840. Patrick Henry's signature on land patent, 1785. Present owner, Atty. Charles Carter. Visitors welcome.

Inverness — Perry Park. KY-355. circa 1849. Architectural example.

Mussel Shoals Baptist Church — 2 mi. E. of Lusby Mill. Erected 1817. Church organized two years prior to formation of Owen County. Beautiful view overlooking Eagle Creek.

Glenwood Hall at Perry Park.

Owen County Courthouse — Owenton, Seminan St. Constructed 1857. Greek Revival Style. N. C. Cook, architect and builder. Occupied during Civil War by Federal troops, although county was strongly Confederate. Legend holds that the four large columns at the front contain kegs of Kentucky Bourbon Whiskey.

Owen County Jail — Owenton, Seminan St. Erected 1876. Italiante brick structure. H. P. McDonald, Louisville architect, was designer of jail. Honeycomb grating in windows gives interesting effect. First known work of McDonald, whose architectural firm later progressed into a nationally known enterprise.

OTHER POINTS OF INTEREST

Eden Shale Farm — University of Kentucky Test-Demonstration Center. KY-22. Farm has an unusual type of soil found only in this 32-county area of Kentucky.

Courthouse in Owenton.

Pendleton County

In 1798, the Kentucky Legislature created the twenty-eighth county in the state from portions of Bracken and Campbell Counties. The new county was named Pendleton County, after Judge Edmond Pendleton, presiding officer of the Virginia Court of Appeals and a Congressman from the Old Dominion.

Falmouth, the county seat, was settled in 1776 and became an incorporated town in 1792. It took its name from Falmouth, Virginia, which in turn was named for Falmouth, England. Here in 1780, British and Indian invaders brought the American Revolution to Kentucky soil. Captain Henry Bird with English guns and artillery, and 1,000 Indians, came up the Licking River and into Central Kentucky. With their heavy artillery, this force of British and Indians blasted the log forts and stations of the settlers. The southerly road they cut for the cannon wheels, now marks the trail of US-27 from Falmouth to Paris and Lexington. Many settlers were killed and 350 were taken prisoner and marched to Canada as a result of Bird's invasion.

Many old communities in Pendleton County have interesting histories connected with their early settlement.

Demossville, on the Licking River and the L & N Railroad line, was named for a French immigrant, Peter DeMoss. Boston Station was founded by the Licking River Lumber and Mining Company, whose logs were floated down river and caught at Boston Station. Hays Station was named for Timothy Hays, a Cincinnati distiller who bought the South Licking Bottoms and built the largest distillery in the county. Callensville, across from Licking River, was a small town where one could find stores, taverns, and a race track adjacent to the town where Kentucky Thoroughbred horses were trained for the racing circuit in Philadelphia, Baltimore, and other eastern cities. It was known as the town where men recruited for the Confederate Army. After the appearance of the railroad, stations were opened along the river. Morgan became the center of attraction, and Callensville was turned into farmland.

FAIRS

Pendleton County Fair — Falmouth. July.

153

PARKS

Kincaid Lake State Park — Falmouth. Off US-27, on KY-159. The park has 448 acres, featuring a lake with recreational facilities, camp sites, cottages, picnic areas, hiking trails, tennis, fishing, boating and swimming.

MARKERS

Bridge Erected — Falmouth. Built 1870, spanning the Licking River. Burned in 1926.

Landing Site of Capt. Bird — Falmouth, Shelby and Main. Landing site in 1780 of Capt. Bird's British and Indian raiders, in American Revolution.

OLD BUILDINGS

Bonar House — Caddo-Concord Pike, off KY-10. circa 1877. Original owner, Henry Bascon Bonar.

Caldwell House — Near Butler. circa 1870. Home of Alec Caldwell, early farmer and politician.

Falmouth Depot — Falmouth, Shelby St. Built 1913-1914. Example of turn of the century rural railroad depot.

Fryer House — Flour Creek, near Falmouth. US-27. circa 1811. Example of fieldstone house. Has been owned by same family since its construction.

Hauser House — Falmouth, 209 Main St. circa 1820. Birthplace of Samuel T. Hauser, Jr., first Governor of Montana.

Minor House — Falmouth, 105 N. Main St. circa 1825. Originally the home of Johnson Minor, a cabinetmaker.

Monroe Homestead — Morgan Pike, near Uma. circa 1855. Architectural example.

Alvin Montjoy House — Falmouth, 203 Chapel St. Built prior to 1800. Oldest house in Falmouth. Used as a meeting place by the county justices in June 1799.

Oldham House — Near Falmouth. KY-159. circa 1825. Home of Thomas Jefferson Oldham, who operated a ferry across the Licking River until a bridge was built in 1853.

Pendleton County Library — Falmouth, Main and Shelby Sts. Built 1884. Architectural example.

Mary Wilson House — Falmouth, Main and 4th Sts. circa 1840. Originally contained a store and dance hall.

Oldham House near Falmouth.

Courthouse in Falmouth.

Fort Harrod Area

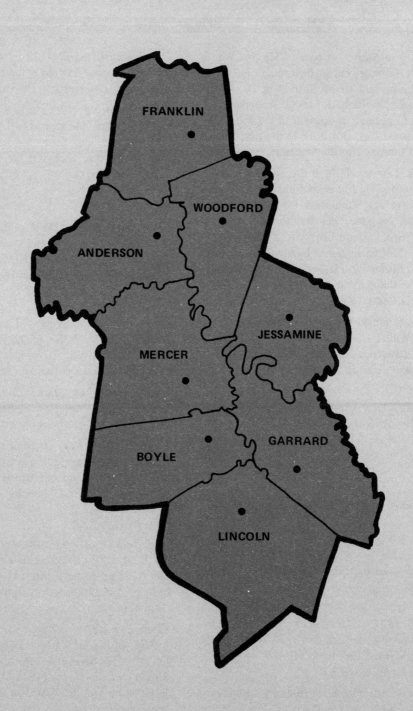

Anderson County

Anderson County territory was part of Mercer, Woodford, and Shelby Counties before becoming the eighty-second Kentucky county to be formed in 1827. The county was named for Richard Clough Anderson, Jr., who served as a Congressman, speaker of the Kentucky House of Representatives, and in 1823 the first American Minister to Columbia, South America.

The county seat, Lawrenceburg, is the point of conversion and diversion for old Indian and buffalo trails, and is the place where the Wilderness Trail divided. The locale of Lawrenceburg has been claimed by five counties at different times. Jacob Coffman, a Pennsylvania Dutchman, was the first settler in Lawrenceburg, arriving in 1776 with his family. He was killed by Indians in 1792, said to be the next to the last slaying of white men by Indians in Central Kentucky.

Lawrenceburg was named for Captain James Lawrence by his brother, William Lawrence, who bought the site in 1814. James Lawrence was an American naval hero whose words "Don't give up the ship!" became a popular naval cry. Lawrenceburg was incorporated in 1820.

Anderson County's largest source of revenue has been its distilleries. By 1818 there were more than fifty in operation. The first distillery was established by "Old Joe" Peyton at Gilbert's Creek.

FAIRS

Anderson County Fair — Lawrenceburg. US-62. Fairgrounds.

PARKS

Fairgrounds Park — Lawrenceburg. US-62.

MARKERS

County Named, 1827 — Lawrenceburg, N. Main St. For Richard Clough Anderson, Jr. (1788-1826). State and national legislator. Appointed Minister to Colombia by President Monroe, 1823.

Hebron Church — 1/2 mi. S. of Bluegrass Parkway. US-127. Built 1844. A Cumberland Presbyterian

church organized in 1827 in a log cabin overlooking McCall's Spring. Visited by an itinerant pastor traveling his circuit on horseback. Interments prior to 1816.

McCall's Spring — 1/2 mi. S. of Bluegrass Parkway. US-127. The McAfee brothers, along with James McCoun, Jr., and Samuel Adams were the first white men to explore this area in 1773. One of county's earliest landmarks.

MEMORIALS

Monument to War Dead — Lawrenceburg, Main St., Courthouse yard. Commemorates Anderson Countians who died in 3 wars. In 1846 Anderson County furnished a company of volunteers for the Mexican War.

CEMETERIES

Lawrenceburg Cemetery — Lawrenceburg. Gravesite of Althea Clark, mother of James Beauchamp (Champ) Clark, marked only by a 120-year old pine tree. Located in northeast corner of cemetery.

New Liberty Christian Church — 17 mi. W. of Lawrenceburg, on New Liberty Rd. US-62. Many Lincoln kin (17 cousins) buried in churchyard.

Grave of the Rev. John Penney — 2 mi. W. of Lawrenceburg, near golf course. US-62. Revolutionary War soldier and pioneer Baptist minister. Great grandfather of retailer, J. C. Penney.

OLD BUILDINGS

Anderson County Courthouse — Lawrenceburg, Main St. Built 1861. Example of French Renaissance architecture. Said to have the first self-winding tower clock built in America. Used in filming motion picture "The Flim-Flam Man."

Clark Birthplace — Lawrenceburg, N. Main St. Built 1830's. Birthplace of James Beauchamp (Champ) Clark in 1850. Congressman from Missouri for 24 years, Speaker of the House (1911-1919), and competitor in 1912 with Woodrow Wilson for Democratic nomination for presidency.

Champ Clark House — Ninevah, near Lawrenceburg. Built 1814. Boyhood home of Champ Clark, 1912 contender for Democratic presidential nomination.

Corner Drugstore — Lawrenceburg, 101 Main St. Built 1827. Rebuilt 1878. Site of oldest continuous business in town.

Gasken Baptist Church — 8 mi. S.W. of Lawrenceburg, Goshen Rd. Off US-62. Oldest church in county, organized 1812. Relocated at present site.

Kavanaugh House — Lawrenceburg, E. Woodford St. Built 1890's. Private school conducted by Mrs. Rhoda C. Kavanaugh, 1904-49. Under her direction it ranked among nation's foremost preparatory schools for Annapolis and West Point.

The Log Cabin — Lawrenceburg, S. Main St. Built in 1818 by early settler, William Routt.

Merry Hall — Near Lawrenceburg, Wildcat Rd. circa 1790. Architectural example.

Pierean Clubhouse — Lawrenceburg, N. Main St. Built 1818. Oldest building currently standing in Lawrenceburg.

Providence School — Near Lawrenceburg, Ninevah Rd. Built 1829. Oldest meeting house and schoolhouse in county.

Salt River Primitive Church — Sand Spring, near Lawrenceburg, Salt River Rd. Built 1842. Organized by the Rev. John Penney in 1798; reorganized in 1842. Now being restored. Marker near old US-127.

Anderson County High School.

Spencer House — Clifton, near Lawrenceburg, circa 1840. Architectural examples.

The Spring House — Clifton, near Lawrenceburg. circa 1790. Log cabin built over a spring by Army spy, Samuel Hutton.

Stone House — Anderson County, Ninevah Rd. Built while Kentucky was still a part of Virginia.

OTHER POINTS OF INTEREST

Beaver Lake — 8 mi. W. of Lawrenceburg. US-62. Noted for fishing and recreation.

Kentucky River Scenic Beauty — Anderson County, Harry Wise Rd. On farm of Hanks Houchin near Sand Spring School.

Panther Rock — On Kentucky River. Setting for the novel Panther Rock by Ariel Burr.

Courthouse in Lawrenceburg.

Boyle County

Boyle County was one of the first regions colonized in Kentucky, although it did not become a county until 1842. James Harrod built a cabin in what is now Danville in 1774. The cabin stood until 1819. After some 30 years of agitation, Boyle County was formed from parts of Mercer, Lincoln and Casey Counties. It was named for John Boyle, a Virginia native, who was elected to three terms in the United States Congress and served as Kentucky's Chief Justice for 16 years.

Danville, the county seat, was founded in 1784 on land donated by Walker Daniel, Kentucky's first district attorney, and was named in his honor. The Supreme Court of Virginia made Danville the seat of government west of the Alleghenies and ordered court buildings erected. The nine conventions preceding the admission of Kentucky into the Union were held at Danville.

Danville is known as the "City of Firsts," because so many important frontier "firsts" occurred in the area.

Agriculture is one of the main industries in the county, with tobacco and cattle as the principal sources of income.

Manufacturing gives employment to many residents as about twenty factories are located in Danville and Boyle County.

The population of Boyle County, including Danville is approximately 21,000.

FAIRS, FESTIVALS, DRAMAS, EXHIBITS

Boyle County Fair — Danville.

Collection Show and Flea Market — Danville.

Perryville Battle Reenactment, Perryville Battlefield — Each year the reenactment of this desperate battle is held on the weekend in October which falls nearest to the date of the battle, October 8.

Pioneer Playhouse — Danville. US-150. Fine plays are presented under the stars in Kentucky's oldest outdoor theater. Performances nightly at 8:30 except Sundays. Dinner 7:30. Mid-June-September 1.

Tri-State Appalachian Folk Festival — US-150. Pioneer Playhouse. Participants come from Tennessee, West Virginia and Kentucky. First week in June.

Forkland Festival — Gravel Switch, Forkland Community Center. KY-37. Celebrating the historic community of Forkland. Historical displays, antique room groupings, heritage skills, crafts and relics displayed, art shop, antique costumes. October.

Wilderness Road Village of the Arts — Pioneer Playhouse. US-150. Village recreates a Kentucky town of the 1800's with shops, restaurant, museums, picnic area, and camp sites. Open April to November.

LAKES

Herrington Lake — KY-34. Fine fishing, especially bass. Tent and trailer camping facilities. Cottages. Home of state's best fish run, the spring migration of white bass into Dix River.

MARKERS

Battle of Perryville — Perryville. US-68, US-150. On October 8, 1862, 16,000 Confederates under Gen. Braxton Bragg fought 22,000 Federals under Gen. Don Carlos Buell. Facing superior forces, Bragg withdrew. There were 7,000 casualties. One of the fiercest and bloodiest battles of modern times. This engagement kept Kentucky firmly in the Union.

Clark's Station — S.E. of Danville. US-150, KY-52. Early pioneer settlement developed by George Clark before 1779. One of first stations erected in vicinity of forts at Harrodsburg and Stanford.

Theodore O'Hara, 1820-1867 — Danville, Main St. Soldier and poet, author of "The Bivouac of the Dead." Born near here.

"Uncle" Charlie Moran — Danville. Centre College Campus. US-127, US-150. Colorful college football coach and National Baseball League umpire. Coached Praying Colonels of Centre College into football prominence, 1916-1923.

MEMORIALS, MUSEUMS

Constitution Square State Shrine — Danville, 1st and Main St. This reproduction of Kentucky's first Courthouse Square contains the original 1792 post office and replicas of the jail, courthouse, and meeting house. Plans were made here in 1784 for Kentucky's independence from Virginia and the first Kentucky Constitution was drawn here in 1792. Was once Virginia's western capital. Open daily.

Perryville Battlefield State Shrine — 2 mi. W. of Perryville on the Mackville Rd. Site of the bloodiest battle ever fought in Kentucky. On October 8, 1862, the armies of Bragg and Buell met in deadly conflict which resulted in the withdrawal of Gen. Bragg and the loss of control of Kentucky by the South. The park, containing 70 acres, has picnic areas, shelter houses, playgrounds, museum and gift shop.

Perryville Museum — 2 mi. W. of Perryville on Mackville Rd., Perryville Battlefield State Park. Honors Civil War dead. Open daily June-October.

Isaac Shelby Memorial — 6 mi. S. of Danville. Off US-127 at Knob Lick. Kentucky's first governor and his descendants lie in this plot near the site of Shelby's home — Traveller's Rest. Open Daily.

OLD BUILDINGS

Ayres Silversmith Shop — Danville. Built before 1792. Believed to be the oldest house standing in Danville. Shop of early silversmiths, Samuel and T. R. Ayres.

John Barbee House — E. of Danville, on Lexington Rd. circa 1788. Originally the home of early settler, John Barbee and family.

Birney Home — Danville, Perryville Rd., W. of city limits. US-150. Built 1800. Birthplace of James G. Birney, abolitionist candidate for President in 1840 and 1844. His 1844 votes caused Henry Clay's defeat.

H. P. Bottom House — Near Perryville, Old Mackville Rd. US-68, US-150. Built early 1800's. Home of H. P. Bottom; one of the first persons to view outcome of Battle of Perryville. He recorded grave sites, burials, etc. House was a key position in Battle of Perryville.

William Crow House — E. of Danville, Lancaster Rd. Built 1783. Example of stone house built for protection against Indians.

Dutch Barn — N. of Danville, Shakertown Rd. Built before 1790. Early log and stone house.

Grayson's Tavern — Danville, 103 E. Walnut St. Built 1786. Early tavern; meeting place of Danville Political Club.

Civil War Battle of Perryville.

W. C. Snider Home built middle eighteenth century.

Jacobs Hall — Danville, 2nd Street. Kentucky School for the Deaf. Built 1850. National historic landmark. Architectural example.

Karrick-Parks House and Cave — Perryville. US-68. This house and the adjacent cave are situated on the site of Harberson's Fort where Perryville had its beginnings. The old cave served the first settlers as a place of shelter and protection while their log houses were being built 1770-71. The house was erected in its present form in the 1850's and served as headquarters for officers and doctors during and after the Battle of Perryville. It is now being restored as a pre-Civil War house.

Lynwood — W. of Danville, Lebanon Rd. Built 1841. Originally owned by James Speed Hopkins. Architectural example.

McDowell House and Apothecary Shop — Danville, S. 2nd St. Built 1789. This restored 18th century house was the home of one of America's most famous surgeons. Here on December 25, 1809, Dr. Ephraim McDowell performed the first successful major abdominal operation, removing an ovarian tumor from Mrs. Jane Todd Crawford, which weighed more than 22 pounds. The patient recovered and lived for over thirty years after the operation. Next door to the McDowell House can be seen the original apothecary shop and office of Dr. McDowell. It is the oldest apothecary shop west of the Allegheny Mountains. Completely restored. Open daily.

Merchant's Row — Perryville. US-68. Across the street from the Karrick-Parks House stands the remains of the Old Perryville business section — an authentic row of quaint old stores and shops that has been there since pre-Civil War days. Of these, Parks Dry Goods Store and Green's Drugstore are in the process of restoration. The Parks Store is now open on Saturdays and by appointment.

Old Crow Inn — Danville, city limits. US-150. Built 1784. The oldest existing stone house in Kentucky is part of this building. John Crow sold it to Walker Daniel in 1784. This was the land on which he established Danville in 1788.

Pleasant Vale — E. of Danville, Lexington Rd. Built in 1784 by Samuel McDowell, father of Ephraim McDowell, the pioneer surgeon.

David Rice House — N. of Danville, Buster Pike. Built in 1793 by David Rice, founder of first 3 Presbyterian churches in Kentucky. Site of founding of Transylvania University.

Roselawn — Built circa 1848 by Governor William Owsley, 17th governor of Kentucky, 1844-48.

St. Patrick's Church — Danville, 141 5th St. Built 1807. Catholic Church from 1807-1833. Oldest Catholic church building now standing in state.

OTHER POINTS OF INTEREST

Centre College — Danville. Jct. US-127, US-150. Founded in 1819, Centre is one of the nation's most highly regarded independent colleges of the liberal arts and sciences. Co-educational, it has about 800 students. Old Centre (administration building) was built in 1820 and is the oldest college building west of the Alleghenies and south of the Ohio River. Many new buildings have been added, including a $6.5 million Regional Arts Center completed in 1973.

Regional Arts Center — Danville, Centre College Campus. This facility houses a concert hall, providing continual offering of first-rate stage productions.

School for the Deaf — Danville, 4th and Main Sts. Founded 1823. First tax-supported school for instruction of deaf children in the U. S.

Dr. Ephraim McDowell Home in Danville.

Franklin County

Franklin County was formed in 1794 from Shelby, Mercer, and Woodford counties. It was named for Benjamin Franklin, one of our leaders for independence.

The first settlement in Franklin County was established in 1775 at Leestown, the oldest continuously inhabited area on the Kentucky River. General James Wilkinson purchased the downtown district in 1786 for $433. Immediately he set about organizing the town. Streets were laid out and named for the general and his friends. It is generally accepted that General Wilkinson originally named the town "Frank's Ford" in memory of a settler, Frank, who had been killed by Indians while fording the river. Over the years the name changed to Frankfort.

On June 1, 1792 Kentucky became the fifteenth state of the Union, and on December 5, Frankfort was judged to be "the most proper place" for the permanent seat of government for the new state. Chief contenders for the capital site were Lexington and Louisville, and the choice of the village on the Kentucky River midway between the two major towns was a compromise in the site selection. Frankfort is the spot where Kentucky's original three counties, Jefferson, Fayette and Lincoln came together.

FESTIVALS, EXHIBITS

Capitol Expo — Frankfort, Capitol Plaza. Kentucky folklore festival. Towns throughout the state exhibit their local foods and crafts.

PARKS, RECREATION

Game and Wildlife Farm — 3 mi. W. of Frankfort. US-60. Kentucky birds and animals on display. Picnic facilities. Supported by fishing and hunting license fees.

Juniper Hills Municipal Recreation Area — Near Frankfort. US-60W. 18-hole golf course. Olympic-sized swimming pool.

MARKERS

Confederates Here — Frankfort, Old Capitol grounds. Kentucky state government moved to Louisville before CSA entered Lexington on Sept. 2, 1862. Richard Hawes was inaugurated 2nd CSA governor on Oct. 4, 1862. Confederates withdrew and Union forces occupied Frankfort on Oct. 7, 1862.

Franklin County Hemp — Franklin County. US-421 Bypass. Last hemp factory to operate in Kentucky. Closed down 1952. Hemp was the state's largest cash crop until 1915.

Leestown — Frankfort. US-127, US-421 Bypass. Surveyed July 16, 1773 by Hancock Taylor. Settled in June, 1775 by Hancock Lee. Second white settlement on Kentucky River.

Lexington and Ohio R.R. — Frankfort. US-421. Built 1833-34. Site of first railroad west of Alleghenies.

Lt. Presley N. O'Bannon, USMC — Frankfort Cemetery, E. Main St. US-60. First American to raise U.S. flag on foreign soil at Battle of Derne on shores of Tripoli on April 27, 1805.

MEMORIALS AND MUSEUMS

Daniel Boone's Grave — Frankfort, Frankfort Cemetery. US-60. In 1845 remains of Boone and his wife, Rebecca, were brought here and reburied. Marked by monument. Scenic overlook view of Frankfort and the Kentucky River.

Capitol Bridge — Frankfort, E. Main St. and Capitol Ave. Dedicated to the memory of World War I casualties. Crosses the Kentucky River at a level that assures highway access in the event of a tragedy similar to the flood of 1937.

Kentucky History Museum — Frankfort, St. Clair St. and Broadway. Artifacts and documents from Kentucky's earliest days. Many oil portraits on display. Confederate Room. Genealogical Library.

Kentucky Military History Museum (Old State Arsenal) — Frankfort, ·Capitol Ave. and E. Main. Established

1973. Military History of weapons and uniforms. Monday-Saturday, 9 a.m. to 4 p.m. Sunday, 1 to 5 p.m.

Old Taylor Hall of Fame Museum — Frankfort. US-60. Glenns Creek and Millville Roads. Colorful exhibits trace history of bourbon in America.

Site of Love House — Frankfort, Wapping and Wilkinson Sts. First meeting of Legislature after Frankfort was made capitol was held here in 1793. A center of political and social life for the capitol.

Veterans of American Revolution To Be Elected Governor of Kentucky — Old State House. Isaac Shelby, James Garrard, Christopher Greenup, Charles Scott, George Madison and John Adair.

Veterans of American Revolution Elected U. S. Senator from Kentucky — Old State House. John Brown, John Edwards, Humphrey Marshall, John Breckinridge, George Walker and John Adair.

CEMETERIES

Frankfort Cemetery — Frankfort, E. Main St., on a hill high above the Kentucky River, overlooking the city. A monument marks the grave of Daniel Boone and his wife, Rebecca. In this cemetery is the state monument to heroes of all wars, an impressive marble shaft surmounted by a statue of Victory. Many of the graves are interesting because of the quaint epitaphs. Open daily until 5 p.m. in winter, in summer until 8 p.m.

OLD BUILDINGS

John Bibb House — Frankfort, 411 Wapping St. Built 1857. Bibb, an amateur horticulturist, developed world-famous Bibb lettuce in his garden here.

Orlando Brown House — Frankfort, 202 Wilkinson St. Built in 1835 by Senator John Brown of Liberty Hall for his son, Orlando. Late Georgian-Colonial architecture. It is one of the few residences designed by Gideon Shryrock. Contains most of the original furnishings. It is open to the public.

Carneal-Watson House — Frankfort, 407 Wapping St. Built 1854. Headquarters for the Military Board of Kentucky during the Civil War.

Devon Downs — Franklin County, near Woodlake. circa 1848-54. Home of Franklin Wilson, son of early settler, Isaac Wilson. Architectural example.

Daniel Boone's grave in Frankfort.

Capitol in Frankfort.

163

Switzer Covered Bridge over North Elkhorn Creek.

Macklin House — Frankfort, 212 Washington St. circa 1850. Example of mid-19th century successful businessman's town house.

Madison House — Franklin County, near Woodlake. circa 1800. Home of George Madison, Kentucky Governor in 1816.

Governor's Mansion — Frankfort, Capitol Ave. The Chief Executive of the Commonwealth of Kentucky is provided with an elegant mansion during his term as Governor. Overlooking the Kentucky River and sharing grounds with the Commonwealth's imposing Capitol on a broad lawn of bluegrass, this has been the home of Kentucky's first families for over 50 years. The first floor of the Governor's Mansion is open to the public on Tuesday and Thursday mornings from 9:30 to 11:30, unless it is being used for official functions. Guides are available at the Capitol information desk.

Old Governor's Mansion — Frankfort, 420 High St. Built 1797-98. Home of 33 governors. Now the residence of the Lieutenant Governor.

Letcher-Lindsay House — Frankfort, 200 Washington St. Built 1840. House of former Governor of Kentucky and Speaker of the U. S. House of Representatives, Robert P. Letcher. In his younger days, he was a bricklayer and helped build the Old Governor's Mansion

which he later occupied. Also was occupied at one time by Senator William Lindsay. The house contains meeting rooms of the Frankfort Woman's Club.

Liberty Hall — Frankfort, 218 Wilkinson St. Built 1796. Visited by 6 U. S. Presidents and Prince Louis Phillippe. The house, under the operation of the Colonial Dames, is open to the public.

Paul Sawyer Library — Frankfort. 305 Wapping St. Built 1887. Originally used by Federal Government for U. S. Post Office, Federal Court, and offices. Site of investigation of first charge of treason against Aaron Burr.

Old Statehouse — Frankfort, St. Clair St. and Broadway. Served as the official capitol from 1827 to 1910. Now the Museum of the Kentucky Historical Society. It has undergone extensive restoration to the period when it was Kentucky's statehouse. Architects received citation for restoration and for removing barriers to the handicapped. America's first Greek Revival capitol building. Open Monday-Saturday, 9 a.m. to 4 p.m. Sunday, 1 to 5 p.m. Admission free.

Justice Todd House — Frankfort, Wapping and Washington Sts. Built 1812. Home of Thomas Todd, Justice on the U. S. Supreme Court, 1807-26. His second marriage was to Lucy Payne Washington, sister of Dolly

Madison, in the first recorded White House wedding, 1812.

Vest-Lindsey House — Frankfort, 401 Wapping St. Built 1816. Childhood home of George Graham Vest, U. S. Senator from Missouri. Vest won fame for his "Tribute to a Dog" oration in court.

Vreeland Mansion — Frankfort, 417 Wapping St. Built 1914. Though modern by comparison with any of its neighbors, the house is notable. Graham Vreeland was publisher of the Frankfort State Journal.

Isaac Wilson House — Franklin County, near Woodlake. circa 1800. Home of Isaac Wilson, early settler and large landowner.

Frank Lloyd Wright House — Frankfort, 509 Shelby St. Built 1909-10. Kentucky's only house designed by Frank Lloyd Wright.

OTHER POINTS OF INTEREST

Corner of Celebrities — Frankfort, Wilkinson St. It is believed that more distinguished men lived on these four acres than on any similar plot of land in the U. S. Old houses of distinguished, early Frankfort citizens.

Floral Clock — Frankfort, W. lawn of Capitol Annex. A cylindrical clockhouse supporting a 100-ton planter. The planter, surrounded by an illuminated reflecting pool, contains thousands of plants and incorporates the name of the state plus stars to represent the hours.

Kentucky State University — Frankfort, Main St.

Old Crow Distillery — Frankfort, off Glenns Creek Rd. Tours 8 a.m. to 3:30 p.m.

Old Grand-Dad Distillery — Frankfort, Georgetown Rd. Tours 8 a.m. to 3:30 p.m.

Old Taylor Distillery — Frankfort, Glenns Creek and Millville Rds. US-60. Built 1887. Only Bourbon castle west of the Atlantic Ocean. Located on exact site of old Leestown, 1773 survey. Hall of Fame Museum. Tours, weekdays 8 a.m. to 3:30 p.m.

Schenley Distillery — 1 mi. from Frankfort, Leestown Rd. US-421. Tours at 10:00 a.m. and 1:00 p.m.

State Capitol — Frankfort, S. end of Capitol Ave. Completed 1910. The interior of the building is finished entirely in marble and accented with murals and paintings depicting historical scenes. A statue of Lincoln stands in the rotunda. Open weekdays 8 a.m. to 4:30 p.m. Sundays, 1 to 5 p.m. Admission free.

Switzer Covered Bridge — Switzer, off KY-1262 over N. Elkhorn Creek. One of few covered bridges in Kentucky. Picnic area available.

Walking Tour — Frankfort. Broadway, Wilkinson, Wapping, St. Clair Streets. Guide through Frankfort's oldest residential district describing 39 points of interest. Brochure printed by Kentucky Department of Public Information.

Old Statehouse in Frankfort.

Garrard County

Garrard County, the twenty-fifth county formed in Kentucky, dates from 1796 and was taken from portions of Lincoln, Madison, and Mercer Counties. The county is nearly surrounded by water, as the Kentucky River, Dix River and Paint Lick Creek form the northern, eastern, and western boundaries. Garrard County was named for the Honorable James Garrard, second Governor of Kentucky and the only governor to serve two full terms in succession.

The county's first settlement was at Kennedy's Fork on Paint Lick Creek in 1775. John Kennedy built cabins there and also raised corn.

Lancaster, the county seat, was established in 1798. It was a namesake of Lancaster, Pennsylvania, home of many of the county's early settlers. Captain William Buford donated land for the town site, and Henry Paulding of Lancaster, Pennsylvania designed and laid out the town.

An historic hamlet in Garrard County is Paint Lick, which was established in 1782. It was so named because the first settlers found Indian symbols painted in bright colors on trees and stones along the creek and around the nearby salt lick.

EXHIBITS

Central Kentucky Saddle Club Horse Show — S. of Lancaster, on the Saddle Club Grounds. US-27. Mainly features walking horses. Early June.

Lancaster Womens Club Horse Show — S. of Lancaster, on the Saddle Club Grounds. US-27. Mainly features walking horses. August.

Walker's Bluegrass Fox Hunt — 3 mi. S. of Lancaster, on Gilberts Creek Rd., at Daniel's Club House at Lake Lorraine, just off Crab Orchard Rd. Usually held in October.

PARKS, LAKES

Camp Nelson — 15 mi. N.W. of Lancaster on Kentucky River. US-27. Camping, swimming, boating, shelter house, houseboat rentals, miniature gold.

Herrington Lake — 7 mi. E. of Lancaster. KY-52. Offers a variety of water sports, fishing, dining and camping facilities.

Lake Lorraine — 160-acre recreational area offering picnic facilities, swimming, beach area, cabins, trailer park.

MARKERS

CSA Starts Retreat — Bryantsville. US-27. In Autumn of 1862, after the Battle of Perryville, CSA began retreat from Kentucky.

Local Authoress — Lancaster, Lexington St. US-27. Eugenia Dunlap Potts was born in Garrard County in 1840 and pursued her literary career here, where she died in 1912. The first of her nine works was *Song of Lancaster.* In 1892, she became the editor of "Illustrated Kentuckian."

James Thompson (1750-1825) — N. of Lancaster. US-27. Dick's River Baptist Church. Burial site of first Lincoln County surveyor. (Daniel Boone was made Deputy Surveyor under him, a nephew of Isaac Shelby.)

The Traveling Church, 1781 — S.E. of Lancaster. KY-39. To find religious freedom, the Rev. Lewis Craig led a congregation of 200 Baptists and 400 other settlers from Spottsylvania County, Virginia and established them here on Gilbert's Creek. This was the largest group of pioneers to enter the District of Kentucky together.

Uncle Tom's Cabin — 4 mi. W. of Paint Lick. KY-52. Harriet Beecher Stowe, author of *Uncle Tom's Cabin,* visited the Thomas Kennedy home while gathering some of the material for her book. Legendary cabin of Uncle Tom was behind the mansion, which was torn down around 1926.

CEMETERIES

Burial Ground — Pain Lick. KY-52. Paint Lick Presbyterian Church. Graves of several veterans of the American Revolution, including the grave of Gen. Thomas Kennedy.

OLD BUILDINGS

Governor Bradley House — Lancaster, 210 Lexington St. Built circa 1850 by A. A. Burton, Lincoln's minister to Bogota. Governor William O. Bradley lived here when elected 32nd Governor of Kentucky, 1895-99. On National Register of Historic Sites.

Forks Dix River Baptist Church — Lancaster, Lexington. US-27. Built 1849. Church was established in 1782 by Lewis Craig. One of the oldest congregations in the State. First church in county.

Thomas Kennedy House — 5 mi. S.E. of Lancaster. KY-1647. Only foundation of the house remains. Gen. Thomas Kennedy, a leader in forming Garrard County, owned 200 slaves and one of the largest plantations in the South, 7,000 acres. Harriet Beecher Stowe is said to have visited this estate when she was in Kentucky gathering material for *Uncle Tom's Cabin.* Gen. Kennedy's daughter is said to have been the inspiration for the "Little Eva" character in the story. Many characters in book were said to be derived from people and stories on this plantation.

Governor Letcher Home — Lancaster, 106 W. Maple St. Built in 1798 by John Boyle for his bride, Nancy Kennedy Letcher, who supposedly was "Little Eva" of *Uncle Tom's Cabin.* They lived here and raised a family of 10 children. Four legislators have occupied this house, John Boyle, for whom Boyle County was named; Samuel McKee; George Robertson, for whom Robertson was named; and Robert P. Letcher, Governor of Kentucky, 1840-44, for whom Letcher County was named.

Carrie Nation House — Near Herrington Lake, off Fisher Ford Rd. KY-34. Birthplace of Carrie Amelia Moore Nation in 1846. She was the famed temperance agitator. Carrie Nation lived here about 7 years.

Governor Owsley Home — 1/2 mi. S. of Lancaster. US-27. Built circa 1820. "Pleasant Retreat" is a beautiful farm with a stately 3-story brick home. Home of William Owsley, for whom Owsley County was named, and Governor of Kentucky, 1844-48.

Old Pain Lick Presbyterian Church — S.W. of Paint Lick. KY-52. circa 1873-75. This congregation was originally established in 1783.

Camp Dick Robinson House — 7 mi. N. of Lancaster. Jct. US-27 and KY-39. First Union training camp south of Ohio River. Organized in 1861 by Gen. William Nelson for enlistment of Union troops in War Between the States. House used as Union headquarters.

Carrie Nation Home near Herrington Lake.

Camp Dick Robinson House near Lancaster.

Courthouse in Lancaster.

167

Jessamine County

Jessamine County, the Commonwealth's thirty-sixth county to be created and the only county to bear a feminine name, was formed in 1798 from the southern portion of Fayette County. Colonel John Price chose the name from Jessamine Creek, which appeared on early maps, and from a flower which flourished in various parts of the county. A legend tells that the creek was named for Jessamine Douglass, the daughter of an early settler, who was tomahawked by an Indian as she rested on the creek bank. Governor Garrard appointed Charles West as the first sheriff, and Samuel Woodson as the new county's court clerk.

Nicholasville, the county seat, was named by the Reverend John Metcalf in honor of Colonel George Nicholas, a prominent lawyer of the time. The town was well-located at the crossroads, and as it grew, Nicholasville's first charter was granted in 1812. Although the first court sessions were held at the tavern of Fisher Rice, Jessamine County was soon to have a courthouse, the first of three on the same site. The present edifice was built in 1878.

The first settlers in Jessamine County were Joseph Drake, reputed to be a descendant of Sir Francis Drake, and Colonel George Nicholas. Drake settled about six miles west of Nicholasville in the early 1780's, while Nicholas settled within the present city limits during the early 1790's. About the same time, Matthew Patton and his sons moved from the Potomac River valley in Virginia to Jessamine County bringing a herd of purebred cattle. It was from this herd that the American strain of shorthorn cattle had its beginning in Kentucky.

Outstanding among the earliest citizens were many Revolutionary War soldiers seeking homes west of the mountains. These early settlers included John, Jacob, and Samuel Hunter, brothers who arrived in 1779; and Benjamin Netherland, the town's first postmaster and host of Mingo's Tavern. Another early settler, William Price, along with 40 veterans of the Revolutionary War, staged the first July 4th Celebration west of the Alleghenies in 1794. General Percival Butler and his sons, all famous soldiers, lived at the mouth of Hickman Creek.

Jessamine County, in the heart of the Bluegrass, has a varied topography. From the scenic Kentucky Palisades bordering the Kentucky River to the fertile fields, this section of Kentucky was rightly termed "an extensive garden" by an early writer.

FAIRS

Jessamine County Fair — Nicholasville, Jessamine County High School. KY-29. Exhibits, carnival, livestock shows. July.

PARKS

Camp Nelson — Camp Nelson. On Kentucky River. US-27. Recreation and tourist community. 650 acres of wooded forests, waterways, and Palisades. Camping, swimming, flea market, shops, riding stable, picnic areas, dining facilities and trails. Civil War Fort and Museum. Currently being restored by the Christian Appalachian Project.

Camp Nelson Marina — Camp Nelson. On Kentucky River. US-27. Boat Rentals.

Rock Fence Park — Nicholasville, W. Oak St. KY-169. Playground equipment, picnic tables.

MARKERS

Butler's Birthplace — S. of Camp Nelson Cemetery. Jct. of Hall Rd. and US-27. Gen. William O. Butler was born here in 1791 and died in Carrollton in 1880. He fought in the War of 1812 in Battles of The River Raisin, Pensacola and New Orleans. He was cited for heroism in the Mexican War in 1846-1848. He served as U. S. Congressman 1839-1843; as Vice President 1848; and in U. S. Senate 1851. He was one of the most prominent and well-liked Democrats in Kentucky.

First Celebration — Jct. of Clear Creek Rd. and US-68. Here on July 4, 1794, Col. William Price, Revolutionary War veteran, held the first celebration of Independence Day west of the Alleghenies. At his plantation,

40 veterans dined to commemorate the "glorious birthday of our freedom."

Jessamine County Hemp — Nicholasville, Courthouse yard, Main St. In 1899 Jessamine was one of the 3 Bluegrass counties which together produced more than one-half of the hemp grown in the entire country.

Dr. Phillip's Birthplace — Nicholasville, 303 S. Main St. Birthplace of Dr. Lena Madesin Phillips, founder of the National Federation of Business and Professional Women's Clubs in 1919. She was born here in 1881. She was also the first president of the International Federation of Business and Professional Women.

Sawyier's Inspiration — S. of Camp Nelson Cemetery. Hall Rd. and US-27. Paul Sawyier, known as the River

Confederate Memorial in Nicholasville.

Artist, painted scenes of Kentucky River gorge while living on a houseboat near here, 1908-1913. Born in Ohio in 1865, he spent most of his life in Kentucky; died in New York in 1917.

MEMORIALS AND MUSEUMS

Former Camp Nelson — Camp Nelson. US-27. Established 1863. One of the leading concentration camps for Federal troops and munitions during the Civil War. Also the main camp in Kentucky for the enlistment of Negro troops and a refuge for slaves. Named for Gen. William Nelson. Remained a military camp until the close of the war. It is now being restored as a recreation and tourist community. Contains museum of military camp days.

CEMETERIES

Joe Drake Burial Ground — Nicholasville, Old Frankfort Drive. Here a reproduction of an original gravestone bearing the inscription "Joseph Drake of Buckland, Monaghorum, England. Born 1694, Died 1777." Joe Drake was described as a descendant and heir of Sir Francis Drake, the English Admiral. His presence in central Kentucky is unexplained.

Maple Grove Cemetery — Nicholasville. US-27.

Camp Nelson Cemetery — Camp Nelson. Established soon after start of Civil War. Contains graves of more than 500 soldiers killed at the Battles of Perryville and Richmond during the Civil War.

OLD BUILDINGS

Brown Family Farm — Wilmore Road. circa 1800. Buildings include brick house and log structures originally used as slave quarters and a meat house.

Cedar Grove — near Spears, Union Mill Pike. Built 1818. Architectural example.

Chaumiere du Prairie — 4 mi. N. of Nicholasville, Catnip Hill Road. Off US-27. circa 1796, 1830-40. Original owner was Col. David Meade, who entertained Aaron Burr, Thomas Jefferson, John Monroe, Andrew Jackson and Zachary Taylor here. Col. Meade spent 3 fortunes on its development. Called the "birthplace of Kentucky hospitality."

Ebenezer Presbyterian Church — Troy. 7 1/2 mi. S.W. of Nicholasville, off Keene-Troy Road. Built 1803-04. Founded by Adam Rankin. Land given by Ephriam January.

Fairview — 5 1/2 mi. W. of Nicholasville, Clear Creek Pike. circa 1790's. Originally called "Pleasant Hill." Excellent example of very early Kentucky brick house.

O. R. Haydens House — 6 1/2 mi. N.W. of Nicholasville, Harrodsburg Road. US-68. circa 1800. Log house architectural example.

The Hedges — 3 mi. S.E. of Nicholasville. Sulphur Well Pike. KY-39. Built early 19th century. Architectural example.

Ephriam January House — 7 1/2 mi. S.W. of Nicholasville, Keene-Troy Road. Built 1786. Example of early stone house.

Jessamine County Courthouse — Nicholasville, Main St. Built 1878. Architectural example.

Keene Springs Hotel — Keene. circa 1840's. One of the few remaining resort hotels or spa buildings of pre-Civil War Kentucky.

John Lancaster House — 7 mi. N.W. of Nicholasville, Keene-Versailles Rd. KY-169. circa 1780's. One of a few stone houses left in county.

Locust Grove — 8 mi. N.W. of Nicholasville, Keene Rd. Built 1833. Farm was originally a hemp farm. First mechanical hemp havesting machine in area was used here. Architectural example.

Metcalf Place — Nicholasville, 209 1st St. Built 1791. Believed to be the oldest house in Nicholasville. Built by the Rev. John Metcalf, Methodist minister who laid out the town of Nicholasville.

Fisher Rice House — 1/2 mi. N. of Nicholasville, Lexington-Nicholasville Rd. US-27. Built late 18th century. First Jessamine County Courts were held here when Jessamine County was separated from Fayette County in 1798.

William S. Scott House — Nicholasville, 305 W. Oak St. Built late 18th century. Believed to be the second oldest house in Nicholasville. Used as a hospital during the Civil War.

Isaac Shelby House — 3 1/2 mi. E. of Nicholasville, Union Mill Rd. KY-169. circa 1840-50.

OTHER POINTS OF INTEREST

Almahurst Horse Farm — Nicholasville. Jct. of US-68 and KY-169. Breeding farm for standard breeds. Site of early tavern. Part of original land grant granted to James Knight for his services in Revolutionary War. Among famous horses bred, foaled and raised here were Greyhound, world's champion trotter of all times; Peter Volo, founder of great trotting family; and Exterminator, known wherever Thoroughbreds are raced.

Asbury College and Asbury Theological Seminary — Wilmore. KY-29. Interdenominational institution founded in 1890. Liberal Arts. The Seminary was

Asbury College in Wilmore.

founded in 1923 and is also an interdenominational institution. Campus tours.

Glass's Mill — 2 1/2 mi. W. of Wilmore on Jessamine Creek Rd. Erected 1782. Said to have been the first gristmill in Kentucky. Later became a paper mill and in 1849 was converted into a distillery, which is no longer in use.

High Bridge — High Bridge, over Kentucky River. KY-29. Erected 1876. Highest railroad bridge in the world over a navigable stream. Rises 317 feet above normal water level of the river and spans 1,230 feet. First cantilever bridge built on American Continent. Most remarkable bridge in U.S. when constructed. Marked the beginning of modern scientific bridge building.

Kentucky River Ferry — Valley View. Runs between Jessamine and Madison Counties. One of the few of its type still operating in the United States.

Kentucky River Palisades — On Kentucky River. US-68 and KY-29. One of the most magnificent views in the state. Great rugged walls of gray limestone rise 300 feet from river's edge. Extends at least 75 miles.

Lincoln County

On November 1, 1780 the Virginia Legislature divided Kentucky County, Virginia into three counties, Fayette, Jefferson and Lincoln. Lincoln County was located south of the Kentucky River and was the largest of the three counties to be created at that time. It was named in honor of Benjamin Lincoln, Revolutionary War officer in command of the Southern army and the soldier who received Cornwallis' sword at the Yorktown surrender. Fifty-eight counties have been cut from the original Lincoln County, which once comprised nearly one-third of The Commonwealth of Kentucky.

Stanford, the county seat, is one of the oldest towns in Kentucky and was founded by an act of the legislature in 1786. Main Street in Stanford was the old buffalo path through this territory in pre-settlement and pioneer days. It is also a part of the first road in Kentucky, the Old Wilderness Trail.

Stanford is near the site of St. Asaph or Logan's Fort, one of three primary wilderness strongholds. It was established by Colonel Benjamin Logan in 1775. When

their efforts to capture it proved unsuccessful, Indians named the settlement Standing Fort, which was later shortened to Stanford. Lincoln County is said to have had seventeen forts or stations since it was created.

Founding fathers who were associated with Lincoln County include Benjamin Logan, Isaac Shelby, William Whitley, John Logan, John, Adam and Conrad Carpenter, and James Knox.

FAIRS

Dairy Day — Stanford, Main St. Parade, dairy breakfast. One-day event. June.

Lincoln County Fair — Stanford. US-150. Horse show, exhibits, beauty contest, dog show, carnival. July.

PARKS

Farm Bureau Youth Center — Stanford. US-150. Shelter house, ball park, fair buildings.

William Whitley State Shrine — 2 mi. W. of Crab Orchard. US-150. Picnic and outdoor cooking facilities on the grounds.

MARKERS

Carpenter's Station — 2 mi. W. of Hustonville. KY-78. Established in 1780 by Adam, Conrad and John Carpenter, brothers and Revolutionary War soldiers. One of the early stations through which settlement of Kentucky was achieved.

Crab Orchard Springs — Crab Orchard. US-150. Site of popular watering place in 1827 until early 1930's. Famed for numerous and excellent mineral springs. Crab Orchard salts are produced here by evaporation.

Captain George Givens — Near Shelby City. Jct. KY-1273 and US-150. Home site and grave. 1740-1825. Forty years service to his country. Noted campaigner.

Logan's Station — Stanford, Waterworks St. Colonel Benjamin Logan settled here after leaving Colonel Henderson's party due to a disagreement over settlement plans. Scene of courageous rescue of fallen companion by Logan in an Indian attack in 1777.

Ottenheim — Halls Gap. US-27 and KY-643. A German-Swiss settlement, 4 miles S.E., started by immigrants in early 1880's. Led by Joseph Ottenheimer, they found their "land of opportunity" to be a wilderness. Undaunted, they developed the land into a highly productive agricultural area.

Site of Traveler's Rest near Danville.

MEMORIALS, MUSEUMS

Harvey Helm Memorial Library — Stanford, Church and 3rd St. Built 1971. This building is a one-floor plan of fireproof brick. It covers 6,000 square feet and has 19,312 books on shelves. There is a cultural arts center, sponsoring art shows, craft exhibits and quilt exhibits several times each year. A Bookmobile operates from this library, making 10 school stops biweekly and about 200 house stops. Contains collections of paintings by Kentucky artists Ray Harm, Nellie Meadows, Thelma Ware, Jo Dunn, Ruth Lyons, and Jim Oliver.

Lincoln County Museum — Stanford, W. Main St. Built on land donated by a sister of Col. Benjamin Logan for a Presbyterian church. The present library and hall were built of logs and used for the first church in Stanford, organized 1788. The building was willed to the people of Lincoln County for a library by the owner, Mrs. Harvey (Mary Bruce) Helm. Now houses the Historic Library and Museum. Contains books on Kentucky history, Kentucky authors and genealogy. Designated a Kentucky landmark and placed on the National Historic Register.

Isaac Shelby Memorial — Hustonville, Knob Lick Pike. US-127. Site of Traveler's Rest, a stone house built in 1786 by Isaac Shelby, Kentucky's first and fifth governor. Home no longer stands. Family burial ground intact inside old stone fence.

CEMETERIES

Buffalo Springs Cemetery — Stanford. KY-78. The land was donated by Col. Benjamin Logan who established Logan's Fort and later the town of Stanford. Burial place of Revolutionary War soldiers and many of Lincoln County's earliest pioneers. Named for the many buffalo that watered there. The path they made to the spring became the "Old Wilderness Road."

Carpenter Graveyard — 3 mi. W. of Hustonville. KY-78. John, Adam and Conrad Carpenter, brothers, established Carpenter's Station, a fort in the wilderness, and later Hustonville, Kentucky. The Carpenter family is buried here near the old Carpenter's Station.

Hustonville Cemetery — Hustonville. KY-78. Resting place of many Lincoln County pioneer families.

Shelby Graveyard — Lincoln County, 6 mi. S. of Danville. Off US-127. Farm owned by Isaac Shelby. Family burial ground of Isaac Shelby, the first Governor of Kentucky. Site of his home, Traveler's Rest, is nearby. The graveyard is a State Shrine.

OLD BUILDINGS

Arcadia — 2 mi. from Danville. US-127. Completed 1836. Home of Isaac Shelby, Jr., eldest son of the first Governor of Kentucky. Handsome Greek Revival, 14-room brick residence. Remained in the Shelby family until early 1960's, when sold at auction.

Bright's Inn — 1 mi. W. of Stanford. US-150. Built in 1816 by John Bright. Operated as a stagecoach inn on Old Wilderness Road for many years. Now privately owned.

Early Boarding School — Stanford, E. Main St. Built 18th century. One of the earliest buildings in Stanford. Used originally as a girls' boarding school.

Lincoln County Courthouse — Stanford, Main St. Built 1787. Land donated by Benjamin Logan. Present courthouse built on same site in 1909. Lincoln County is one of the three original counties of Kentucky. This courthouse contains some of the oldest records in Kentucky, some of which are written on sheepskin.

John Logan Home — Stanford. US-150 and Goshen Rd. Built 1780-1790 of stone by John Logan on Logan's Creek. Logan was first treasurer of the Commonwealth. Now privately owned.

McCormack Christian Church — On Hanging Fork Creek. KY-1194. Built 1819. Well-preserved and in constant use since its construction.

Valentine Payton Home — Lincoln County. Payton Well Road on Hanging Fork Creek. circa 1792-1793. Built of logs by Revolutionary War soldier, Valentine Payton. Later weatherboarded and modernized. This section of county is named for famous sulphur well on the property.

William Whitley House — 2 mi. W. of Crab Orchard. US-150. State Shrine. Built 1792. First brick house west of the Allegheny Mountains. Owned by William Whitley, Indian fighter, pioneer and Revolutionary War soldier. Whitley commanded troops patrolling the Wilderness Road to protect settlers from Indians. Called Sportsman's Hill, because of the circular race track he built nearby. This was the first circular race track in America, and it ran counter-clockwise instead of clockwise, as in England. Over the front entrance, made from glazed brick, are the initials W. W., standing for William Whitley, over the back entrance are the initials E. W. for his wife, Esther Whitley. This home was a favorite with the important persons of the day, such as George Rogers Clark and Isaac Shelby. Listed on the National Historical Register.

OTHER POINTS OF INTEREST

Ft. Logan Square Dances — Stanford, Main St. Opera House.

Courthouse in Stanford.

Mercer County

Mercer County was formed in 1785 from Lincoln County and named for Hugh Mercer, a native Scotsman who was killed in the American Revolution. It was the sixth county to be created in Kentucky. Among early settlers in the county were Captain Thomas Bullitt and the McAfee brothers of Virginia, James, George, Robert, and Samuel. The settlement of the area around Mercer County started in June of 1774, when a Pennsylvanian, James Harrod, led a company of 31 adventurers to the headwaters of the Salt River and set about establishing Harrodstown. Five or six cabins were built that summer near a "boiling spring." Several parties of surveyors were also at work in the area laying off choice bluegrass land for the officers of the French and Indian War. The Indians were alarmed at this encroachment on their hunting grounds and hostilities broke out. Harrod's men and the surveyors temporarily withdrew to safer settlements. The Indians were defeated at the Battle of Point Pleasant on October 10, 1774 and the way was opened for settlement of Kentucky.

Harrodstown was reoccupied on March 15, 1775 and never again abandoned. On higher ground, Harrod's party built a fortified village for added protection. The American Revolution was breaking out in the East. On the frontier, the Revolution provoked a period of constant harassment and danger. In 1777, conditions were so bad that all stations in Kentucky were abandoned except Harrodsburg, Boonesborough and Logan's Fort.

The first court for Kentucky County met at Harrodsburg and selected St. Asaph's, now Stanford as the county seat. Now, 200 years later, Harrodsburg survives and flourishes as the oldest permanent settlement in Kentucky and the first English settlement west of the Alleghenies. Often Harrodsburg is referred to as the "Mother Town of Ole Kaintuck." Today Harrodsburg is a trade center for a leading agricultural county, a busy tourist area, a thriving industrial city, and a charming residential town.

FAIRS, FESTIVALS, DRAMAS, EXHIBITS

Legend of Daniel Boone — Harrodsburg. US-127. Old Fort Harrod State Park amphitheater. This outdoor drama describes some of Boone's adventures and the settling of Kentucky. Summer evenings.

Ann Pogue McGinty Arts and Crafts Festival — Harrodsburg, W. Lexington St. Old Fort Harrod State Park. Arts festival named in honor of the resourceful teacher-pioneer-homemaker extraordinaire in Old Fort Harrod. Sponsored by Harrodsburg Guild of Creative Arts.

Mercer County Fair and Horse Show — Harrodsburg, Linden Ave. Fairgrounds. Features a horse show, industrial exhibits, livestock shows, homemaking and 4H exhibits, beauty contest, baby contest, pet show, etc. Organized in 1839, it is reputed to be oldest continually running fair in America. Largest county fair in Kentucky. Annually in July.

Shakertown Arts Festival — Pleasant Hill, 6 mi. N.E. of Harrodsburg. US-68E. Displays, exhibitions, demonstrations of arts and crafts. Lectures on Fridays and craftsmen's demonstrations on weekends. Shaker ballet. September.

PARKS, RECREATION, LAKES

Chimney-Rock Resort — Herrington Lake. Off KY-152. Natural rock formation.

Harrodsburg Community Center, Lion's Park — Harrodsburg, Factory St. Park facilities, shelter house.

Herrington Lake — 11 mi. E. of Harrodsburg. KY-152. 3600-acre lake. Excellent fishing, boat docks, cottages, tent and trailer areas.

Old Fort Harrod State Park — Harrodsburg, College St. US-127. Oldest permanent English settlement west of the Allegheny Mountains. Founded in 1774 by Captain James Harrod and his band of 30 rugged pioneers. Park contains mansion museum, reconstruction of Fort Harrod. Lincoln Marriage Temple, amphitheater, picnic ground and shelter house.

Young's Shelter House and Park — Harrodsburg, Linden Ave. Shelter houses. Some outdoor cooking facilities. Playground area.

MARKERS

"The Big Spring" — Harrodsburg, behind school. US-68 and US-127 Bypass. This spring, with its abundant, never-failing flow of water, was the reason for the location of Harrodsburg. Capt. James Harrod and party, on June 16, 1774, began building the first settlement in Kentucky along this "town branch." In the previous year Harrod had visited area and chosen this site for the town.

Boone Cabin Site — Harrodsburg, E. Lexington St. Granite stone relates that Daniel Boone and Evan Hinton built double log cabin on this site in 1774. Boone assisted James Harrod in laying off Harrodstown.

Boone's Cave — 5 mi. N.E. of Harrodsburg. US-68. Only cave in Kentucky historically verified as having been used by Daniel Boone. Spent winter 1769-1770 here.

An Early Derby Winner — Harrodsburg, Linden Ave., Young's Park. Harrodsburg was home of Leonatus, 1883 Kentucky Derby winner. He was owned by Col. Jack Chinn and George Morgan. Another Derby winner, George Smith, was also from Mercer County. He won considerable money for that time, $42,884 in 31 starts.

Early Gun Shop Site — Harrodsburg, Moreland Ave. Here Benjamin Mills made some of finest rifles in U. S., circa 1830-1850. Used by Kit Carson at the Alamo, and on the Fremont expeditions.

Early Vital Junction — Burgin, Schoolyard. KY-33, KY-152. Crossroads for pioneer defense. Harrodsburg in 1774, Harrod's Fort in 1775, and Bowman's Fort in 1777 were earliest defenses in area. In 1779-1780, eight fortified stations were built nearby. Col. John Bowman was a leader of defense against Indians.

McAfee Station — McAfee. US-127. Site of stockade built in 1779, 1 1/2 mi. W. on Salt River on land owned by James McAfee. He and his brothers marked and improved land in the area.

Mercer County Before Kentucky Became A State — Harrodsburg, Chiles St., Courthouse yard. Describes development of town and county. Lists Mercer County firsts in Kentucky; which include first settlement, corn

Legend of Daniel Boone in Harrodsburg.

Lincoln Marriage Temple in Harrodsburg.

crop, religious services, physician, school, woven fabric, wheat sown, gristmill, horse racing, jail and census.

Mercer Governors — 5 mi. N.E. of Harrodsburg. US-68. Christopher Greenup, 1804-08; Gabriel Slaughter, 1816-20; John Adair, 1820-24; Robert Letcher, 1840-45; Beriah Magoffin, 1859-62.

MEMORIALS, MUSEUMS

Bataan War Memorial — Harrodsburg, city limits. US-127. World War II M-4 tank and monument dedicated to the 66 Mercer countians who endured the "Bataan Death March" in the Philippines campaign.

George Rogers Clark Monument — Harrodsburg, in Old Fort Harrod State Park. Commemorates Clark's northwest conquest which was planned at Fort Harrod. Granite base relief depicting Clark and frontier soldiers. Dedicated in 1934 by President Franklin D. Roosevelt.

James Harrod Memorial Bridge — Harrodsburg, College St. and Broadway. Over "town branch" waters of historic "Big Spring." Lists citizens who were first in settlement, in education, in medicine, in religion, in law, in industry and in agriculture.

Mansion Museum — Harrodsburg. US-127. Old Fort Harrod State Park. Built 1835. Striking example of Georgian Colonial architecture. Houses authentic household items of early Kentucky and a fine collection of old firearms.

Morgan Row Museum — Harrodsburg, Chiles St. Museum maintained by Harrodsburg Historical Society. Contains county documents, portraits by Kentucky artists, antique furniture, pioneer household items. Personal items of James Harrod and Daniel Boone. Genealogical and research library. Early Kentucky green garden.

Courthouse in Harrodsburg

Shakertown at Pleasant Hill.

Shaker Museum — Pleasant Hill, 6 mi. N.E. of Harrodsburg. US-68. Exhibits tell the story of the Shaker colony and describe their way of life.

CEMETERIES

Burgin Memorial Gardens — Burgin, Buster Pike. Dates to 1897 or possibly even earlier.

Grave of the Unknown Belle — Harrodsburg, Linden Ave., Young's Park. Romantic story maintains that during the era when Harrodsburg was considered the "Saratoga of the South," this unidentified belle died while dancing at one of the grand balls.

Memorial Acre — Harrodsburg, Old Fort Harrod State Park. US-127. Burial site of Revolutionary War Veterans. When a grave of a Revolutionary War soldier is discovered elsewhere in the county, part of its earth is scattered here.

Mud Meeting House Cemetery — Harrodsburg, on Dry Branch Rd. Off US-68. Dates from early nineteenth century. Grave of the first pastor, Dominie Thomas Kyle.

Pioneer Cemetery — Harrodsburg, Old Fort Harrod State Park. Contains graves of over 500 early settlers and soldiers. Oldest in the west. Tombstone of first child to die in this settlement.

Shaker Cemetery — Pleasant Hill. US-68. Shaker rule maintained that gravestones bear no epitaphs, names or dates. Graves marked only by slab of wood or limestone with intials of the deceased.

Spring Hill Cemetery — Harrodsburg, N. Greenville St. circa 1860. Burial ground of many unknown victims of the Battle of Perryville. Monument to Confederate dead. Burial site of Governor Beriah Magoffin.

OLD BUILDINGS

The Academy — Harrodsburg, 101 Moreland Ave. circa 1847. Originally used for Presbyterian Female Academy; later for boys school, Hogsett's Academy. Now private apartments.

Aspen Hall — Harrodsburg, 558 Aspen Hall Dr. Built 1840. Once owned by John B. Bowman, one of the founders of University of Kentucky. Fully developed classic Greek Revival architecture. Presently an inn.

Beaumont Inn — Harrodsburg, 638 Beaumont Dr. Original site of Greenville Springs, a spa-resort from 1806-1853, offering mineral water, gambling, horse racing, and gala entertainment at this "Saratoga of the South." Later it was converted into the Greenville Female Academy which burned. Present structure built in 1851 housed Daughters College which later was known as Beaumont College.

Bellevue or Bowman-Curd House — 2 mi. E. of Burgin, Kennedy Bridge Rd. Built 1777. On site of original Bowman Fort.

Burford Hill — Harrodsburg, at end of N. Greenville St. County's best example of Georgian style architecture. Has escaped architectural alterations.

Cardwellton — Harrodsburg, 103 N. Broadway. circa 1830-37. Constructed around a log cabin. Early Greek Revival architecture. Now privately owned.

Clay Hill — Harrodsburg, 433 Beaumont Ave. circa 1790-1812. Birthplace of Beriah Magoffin, Jr., 21st Governor of Kentucky. Georgian mansion. One of the county's most magnificent structures. Now privately owned.

Diamond Point — Harrodsburg, College St. and Price Ave. Built 1819. Off-center doorway is unusual in Greek Revival style. New Orleans influence.

Doricham — Harrodsburg, 409 N. College St. circa 1835-39. Originally owned by Daniel Stagg. Once home of Terah T. Haggin, father of multi-millionaire James Ben Ali Haggin. Georgian and Greek Revival style. Now privately owned.

Fair Oaks — Harrodsburg, 712 Beaumont Ave. circa 1840-45. Battenburg grille on second story; side galleries unique in Kentucky architecture. Built by Dr. Guilford Runyon, former member of Shaker colony, for his bride-to-be. She died before they could marry.

Glenworth — E. of Harrodsburg, Buster Pike. Built 1848. Greek Revival structure with slave quarters, ice house, barns and other outbuildings. Property has connections with Rachel Robards, wife of Andrew Jack-

Shakertown at Pleasant Hill.

Centre Family Dwelling House at Shakertown.

son. Exists today as when it was built. Now privately owned.

Lincoln Marriage Temple — Harrodsburg, Old Fort Harrod State Park. US-127. Cabin in which Abraham Lincoln's parents were married. Transferred to the Park from original site on Beech Fork of Salt River in 1911.

Lynnwood — 5 mi. E. of Harrodsburg. KY-33. Built 1850, by A. H. Bowman. Example of country estate manor house.

Millwood — N. of Harrodsburg on banks of Salt River. Built late 1700's. Home of Daniel Brewer, pioneer. Still occupied by same family.

Morgan Row — Harrodsburg, Chiles St. Built in 1807 by Squire Joseph Morgan. Unique four-unit 2-story row house which is the oldest one of its kind in the state. This type of architectural construction is rare west of the Allegheny Mountains. Early social and business center.

James McAfee House — Near McAfee, Talmadge Rd. Built in 1790 by the oldest McAfee brother, one of first settlers in county. One of the three oldest stone houses still standing in area.

Samuel McAfee House — Near McAfee, N.W. of Harrodsburg. Built 1774. Log and stone house. Originally home of Samuel McAfee, one of county's first settlers.

Old Mud Meeting House — Near Harrodsburg, on Dry Branch Rd. Off US-68. Built 1800. Public shrine to the Dutch Reform church which came to Mercer County as early as 1787. Original construction was handhewn logs with mud and straw daubing. National historic landmark.

Round Ridge — Harrodsburg, Moberly Road. Built 1817. House and outbuildings owned by Joseph Morgan, member of early community. Morgan's descendants still occupy home and farm. On site of old McAfee Fort. Now privately owned.

Shakertown — Pleasant Hill 6 mi. N.E. of Harrodsburg. US-68E. Restoration of a religious colony which flourished from 1805 until 1912 and developed many modern concepts of farming, packaged seeds for sale, shipped produce as far as New Orleans, built remarkable stone and brick buildings which are still standing. One of nation's outstanding restorations of early American life.

Shawnee Springs — Near Harrodsburg, Curry Rd. circa 1788-92. Originally home of Col. George Thompson. Unusual brick arcade in the Italian style.

179

Woods House — Harrodsburg, 129 N. East St. circa 1820's by Archibald Woods, original owner. Occupied by same family. Stands within 50 yards of the site at which Harrod built cabins in 1774.

OTHER POINTS OF INTEREST

Kentucky Palisades — Mercer/Jessamine County line, Valley of the Kentucky River. US-68. Rugged walls of gray limestone rise 300 feet from river to the plain above. One of the most beautiful views in the Middle West.

Pioneer Red Arrow Tour — Harrodsburg, Lexington St. Chamber of Commerce. Guide to a driving tour listing 49 points of interest.

Shakertown at Plesant Hill — Plesant Hill, 7 mi. from Harrodsburg. US-68. This quaint village and surrounding farmland once owned by a religious sect, the Shakers, who flourished from about 1810-1910. Village has been completely renovated and restored. Contains a museum, inn, restaurant, and shops. Open to public.

Fort Harrod State Park in Harrodsburg.

Woodford County

Woodford County was formed from Fayette County in 1788, and was the last of the nine counties created by Virginia before Kentucky became a separate state. It was named in honor of General William Woodford, an officer in the Revolutionary War.

Versailles, the county seat of Woodford County, was laid out on May 13, 1793, on 80 acres of land. General Marquis Calmes, one of the town's founders, named it after the city of Versailles, France, as a tribute to that country for its help during the Revolution. Previously, the settlement was known to the pioneers as "Falling Spring" because of the large stream that gushed from a hearty cavern. The stream still runs with its original vigor and falls into Big Spring Park. Versailles is one of Kentucky's oldest towns, and Woodford County is known as "The Asparagus Bed of the Bluegrass" due to its extremely fertile soil. For several years Woodford County citizens have been preserving and restoring public buildings and homes.

The town of Midway was planned and built largely through the efforts of the L & N Railroad. The town streets are, in fact, named for members of the railroad company's board of directors in the 1840's. The name Midway refers to General Francisco's log house built here in 1795, midway between Lexington and Frankfort. Many of the houses and buildings date from 1840 to 1890 and most have been either well kept or recently restored.

FAIRS, FESTIVALS

International Dinner and Program — Midway, Midway College. US-62. October.

May Day Program — Midway, Midway College. US-62. May.

Woodford County Fair — Woodford County High School. June.

PARKS

Big Spring Park — Versailles, on Park St. Behind Methodist Church.

Versailles Historical Park — Versailles, S. Main St. Honors eight Civil War generals.

MARKERS

Morgan's First Raid — Versailles. US-60, US-62. Describes CSA Gen. John H. Morgan's first Kentucky raid. Covered 1,000 miles in 24 days, raiding 17 towns.

Morgan at Midway — Midway. US-62 at railroad. Morgan took 300 abandoned Union horses and mules at Versailles and came here July 15, 1862. Attempted to abort approach of Union troop train.

"Sue Mundy" Here — Midway. US-62. Relates guerrilla action of Jerome Clarke, called "Sue Mundy," who formed his own guerrilla band after Gen. John Hunt Morgan's death. September, 1864.

MEMORIALS AND MUSEUMS

General Marquis Calmes Tomb — E. of Versailles, Payne's Mill Rd. Founder of Versailles, built and erected tomb himself.

Old Taylor Distillery and Museum — Millville. KY-1659. Oldest bonded warehouse in the world. Constructed of the lovely pink brick for which Kentucky is famous.

Buckley Wildlife Sanctuary.

Midway College Library.

CEMETERIES

Pisgah Cemetery — Versailles, Pisgah Pike, 3/4 mi. off US-60. Flat tombs of pioneer ancestors of citizens in the neighborhood, and 5 Revolutionary War soldiers.

OLD BUILDINGS

Adam Childers House — Versailles, Morgan St. circa 1835. Greek Revival style, with unique portico. The Woodford County Board of Education is located in this building and the school Superintendent's office is in the adjacent building, the former slave quarters.

Airy Mount — Versailles, McCowan's Ferry Rd. circa 1790-1800. Second brick house built in Kentucky. Built by Col. William Fields, a Revolutionary War officer from Culpepper, Virginia. This is one of three houses in Woodford County with murals painted on the plastered walls by the traveling muralist, William Cohen.

Baptist Meeting House — Versailles, Rose Hill. circa 1820. First church in Versailles. Being restored by the Historical Society.

Buck Pond — 1 1/2 mi. E. of Versailles, Payne's Mill Rd. circa 1783. Originally the home of Col. Thomas Marshall, hero of the Battle of Brandywine and father of U. S. Chief Justice John Marshall.

Carter House — Versailles, 110 Morgan St. circa 1790-1820. One of the oldest brick houses in Versailles. Doctor Carter's family lived here when it was so near the Indians' trail that a little cousin was kidnapped by the Cherokees. Four years later she was rescued.

Cleveland House — Versailles, Morgan St. Built 1854. Federal-style house with Palladian windows and a fan-lighted door.

Crittenden Cabin — E. of Versailles. US-60. Built 1782, land owned by the Methodist Home. Birthplace of John J. Crittenden, Governor of Kentucky, and U. S. Attorney General.

Edgewood — near Versailles. US-60. 1 1/2-story house built in 1810 by Joel DuPuy. The bricks laid in Flemish bond throughout were fired on the place. A double door with fan and side lights opens off the front porch. Over the porch is an unusual Palladian window, the side lights of which are diamond-shaped panes. Much of the original hand-blown glass is retained.

Guyn House — Buffalo Springs Farm — 1 mi. from Troy. KY-33. The original four rooms of this stone house were built in 1802 by Thomas Hogan. The 1/2-story wing was built in 1827. The walls of the dining room and kitchen are of solid cherry. Buffalo Springs Farm was so named since buffalo came to drink from the 3 springs at the foot of the hill.

Jack Jouett House — Versailles, Craig's Mill Pike, off McCowan's Ferry Rd. circa 1792. Home of Capt. Jack Jouett, famed for the night ride to save Thomas Jefferson from capture by the British.

Mundy's Landing — Mundy's Landing Rd. KY-33. In 1847 John Mundy built a large white clapboard house. At the height of steamboat travel on the Kentucky River, he opened his house as a tavern, and Mundy's Landing became one of the most popular stopping places on the river.

Offutt Inn — Cole's Tavern — Jct. US-62 and Old Frankfort-Lexington Pike. circa 1780. Originally the home of the Lee family; later operated as a fashionable inn and stagecoach tavern by Horatio Offutt, then by Richard Cole. Many political meetings and rallies were held here in the antebellum days by and for noted politicians of the period.

Old Moss House — S. of Versailles, McCowan's Ferry Pike. KY-1964. circa 1812-1816. Two-story brick

Welcome Hall near Versailles.

house with a wing on the right and a detached stone kitchen. Owned at one time by Henry Clay.

Pisgah Presbyterian Church — E. of Versailles, Pisgah Pike. Off US-60. circa 1813. Pioneer church organized in 1784. Pisgah was the site of Kentucky Academy opened in 1797. The stone building was remodeled in 1868 with arched windows and other Gothic features.

Stone Castle — Woodford County, on Clear Creek. 1 mi. off KY-33. Built late 1700's. An example of early stone architecture.

Stonewall — Woodford County. US-62. Built 1830's. Originally the home of James Coleman, then later of Warren Viley, Thoroughbred horse breeder.

Stoney Lonesome — Woodford County, Grier's Creek Rd. circa 1784. Early stone house; originally owned by Joel DuPuy, gristmill operator.

Lewis Sublett Log House — Woodford County, McCowan's Ferry Pike. circa 1780. The front of the house is 2-story with chimneys. A dog trot connects the house to the kitchen. Location was partially determined by its nearness to water. The remnants of the old springhouse still stand. Many descendants of Lewis Sublett still live in Woodford County.

Sycamore Park — E. of Versailles, Shannon Run Rd. KY-1967, 2 mi. from US-60. In 1828 the brick house was built in front of the more ancient stone dwelling.

Thornton House — Versailles, 200 Morgan St. Built in 1821 by David Thornton, first president of the Woodford Bank and Trust Co. Federal Style, 1 1/2-story house. The slave quarters in the yard and the cutting garden have been restored.

Waverly — Woodford County, Frankfort-Versailles Pike. US-60. Built 1837. A Federal Style house which is quite extensive due to several additions. Slave quarters, meat house and storage cellar are in the side yard.

Welcome Hall — 5 mi. W. of Versailles, Clifton Rd. KY-1964. circa 1795. This fine home is one of the oldest in Kentucky. In 1790 the rock for the 24-inch walls was quarried on the farm for the 2-story central portion of the house. The right and left wings were added later, in 1806 and 1816.

Weisenberger Mill — near Midway, at S. Elkhorn Creek. US-421. Meal and flour mill operated since 1865.

Woodburn — Woodford County, Old Frankfort Pike (Shady Lane). KY-1681. Located on one of the most beautiful roads in the state, the main part of this house was built in 1800 by Dr. Alex J. Alexander, who bred the first Thoroughbred horse in Kentucky. The famous Thoroughbred, Lexington, was bred at Woodburn, as well as many other famous horses. The Alexanders were well known doctors in early Kentucky history, and succeeding generations of Alexanders have added onto the house which has often been called one of the most magnificent country estates in the U. S.

Wyndehurst — Woodford County, McCowan's Ferry Rd. Built in 1790 by Gen. James McConnell. Now known as Wyndehurst. Georgian architecture. There are several murals on the walls painted by William Cohen.

OTHER POINTS OF INTEREST

Clyde E. Buckley Wildlife Sanctuary — Northwestern corner of Little Germany. Germany Rd. From US-60 follow KY-1659 to KY-1964. 285 acres of Kentucky hill land overlooking bluffs of the Kentucky River. Operated by the National Audubon Society in cooperation with the Buckley Hills Audubon Society. Trail walks, bird-watch house.

Midway — Railroad Street — Between Lexington and Frankfort off Leestown Pike. I-64. Both sides of railroad street are lined with shops, boutiques and dining places in buildings restored by their owners since 1972. The quaint city hall has a lovely iron stairway on the side.

Midway College — N. of Versailles. US-62. Historical college for women founded in 1847 and is affiliated with Disciples of Christ Church.

Thornton House near Versailles.

Bluegrass Area

Bourbon County

In 1785, Bourbon County was formed from territory of the Fayette district and was the fifth county in order of formation in Kentucky. Bourbon County was named for the House of Bourbon to honor French assistance in the Revolutionary War. Bourbon County abounds with examples of early Kentucky architecture. Many fine examples of log, frame and stone houses are found in the county, as are lovely country manor homes.

Paris, the county seat, received its name from the French capital city. The first court was held at Mt. Lebanon, at the home of James Garrard on Tuesday, May 16, 1786. At this time, the first county government was formed.

Bourbon County is the namesake for the world's largest selling whiskey, as it is the county where bourbon was first created. Bourbon County also boasts of some of the most fertile land in the world.

FAIRS AND FESTIVALS

Bourbon County Fair — Paris. Art show. Usually held the 4th week in July.

Paris-Bourbon County Home-a-Rama — Paris, Normandy Place Shopping Center. Sponsored by the newspaper, *Paris Daily Enterprise.* Involves art exhibits, crafts, tours of homes, ideas for leisure living, and Blessing of the Arts. Held during summer months.

Tours of Homes and Gardens — Paris and Millersburg. May.

PARKS

Garrard Park — Paris, off E. Main St. 30-acre picnic area and playground.

MARKERS

Birthplace of John Fox, Jr. — 6 mi. from Paris, Winchester Rd. KY-627. Author of *The Little Shepherd of Kingdom Come.*

Edward Boone — Paris, on the farm of Carl Calvert on the See Pike. Original resting place for Edward Boone, who was killed by Indians in 1780 while hunting with his brother, Daniel, along the banks of Boone's Creek. Inscription on marker: Edward Boone, Virginia Militia, Revolutionary War. Remains are now in Rock Bridge Graveyard, 1 mi. from the Levy. KY-57.

Hopewell — Paris, on banks of Houston Creek near the 2nd St. Bridge. Hopewell was the original name of Paris and was established in 1789. The name was changed to Paris in 1790.

Martin's Fort — 3 mi. from Paris, Cynthiana Rd. US-27. Established in 1779 by John Martin. It was destroyed by the Indians and British in 1780. Cooper's Run Meeting House was built on this site.

McGuffey's Readers — Paris, High St. Located by the 1-room school where William Holmes McGuffey, compiler of the famous McGuffey Reader, taught from 1823-1836.

Mt. Gilead — Paris, Millersburg Rd. Site of first Methodist church in 1792.

Ruddell's Mills — Bourbon County. KY-1940. Near his home, Isaac Ruddell built a gristmill in 1788, and a sawmill in 1795. A cotton mill was erected in 1828.

MUSEUMS

Duncan Tavern (1788) and Anne Duncan House (1801) — Paris, Courthouse Square. Historical and genealogical libraries are housed at the Tavern, as well as manuscripts of John Fox, Jr., author of *The Little Shepherd of Kingdom Come.* Anne Duncan house has fine antique furnishings.

CEMETERIES

Banta Graveyard — Little Rock. KY-536. Burial place of Henry Banta, who fought in the American Revolution, and of his son Peter, who fought in the War of 1812.

Cane Ridge — 6 mi. E. of Paris. KY-536. Where Barton W. Stone and some of his family are buried. On grounds of Cane Ridge Shrine.

Paris Cemetery — Paris, Main St. Where author John Fox, Jr. is buried.

OLD BUILDINGS

Cane Ridge Meeting House and Shrine — 6 mi. E. of Paris. KY-536. Built before 1791. In Aug. 1801, this was the site of the "Great Revival" with preachers of many denominations participating. On June 28, 1804, Barton W. Stone and his colleagues made the first united plea on American soil for the union of the followers of Christ. Thus was born the older of 2 movements for Christian unity known as the "Christian Church" or the "Disciples of Christ". The "Great Revival" was attended by 20,000 to 30,000 persons. The original structure is now sheltered inside a new stone building.

Clark's Run — Near Paris, Hume Bedford Rd. Built 1784. Early log house with portholes. Originally the home of Robert Clark, and served as place of refuge from Indians.

Duncan Tavern — Paris, 323 High St. Built 1788. It is state headquarters for the Daughters of the American Revolution. Originally a tavern operated by Maj. Joseph Duncan. One of the best preserved buildings of its period. Daily tours.

The Grange — 4 mi. N. of Paris. US-68. Built in 1818 by Edward Stone, an early slave dealer. From a structural standpoint, one of the most beautiful homes in Kentucky.

Johnston's Inn — 5 mi. W. of Paris. KY-227, US-460. Built in late 1700's. Famous stopping place for trav-

Duncan Tavern in Paris.

elers from Limestone (now Maysville) to Lexington. Inn was operated as a tavern by Robert Johnston, Revolutionary War captain, and his wife in 1796-1812.

Little Rock Christian Church — 12 mi. from Paris. KY-536. Formerly Flat Rock. Organized in 1851, and present building was constructed in 1878.

Millersburg Military Institute — Millersburg. US-68. Founded in 1893. Fully accredited college preparatory school, grades 6-12.

Mt. Lebanon — 3 mi. N. of Paris, Peacock Pike. Built before 1785. Home of James Garrard, second Governor of Kentucky.

Paris Courthouse — Paris. Occupied June 1, 1905. The original court records are preserved here dating back to the founding of the County of Bourbon in 1785. Priceless books and documents are also found here, including the marriage record of Simon Kenton to Martha Dowden on May 16, 1787. A memorial tablet containing the names of 156 citizens of Bourbon County who gave their lives in the American Revolution is also housed here.

Aaron Smedley House — Paris, Main St. Built before 1805. One of the 2 oldest houses in Paris.

Jacob Spears Distillery — Near Paris, Clay-Kiser Rd. circa 1800. Early distillery owned by Jacob Spears, who used charcoal in the distilling process earlier than had been generally believed.

Stephens-Davis House — Paris, 902 Pleasant St. Built 1821-1822. Original owner of house, Robert Baylor, was a member of the family that founded Baylor University in Texas.

Trabue House and Barn — Trabue Lane, near Ruddell's Mill Rd. Built 1785. Log house and barn originally owned by James Trabue. Daniel Boone helped to build the barn.

Cane Ridge Meeting House and Shrine near Paris.

OTHER POINTS OF INTEREST

Old Colville Covered Bridge — S. of Millersburg, at Hinkston Creek. 11 mi. from Paris on the Colville Rd. Off US-68. Built 1877. Wood covered bridge still in use. One of 16 left in state.

Claiborne Farm — Paris, Winchester Rd. KY-627. Present home of the stallion Secretariat, Triple-Crown winner in 1974. Considered the largest Thoroughbred breeding farm in the world. Private farm.

Golden Chance Farm — 6 mi. from Paris, on N. Middletown Rd. US-460. Former home of Dust Commander, Kentucky Derby winner in 1970, and sire of Master Derby, winner of Bluegrass Stakes, Louisiana Derby, and Preakness in 1975.

There are many other well-known horse farms in Bourbon County. The 2 named above have produced or now house former Kentucky Derby winner. A very well-known horse hospital is located at Sunnyside Farm on the Cynthiana Rd. US-27.

Cane Ridge Meeting House.

State Garden Club Headquarters — Paris, Pleasant St.

Paris Fine Arts Center — Paris, 7th and Houston St. Community programs.

Clark County

Clark County was named for General George Rogers Clark, the Revolutionary War hero and famous explorer of the Northwest Territory. The county was established by act of the second session of the Kentucky General Assembly at Lexington in 1792. This makes Clark County the same age as the Commonwealth of Kentucky.

Winchester, the county seat, was established by an act of the General Assembly in 1793, and was named for the town of Winchester in Frederick County, Virginia, which was the former home of John Baker, the founder of Winchester, Kentucky.

Many of the original settlers came from Frederick County, Virginia. Long before white settlers came to this area, it was a crossroads of Indian warrior's trails.

FAIRS, FESTIVALS, DRAMAS

Clark County Fair — 4 mi. from Winchester. KY-15. Second week in July.

Children's Theater — Winchester. January.

Legal Secretaries Variety Show — Winchester. May.

Clark County-Winchester Minstrel Show — Winchester. Sponsored by Lions Club for sight conservation. Local talent. April.

PARKS

Community Park — Winchester, Friendship Dr. Near US-60. This is a 3-4 acre park with facilities for swimming, basketball, badminton, and picnicking.

MARKERS

Morgan's Men Here — Winchester, Courthouse yard. US-60, KY-227. Traces movement of CSA Gen. John H. Morgan's Raiders as they came through this area during raids in Kentucky.

Rare 1860 Tombstones — 3 mi. S. of Winchester. US-60. In the burial ground, 1/4 mi. E., are 2 rare Carrara marble tombstones carved in Italy by Joel Tanner Hart, Kentucky's world-renowned sculptor and poet.

Sculptor's Birthplace — 1 mi. E. of Winchester. US-60. Birthplace of Joel Tanner Hart.

Strode Station — 1 mi. W. of Winchester. US-60. Stagecoach stop. Founded by settlers from Boonesboro in 1779, and led by Capt. John Strode. This station was the most important fortified area in Clark County to early settlers during Indian wars.

MEMORIALS

Indian Old Fields — 11 mi. S.E. of Winchester, Iron Works Pike. KY-15. Site of "Eskippakithiki," located on the Warrior's Path. This meeting place for traders and Indian hunters was the last of the Kentucky Indian towns. Occupied by the Shawnees circa 1715-1754. John Finley had a store here and traded with the Indians in 1752. Daniel Boone viewed "the beautiful level of Kentucky" from this point on June 7, 1769.

CEMETERIES

East Broadway Cemetery — Winchester. US-227. First cholera epidemic in U. S. reached here. There were 75 victims buried here in 1833. Epidemic caused town trustees to purchase this acre for public burial ground. Maintained as a memorial to that tragedy.

Thacker Cemetery — 12 mi. E. of Winchester.

Winchester Cemetery — Winchester. US-60. Old grave sites.

OLD BUILDINGS

Athlone Hall — Winchester, Winn Ave. KY-15. Built 1855. Home of James Halley. Architectural example.

Gen. Thomas Barbee House — Winchester, 115 S. Main St. Built 1804.

Caveland — Near Winchester, Jones Nursery Rd. Built 1797. Home of Richard Hickman, one of the first trustees of Winchester, member of the 1799 Constitutional Convention, member of the Kentucky Legislature, Lt. Gov. of Kentucky. He was acting governor while Governor Isaac Shelby led troops during War of 1812.

Clark County Courthouse — Winchester, S. Main St. Built 1853-1855. Considered one of the most beautiful courthouses in the state. Henry Clay made his first and last public speech here. Houses some of the oldest documents in Kentucky.

Colbyville Tavern — 5 mi. W. of Winchester, Colby Rd. Built 1821. Famous stagecoach stop of antebellum days. In 1832, President Andrew Jackson visited here on trip to Winchester.

Croxton House — Winchester, Lexington Rd. Built 1820. Architectural example.

Hart House — Near Winchester, Ecton Rd. Built 1800. Home of Gen. Thomas Hart, member of Kentucky Legislature, who helped lay out town of Winchester when area was enlarged in 1831.

William Hickman House — Winchester, corner of W. Hickman and Maple Sts. Built 1814. Was originally a tavern. Seen by appointment.

Holly Rood — Winchester, S. Burns Ave. Built 1813. Home of James Clark, 12th Governor of Kentucky. Most historic house in Clark County.

Holmhurst, Goff House — Near Winchester, Van Meter Rd. Built 1840. Architectural example.

Dr. Andrew Hood House — Winchester, French Ave. Built 1830.

George Rogers Clark High School in Winchester.

Martin House — Near Winchester, Basin Springs Pike. Built 1791 by Maj. John Martin, Revolutionary War soldier. It was later owned by his son, Dr. Samuel Martin, early Winchester physician. Oldest house in county.

Old Stone Meeting House — 6 mi. S. of Winchester, on Howard's Creek. Off KY-627. Built 1792. In terms of continuous worship, this is the oldest church west of the Appalachians. Place of worship for Daniel Boone and his family.

Spring Hill — Near Winchester, Todds Rd. Pine Grove. Built 1788-1790. Home of Hubbard Taylor, member of 1792 State Constitutional Convention, member of first Kentucky legislature, and State Senator.

Samuel Taylor House — Winchester, 315 S. Maple St. Built 1809. Originally home of Samuel Taylor, County Court clerk.

Capt. John Tramel House — Winchester, 26 W. Hickman St. Built 1834.

Vinewood — 4 1/2 mi. E. of Winchester, Mt. Sterling Rd. Built 1860 by Benjamin Groom, well-known cattle breeder. Replica of 19th century English manor house.

Welcome Hall — Winchester, Van Meter Rd. Built 1833. Home of Thomas Moore, a man quite popular in the county's early social life. Recently restored.

OTHER POINTS OF INTEREST

Bwamazon Horse Farm — S. side of Winchester. Has bred several Kentucky Derby contenders. Visitors invited.

Ride to the Hounds — 8 mi. W. of Winchester. Iroquois Hunt Club. Rides held on Pursley farm on Coomes Ferry Pike. Late October and November.

Estill County

In 1808, Estill County was taken from Madison and Clark Counties and named for Captain James Estill, one of the bravest of Kentucky's pioneers. Estill County became a popular center for settlers. Captain Estill was killed at Estill's Defeat, a fierce battle with the Indians in March of 1782. A statue of him now tops a monument erected in his honor in the Richmond, Kentucky Cemetery, and is considered the state's most accurate figure of a Kentucky pioneer.

For nearly eighty years, a resort known as Estill Springs drew the most fashionable and distinguished persons from all over Kentucky and the East. At that time, it was generally believed that the pure, foul-smelling water was conducive to good health. Local residents still take advantage of the accessibility of the Springs. About one-half of Estill County's area is situated in Daniel Boone National Forest, making it quite a scenic area that is popular with vacationers and sight-seers.

FAIRS

Estill County Fair and Horse Show — Irvine. KY-89. Usually first week of August.

PARKS, RECREATION, LAKES

Cottage Furnace Recreation Area — Located in Daniel Boone National Forest.

Daniel Boone National Forest — KY-52, KY-89. Leads into the National Forest, which covers half the county.

Kiwanis Memorial Park — Irvine. KY-89. Tennis courts, playground.

U. S. Locks on Kentucky River — E. of Ravenna. 1/4 mi. W. of Jct. KY-1571 and Old Pike. On Kentucky River. Features beaches, as well as swimming and picnic areas.

MARKERS

Estill Springs — 1/2 mi. N. of Irvine. KY-89. Known as Sweet Springs, these mineral springs drew distinguished persons for nearly 80 years. The hotel was the oldest summer resort in the state. Built in 1845 the hotel was destroyed by fire in 1924. The original springhouse was built in 1846.

Irvine — Irvine, Courthouse yard. Honors Col. William Irvine, who sought separation from Virginia and statehood for Kentucky.

CEMETERIES

Station Camp Cemetery and Church — Station Camp. KY-594. Graves of famous persons of Civil War.

OLD BUILDINGS

Cottage Furnace — Union Hall Community, Marbleyard Rd. KY-52E., KY-213. From 1830 to the close of the Civil War, Estill County was a great iron producing and manufacturing county. Cottage Furnace, named because it has the appearance of a stone cottage, stands hidden in the wilderness of Estill County near the community of Marbleyard. Constructed of massive blocks of native stones, it stands about 25-ft. square and 35-ft. high.

Fitchburg Furnace — Fitchburg. Built 1858. Last iron furnace built in Estill County, and it was considered the largest in the world at the time it was built.

Col. Henry Clay Lily House — Irvine, 208 Broadway. Built 1859. Circuit judge and lawyer who organized the 14th Cavalry Regiment in the Civil War.

Station Camp Christian Church — S. on Station Camp Creek. KY-594. Built 180 years ago. Daniel Boone spent his first winter in Kentucky here in 1769-1770.

Capt. John Wilson House — Station Camp. Built 1846. Wilson was a captain during the Civil War for the Union Army. In 1863, he led the group which planted the American flag at the peak of Lookout Mountain.

Fitchburg Furnace.

OTHER POINTS OF INTEREST

Aldersgate Youth Camp — Fitchburg, near Fitchburg Furnace. KY-52, KY-975. The 190 acres adjacent to the furnace property have been purchased by the Board of Education, Kentucky Conference of the Methodist Church, and a church camp was established. The camp is situated across the highway from the furnace at the foot of the mountain range.

Red Lick Valley — On KY-594. Scenic valley that was the first section of the county to be settled by pioneers from Berea, Kentucky.

L&N Railroad Station at Ravenne.

Fayette County

In 1780, Fayette County was one of the three original counties formed when Kentucky County, Virginia was divided. It then included thirty-seven present-day counties and parts of seven others. The present boundaries were established in 1799. Fayette County was named in honor of the French General Lafayette, an aide to General George Washington in the American Revolution.

Lexington, the county seat of Fayette County, was named on June 4, 1775, although not officially founded until 1780. A group of young men including John Maxwell, Levi Todd, John McCracken, Hugh Shannon, Isaac Greer, James Dunkin, William McConnell and a few others were discussing what name should be given to the city they were planning on this beautiful site. John Maxwell, recalling the exciting news just received of the Battle of Lexington and the beginning of the American Revolution, said "Let us call our city, Lexington, in memory of the first blood shed for liberty."

FAIRS, FESTIVALS, DRAMAS, EXHIBITS

Antiques Fair — Lexington, 847 S. Broadway. Red Mile Trotting Track. Exhibits by area antique dealers. Sponsored by Fayette County Medical Auxiliary.

Blessings of the Hounds — Near Lexington, at Grimes Mill. Sponsored by the Iroquois Hunt Club. An Episcopal Bishop invokes the blessing of St. Hubert, patron saint of the chase. Marks the beginning of the hunting season. First Saturday in November.

Bluegrass Fair — Lexington, Masterson Station Park. US-421. Midway, exhibits, entertainment. July.

Bluegrass National Open Sheep Dog Trails — Walnut Hall Farm, Newtown Pike. US-460. June.

Canterbury Pilgrim Playhouse — Lexington, Rose St. Community theater presents quality performances to central Kentucky residents.

Carrick Theater — Lexington. Transylvania University campus, Mitchell Fine Arts Center. Presents 3 major productions and 3 studio productions per year.

Central Kentucky Youth Symphony Orchestra and Concert Orchestra — Lexington. Comprised of young students representing 15 counties in the central Kentucky area. Local concerts annually.

Diners Playhouse — Lexington, 434 Interstate Ave. Features a buffet dinner and a play.

Guignol Theater — Lexington, Rose St. University of Kentucky campus, Fine Arts Building. Theater for University of Kentucky dramatic arts students. Seasonal performances.

Junior League Horse Show — Lexington, 847 S. Broadway. Red Mile Trotting Track. World's largest outdoor horse show for American Saddlebreds. Proceeds to charity. Held each year in July.

Lexington Children's Theater — Lexington. Transylvania University. Presents productions for and by children of central Kentucky.

Lexington Philharmonic Orchestra — Lexington, at the Opera House. Gives a series of 6 concert-pairs. October-April.

Lexington Singers, Inc. — Lexington. A community chorus formed in 1959. Christmas, Spring, and Pops concerts.

Horse Farm Tour — Lexington. Motor-coach tour of 5 horse farms and houses of interest. Sponsored by Suburban Woman's Club. Four-hour tour on Saturday and Sunday. Latter part of June.

The Opera House — Lexington, 145 N. Broadway. Opera house, renovated 1886. Showcase for the arts. In 19th century, contributed to Lexington's designation as "Athens of the West".

Shrine Circus — Lexington. Red Mile Trotting Track. August.

Studio Players — Lexington, Bell Carriage House on Bell Court. Community theater. Open to all.

Tours of Homes and Gardens — Lexington. May.

Vine Street Horse Race and Arts and Crafts Fair — Lexington, Vine St. Parade, race, street dance, arts and crafts exhibits. Sponsored by Historic Commission. Held during spring or summer.

PARKS

Cheapside Park — Lexington, Cheapside off Main St. Throughout the years, Cheapside has been an open-air forum for the opinions of politicians. Site of John C. Breckinridge statue.

Gratz Park — Historic Area of Lexington, named after a Jewish family that helped finance the American Revolution. Original site of Transylvania University campus.

Kentucky Horse Farm Park — Lexington, Iron Works Pike. Purchased by the state for use as a park, this land retains the features of the famed Thoroughbred farms.

Shillito Park — Lexington, off Reynolds Rd. Recreational facilities and picnic areas.

Jacobson Park — Lexington, off Richmond Rd. Water sport facilities, golf course and sheltered picnic facilities.

MARKERS

A Founder of D.A.R. — Lexington, Maxwell and Mill Sts. Mary Desha (1850-1911), a Lexington native, was one of 4 founders of the Daughters of American Revolution in 1890. She taught public school here.

Alanant-O-Wamiowee (Warrior's Trace) — Lexington, N. Limestone. Ancient buffalo trace carved by prehistoric animals seeking salt. Later used by buffaloes, mound builders, Indians and pioneers.

Architects Shryock — Lexington, 149 N. Broadway. Family home of Matthias Shryock and his son Gideon, who shared the best known surname in Kentucky architecture.

Boone's Station — Fayette County, Athens-Boonesboro Rd. Established in 1779 by Daniel Boone who resided there several years with his family.

John Breckinridge — Lexington, Courthouse yard, Main St. One of 4 Kentuckians who was Vice President of U. S. — more than any other state except New York.

Bryan's Station — 5 mi. N. of Lexington, Bryan's Station Pike. A fortified station occupied by the Bryan brothers, who repelled a seige by Indians and Canadians. Mary Boone, Daniel Boone's sister, and a group of other ladies, carried water to the station, fooling the Indians until help could arrive from Lexington.

First Race Course — Lexington, S. Broadway. Established 1780 near this spot by pioneers as starting point of the first race path in Kentucky.

Ashland in Lexington.

Lexington and Ohio R.R. — 3 mi. N.W. of Lexington. US-421. Built 1833-1834. Site of first railroad west of the Alleghenies.

Mary Todd Lincoln — Lexington, 501 Short St. On this site, Mary Todd, wife of Abraham Lincoln, was born Dec. 13, 1818, and spent her childhood here.

Samuel Boone — Fayette County, Athens-Boonesboro Rd. Grave of Samuel Boone (1728-1816), eldest brother of Daniel Boone. Settled Boone's Station.

Site of First Kentucky Legislature — Lexington. US-421. The 2 sessions were held Monday, June 4 and Monday, November 5, 1792.

Wing Commander — Lexington, Jct. Iron Works Rd. and Mt. Horeb Rd. KY-1973. Famous 5-gaited saddle horse. Undefeated for 7 years (1948-1954). Won over 200 championships in 9 years of competition. Defeated only twice. Trained and owned by Earl Teater.

MEMORIALS AND MUSEUMS

Man O' War Memorial Park — Fayette County. Kentucky Horse Park, Iron Works Rd. Lexington's most popular tourist attraction. Large statue and burial plot dedicated to the great Thoroughbred who broke many track records 1919-1920. "The horse of the century."

The Headley Museum — Lexington, La Belle Farm, Old Frankfort Pike. Unique, non-profit museum housing jeweled bibelots, oriental porcelains, the famous Fleischmann art collection, a collection of rare and unusual shells, as well as a fine art book collection.

Kentucky Life Museum and Waveland State Shrine — S. of Lexington, Higbee Mill Pike. Off US-27. Gives a total picture of Kentucky life from pioneer days through the period of plantations to more recent times. Restored mansion.

Doctors Park Art Gallery — Lexington, S. Limestone. Changing exhibits with a reception held the first Sunday of each month from 3 to 5 p.m.

University Gallery — Lexington. University of Kentucky campus, Fine Arts Building. Rose St. Art Exhibits.

Living Arts and Sciences Center — Lexington, 362 Walnut St. Open Monday through Saturday from 10 a.m. to 4 p.m.

Lexington Public Library Gallery — Lexington. 2nd and Mill Sts. Provides programs in art, science, drama, photography, and film making for young people. Changing monthly exhibits year round.

Bryan's Station Monument-1896 — 5 mi. N. of Lexington, Bryan Station Pike. KY-1970. Erected by the Daughters of the American Revolution to commemorate the deeds of the women of Bryan's Station that made possible the defense of the station under Indian attack, 1782.

Henry Clay Memorial — Lexington Cemetery, W. Main St. Erected 1857. A single Corinthian column supporting a statue of Clay. Within the base of the monument are the sarcophagi of Clay and his wife.

CEMETERIES

Lexington Cemetery — Lexington, 833 W. Main St. Known nationwide for its beautiful gardens, as well as being the burial place of Henry Clay, James Lane Allen, and King Solomon, who was the hero of the cholera plague of 1883.

Lexington's Westminster Abbey — Lexington, E. 3rd St. between Walnut and Deweese Sts. Local name for several old cemeteries dating from 1830's.

Keeneland Race Track in Lexington.

OLD BUILDINGS

Adam Rankin House — Lexington, 317 S. Mill St. Built in 1784, for Adam Rankin, pioneer minister. Oldest house in Lexington. In 1971, house was moved from original location on High St. to prevent its destruction.

Ashland — Lexington, Richmond Rd. circa 1857. Now a national shrine. This was the estate of Henry Clay, statesman, politician, and diplomat. Includes a 20-room mansion and lovely surrounding grounds.

Fairfield — Near Lexington, Iron Works Rd. circa 1788. Originally the home of pioneer editor John Bradford, founder of the first newspaper west of the Alleghenies.

Grimes House — 9 mi. E. of Lexington, on Grimes Mill Rd. Built 1813. Finest stone house in county. Owned by Iroquois Hunt Club.

Henry Clay's Law Office — Lexington, 176 N. Mill St. Built 1803. Used as law office by Henry Clay until 1810. Believed to be the only remaining early 19th century professional office building in downtown Lexington. Recently restored.

Historic North Side — Lexington. Many beautiful old homes comprising a wide range of architectural styles may be seen. Between 2nd and 3rd Sts. and bounded by Mill and Market Sts. is Gratz Park, bordered by homes reminiscent of the days Lexington was known as the "Athens of the West."

Hunt-Morgan House — Lexington, 201 N. Mill St. Built circa 1814 by John Wesley Hunt, Kentucky's first millionaire. Later, the home of his grandson, the brilliant CSA general, John Hunt Morgan, as well as Thomas Hunt Morgan, the Nobel prize winner in genetics.

Hurricane Hall — About 6 mi. from Lexington, Georgetown-Lexington Pike. W. side of US-25. Built 1794. Fine old pioneer home. Historic associations.

Keen Place — 5 mi. W. of Lexington, Versailles Pike. Built 1805. Magnificent 2-story brick house. Homeplace of Keen family. J. O. Keen laid out race course and built the Keeneland Clubhouse.

Mary Todd Lincoln House — Lexington, 574 W. Main St. Built 1811. Home of Mary Todd's parents at the time of her marriage to Abraham Lincoln; visited by Lincolns later.

Morton, William (Lord) House — Lexington, 518 N. Limestone St. Built 1810. From 1838-1850 it was the home of Cassius Marcellus Clay. Built and furnished by the younger son of a titled English family.

Old Morrison — Lexington, 3rd St. An early Greek Revival design by Kentucky architect Gideon Shryock. Trustee and teacher, Henry Clay guided the construction, supported by bequest of Col. James Morrison. Building dedicated on Nov. 4, 1833. Listed in National Register of Historic Places.

Patterson Cabin — Lexington, 3rd and Broadway. Transylvania University campus. Built 1778. Log cabin of Col. Robert Patterson, founder of Lexington and Cincinnati. Oldest building in Lexington.

Dr. Ridgely Home — Lexington, Corner of Market and 2nd Sts. Built 1800-1805. Eighteenth century in style. Several illustrious owners, among them John W. Hunt, "first millionaire in the west."

Thomas Hart Home — Lexington, 193 N. Mill St. Built in 1794 for Thomas Hart. Georgian-Colonial brick house. His daughter, Lucretia, married Henry Clay here.

OTHER POINTS OF INTEREST

Kentucky Educational Television — Lexington, Cooper Drive. Kentucky ranks first among the states in its Educational Television Network.

High Hope Steeplechase — Lexington, Iron Works Pike. Kentucky Horse Park. April.

Horse Farms — Lexington, on Iron Works Pike, Paris Pike, Newtown Pike, and US-60, US-27, US-68. It is considered the horse capital of America. There are over 300 horse farms located within a 35-mile radius of the city. Good views of the farms can be seen.

Keeneland Race Course — 6 mi. W. of Lexington, Versailles Rd. US-60. The mile-and-one-sixteenth oval is one of America's most beautiful race tracks. Horses may be seen working out in the very early morning year round. Thoroughbred racing in April and October.

Keeneland Sales — Lexington, Versailles Rd. Periodic sales of world's finest Thoroughbreds.

Lexington Theological Seminary — Lexington, 631 S. Limestone. Established 1865.

The Red Mile Trotting Track — Lexington, off S. Broadway. The 100-year old track is the world's fastest for harness racing. The oldest stop on the Grand Circuit where may be seen harness racing's finest horses and drivers. Spring and fall meets.

Tattersalls Sales — Lexington, S. Broadway. Periodic sales of standard breds.

Transylvania University — Lexington, 300 N. Broadway. First institution of higher learning west of the Allegheny Mountains.

University of Kentucky — Lexington. Limestone St. Established 1865 as land grant university. Includes Albert B. Chandler Medical Center. 15 colleges and schools.

World's Largest Loose-Leaf Tobacco Market — Lexington. Auctions held December, January and February.

Harrison County

Harrison County was created from parts of Bourbon and Scott Counties. It was the seventeenth county in order of formation in Kentucky, and the eighth to be created after Kentucky had become a state. The county was named for Colonel Benjamin Harrison, who came to the area in 1776 from Pennsylvania. He served in the American Revolution, and afterwards, served in many areas of Kentucky politics. Both Harrison County, and Cynthiana, the county seat, were formed on December 23, 1793, by an act of the General Assembly. The town was established on one hundred fifty acres of land belonging to Robert Harrison, and Cynthiana was named for his two daughters, Cynthia and Anna.

Cynthiana was first settled in the spring of 1775 when Captain John Hinkton led a party of fifteen men from Pennsylvania down the Ohio River and up the Licking River in canoes, in search of land to settle. He soon abandoned the site, which was rebuilt in 1779 by Isaac Ruddle, and called Ruddle's Station. In 1780 the settlement was destroyed by British and Indians during their northern Kentucky raid under Captain Henry Bird. Later, Captain Hinkton returned to settle the area permanently.

FAIRS AND FESTIVALS

Christmas Festival — Cynthiana. Sponsored by the Chamber of Commerce. First week in December.

Harrison County Fair — Cynthiana, at 4-H Center. US-27. Usually held the 3rd week in July.

Iris Festival — Cynthiana, site varies. Contest for landscaping, Iris show, tour of homes and businesses. Sponsored by Harrison County Iris Society. Mid-May.

MARKERS

Cynthiana – Two Battles — Cynthiana. US-27. Battle of Cynthiana took place here. Twice, in 1862 and 1864, CSA Gen. John H. Morgan and his Raiders captured Cynthiana from Federal troops.

Indian Creek Baptist Church — Harrison County. KY-32, KY-36. Church was constituted in 1790. This is the original building erected on this site by pioneer families of the Indian Creek settlement. In continuous use until 1965.

The Old Cemetery — Cynthiana, adjacent to Main St. US-27. Only burial ground in Cynthiana from 1793 to 1863. Prominent early citizens buried here. First school in city, Harrison Academy, situated on corner of this plot.
Ruddles's Station — 4 mi. S. of Cynthiana. US-27.

MEMORIALS

Confederate Monument — Cynthiana, Battle Grove Cemetery. KY-36. Memorializes Gen. John H. Morgan's defeat of Cynthiana in 1864. Erected in memory of 48 CSA soldiers.

Ruddles's Monument — Lair, S. of Cynthiana. 8-ft. shaft marks the site of pioneer station built by Capt. Isaac Ruddle in 1779. Erected in memory of the 1780 massacre and destruction of Ruddle's Station, and the hardships suffered by the prisoners of the Indians and British. From forts all across northern Kentucky 400 prisoners suffered a 14-year captivity. One of the most tragic episodes in Kentucky history.

CEMETERIES

Battle Grove Cemetery — Cynthiana. KY-36. Site of Civil War battle between CSA Gen. John H. Morgan's Raiders and Union troops.

Burying Ground — Cynthiana, N. Main St. Established 1793. Contains many old gravestones.

Indian Creek Baptist Church — Harrison County. KY-32, KY-36. Graves of Revolutionary War soldiers Moses Endicott, Edward McShane, Henry Talbert, Hugh Wilson, and many other first settlers.

Lindsey Cemetery — 1 1/2 mi. N. of KY-36, on KY-1743. Located 1/2 mi. E. of Pioneer. Cemetery of settlers and 4 Revolutionary War veterans.

OLD BUILDINGS

Amende House — Near Broadwell, Leesburg Pike. circa 1784-1789. Home of Samuel McMillan, early justice of the peace and organizer of county's early school system. Oldest house standing in county.

The Cedars — S. of Cynthiana, Old Lair Rd. Built 1794. Originally the home of Mathias Lair, Revolutionary War officer. Ruddle's Fort was located here.

The Church of the Advent — Cynthiana, 120 N. Walnut St. Built 1855. Oldest church in Cynthiana. Used as hospital during Civil War.

Crown Jewell Mill — Cynthiana, S. Main St. Constructed 1808. Oldest industrial building in Cynthiana.

Cynthiana Courthouse — Cynthiana, Main St. Constructed 1854. Henry Clay practiced law here. Clay's papers exhibited. Listed in the National Register of Historic Places.

Funeral Home — Cynthiana, Main St., at John Hunt Morgan Bridge. Built early 1800's. Believed to be the headquarters for Gen. John H. Morgan and his troops while they held Cynthiana during the Civil War.

Hell's Half-Acre School — Near Cynthiana, Lafferty Pike. circa 1920-1930. One-room country school.

Howk House — Cynthiana, Tricum Pike, off Pleasant St. At one time, this was the home of Governor Joseph Desha. Later, the home of Dr. George Perrin, founder of the Church of the Advent in Cynthiana.

Mr. Dave Rees Home in Cynthiana.

Mr. Dave Rees Home — Cynthiana, Court St. Built 1790. Guthrie's Arithmetic, first published textbook west of the Alleghenies, was printed here. Oldest house in Cynthiana.

Old Lair Distillery — Lair. The oldest distillery in this part of the county.

Old Log Courthouse — Cynthiana, behind Courthouse Square. Built 1790. Original courthouse. Has served many purposes, including the printing office for the *Guardian of Liberty,* Cynthiana's first newspaper.

Stony Castle — KY-1054 off KY-36. First post office between Lexington and Cincinnati.

OTHER POINTS OF INTEREST

Abdallah Park Trotting Track — Cynthiana, on the Old River Rd. 1/2 mi. off US-27. Established 1875.

Birthplace of "Death Valley Scotty" — Cynthiana, N. Main St. Walter E. Scott, born in 1872, misled many visitors in Death Valley, California with tales of lost gold mines. The hoax was exposed in 1941, but legend persisted, and "Death Valley Scotty" became well established in American folklore.

Kentucky Central Railroad Bridge — 8 mi. S. of Cynthiana, at Kiserton Station. Old stone-arch bridge is the last remaining vestige of the old Kentucky Central Railroad.

Madison County

Madison County was one of the nine counties already in existence when Kentucky became a state in 1792. It was named in honor of President James Madison. Boonesboro, located in Madison County, was the first seat of government in what is now the Commonwealth of Kentucky. Two notable "firsts" occurred in Boonesboro. The first tobacco was grown at Boonesboro, and the first wedding in the state was performed here, as well.

FAIRS, FESTIVALS, DRAMAS, EXHIBITS

Berea College Mountain Day — Berea, Berea College. All day annual hike into the mountains. Usually held in October.

Country Music Show — Valley View. KY-169. Entertainment by local and visiting music stars. Saturday nights.

Crafts Demonstration Center — Berea, at Appalachian Museum of Berea College. Old log smokehouse on museum grounds is center of demonstration area. Periodically special events and workshops are held. In late summer and early fall, students and craftsmen demonstrate craft processes.

Eastern Kentucky University Concert Choir and University Singers — Richmond, at Eastern Kentucky University campus. Concerts in Gifford Theater and Hiram Brock Auditorium. October-May.

Founders' Festival — Downtown Richmond, Main St. Hog calling, fiddling, parade and auctions are among the featured events.

Henrietta Children's Theater — Berea.

Home and Garden Tours — Richmond. May.

"In Celebration" — Berea, at Berea College, Phoenix Theater. Major dramatic production offered in spring season.

Kentucky Guild of Artists and Craftsmen Fair — Berea. Indian Fort Theater. KY-21E. Guild members display, make, and sell arts and crafts items. Entertainment on stage of Indian Fort Theater. May and October.

Kress Study Collection of Renaissance Paintings — Berea, at Berea College Art Building. An invaluable collection, often loaned to other art galleries.

Madison County Fair — Richmond, Irvine Rd. KY-52E. Features horse show, livestock show, and display of fair items. August.

Mountain Folk Festival — Berea, Seabury Gymnasium. Sponsored annually by Berea College. April.

Whitehall Art and Antique Revue — N.W. of Richmond. Boonesboro-Winchester Exit to US-25, off I-75. Reenacted Civil War Battle. Flea market and tour of Whitehall. Labor Day Weekend.

Wilderness Road Drama — Berea. Indian Fort Theater.

KY-21E. Outdoor historical drama. Musical story set during the Civil War based on drama written by Paul Green and produced by Berea College. Nightly except Sunday, June to September.

PARKS

Fort Boonesboro State Park — Boonesboro, 12 mi. N. of Richmond. KY-388. Reconstructed from original drawings. Costumed artisans demonstrate making soap, candles, weaving, and other crafts. Gift shop sells Kentucky crafts. 90-acre park. Park camping, swimming, beach, playground, picnic area. April-October 31.

McDowell Irvin Park — Richmond, Lancaster Ave. Site of Irvineton. Playground facilities and picnic grounds.

MARKERS

Battle of 1862 — Madison County, 2 mi. S. of Jct. US-25 at Terrill. US-421. Site of one of the greatest victories for the CSA during the Civil War.

Big Hill Skirmish — S. of Madison, at Rockcastle County line. US-421. On Aug. 23, 1862, CSA army under Gen. Kirby Smith routed the Union forces under Col. Leonidas Metcalfe, who were trying to seize Kentucky. First CSA victory in Kentucky.

Daniel Boone's Trace — Northbound Rest Area. I-75. Two miles east is the location of the trail blazed by Daniel Boone in 1775, as agent for the Transylvania Company. This famous road was used by thousands of settlers traveling to Kentucky.

Christopher (Kit) Carson — 10 mi. N.W. of Richmond. KY-169. Born near here on Dec. 24, 1809. Famous scout, hunter, fur trader, and guide. Died in 1868.

For Mountain Youth — Berea, at Berea College campus. US-25. Founded in 1855 by John G. Fee, with the support of Cassius M. Clay, in a one-room school built by the community. Its 1858 constitution made it Christian, nonsectarian, antislavery. Dedicated to the service of the mountain people, Berea is an historic monument to equality.

Pilot Knob — Near Big Hill. US-421. Served as a landmark to guide the settlers as they followed trailblazers to Boonesboro. From this knob, Daniel Boone first viewed the Kentucky Bluegrass area.

Twitty's, or Little Fort — 2 mi. S. of Richmond. US-25, US-421. Site of first fort in Kentucky. Built in March, 1775 by Daniel Boone and party.

Valley View Ferry — 12 mi. N. of Richmond at Kentucky River. KY-169. Oldest continuous business of record in Kentucky. Authorized 1785. Last ferry on the Kentucky River.

MEMORIALS AND MUSEUMS

Appalachian Museum — Berea, Jackson St., on Berea College Campus. Excellent exhibit of early pioneer articles, such as farm tools, cooking utensils, guns, and related articles.

Daniel Boone Statue — Richmond, on Eastern Kentucky University campus. Exact duplicate of statue by Enid Yandell which stands in Cherokee Park at Louisville.

Squire Boone Rock — Richmond. Kentucky's oldest monument marked by the hand of a man, showing inscription "1770 Squire Boone." Now encased in glass inside Madison County Courthouse.

Whitehall State Shrine near Richmond.

Fort Boonesboro State Park.

Jonathan Trueman Dorris Museum — Richmond, on Eastern Kentucky University campus. Contains many original and photocopies of historical manuscripts, pictures, and items of historical interest. Many Kentucky and Civil War exhibits.

Wallace Nutting Furniture Museum — Berea. US-25. In the Log House. Exhibits of early American furniture, including rare authentic Colonial furnishings.

CEMETERIES

Richmond Cemetery — Richmond. US-25. Grave sites of both Union and CSA forces. Memorials of interest to students of Madison County and Kentucky history.

OLD BUILDINGS

Banks House — Richmond, Lancaster Ave. Built 1803. Believed to be the oldest house still standing in Richmond.

Bernard Hall — 6 mi. N. of Richmond. US-25. Built 1812. One of the largest and most beautiful homes of Georgian architecture. Spacious grounds and gardens.

Brighton — Richmond, Lancaster Ave. circa 1837. Georgian-style architecture. Built by Daniel Breck and his wife, the aunt of Mary Todd Lincoln. It is thought that Abraham Lincoln and wife once stayed here.

Cane Springs Baptist Church — Near College Hill and Red River Pike. Built 1803. Oldest church in Madison County.

Dunsinane — Near Paint Lick on Walnut Meadow Pike. Built 1821. Well-preserved brick home painted white. Currently home of Mrs. Earle B. Combs, widow of New York Yankee baseball great.

Galey House — Near Richmond, Curtis Pike. Built 1790. Example of an early stone house.

Grant House — 1 1/2 mi. S.E. of Berea, and the foot of Big Hill. US-421. circa 1850. Simple wooden cottage was used as Merritt Jones' Tavern during Civil War. While Jones was serving with CSA forces, Mrs. Jones had to entertain Gen. U. S. Grant and his staff at the tavern. Listed on National Register of Historic Places.

Irvineton Home — Richmond, McDowell Irvin Park on Lancaster Ave. Built 1824. Used as a trachoma hospital from 1926-1950. Houses City-County Library. Listed on the National Register of Historic Shrines.

Madison County Courthouse — Richmond, Main St. Built 1849. Example of classic architecture. Records here date back to 1786 and contain valuable informa-

tion concerning the history of the county as well as the state.

Miller House — Richmond, W. Irvine St. Built 1818. Now houses Richmond Chamber of Commerce, a source of information for points of interest in Madison County. Gift shop for sale of crafts and souvenirs. Recently restored.

Reuben Staff House — Newby, Madison County. Built late 1700's. Two-story log cabin, one of the oldest houses in the county.

Whitehall State Shrine — N.W. of Richmond. US-25, at Boonesboro-Winchester exit. I-75. Restored Italianate mansion of Cassius Marcellus Clay (1810-1903), early antislavery leader and politician. Contains works of art, china, mirrors and furnishings that reflect its prestige and glory. Daily tours.

OTHER POINTS OF INTEREST

Berea College — Berea, US-25. A liberal arts school founded in 1853 as a university for all races. Nationally known for high standards of teaching and for its student-work industries program. Tours Monday-Friday, 9 a.m. to 2 p.m., and Saturday, 9 a.m.

Boone Tavern Hotel — Berea. US-25. Famous eating place and inn. Operated by Berea College. Offers traditional Southern cooking and recipes created especially for the tavern menu.

Bybee Pottery — Bybee, 9 mi. E. of Richmond, near Waco. KY-52. Oldest existing pottery west of the Alleghenies. Hand-turned pottery produced by the Cornelison family for 4 generations. Originally established in 1809. Visitors welcome year round, Monday-Saturday, 8 a.m. to 4:30 p.m.

Churchill Weavers — N. Berea. US-25. Country's largest hand weaving plant. Hand weaving of fabrics suitable for linens and clothing. Demonstrations, displays, and retail sales room.

Eastern Kentucky University — Richmond. Institution of learning established originally to train teachers. Now offers diversified curricula and is the only university in Kentucky offering an Associate of Arts degree in law enforcement. Kentucky Civil War displays in Crabbe Library.

Indian Mound — Round Hill, near Kirksville. circa 475. Mound about 25-ft. high and 250-ft. in circumference.

Palisades of the Kentucky River — In N.W. Madison County, on the Kentucky River, from Boonesboro to Garrard County line. The Kentucky River passes between towering rock cliffs. The area abounds in unusual geologic formations and rare natural and scenic beauty.

Student Craft Industries — Berea, at Berea College campus. A program of Student Arts and Crafts is carried on at Berea College. Includes woodcraft, broomcraft, weaving, needlecraft, ceramics, and lapi-dary arts. Tours may be arranged by writing to: Development and Office of Information, Box 2316, Berea, KY, 40403.

Sycamore Hollow — Boonesboro. One of the largest sycamore groves in the U.S. Used as camp sites for Fort Boonesboro State Park.

Nicholas County

Nicholas County was the forty-second in order of formation in Kentucky. It was taken from portions of Bourbon and Mason Counties. The county was named for a son of the Virginia Burgess, George Nicholas. Colonel Nicholas was a member of Kentucky's first Constitutional Convention.

John Kincart gave the town site for Carlisle, the county seat. Court sessions were held in Kincart's house until a brick courthouse was completed in 1818. Some of the early settlers in the county were Samuel Peyton, James Stephenson, George M. Bedinger, and the Metcalfes.

FESTIVALS

Carlisle Blackberry Festival — Carlisle. Festivities include selection of a Blackberry Queen, a parade, amusements, and all the blackberries visitors can eat. Homecoming event for Nicholas Countians. Held annually in July, when Kentucky's blackberries are at their peak.

Central Kentucky Fox Hunt — Site of Hunt varies. Often held on Skyview Farm, one of the best field trail sites in the country. Three-day field trail is open to hunters from any state. Beautiful landscape and colorful proceedings. Sponsored by Central Kentucky Fox Hunters, Inc. Usually held in October or early November.

Jaycee Horse Show — Grounds of Nicholas County School. KY-32. Events held on 2 evenings. Early June.

PARKS

National County Recreational Park — Carlisle. KY-36. Tennis courts, baseball diamonds, football fields, playgrounds. Supervised recreation programs in Summer.

MARKERS

County Named — Carlisle, Courthouse yard. KY-32, KY-36. Named for George Nicholas, (1743-1799), born in Virginia and a Revolutionary War Colonel. "Brightest luminary" in Kentucky's first Constitutional Convention. First Attorney General of Kentucky. First Transylvania law professor.

Courthouse at Carlisle.

199

Patriot-Pioneer — Blue Licks Union Church. US-68. Site of the home and grave of Maj. M. Bedinger, (1756-1843). Served in Revolutionary War in the defense of Boonesborough, and at the siege of Yorktown. In 1784 he came back to Kentucky. First to survey this area.

Tollgate House — 6 mi. W. of Carlisle, at Bourbon County line. One of last tollgates operated in Kentucky. There were 13 of these along the Maysville to Lexington Road. In late 1890's, a tollgate war raged against the turnpike companies until the counties bought the turnpikes.

Upper Blue Licks — Moorefield. Jct. KY-36, KY-57. On Aug. 12, 1782 Capt. John Holder and 17 militiamen attempted to retrieve 2 captured boys from Wyandot Indians. Jones Hoy was held captive 7 years.

Old Concord Church — Carlisle, Dorsey St. KY-36. Organized in 1793. Site of Presbyterian Church and School made famous by its pioneer pastors. Recently destroyed by wind.

CEMETERIES

Carlisle Cemetery — Carlisle. KY-36.

OLD BUILDINGS

Daniel Boone Cabin — N.W. of Carlisle. Off US-68. circa 1795. Restored log cabin which was Daniel and Rebecca Boone's last home in Kentucky before they moved to the Louisiana Territory in 1799. Originally located at Hinkston Creek.

Forest Retreat — N.W. of Carlisle. US-68. Built 1820. Home of Thomas Metcalfe, 10th Governor of Kentucky (1828-1838), and U. S. Senator. Now a successful racehorse farm.

McClintock-Hamilton House — Nicholas County, Collier Pike. circa 1810-1820. Early stone house built by William McClintock, Jr., whose family came to Kentucky in 1775.

Thompson House — Nicholas County, Collier Pike. circa 1840-1850. Example of plantation house in early stone style. Built by John Henry Thompson, grandson of early settler Henry Thompson.

Nicholas County Courthouse — Carlisle, Main and Locust Sts. Built 1893. Architectural example.

Stone Tavern — Ellisville. US-68. Built 1807. Tavern, originally owned by James Ellis, was important stopping place on "Smith Wagon Road" from Limestone (Maysville) to Lexington.

Henry Thompson House — 10 mi. W. of Carlisle, S. of Head Quarters, Arthur Pike. circa 1790. Example of early stone house.

Tollgate House — Bourbon County line, near Millersburg. US-68. circa 1830. Toll collection point for Maysville to Lexington Road.

Lott Young House — 15 mi. S. of Carlisle, near Hinkston Creek, Somerset Pike. circa 1812. Architectural example.

OTHER POINTS OF INTEREST

Blue Licks — N. of Licking River. US-68. Site contains bones of late Pleistocene Age animals and stones worked by early man. In 1778, Daniel Boone and 30 companions were captured by Indians while making salt here.

Iron Bridge — Bourbon County Line, Lower Jackstown Pike, over Hinkston Creek. circa 1890. Iron truss bridge with wood plank surface. Still in use.

Lake Carnico — Carlisle. KY-1455. Golf course, country club, beach and camping area.

Powell County

Powell County was named for Lazarus W. Powell, who became governor of Kentucky in 1851. In 1852, Powell County was created from Estill, Montgomery, and Clark Counties. It was settled almost one hundred years before, soon after Daniel Boone came to Kentucky. Prior to Boone's era, the region was a sacred hunting ground for Shawnee and Cherokee Indians. The extreme northwestern portion of the county served as the location of the last Indian village in Kentucky. In 1769, Daniel Boone and John Finley camped at Oil Springs, near Pilot Knob, the county's highest elevation. From this summit, Boone first saw the Bluegrass uplands in the distance.

Stanton, the county seat, was first called Beaver Pond, then renamed for Richard H. Stanton, a member of Congress from 1849-1855.

FAIRS, FESTIVALS, EXHIBITS

Annual Mountain Music Festival — Slade, Natural Bridge State Resort Park. KY-15. July 4 Weekend.

Country Music Show — Slade, Natural Bridge State Resort Park. KY-15.

Kentucky Mountain Music Shindig — Slade, Natural Bridge State Resort Park. Springtime.

Lion's Club Fair and Horse Show — Slade, Lion's Club Park. KY-213. Begins Labor Day weekend.

National Mountain-Style Square Dance Contest — Slade, Natural Bridge State Resort Park. KY-15. June.

Powell County Art Exhibit — Slade, Natural Bridge State Resort Park. KY-15. August.

Western Square Dance Festival — Slade, Natural Bridge State Resort Park. KY-15. Late summer.

PARKS

Daniel Boone National Forest — Slade. Some 26 miles of the wandering Red River has carved Red River Gorge, which has received national attention for its rock formations, streams, rugged forest, and scenic beauty.

Natural Bridge State Resort Park — Slade, 2 1/2 mi. from Mountain Parkway. KY-15. A wonder of nature carved by wind and rain out of the porous sandstone of the area. The bridge is 78 ft. in length and 65 ft. high. There are 12 natural arches and rock formations in the park.

MARKERS

Courthouse Burned — Stanton Courthouse yard. KY-11, KY-15. 22 Kentucky courthouses were burned during Civil War. Courthouse and records at Stanton and other buildings were burned by guerrillas, Spring of 1863. Jail and records again burned June 1, 1864.

Pilot Knob — W. of Clay City. KY-15. Point from which Daniel Boone and his party first viewed the Bluegrass on June 7, 1769.

MUSEUMS

Red River Historical Museum — Clay City, Main St. Built 1899. Oldest public building in Clay City. Clay City's population was 1,000 and the lumber and Red River iron ore made it a booming town. Museum contains relics of the region and Indian artifacts. Clay City once had the second largest lumber industry in the world. Museum also contains implements of Adena Culture 2,000 years ago.

CEMETERIES

Old Amburgy Cemetery — Bowen, Amburgy Hollow. Exit KY-15 to KY-613, KY-1067. Revolutionary War privates buried here in 1839. Joseph Horne, Sr. and William Cave buried here.

Old Kennon Cemetery — Hardwick's Creek Rd. KY-1057, S.W. Unmarked graves of Lee family and Swope family, early 1800's. Early settlers on Hardwick's Creek came from Ohio, Pennsylvania and Virginia to work in old iron ore furnace and forge.

McKinney Cemetery — KY-1057. The Clarks and Smiths buried in 1776, across from Hardwick's Creek Methodist Church. Five generations of Clarks buried here.

Roberts Cemetery — N. of Clay City, between Pompii and Beech Fork. circa 1850.

OLD BUILDINGS

Clay City National Bank — Clay City. Built 1889. First bank in Powell County, established during lumber industry boom. Example of commercial architecture. Now houses Red River Historical Museum.

County Building — Stanton, N. Main St. Built 1909. Beginning of row houses.

Louisville & Nashville Railroad Depot — Stanton. Built 1891. Utilitarian architecture.

McQuire House — Clay City, 9th St. Opposite Clay City Baptist Church. Oldest house in Clay City.

Nada Tunnel through Red River Gorge.

Old Boone Hotel — Stanton, Main St. circa 1899. Oldest public building on Main Street.

Old Stanton Academy — Stanton. KY-15. circa 1907. Run by Presbyterian Church Board of Pennsylvania.

Ouida Newkirk House — Waltersville. Jct. KY-15, KY-11. Oldest continuously occupied house in Powell County.

Powell County Courthouse — Stanton, Breckinridge and Court St. Burned by guerrillas during Civil War, Spring of 1863. Rebuilt June 1, 1864.

Smather's Grocery — Stanton, Main St. Built 1907. Store is believed to be the oldest continuously operated grocery store in the county.

Stanton Christian Church — Stanton, Church St. 1 block from KY-213. Built 1874. Stanton's oldest church building.

OTHER POINTS OF INTEREST

The Abner Shelter — 3 mi. S.W. of Stanton. KY-213, at forks of Hatton Creek Rd. Indian artifacts, also quarry for grindstones used in granary and flour mills.

Fireside Craft Industries — Slade. KY-15. The Kentucky Mountain Quilting and Craft Coop., Inc.

Gray's Arch — Slade. Between King Branch and Martin Fork. Large sandstone arch.

Hidden Valley Ranch Resort — Clay City. Old western town and resort farm. Correctional Institute.

Mountain Park Dragway — Clay City. KY-1057. Cars from many states competing for cash and trophy. Racing every Saturday night.

Nada Tunnel — KY-77. Through Red River Gorge, one of the most scenic drives of South. Tunnel was completed in 1912 for logging railroad that hauled timber out of the forest. The old railroad bed is now KY-77 which goes through Old Nada Tunnel, handmade with pick and shovel, and only 13 ft. high and 10 ft. wide.

Red River Canoe Race — Stanton. Sponsored by Stanton Jaycees. Annually in May.

Stanton-Woodcraft Shop — Stanton, Airport Rd. Handmade wooden furniture and wooden accessories.

Stump Cave — KY-1639, S. of KY-15. Indian artifacts in a cave near Tin Town Church.

Scott County

In 1792, the year Kentucky was admitted to the Union, Scott County was formed, and Georgetown was made the county seat. The county was named for General Charles Scott, a Revolutionary War hero who later became Governor of Kentucky.

The first surveying of Royal Springs, later the site of Georgetown, was done in July of 1774. McClelland's Fort was first established on the spring, as it was McClelland, along with John Floyd and Elijah Craig, who was credited with the early development of Georgetown and Scott County. In December, 1790, the General Assembly of Virginia established Georgetown, then called George Town, in honor of George Washington.

FAIRS, FESTIVALS

Christmas Parade — Georgetown. Parade runs from College Street to Main Street to Broadway. Sponsored by Junior Chamber of Commerce. Floats, marching units, exhibits. 1st Monday in December.

Fall Festival — Georgetown, Main St. Sidewalk bake sales, arts and crafts. Sponsored by JayCees. September.

Georgetown College Homecoming — Georgetown, Georgetown College campus. US-62. Football game, class reunions, parade, Homecoming queen, trophies for decorated floats and dormitories. Usually late October.

Holiday Heritage Tours — Georgetown. Tours of 4 or 5 historic homes, featuring traditional Christmas theme. Descriptive booklets. Sponsored by Scott County Woman's Club and the Little Garden Club. Usually 1st Sunday in December.

Rotary Club Horse Show — 1 mi. N. of Georgetown, Scott County Community Park. US-25. General show with 20 classes. Usually 2 nights. Early in June.

Scott County Fair — 1 mi. N. of Georgetown, corner of Long Lick Rd. US-25. Exhibits, carnival, livestock shows. Usually week after July 4th.

PARKS

Scott County Community Park — 1 mi. N. of Georgetown. US-25. Playground equipment, barn, horse show ring, community building planned, baseball diamond, tennis, basketball, croquet, archery, picnic tables.

MARKERS

Patriot's Stage Stop — White Sulphur. Jct. Iron Works Pike and US-460. This house, a stagecoach stop from 1800-1832, was owned by Julius Gibbs, pioneer settler, who enlisted in the American Revolution in 1775 under Col. Patrick Henry.

Remember the Raisin! — Georgetown, Courthouse yard. US-25, US-460. Rendezvous of Kentucky Volunteers who on Aug. 15, 1812, were ordered to relieve Gen. Hull at Detroit. Kentuckians took Frenchtown (Monroe) on the Raisin River Jan. 18, 1813. Four days later enemy attacked. Of 1050 men sent, less than half returned home.

Royal Spring — Georgetown, Main St. Discovered July 9, 1774 by Col. John Floyd and party. This has been Georgetown's water supply since earliest settlement. Site of McClelland's Station in 1775. Also site of first paper mill in state and possibly the first bourbon still.

Scott County Courthouse — Georgetown Courthouse yard. US-25, US-460. Built 1877. Present structure is Scott County's 4th courthouse. Outstanding example of the French Second Empire style.

Stamping Ground — Stamping Ground. US-227. This area first explored in April, 1775. Buffalo herds had stamped down undergrowth and ground around the spring, hence the origin of town's name.

U. S. Vice President — 3 mi. W. of Georgetown. US-460. Richard M. Johnson (1780-1850) one of 4 Kentuckians who became U. S. Vice President. Held office during term of President Martin Van Buren, 1837-1841.

MEMORIALS

Edward Troye Monument — Georgetown, in Georgetown Cemetery. US-25S. Eight foot marble monument to Kentucky's great animal and portrait painter. Troye was at his best in portraying the American-blooded horse. His work was accomplished from 1832-1873.

CEMETERIES

Georgetown Cemetery — Georgetown. US-25S. Resting place of three governors, the founder and first president of Kentucky Medical Association and other outstanding people. 100 years old and of interest to botany students also.

OLD BUILDINGS

Wright Allen Log House — 8 mi. N.W. of Georgetown, Sebree Pike, near Long Lick Pike and McConnell's Run. circa 1790's. Example of log house.

Allenhurst — Georgetown, on Cane Run Pike. Between US-460 and Iron Works Pike. circa 1844-49. Greek Revival style.

George Allgaire House — Georgetown, 32 E. Main St. West wing built 1790's; east wing in 1844. In mid-19th century, this home was the Catholic mission station in Georgetown for circuit-riding priests.

John C. Buckner House — Georgetown, 355 E. Main St. circa 1814. Home of George W. Johnson, Confederate Governor of Kentucky, 1833-1835. He was born in 1811 in Scott County. Architectural example.

Cantrill House — Georgetown, 324 Jackson St. Built late 1790's. Associated with hemp industry.

Cardome — Georgetown. US-25N. Built 1821 Convent of Sisters of the Visitation, girls' school. Home of Governor James F. Robinson from 1844 until his death in 1882.

Cast Iron Store Fronts — Georgetown, E. Main St. Built 1869, after a series of fires. Victorian Era Architecture.

Holy Trinity Episcopal Church.

Choctaw Indian Academy — Near Great Crossing on Owenton Pike. Blue Spring Farm. Built 1825. Academy for education of Choctaw children. Operated as Mission project of Baptists from 1818 to 1844. At this location 1825 to 1833. Became a national academy.

Governor Joseph Desha House — Georgetown, Kelly Ave. off W. Main St. Built 1815. Home of Kentucky's governor from 1824 to 1828.

James K. Duke House — 5 mi. S.E. of Georgetown, Lisle Pike. circa 1820's — early 1830's. Example of a Kentucky antebellum home. Birthplace of Gen. Basil Duke, who succeeded Gen. John Hunt Morgan as leader of his command. The large pasture in front of the home was the favorite dueling ground of Central Kentucky.

Echo Valley — S. of Georgetown, Lexington Pike. Built 1798. Originally the home of Col. Robert Sanders, who brought the first Thoroughbred racing horse to Central Kentucky and operated the first race track in Scott County.

Giddings Hall — Georgetown, Georgetown College campus. Built 1839. Greek Revival. Erected entirely by student and faculty labor, from bricks fired on grounds. Listed on National Register of Historic Places.

Grant House — Georgetown, E. Washington St. circa 1800. One of the oldest houses in Georgetown.

Greathouse Place — 7 mi. W. of Lexington, Payne's Depot near Leestown Pike crossing. circa 1800. Stone house thought to have been built by stonemason, Thomas Metcalfe, who later became governor.

Alexander Hamilton House — Minorsville. Built late 1700's — early 1800's. Founder of the Minorsville Community.

William Brown's Hatter's Shop — Georgetown, 144 S. Broadway. Built early 1800's. One of 2 leading hatter's shops when Georgetown was first stopping place for Northern Kentucky hunters.

Hockensmith House — Near Stamping Ground, Cedar Pike. circa 1790. Probably the oldest house in the Stamping Ground vicinity.

Lindsay House — Near Stamping Ground, Locust Fort Pike. circa 1790. Marriage place of Jesse James' parents.

Longview — W. of Georgetown, on Galloway Pike. Off US-460. Built 1819. Home once owned by Richard M. Johnson during his term as U. S. Vice President.

Newtown Christian Church — Georgetown, Paris Pike. US-460. Typical of mid-nineteenth century Greek "meeting houses."

Osburne House — Georgetown. US-25N. One of the first rustic cabins of the area; was at one time a stagecoach stop during 1790-1842.

Gen. John Payne House — 2 mi. W. of Georgetown. US-460. circa 1787-1791. This is one of the oldest houses in Kentucky. Fine example of Kentucky "stone age" architecture.

Pence House — near Great Crossing. Off US-227. circa 1859. Original owner was Josiah Pence who helped Cyrus McCormick develop the reaping machine in the 1830's.

Walter Perry House — Great Crossing. US-227. circa 1820-40. One of the few remaining original houses in Great Crossing.

Robinson House — Georgetown, W. Washington near Water St. Built late 18th-century. One of 2 log houses standing in Georgetown.

Royal Bridge — Georgetown. US-460. W. Main Street. Built 1796 by Rev. Elijah Craig. Believed to be site where he first made Bourbon whiskey in 1789. This area was part of Bourbon County, Virginia at the time.

Row Houses — Georgetown, E. Main St. Outstanding contribution to Georgian period.

Scott County Courthouse — Georgetown, E. Main St. Built 1877. Noted example of Second Empire style.

Shropshire House — Georgetown, E. Main St. Built 1814. One of the most interesting architectural examples to be seen.

Showalter House — S. of Georgetown, W. Hamilton St. circa 1815. Site of an old slave market. Still has auction block in the yard.

St. Francis Mission — White Sulphur. US-460. Built 1820. The second oldest Catholic church in Kentucky. Neo-Gothic in style.

Sunny Acres — Near Georgetown. Near Jct. US-460 and US-227. circa 1783. Home of Col. Robert Johnson and site of his fort at the Great Crossing, first permanent station in Scott County.

Weisenberger Mill — S. Elkhorn at Mt. Horeb Pike. Dam is 18th century, mill is 20th century. Last flour mill in Scott County. Other mills have been located on this site since early 1800's.

OTHER POINTS OF INTEREST

Georgetown College — Georgetown, Jackson and College Sts. Established 1829. Second oldest Baptist college in U. S. Giddings Hall was built in 1840 by students from bricks fired on grounds.

Licking River Area

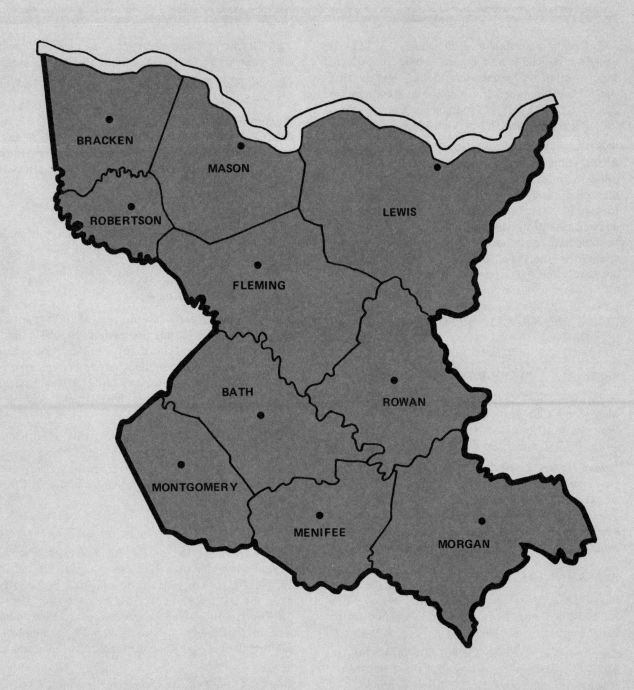

Bath County

Bath County was established on January 15, 1811. Its name was derived from the great number of medicinal springs within its borders. Bath County was the fifty-sixth county in order of formation in Kentucky and was taken from part of Montgomery County. Noted for its limestone soil, it also ranks high as an agricultural area.

At the time Bath County was formed, only a few cabins were located on the present site of Owingsville, the county seat. Colonel Thomas Deye Owings and Richard Menifee, Sr. owned adjoining properties. Each donated part of his land for the town site and each felt he sould have the honor of naming it. According to one account, it was agreed the town would belong to the one who erected the finest home in the shortest time. The Owings mansion was started in 1811 and completed in 1814, at an estimated cost of $60,000. As Richard Menifee lost, the name Owingsville was chosen for the town.

FESTIVALS AND EXHIBITS

Owingsville Lion's Club Horse Show — S. of Owingsville, Lion's Club Park. KY-36. It draws many horses from many other states. Held in natural amphitheater setting on Slate Creek. Second Saturday in May.

Walnut Harvest Festival — Owingsville. Sponsored by the Chamber of Commerce. A Princess and her court are selected. There are crafts and hobby exhibits, demonstrations of quilting, embroidery, ceramics, and other articles for sale. There are also walnuts of all kinds for sale, a fashion show and an open house.

PARKS AND LAKES

Daniel Boone National Forest — Off I-64, on US-60 and KY-36. Consists of 20,000 acres in southeastern Bath County.

Cave Run Lake — Owingsville. KY-801, off US-60. This 8,270-acre lake was constructed for flood control and downstream control of Licking River. Kentucky's 4th largest water impoundment; includes Minor E. Clark Fish Hatchery. There are numerous recreation facilities, boat ramps, marinas, camping areas and a beach.

Olympia State Forest — Near Olympia Springs. I-64, on KY-36. Southern part of Bath County.

Pioneer Weapons Hunting Area — Owingsville. S.E. of Salt Lick, off US-60 and KY-211. Over 7,000 acres of forest land preserve. Features nature trails, natural arches and a lookout point. Hunting with primitive weapons only.

MARKERS

Joe Creason Historical Marker — N. of Bethel at Longview Cemetery. KY-11. Grave site of one of Kentucky's most noted and best-loved journalists. Renowned for his column "Joe Creason's Kentucky" in the Louisville *Courier-Journal.*

Gen. John Bell Hood — Owingsville, Main St. Famous CSA General born in this city on June 29, 1831. Graduate of West Point. Gained distinction as commander of the Texas Brigade. Fought at Fredericksburg, Gettysburg, and Chickamauga. Lived in New Orleans after the Civil War and is buried near Nashville, Tennessee.

Capt. John "Jack" Jouett — Owingsville, Courthouse yard. Famous Revolutionary War hero who rode 40 miles to warn Thomas Jefferson, Patrick Henry and other legislators of British approach on June 3, 1781. He is buried in Bath County.

OLD BUILDINGS

Owings House — Owingsville, Main St. Col. Thomas Deye Owings' Federal-style mansion was erected in 1811-1814, part of which is now a bank. In the early days, the Owings' house was a stagecoach stop. Henry Clay was a visitor there, as was Andrew Jackson on his way to Washington to be inaugurated as President. Louis Phillippe, later King of France, reportedly stayed here.

Springfield Presbyterian Church — Between KY-11 and US-60 on Gudgell Hill Rd. One of the oldest Presby-

terian churches in Kentucky. Originally organized by
the Rev. Joseph Price Howe in 1794. The congregation
petitioned on June 12, 1793 to erect a building for
public worship. This was the mother church for congregations at Mt. Sterling, Sharpsburg, and Mt. Gilead. It
is surrounded by an old cemetery which is being restored, and is visited annually by hundreds of persons
searching for their roots. Services are still being held in
this lovely old church.

OTHER POINTS OF INTEREST

Clear Creek Furnace — Salt Lick on Clear Creek Rd.
KY-211. Early iron furnace. Picnicking and camping
facilities.

Memorial Library — Owingsville, Main St. New facilities remodeled in 1967. Community meeting room upstairs. All county meetings are held here. Several exhibits each year. Programs for children.

Old State Furnace, Bourbon Furnace, Owings Furnace
— Olympia Rd., S. of Owingsville. KY-36. Land around
furnaces was granted to Jacob Myers in 1782. Furnaces
were built in 1781. The Bourbon furnace was built to
make utensils and tools to supply settlers. In 1810
began to make cannon balls and grape shot for U. S.
Navy. The ammunition was floated down the river to
Andrew Jackson at New Orleans. The Owings furnace
was built to make cast iron kettles. These were the first
built west of the Alleghenies. Closed 1838. Area has
been converted to roadside park with picnic and playground facilities.

Boating on Cave Run Lake near Owingsville.

Owings House in Owingsville.

Horse Show at Lions Club Park in Owingsville.

Bracken County

As early as 1773, surveys were made in the Bracken County region by John Hedges, Thomas Young, Thomas Bullitt and John Fitzgerald. Bracken County, the twenty-third county in order of formation in Kentucky, was created in 1796 from parts of Mason and Campbell Counties, and indirectly named for William Bracken, a pioneer who came to the area in 1773. Big and Little Bracken Creeks were named for him, and the county then took its name from the creeks.

Brooksville has been the county seat since 1832, but the river town of Augusta, first settled in 1792, dominates the county's past. Augusta was Bracken County's first seat of government. Planted on a bank high above the Ohio, the fine harbor of "Augusta the Beautiful" was an important shipping point for tobacco. In 1867 the first white burley tobacco was grown from Bracken County seed. The region around Brooksville, originally known as Woodward's Crossroad, chiefly produces burley tobacco today.

During the 1870's Bracken County was one of the leading wine-producing counties in the United States. German immigrants found the soil similar to that of their homeland, and developed the grape production and wine-making in the country. Disastrous weather and blight destroyed the dream of creating the "Rhineland of America" in Bracken County.

Many sources maintain that the entire town of Augusta is built over a prehistoric burial ground of Indians or their predecessors.

Among the distinguished residents of Bracken County have been John Fee, who founded Berea College in 1855, and Dr. Joshua Bradford, world-renowned surgeon.

MARKERS

Augusta in the Civil War — Augusta. KY-8. By September 1862 Union troops had left this district, leaving only 100 Home Guards. An attack by 350 of Morgan's Raiders burned and cannonaded houses, but CSA losses forced abandonment of raid into Ohio.

Augusta College, 1822-1849 — Augusta. KY-8, KY-19. In 1822 the trustees of Bracken Academy with conferences from the Methodist Church of Kentucky and Ohio merged to establish Augusta College, the first established Methodist college in the world.

Bracken County Wine — Augusta. KY-8, KY-19. During the 1870's Bracken was the leading wine-producing county of United States, furnishing over 30,000 gallons annually, half the entire national production. This is the last remaining wine cellar and has 3-ft. thick walls and a vaulted ceiling.

Casto-Metcalfe Duel — Bracken County, on Mason County line. KY-8. Near site of one of the last duels in Kentucky which was between William T. Casto and Col. Leonidas Metcalfe. Casto believed Metcalfe was responsible for his imprisonment during the Civil War and challenged him to a duel on May 8, 1862. Casto was mortally wounded on the first fire.

A Foster Inspiration — Augusta, Frankfort and 5th Sts. KY-8. In 1833 Stephen C. Foster visited his uncle, Dr. Joseph S. Tomlinson, president of Augusta College. The harmonious voices from the Negro church on the hill floated over the town. Foster later put the sorrow in their voices into song.

Wine cellar near Augusta.

208

OLD BUILDINGS

Armstrong-Bradford Home — Augusta, Riverside Dr. Built in early 1800's. Became "Piedmond," home of Dr. Joshua Bradford, surgeon famous for performing over 30 ovarian surgical operations.

Philip Buckner House — Augusta, 202 W. 3rd St. Built 1796. Oldest house still standing in the county.

George Doniphan House — Augusta, 302 E. 4th St. Built about 1820 as a brick addition to an older log-frame house.

OTHER POINTS OF INTEREST

Ferryboat — Augusta, Main St. KY-19. One of the vanishing modes of transport across the Ohio River. Carries passengers and automobiles.

Old Winery — Augusta, intersection of KY-19 and KY-8. A reminder of the 1870's period when Bracken was a leading wine-producing county.

Ferry to Augusta across the Ohio River.

Wolcott Covered Bridge — Near Wellsburg on Locust Creek. KY-1159. Built 1835. Wooden log bridge is one of few remaining in Kentucky.

Fleming County

Fleming County, formed from part of Mason County and named in honor of Colonel John Fleming, was the twenty-sixth county to be created in Kentucky and the first of 13 counties established in 1798.

Flemingsburg, located in the central part of Fleming County, is the county seat and was incorporated in 1812. Before its founding in 1796, Flemingsburg was centered between Stockton Station, Fleming Station, and Cassidy Station, the three forts which played an important part in the early history of Fleming County.

FAIRS, FESTIVALS

Fleming County Court Day — Flemingsburg. October.

Fleming County Fair — Between Ewing and Fairview. July.

PARKS, RECREATION, LAKES

Fox Valley Recreation Area — Wallingford. KY-32. Camping and fishing facilities.

MARKERS

James J. Andrews — Flemingsburg, Courthouse yard. KY-11, KY-32. Andrews, who lived here 1859-62, led 22 Union soldiers into Georgia to cut the railway between Marietta and Chattanooga in 1862. Their capture of the locomotive "The General" and the CSA pursuit of them was a dramatic incident of the Civil War.

Michael Cassidy — W. of Flemingsburg, on Cassidy Road. 1 mi. from Jct. KY-32. Cassidy (1750-1829) was born in Ireland and came to Virginia as a cabin boy in 1767. Enlisted in the Revolution and was with Gen. Washington at the British surrender at Yorktown in 1781. Came to Kentucky, first to Clark County and then to Fleming County, where he established Cassidy Station in the late 1780's. Fought in over 30 battles against the Indians, and from 1797-1822, served 5 terms in the Kentucky House and one in the Senate.

Site of Finley Home — Near Hilltop. KY-57, KY-170. John Finley (1748-1837), pioneer-surveyor, came to

Kentucky in 1773. He discovered Upper Blue (Salt) Licks and surveyed land to Kentucky River near present-day Frankfort. He was a soldier and legislator.

Stockton Grave — E. of Flemingsburg. Jct. KY-32, KY-1013. Robert Stockton was buried after being killed by Indians in 1789 while hunting. His wounded companion, Blacham Rhodes, made his way back to Stockton's Station. On returning to the site with friends, they found his faithful dog standing guard, "a circle of torn earth all around the body marking the rage and disappointment of wolves."

Stockton's Station — W. of Flemingsburg city limits. KY-11. Site of the station built in 1787 by Maj. George Stockton, who raised a crop here in 1786 while living at Strode's Station. This was the first of three forts in the area that became Fleming County in 1798.

OLD BUILDINGS

Fleming Hotel — Flemingsburg, Court Square. Capture of Confederate locomotive, "The General," was plotted at this hotel in 1862 by James Andrews.

OTHER POINTS OF INTEREST

Atomic Burial Ground — Maxey Flats. KY-32.

Goddard Covered Bridge (Grange City Bridge) — Goddard. Off KY-32. Built 1867-1868. It is 158 feet long.

Hillsboro Covered Bridge — Fox Creek. KY-111. Built 1865-1870.

Fleming County High School.

Ringo Mill Covered Bridge — Fox Creek. KY-158. Built 1867.

Sand Lick Covered Bridge — Goddard. KY-32. Timbers are held together with wooden pegs.

Sherburne Covered Bridge — S.W. of Flemingsburg. KY-11. Built 1867-1868. This "suspension" bridge is the most unusual of Kentucky's covered bridges. In the early days, a stagecoach route from Mt. Sterling to Maysville crossed this bridge, which was then privately owned. Bridge is 266 ft. long, with a single roadway 14-ft. wide. Heavy steel suspension cables and reinforcing timbers were added in 1951.

Goddard Covered Bridge.

First Presbyterian Church (1799) in Flemingsburg.

Lewis County

Lewis County is located in the northeastern part of the state, bordering the Ohio River. It is located in "the knobs" area and was Kentucky's forty-eighth county to be created. Lewis County was organized in 1806 from part of Mason County and was named for Captain Meriwether Lewis of Virginia who commanded the famous expedition up the Missouri River, across the Rockies, and down the Columbia River to the Pacific.

Vanceburg is the Lewis County seat, and is located at the mouth of Salt Lick Creek on the Ohio River. Emigrants coming from Pennsylvania down the Ohio on flatboats landed at the mouth of Salt Lick Creek, then headed for the famous hunting grounds of "Old Kaintuckie."

PARKS, RECREATION, LAKES, DAMS

Meade Forest Wildlife Area — Vanceburg. KY-10. Located on KY-59, KY-344. 6,000 acres. Hunting in season.

Kinniconick Creek — Near Vanceburg. Famous fishing spot, due to its crystal-clear water. Boating and picnicking. April-October.

Dam 32 – Picnic Area — Near Vanceburg. KY-8. Scenic area on Ohio River.

Ruggles Campground — Epworth Community, near Burtonville. KY-1237. A Methodist summer camp established 1872 on land donated by the Ruggles Family. Now privately owned.

MARKERS

Cabin Creek — Tollesboro. KY-10, KY-57. Early point of entry into Kentucky for explorers and pioneers. From here, marauding Indians crossed the Ohio River. War roads, marked with drawings of animals, the sun, and the moon, led from its mouth to Upper Blue Licks.

Route for Horses and Cattle — W. of Vanceburg. KY-8, KY-10. In 1775 Col. Robert Patterson, William McConnell, David Perry, and Stephen Lowry brought the first horses and cattle into northern Kentucky. Animals were brought by boat from Fort Pitt and driven overland from here to the early inland settlements.

Magnificent Pin Oak — 1 mi. E. of Charters. N. of KY-10. One of the largest and oldest pin or swamp oak trees in the world. In 1970 when the highway was relocated, this oak was determined to be about 150 years old; its trunk circumference was 16.2 feet; the diameter at breast height was 5 feet, and total height was 58 feet. This historic oak is preserved as one of nature's beautiful achievements.

MEMORIALS

Union Monument — Vanceburg, 2nd St. Courthouse lawn. Only Union monument south of the Mason-Dixon Line. This unique memorial was dedicated in 1884 to the 107 Lewis County soldiers who gave their lives for the Union during the Civil War.

Union Monument in Vanceburg.

OLD BUILDINGS

Commercial Hotel — Vanceburg. Oldest building (cook-house before 1800) before 1806. Since Salt Lick Creek seems to be connected with the first route back to the settlements, it was supposed settlers would be attracted to it sooner than to other parts. A first settler, Dudley Calvert, related that the first cabins in the Salt Lick Valley were where the remains of the first salt furnaces can still be seen (about one mile from Vanceburg).

Walnut Grove Church — Emerson Community. KY-59 and KY-344. First Methodist Conference held here in the early 1800's.

OTHER POINTS OF INTEREST

Wooden Covered Bridge — Near Tollesboro Community. KY-984. Junction of Little and Big Cabin Creeks. One of few covered bridges still in public use.

Mary Inglis Trail — Near Vanceburg. KY-8. Trail named after a pioneer woman who was captured by the Indians, then escaped and fled homeward along the Ohio River.

Commercial Hotel in Vanceburg.

Esculapia Springs Historical Health Spa — Near Glen Springs at head of Salt Lick. KY-989. Former site of a mineral health spa known as Esculapia Springs in late 1800's and early 1900's. Historian Lewis Collins, a frequent visitor, described the area as a "romantic valley surrounded by tall hills of easy access from which the view is picturesque and enchanting."

Mason County

Mason County, organized in 1788 from part of Bourbon County, is one of the oldest Kentucky counties. Eighth in order of creation, it was named for George Mason of Virginia, author of the Virginia Declaration, which was the foundation for the United States Bill of Rights.

Mason County was the port of entry into Kentucky for settlers voyaging down the Ohio River. Christopher Gist made surveys of the area in 1751 for the Ohio Land Company. In 1775-1776 Simon Kenton, pioneer "patron saint" of the area, built a station near present-day Washington, Kentucky. Well known to settlers, the area was too close to hostile Indian lands to have permanent settlers until 1784.

Limestone, later renamed Maysville, was settled in 1784. Washington was established in 1786, and was the county seat and second largest town in Kentucky by 1790. Maysville became the county seat in 1848. Maysville changed its name from Limestone to honor a pioneer landowner, John May.

Arts Festival — Washington. US-62, US-68. August.

Court Day — Maysville. October.

Frontier Christmas — Washington. US-62, US-68. Tour of restored homes and churches. December.

Geranium Day Festival — Washington. US-62, US-68. May.

Hayseed Festival — Washington. US-62, US-68. June.

MARKERS

First Courthouse — Washington, off Main St. Built 1794. Site of Mason County's first courthouse.

Old Jail — Washington, off Main St.

Limestone — Maysville, Courthouse yard. US-62, US-68. Settled in 1784 by John and Edward Waller, and George Lewis. Pioneer river gateway to the west. Named Maysville 1787. Lands were owned by John May and Simon Kenton.

Morgan's Last Raid — Mays Lick. US-68. After taking Mt. Sterling, Lexington and Cynthiana during June 1-11, 1864, CSA Gen. John H. Morgan was defeated by USA Gen. G. G. Burbridge. Morgan retreated through here. Raiders never recovered from this defeat.

National Post Road — S. of Washington city limits. US-68. Road follows the Buffalo Trace from the Ohio River to the Licking River. In 1816 it became the "National Road" from Zanesville, Ohio to Florence, Alabama, and the first macadamized road west of Alleghenies.

Simon Kenton's Station — 4 mi. S. of Maysville. US-68. About 1/2 mile west is site of Simon Kenton and Thomas Williams' 1775 camp. Later fortified, it became the major stronghold north of the Kentucky River.

MEMORIALS, MUSEUMS

Mason County Museum — Maysville, 215 Sutton St. Built in 1876 as a Public Library. It has been restored and enlarged. Listed on National Register of Historic Places, 1974.

Paxton Inn Museum — Washington, National Post Rd. circa 1810. This old inn has been restored and furnished in the style of the period. Houses a genealogy library.

CEMETERIES

Early Graveyard — Maysville, 221 Sutton St. Directly behind the library. Perhaps the town's first cemetery. Contains quaint old gravestones of early residents, among whom are Jacob Boone, first trustee of Maysville; Charles Erb Wolfe, first Mayor; and Peter Grant, uncle of U. S. President Ulysses Grant.

OLD BUILDINGS

Armstrong House — Maysville, Front St. Built 1834. Home and store of John Armstrong. Unique arch and cobblestone pavement. First brick house in Maysville.

Armstrong Row — Maysville, 2nd St. Built in the early 1800's by enterprising merchant, John Armstrong. He is said to have arrived in Maysville as a peddler, and made a fortune.

First Branch Bank in Kentucky — Washington, Main St. Built 1809.

Bank of Maysville — Maysville, 2nd St. Established 1835. Present building houses beautiful murals of Mason County scenes.

Baptist Church — Maysville, Market St. Third edifice on same site. Was first a log building, then frame, and now brick.

Bayless-Forman-Taylor House — Washington, Main St. Built 1802.

Bierbower House — Maysville, 4th St. Built by one of Maysville's first carriagemakers.

Indian Fort — Washington, Main St. Built prior to 1800 as protection from Indians.

Cane Brake Shop — Washington, Main St. Built 1790. One of the original log houses of the town which typifies the structures of Simon Kenton's day. Now an antique shop. Handicrafts and refreshments.

Christian Church — Maysville, 3rd St. Built 1823.

Washington Christian Church — Washington, Main St. Built 1848.

Church of the Nativity — Maysville, 3rd St. Built 1823. Services first held in 1850. Church is noted for late 19th century brass fittings and altar. Tudor-Gothic style. Designed by the first bishop out of Kentucky, Bishop Smith.

Clerk's Office — Maysville, 3rd St. Built 1860. Contains

Macon County Library-Museum in Maysville.

many records of pioneers, such as Boone, Kenton, and of John May, for whom the town was named.

Rosemary Clooney's Childhood Home — Maysville, Rosemary Clooney St. Famous singing star lived in red brick house at top of street. Named for her when her first motion picture premiered in her home town.

Coburn-Stevenson Home — Washington, National Post Rd. Built 1800.

Lewis Collins' Home — Maysville, 4th St. Noted historian lived in this house. It was also a school, then a funeral home. Now privately owned.

Collins-Davis Home — Washington, Main St. Known for Gothic architecture commonly known as carpenter's Gothic.

The Courthouse — Maysville, 3rd St. Built City Hall, 1844. Then Mason County Courthouse, 1848.

Dr. Basil Duke-Judge John Coburn McMurty School for Girls — Washington, Green St., Malone. Built 1810.

Dr. Louis Frazee House — Maysville, 3rd St. Built 1856. Home and office.

Dr. John Shackleford House — Maysville, 4th St. Built prior to 1850. Office for early Maysville physician.

Dover Bridge — Dover, over Lock Run of Lee's Creek. KY-8. Built 1835. Kentucky's oldest covered bridge. 62 feet long.

Early Building — Washington, Main St. circa 1839. John Marshall-Combess-Hesler, owners of the original building.

Federal Hill (Marshall-Fryman) — Washington. US-68. Built in 1800 by Thomas Marshall, brother of Chief Justice John Marshall. Home of 7 generations of Marshall family.

Ficklin House — Maysville, 4th St. House has fort room built as protection from Indians in early days.

Arthur Fox, Sr. — Washington, Main St. circa 1795. One of the men who laid out the town of Washington. Only rock house in Washington, first rock house in Washington, first rock house in the county.

Fox-Bickley — Washington, Main St. Built 1785. First frame house in Mason County.

Hayswood Hospital — Maysville. Mary Wilson presented old Hayswood Seminary to the city for use as a hospital.

A. M. January House — Maysville, 3rd St. Built 1838. Continuous residence by descendants of the January family.

Meddford's Fort in Washington.

January & Wood — Maysville, W. 2nd St. Established 1834. Oldest industry, and second oldest cotton mill in the state. Became January & Wood in 1851.

Albert Sidney Johnston Home — Washington, off Main St. Built 1797. The childhood home of the Commander of the Confederate Army of the West. Now houses antiques and relics of Washington's history.

Lee House — Maysville, Sutton St. and McDonald Parkway. Formerly Lafayette Apartments, this was a famous old hotel, and its early register, now at public library, lists Henry Clay as a visitor. An earlier building was the inn where Lafayette visited, hence, the first name.

Marshall Key House — Washington, Main St. Allen, circa 1800. Harriett Beecher Stowe was visiting the daughter of Marshall Key when she witnessed a slave sale that inspired *Uncle Tom's Cabin.*

Mason County Jail — Maysville. Built 1884. First jail was attached to Jacob Boone's Tavern on Front Street, built 1820.

Mefford's Fort — Washington, National Post Rd. Built in 1789 by George Mefford. Believed to be one of the last existing flatboat houses in the United States. It has been moved from its original site and restored from timbers of the flatboat on which Mefford, his wife and 13 children came down the Ohio from Maryland.

Methodist-Episcopal Church — Washington, National Post Rd. Built 1848. The Old Church Museum. This church was adapted as a museum when a newer church was built. It contains the original furniture of the original church. Also, fine paintings of the four apostles, Matthew, Mark, Luke and John. Special activities still held here.

Moose House — Washington, National Post Rd. Built 1805. Owned by descendants of the Moose family.

Newdigate Tavern — Maysville. US-68. Log summer home of former Supreme Court Justice Stanley F. Reed.

Old Well — Washington, Main St. Washington was the first town west of the Alleghenies to have a public waterworks. In 1798 the Kentucky Legislature appropriated $1,000 for fire protection for the town. Twenty-two wells were dug and several of them are still in use today, as are the original flagstone sidewalks.

Opera Theater — Maysville, 2nd St. Built on site of "Old Blue" church, first Presbyterian church. Later a

Row of brick houses in Maysville.

City Hall. A theater built in 1885 burned to ground in 1898, and was rebuilt the next year. Another fire caused damage in 1930, when the Fire Department was housed in part of the building.

"Phillip's Folly" — Maysville, Sutton St. This house was started in 1825 by William B. Phillips, who ran out of money before construction was completed. Rumor persists that after winning at gambling, he completed the house in 1828. Constructed on a dry foundation of hand-quarried stone.

Pillsbury School — Washington, off Main St. circa 1820.

Platt Stout House — Maysville, Wall St. Built 1823. Very old home.

Presbyterian Church — Maysville, 3rd St. Present building erected in 1850. A disastrous fire burned the "Old Blue" church which stood on grounds where Washington Opera House now stands. On Aug. 13, 1854, an explosion of gunpowder more than half a mile away knocked a hole in the side of the new church, and ths hole has been preserved as a bit of Maysville history.

Presbyterian Church South — Washington, Main St. First church erected 1806, second 1844, present church 1870.

Public Library — Maysville, Sutton St. Contains collection of rare books of local history and a self-portrait of Asron Corwin, the famous artist, who was born here. Also has museum pieces on display, and portrait of Lewis Collins, noted author of "History of Kentucky."

Residence — Maysville, 2nd St. Listed in City Directory of 1860, as "McCarty's Hotel." Present owner was told that the cornerstone of Maysville forms part of old basement wall.

Rev. Edgar House — Maysville, 3rd St. Built in 1820's. House of first Presbyterian minister, John T. Edgar. Made of logs covered by clapboard.

Rhoden Hord House — Maysville, 3rd St. Built 1822. Oldest brick house in the block.

Row of Brick Houses — Maysville, 3rd St. circa 1850. Iron grillwork shows New Orleans influence, a result of great river trade. Most of the row was built by John Armstrong, wealthy merchant of early Maysville.

St. Patrick's Church — Maysville, 3rd St. Built 1910.

Scott House — Maysville, Front St. Early home where first Catholic Mass was said in city.

Sheriff's Office — Maysville, 3rd St. Built prior to 1817. Home of Pleasant H. Baird, early Maysville jeweler.

Tavern — Washington. Tavern operated by Daniel Boone and wife.

Robert Taylor Home and Store — Washington, Main St. Morris, circa 1830.

Trinity Methodist Church — Maysville, 3rd St. Original building constructed in 1847. Present structure built in 1955 on site of older church. Ground was given for church by John Armstrong.

Washington Hall — Washington, Main St. Built 1845. Hotel.

Washington Slave Block — Washington, Main St. Harriet Beecher Stowe witnessed slaves sale here which inspired her to write *Uncle Tom's Cabin.*

Isaiah Wilson House — Maysville, 3rd St. Built 1824.

Wood-Barnett-Wood — Washington, US-68. circa 1800.

OTHER POINTS OF INTEREST

Covered Bridge — S.W. of Dover to KY-1235. Erected 1835. One of the oldest covered bridges in Kentucky still in use, it was originally a toll bridge. The 62-foot span was built in an unusual Queensport truss design similar to early barn construction. Major repairs were made by Bower Bridge Co. in 1928. Restoration of bridge was completed by the Kentucky Highway Department in 1966.

Fox Field — Mays Lick. Large Mississippian Indian village and burial site. One of the best representations of Fort Ancient Culture in Kentucky.

"Old Tip" — Maysville, 3rd St. Cannon used in Battle of Tippecanoe in 1811. Buried in ground after several accidents, and used for a hitching post. Now located in courthouse yard.

Site of First Blockhouse — Maysville, corner of Limestone and 2nd St. In 1785 a double log cabin and blockhouse was erected by three Virginians, Edmund Waller, John Waller, and George Lewis. The first permanent building in city.

Site of First Ferry — Maysville. Operated by Benjamin Sutton.

Site of First Post Office — Washington, National Post Rd. Established in 1790's. Site of first post office west of Allegheny Mountains, and distribution point for mail going to seven states.

Site of the Office of the "Eagle" — Maysville, Court St. Founded in 1814. The *Maysville Eagle* was first newspaper published in Maysville.

Site of Old Markethouse — Maysville, the middle of Market St.

Washington Guided Tours — Washington. March-December, except Sunday-Monday.

Bridge across Ohio River at Maysville.

Menifee County

Menifee County, the one hundred thirteenth county to be established in Kentucky, was formed in 1868 from parts of Bath, Montgomery, Powell, Wolfe, and Morgan Counties. It was named in honor of Richard H. Menifee, a native of Bath County and one of the state's most brilliant young statesmen, who was elected to Congress when only 27 years old.

The county is located in east central Kentucky, a heavily forested and mountainous area lying between two important superhighways, Interstate-64 and the Mountain Parkway. About eight percent of the county is in the Daniel Boone National Forest, an important part of the scenic beauty of the area. Three-fourths of the Red River Gorge is in Menifee County, also.

Frenchburg, the seat of justice for Menifee County, was named in honor of Judge Richard French, a lawyer and political leader. Judge French was the popular, although unsuccessful, opponent of Mr. Menifee in the race for U. S. Representative in 1837. French was also the Democratic candidate for governor in 1840. He was defeated by the Whig candidate, Robert P. Letcher. Frenchburg is located twenty-one miles east of Mt. Sterling.

FESTIVALS

Cave Run Country Music Barn — Korea. KY-1693. Country music on weekends.

Menifee County Mountain Festival — Frenchburg. Third week of August.

RECREATION, LAKES

Broke Leg Falls — Wellington. US-460. Rough trails lead to Bear Hole and saltpeter caves. Scenic terrain.

Cave Run Lake — Frenchburg. KY-1274. Longbow boat access ramp. Marina.

Primitive Weapons Hunting Area — Frenchburg. Off KY-1274. Hunting with only primitive weapons such as bow and arrow, muzzle-load rifle, etc., are allowed.

MARKERS

Beaver Dam Furnace — Scranton. KY-1274. Erected in 1819 by J. T. Mason. Began operations under Robert Crockett, ironmaster. The furnace was a big truncated pyramid of sandstone blocks, 35-ft. high with a 28-ft. square base. Some furnace products included nails, "plough plates," kettles, skillets, and flatirons. The goods were shipped down river to the markets in flatboats. The furnace went out of business in 1870-1873.

Murder Branch Massacre — 10 mi. E. of Frenchburg. KY-1274. In April 1793 Indians captured 19 women and children at Morgan's Station in Montgomery County. Overtaken north of here by a posse, the Indians massacred some captives, and took others across Ohio River. Thought to be the last Indian raid in Kentucky.

Broke Leg Falls State Park.

217

OTHER POINTS OF INTEREST

Carrington Rock — Sudith. KY-36. Prominent in Civil War activity. A tannery was located at the foot of the mountain, and the rocks were used as a lookout point. It is a 1 1/2 hour hike to here from KY-36. See Forest Rangers for location.

Donathan Rock — Frenchburg. KY-36 and US-460. A unique, balanced rock that crowns a stone-topped mountain. Several rough trails lead to this spectacular overlook from downtown Frenchburg. See Forest Rangers for location.

Greenwade Rock — Frenchburg. KY-1274. Tom Greenwade came from Pennsylvania to operate the Scranton furnace, and was also superintendent. Mr. Greenwade built the first hotel in Frenchburg.

McCausey Ridge Lookout Tower — Frenchburg. Off US-460. At the end of McCausey Ridge.

Natural Bridge Formation — Frenchburg. US-460.

Located at Byrd Ridge, on the farm of Willard Welch.

Old-Fashioned Sawmills — Sudith, near Post Office. KY-36. Another is located off US-460, on Amos Ridge.

Red River Gorge — Menifee County. KY-715. Douglas Trail, Moonshiner's Arch, and Tower Rock are attractions of the gorge in Menifee County.

Sorghum Mills — Frenchburg. On Fletcher Ridge, off KY-77. Another is located S. of Frenchburg. US-460. Others are located throughout the county. Mills operate in late September and through October before frost.

Tater Knob Lookout Tower — Frenchburg. Off KY-36, on KY-211. Natural arches, trails.

Town Cliffs — Frenchburg. On US-460.

Twin Falls — US-460. Falls located above Broke Leg Falls.

Weather Observation Station — Fletcher Ridge Road. KY-77.

 # Montgomery County

Montgomery County, the twenty-second county to be created in Kentucky was formed in 1796 and taken from part of Clark County. The county was named for General Richard Montgomery, an Irishman who fought in the Revolution. He commanded an attack on Quebec and was killed. Eighteen counties have been formed out of the original Montgomery County.

Mount Sterling, the county seat, was established in 1793. It was originally called Little Mountain Town. Hugh Forbes, an early surveyor, changed the name to Stirling. Through an error in spelling, it became Mount Sterling.

FAIRS

Court Day — Mt. Sterling. Traditional swapping and marketing of goods and articles. Originally held when judges held court. Unpromoted event with larger attendance each year. Third Monday in October.

Montgomery County Fair — Mt. Sterling. US-60W. American Legion Park. Annually in July.

MARKERS

Battle – June 8, 1864 — Mt. Sterling. US-460. Early on

this date, CSA forces under Gen. John H. Morgan attacked a Union camp here, on his tragic last raid. Next morning, CSA were driven out.

Battle of Mt. Sterling — Mt. Sterling, Courthouse yard. US-60. On March 22, 1863 about 300 Confederate cavalrymen took 438 prisoners, 222 wagon loads of military stores, 500 mules and 1000 stand of arms. Confederate losses were 80 killed, 13 wounded. Union losses were 4 killed, 10 wounded.

Estill's Defeat — Mt. Sterling. US-60. On March 22, 1782 in Battle of Little Mountain, Capt. James Estill and seven of his force of 25 pioneers were killed in desperate hand-to-hand fighting with a band of 25 marauding Wyandot Indians.

OLD BUILDINGS

Ascension Episcopal Church — Mt. Sterling, High St. The cornerstone for the new Ascension Episcopal Church, the oldest church building still in use in Mt. Sterling, was laid in March, 1878. Beautiful Gothic church.

Camargo Methodist Church — Mt. Sterling. circa 1800-1805. The ground for old Fort Meeting House was the first in the county to be deeded to a Methodist Church. The log meeting house had been constructed previously. In 1850 the congregation built the present church at Camargo. About 3/4 mi. E.S.E. of the present Camargo Church property is the Old Fort woods. At one time a fort was built in these woods for protection against the Indians.

The First Christian Church — Mt. Sterling, Main St. In 1826 "Raccoon" John Smith led a group of followers out of the Particular Baptist Church due to the influence of Barton W. Stone and Alexander Campbell. From July, 1827 to July, 1828 he baptized 114 people into his church. The present church, constructed in 1927, is the sixth built by the congregation.

Grassy Lick Methodist Church — Mt. Sterling, on Prewitt-Grassy Lick Pike. US-60W. Present brick building erected in 1868. Church designated a Methodist shrine in 1967. A bronze plaque in churchyard states, "Grassy Lick Methodist Church — Founded before 1790. First church erected in 1793, oldest continuous Methodist church in Kentucky. Bluegrass was first

found at a Salt Spring 100 yards northeast of this church."

Gen. John Bell Hood's Boyhood Home — Mt. Sterling, US-60W. John Bell Hood was a West Point graduate who resigned from the U. S. Army and returned to Texas to join the Confederate Army. Hood led the troops in the campaign of Atlanta, Franklin and Nashville. Died at the age of 48 in 1879.

Mt. Sterling Library — Mt. Sterling, High St. In 1879 Lewis Apperson, Howard R. French, D. B. Garrison, and M. S. Tyler, all under the age of thirty, felt that the town needed a library. One of the few remaining libraries in the state that operates without a tax levy.

Morgan's Station — Mt. Sterling, Harpers Ridge, 6 mi. E. on county road. House on site of stockade station built in 1789 by a group of settlers led by Ralph Morgan, cousin of Daniel Boone. On April 1, 1793 Indians attacked, burning the stockade and killing nineteen people. Last organized Indian raid in Kentucky. The house as it now stands was constructed in 1796.

Old Salem Church — 4 mi. S. of Camargo. KY-40. The present church, a frame building, was built in 1865. The estimated date of the original church building is 1815.

Battle of Mt. Sterling in Courthouse yard at Mt. Sterling.

Morgan County

Morgan County, the seventy-third county to be created in Kentucky, was established in 1822. Taken from portions of Floyd and Bath Counties, this new county was named for General Daniel Morgan of Virginia, an officer of the Revolutionary War.

Morgan County is primarily an agricultural county, with dairy products and tobacco being of major importance. Tobacco, the major money-making crop, brings one-half million dollars to the county annually.

West Liberty, located on the Licking River, was established in 1823 and is the county seat.

FAIRS, FESTIVALS

Morgan County Fair — Malone, RECC Fairgrounds. KY-191. September.

Sorghum Festival — West Liberty. US-460. Sorghum making, arts and crafts, quilting, mountain music, and square dancing. Second weekend in October.

MARKERS

West Liberty-Civil War — West Liberty. US-460. The first important Civil War engagement in eastern Kentucky occurred here on Oct. 23, 1861. USA forces led by Brig. Gen. William Nelson surprised Confederates under Capt. Andrew J. May. Civilian secessionists were captured and jailed and Unionists released. Confederate losses included 21 dead, 40 wounded, 34 captured. Only one Union soldier was wounded. On Nov. 4, 1861, Gen. Nelson captured Prestonsburg.

CEMETERIES

Caney Graveyard — Caney, near Cannel City. KY-191. Burial place of early Morgan County settlers. The Daniel C. Williams Historical Society is erecting log cabins as a memorial to Mr. Williams near the cemetery.

OTHER POINTS OF INTEREST

Hell's Half-Acre — 15 mi. W. of Paintsville, at intersection of Johnson, Magoffin, and Morgan counties.

KY-437. Rough, primitive tributary featuring exposed cliffs, caves, crags, and boulders.

Riffle Springs — 8 mi. N. of West Liberty, Wrigley Hill. KY-7. Formerly consisted of 2 hotels and mineral springs. Remaining today are the partially covered mineral springs.

Teakettle Rock — 20 mi. E. of West Liberty. Near Hell's Half-Acre. Balanced rock teakettle-shaped overlooking Paint Creek Gorge. Said to carry markings descriptive of the famed "Swift silver mine" location.

Wrigley Arch — Near the Village of Wrigley. North of KY-7, 1/2 mi. on KY-711. One of over 100 known arches in or near the Daniel Boone National Forest.

Yocum Falls — 10 mi. N. of West Liberty, near community of Yocum. KY-519, KY-1002. Scenic waterfall spills into gorge near road.

Wrigley Arch in Daniel Boone National Forest.

Robertson County

Robertson County is Kentucky's smallest county in population, and the second smallest in area. It was the one hundred eleventh to be established in Kentucky and was formed in 1867 from parts of Bracken, Nicholas, Harrison, and Mason Counties. It was named for Judge George Robertson of Mercer County, who was the Chief Justice of the Court of Appeals.

Mount Olivet, the county seat, is now a small, serene little town with 600 citizens. Once known as "Hell's Half-Acre," various businesses once flourished there — including the 23-room Louisiana Hotel which was built in 1869. The hotel is now a family residence on Main Street, Mount Olivet.

Other county communities include Kentontown, Piqua, and Pinhook (Bratton's Mill). The tobacco term "pinhooker" is still used to identify small speculators who buy crops occasionally in the hopes of turning a profit. Although these communities are considerably smaller now than in days gone by, they still serve as a source of identity and community spirit for those living near them.

PARKS

Blue Licks Battlefield State Park — Mount Olivet. KY-165. 100-acre state park includes picnic and recreation area, pool, hiking trails, fishing. The Battle of Blue Licks, Kentucky's most important historic battle took place here on August 19, 1782, after the British surrender at Yorktown. It is called the "Last Battle of the Revolution" and represents Kentucky's strongest link with the American Revolution.

MARKERS

Mount Olivet Courthouse Marker — Mount Olivet, Court St. County named 1867 for George Robertson (1790-1874). Member of Kentucky Court of Appeals, Speaker and member of State Legislature.

MEMORIALS, MUSEUMS

Blue Lick Museum — Blue Lick Battlefield State Park, Mount Olivet. KY-165. Museum has large collection of pioneer artifacts. The Blue Licks story is graphically presented from the Ice Age through the last battle of the Revolutionary War. April-October.

Granite Monument — Blue Licks Battlefield State Park. KY-165. Names of 60 Kentuckians killed in an Indian ambush. One was a son of Daniel Boone.

OLD BUILDINGS

Baptist Church — Mount Olivet, Main Street. Oldest concrete block building in the county (1907). Blocks were made on the church grounds.

Courthouse — Mount Olivet, Court Street. Original brick building. Considered an architectural example by Kentucky Heritage Commission and listed in the Spindletop Survey of Historic Sites.

Oldest Stone House — Kentontown, KY-617. Built by Governor Thomas (Old Stone-Hammer) Metcalfe for his son.

OTHER POINTS OF INTEREST

Johnson Creek Covered Bridge — Mount Olivet, on Old Blue Licks Road. Built 1878. In original condition. Picnic tables available.

Courthouse in Mt. Olivet.

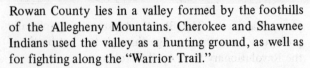

Rowan County

Rowan County lies in a valley formed by the foothills of the Allegheny Mountains. Cherokee and Shawnee Indians used the valley as a hunting ground, as well as for fighting along the "Warrior Trail."

In 1856 Rowan County was the one hundred fourth to be created in Kentucky, and was formed from parts of Fleming and Morgan Counties.

Rowan County received its name from Judge John Rowan, a distinguished jurist, a United States Senator from Kentucky, an uncle of Stephen Collins Foster, and the builder and owner of "My Old Kentucky Home."

Morehead, the county seat, was named in honor of James T. Morehead, once Governor of Kentucky.

FAIRS

Northeast Gateway Regional Fair — Morehead. July.

PARKS

Daniel Boone National Forest — Morehead. U.S.-60, I-64. Scenic. Picnic grounds.

Rodburn Hollow — 2 mi. from Morehead. Off US-60E. Narrow, steep-sided valley in Daniel Boone National Forest. Camping units, picnic tables, shelter, hiking trails, many varieties of wild flowers.

Tripwood Park — Holly Ford Road. Off KY-799. Picnic tables, grills, shelter house. Community-owned.

MARKERS

First Moonlight School — Morehead, Main St. Established in 1911 by Mrs. Cora W. Stewart, "to emancipate from illiteracy those enslaved in its bondage." Because the people had to labor by day, it was decided to have classes on moonlight nights so the moon could light the way to the school. The schools were taught by volunteer teachers. Movement soon spread nationally and internationally.

Morgan's Raiders — Farmers. US-60. Site of Morgan's Raiders' foray into county during Civil War. Camped here before returning to Virginia.

OLD BUILDINGS

Bratton Branch School — Left, 1/4 mi. past I-64 interchange. KY-32N. Local interest in restoring this old school. Now privately owned.

Old Cranston School — At Cranston, on Clearfork Road. Off KY-377. Church youth center.

OTHER POINTS OF INTEREST

Abandoned Brick and Coke Plant — Haldeman, 5 mi. E. of Morehead. US-60. Right 1 mile on KY-174. Abandoned plant. Now privately owned.

Amburgey Rock — 5 mi. from Clearfield, Mill Branch Road. Large rock formation in the Daniel Boone National Forest.

Bangor Indian Mounds — Off KY-1274. Excavating done by Morehead State University. Now privately owned.

Big Limestone Knob — Off Lockege Road, KY-1274 onto Big Limestone Road. One of the highest points in Rowan County. All of Morehead and the entire Triplett Valley may be seen. National Forest. See Forest Ranger for detailed information.

Claude Brown Stables — N.W. of Morehead. KY-32. Home of Major Wilson, world champion walking horse. Now privately owned.

DAR Memorial Plantation — Cranston, near Post Office. Off KY-377. Beautiful 30-acre stand of short-leaf pine and yellow poplars planted in 1940. U. S. Forest Service.

Kentucky Division of Fish and Wildlife Fish Hatchery — 2 mi. from Farmers. KY-801. Largest fish hatchery in the state. State-owned.

Laurel Cliff — Near Elliott County line. Off KY-173. Scenic rocky cliff. National Forest.

Licking River Bridge — Follow KY-1274 (Pretty Ridge Road) to near Menifee County line. High bridge, and scenic view. Land now privately owned.

Limestone Quarries and Clay Mines — 3 mi. S. of Clearfield. KY-1274 (Pretty Ridge Road). Excavation reveals several interesting geologic formations.

Lockege Rock (Lover's Rock) — Morehead to Clearfield on KY-519 to Clack Mountain and Jct. with KY-1274. Large rock formation. National Forest. See Forest Ranger for location.

Morehead State University — Morehead. Established 1887. Became State University in 1966. Museum on campus in Lappin Science Hall. Museum has many relics from archaeological excavations.

Paragon Tunnel (Poppin Rock) — 10 mi. from Clearfield, S. on KY-519. Clack Mountain.

Scenic Drive — 15 mi. from Morehead. KY-377, KY-799. Through beautiful valley with view of distant peaks and through wooded mountain area.

Triangle Tower — From Morehead, take KY-519 to Clearfield. A pinnacle with 1,386 ft. elevation. Lookout tower, scenic overlook. Nearby are caves once used as tobacco barns. National Forest. See Forest Ranger for location.

Morehead State University at Morehead.

Lockege Rock in Daniel Boone National Forest.

Cave Run Lake.

Northeast Area

GREENUP

BOYD

CARTER

ELLIOTT

LAWRENCE

JOHNSON

MARTIN

MAGOFFIN

FLOYD

PIKE

Boyd County

In 1860 the one hundred seventh county established in Kentucky was formed from portions of Greenup, Carter and Lawrence Counties. This new county was called Boyd County in honor of Linn Boyd of McCracken County. He was spoken of in an old history book as a "long resident of Kentucky and prominent in public life."

The county was established and settled because of the iron, coal, and other natural resources of the Ohio River and Ohio River Valley. It is historically known as the area where coal meets iron. Numerous charcoal furnaces used in the early 1800's still remain in the county today.

Ashland, the seventh largest city in Kentucky, is in Boyd County and is located on the Ohio River. Known for its oil and steel production, Ashland was first called Poage's Landing, for one of the families who first settled in the area. The name was later changed to Ashland in honor of the home of Henry Clay in Lexington.

Catlettsburg is the county seat. It was named for a family who were among the earliest settlers. The town's first merchant, Catlett was in business at the time the town was laid out in 1849. At this time, Catlettsburg was the largest town in the county, so it was chosen as the location for the courthouse. Many descendants of early families still live in this area and our early heritage is still appreciated in this beautiful little city.

DRAMAS AND EXHIBITS

Paramount Arts Center — Ashland, 1310 Winchester Ave. Concerts and plays feature professional and amateur talent.

Ashland Arts Gallery — Ashland, 501 15th St. Open daily.

Parade of Skills — Ashland, Mid-Town Shopping Center. Organized by Boyd County Extension Homemakers, its purpose is to display arts and crafts and to interest prospective members. September.

PARKS

Central Park (Indian Mounds) — Ashland, Central Ave. between 17th and 22nd Sts. Indian mounds are located at the 17th St. entrance. They have been restored to their original proportions. The 5 mounds date from the Adena period (800 B.C.-800 A.D.) This 52-acre park contains recreation facilities.

MARKERS

Buena Vista Furnace — Summit, 3 mi. S.W. of Ashland. KY-5 at KY-884. Built in 1847 by William Foster and Co. It was named for a Mexican War battle fought in that year. The furnace was an important factor in the Hanging Rock iron industry until dismantled in 1876. Stone stack was 40 ft. high with a maximum inner diameter of 10 ft.

Norton Furnace — Ashland, Winchester Ave. at 23rd St. US-23, US-60. In 1967 the world's oldest known operating blast furnace. Built by Norton Iron Works Co. in 1873, an iron shell stack 67 ft. high with maximum inner diameter of 18 ft., burning "stone coal." Operated by Armco Steel Corp. after 1928.

MEMORIALS, MUSEUMS

McGuffey Log School Museum — Ashland, 3201 Cogan St. US-60. Log cabin school has copies of McGuffey's Readers and memoirs of William H. McGuffey (1800-1873) who started work on readers while teaching in Bourbon County, Kentucky. McGuffey's Eclectic Readers were used in all parts of the United States. Over one million copies were sold in the 1800's. His stories were designed to win the interest of students. Words in McGuffey's stories taught pronunciations and accents.

CEMETERIES

Old Catlettsburg Cemetery — Catlettsburg. Off US-60. In this cemetery are the graves of the Horatio Catlett family and many of their descendants. It is one of the oldest cemeteries in the area.

Lockwood Cemetery — Lockwood. US-23. This is a typical old family cemetery. Graves date back to the time the area was being settled. The Lockwoods were one of the most prosperous farm families in the area.

OLD BUILDINGS

Dr. Hugh Martin Home — Ashland, 1520 Chestnut Dr. Built in 19th century. An interesting home, it has been modernized for today's living.

Mayo Manor — Ashland, 16th St. and Bath Ave. This beautiful old home was once the hub of social life in the area. Now an office building.

First United Methodist Church — Catlettsburg, 2712 Louisa St. Built in 1867 by the Methodist-Episcopal South Congregation, one of two groups formed when a split occurred during 1844 from the General Methodist Conference. The two factions of the church were re-united in this building in 1939.

First Presbyterian Church — Ashland, 1600 Winchester Ave. Oldest church in Ashland. The present structure was built in 1858. Extensively remodeled twice. Church was organized June 11, 1819 at home of Maj. James Poage, as Bethesda Presbyterian Church by Rev. Robert Wilson with 20 members.

OTHER POINTS OF INTEREST

Armco Steel Corporation — Ashland. US-23. Site of the largest blast furnace in the free world. Tours by appointment.

Ashland Community College — Ashland. 1400 College Drive. Established 1957. College is now under the University of Kentucky Community College system.

Ashland Oil and Refining Company, Inc. — Ashland and Catlettsburg. Ashland oil ranks among the top 150 corporations in the country. Offices are in Ashland but the factory is located on US-60 out of Catlettsburg. Guided tours can be arranged for organized groups. Open to public.

Stone Serpent Mound — Catlettsburg. US-60 and I-64. Mound estimated to be 5000 years old. The 600-to-800 ft. formation is of stone laid in the shape of a serpent. Thought to be the only one of its kind in the U. S. Not open to the public at present, but future plans are for a park.

226

Ashland Community College in Ashland.

Poage's Landing Settlement Play in Ashland.

McGuffey Log School Museum in Ashland.

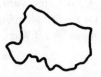

Carter County

In 1838 Carter County became the eighty-eighth county to be established in Kentucky. It was formed out of parts of Greenup and Lawrence Counties, and was named in honor of Colonel William G. Carter, who was then State Senator from Lewis, Greenup and Lawrence Counties.

The first settlement in Carter County is believed to have been established in 1808 at the Sandy salines by persons engaged in the salt business. Grayson, the county seat, was named in honor of Colonel Robert Grayson, who was once aide-de-camp to General George Washington. Grayson is located on the Little Sandy River.

Carter County is known for its brickyards. Fired brick has been made here for many years. It has been said "The Good Lord knew what he was doing when he made so much red clay in Carter County, for it has furnished a livelihood for more people than any other industry."

Today Carter County has become a sportsman's paradise since the Grayson Reservoir was built. Thousands come to this lake each year to camp, fish, picnic and water ski.

FESTIVALS

American Folk Song Festival — Grayson. Carter Caves State Resort Park. KY-182 off US-60 and I-64. Authentic folk music presented by descendants of the early settlers. Music with the Elizabethan flavor of the sixteenth century is played on quaint lutes, fiddles, dulcimers and recorders. Traditional mountain hymns, which are uniquely Kentuckian, are chanted in the Gregorian musical mode, which dates back to 550 to 600 A.D. The festival was founded by Miss Jean Thomas, "the Traipsin' Woman" in 1930. June.

Davy's Run Homecoming Festival — Hitchins. KY-1. Special homecoming for all the "old timers."

Fraley Family Festival — Olive Hill. Mountain music. August.

Grayson Memory Day — Grayson. Street dancing, displays, horse shows. The entire week bustles with activities, leading up to one big day. Annual in May.

Olive Hill Homecoming Celebration — Olive Hill, Downtown area. Parade, arts, crafts, music, and fireworks. June-July.

PARKS, RECREATION, LAKES, DAMS

Carter Caves State Resort Park — Olive Hill. KY-182, off US-60 and I-64. This 1000-acre resort park is located in a region abounding in natural bridges, rugged cliffs and mountain streams. The mountain-top lodge overlooks the 45-acre Smoky Valley Lake. Year-round guided tours through three electrically lighted caves, Saltpetre Cave, "X" Cave and Cascade Cavern. Each has its own peculiar geological character and a number of rare natural formations. Two other caves, Bat and Laurel, may be toured through special arrangement. Bat Cave is of particular interest because of its extraordinary bat population, numbering in the hundreds of thousands. Lodge, cottages, campground, fishing, hiking, horseback riding, swimming, boats and miniature golf are available.

Grayson Lake State Park — Grayson. Off KY-7 on Little Sandy River. An earth and rock-fill dam has created a lake in Carter and Elliott Counties with a seasonal pool of 1,500 acres, approximately 20 miles long. It serves for water quality and flood control, as well as recreation. Camping, beach, boating, fishing, picnic areas available.

Grayson Lake Wildlife Area — Grayson. Off KY-7 on Little Sandy River. State-regulated hunting in season.

Tygart's State Forest — Olive Hill. Off US-60 and I-64, near KY-182. Western boundary of Carter Caves State Resort Park. Picnicking, hiking, and state-regulated hunting in season.

MARKERS

Aviation Pioneer — US-60 and KY-182. Matthew Sellers was among the first to experiment with gliding and power flight from 1897-1911. Built most advanced wind tunnel of his day to study lift and drag of various wing designs, 1903. Developed first use of retracting wheels on powered plane 1908; it is said to be lightest plane ever flown.

Beckham County — Olive Hill. US-60. It was created from parts of Carter, Lewis and Elliott Counties. The county seat was established here by legislative act February 9, 1904 by Governor J. C. W. Beckham, for whom it was named. On April 29, 1904 the Court of Appeals ruled that it failed to meet constitutional standards of size and population and ordered it dissolved.

Mt. Savage Furnace — E. of Grayson. Jct. US-60 and KY-1. 6 miles S. is site of famous iron furnace erected in 1848 by R. M. Biggs and others. Operated for 37 years, averaging 15 tons of pig iron daily, which was hauled by ox teams to the Ohio River for shipment.

Pactolus Furnace — Pactolus. KY-1. Built in 1824 by Joseph McMurtry and David L. Ward on the site of an earlier bloomery forge. Its stone stack used charcoal fuel and its air blast machinery was powered from a dam 5 1/2 ft. high in Little Sandy River. Last blast before 1835.

MEMORIALS

World War I Monument — Grayson, Courthouse yard. Monument was placed here in memory of those who served their country and gave their lives in World War I.

OLD BUILDINGS

Governor Fields Home — Olive Hill. US-60. Home of thirty-fourth Governor of Kentucky, William Jason Fields (1874-1954), "Honest Bill from Olive Hill." Governor from 1923-1927. U. S. Congressman, 1911-1923.

Matthew Sellers Home — 6 mi. S. of Jct. US-60 and KY-182. The palatial home was destroyed by fire in 1975. The building where Mr. Sellers worked on his airplane is still standing but will soon be dismantled and moved to the Aeronautical Museum in Connecticut.

OTHER POINTS OF INTEREST

Kentucky Christian College — Grayson. KY-1, KY-7. Established 1919. Christian Church and Church of Christ.

World War I Monument in Grayson.

Elliott County

In 1869 Elliott County became the one hundred fourteenth county to be established in Kentucky, carved from parts of Morgan, Carter and Lawrence Counties. A settlement at present-day Sandy Hook developed due to timber harvesting during the 1820's. The Little Sandy River was navigable to this point, so that rafts of logs could be floated downstream to the Ohio River. When Elliott County was organized, Sandy Hook became the county seat, but its name was changed to Martinsburg. Ten years later the town changed its name back again to Sandy Hook.

Elliott County was named for Judge John M. Elliott of Bath and Floyd Counties. Judge Elliott was assassinated by a disappointed litigant in a land case decided by the court.

Most of the industries in this county are related to the natural resources the area provides. There is still a large quantity of good-quality coal mined from the hills. Most mining is being done by strip mining, and the land is being reclaimed.

Many families now living in Elliott County are descendants of settlers who migrated here through the Cumberland Gap and they are very proud of their heritage.

PARKS, RECREATION

Grayson Lake — N.W. of Sandy Hook. KY-7. Much of the 1,500-acre lake lies in Elliott County, with a State Park in adjoining Carter County. Excellent fishing. Recreational spots being developed for picnicking, camping, boating and swimming.

MARKERS

A Masterful Retreat — Sandy Hook, Courthouse yard. KY-7, KY-32. Gen. George W. Morgan's 9,000 USA forces occupied Cumberland Gap June 18 to September 17, 1862. Cut off from supplies, he began 200-mi. retreat. Passing through Elliott County, the troops were harrassed by CSA Morgan's Raiders. Failure to combine with reinforcements caused CSA Raiders to withdraw at Grayson on October 1. The Union retreat from Cumberland Gap to Greenup on Ohio River was made in 16 days.

Skirmish Here — 2 mi. S. of Sandy Hook. On KY-7. This burial ground is the final resting place of 7 unnamed soldiers who were killed in a Civil War skirmish here in late September, 1862, between forces of USA Gen. George W. Morgan and CSA Gen. John H. Morgan. Union forces retreating from Cumberland Gap to Greenup were harrassed by Confederates from West Liberty to Grayson.

OTHER POINTS OF INTEREST

Diamond Mine — Little Fork, S.E. end of county.

"The Narrows" — 1 mi. from Sandy Hook. KY-32. In the Laurel Cliffs, beautiful rocks and stream.

Scenic Area — Little Sandy Palisades.

Scenic Areas — Along KY-7 and KY-32.

Scenic view from Highway 32.

Floyd County

Floyd County was created in 1799 as the fourteenth county to be established in Kentucky. The county was named for Colonel John Floyd, the noted Indian fighter and early Kentucky surveyor who founded Floyd's Station.

Prestonsburg, settled in 1797 and located on US-23, US-460 and KY-114, is the county seat. It is a beautiful little town on the Big Sandy River. After much growth, the town is now divided by the river. A University of Kentucky Community College is located here, giving local residents new opportunities for education.

Floyd County was Indian country when the first settlers arrived from Virginia. Solomon Stratton was one of the earliest settlers, and he settled where Mare Creek Road now meets US-23.

Coal has made Floyd County important and quite prosperous.

FAIRS, FESTIVALS, DRAMAS, EXHIBITS

Concert Series — Prestonsburg Community College, Bert Combs Drive. October-May.

Floyd County Fair — Prestonsburg, Archer Park. US-23. Annual project for business people and University of Kentucky Extension organizers. September.

Highlands Folk Festival — Jenny Wiley State Resort Park. KY-304. Arts and crafts exhibits, folk music and dancing. August.

Mountain Dew Festival — Prestonsburg, Downtown. Exhibits, athletic events, dancing. April.

Red, White and Blue Day — Prestonsburg, Mt. Parkway and US-23. Floats, bands, dignitaries. Has received national publicity. Founded by Mrs. Marcella Bailey. October.

Summer Theater — Jenny Wiley State Resort Park. KY-304. Continuous plays and musicals in the amphitheater. June-August.

PARKS, RECREATION, LAKES, DAMS

Archer Park — Prestonsburg. US-23. Recreation area, horse show arena and drama theater.

Dewey Lake — Jenny Wiley State Resort Park. KY-304. Recreation area, fishing, camping.

Jenny Wiley State Resort Park — Prestonsburg. KY-304 off US-23, US-460 and KY-114. The 1700-acre park is on Dewey Lake, surrounded by 12,000-acre forest. The park was named for the pioneer woman, Jenny Wiley, who was captured by the Indians and endured eleven months of captivity before she escaped unaided and made her way back to Prestonsburg. Recreation area and camping.

Sugar Camp Mountain Skylift — Jenny Wiley State Resort Park. KY-304. Chair lift skyride (4700 feet). On top of mountain are scenic trails, picnicking, recreation area.

MARKERS

Battle of Middle Creek — 1 mi. W. of Prestonsburg. KY-114. Deciding factor in control of Big Sandy Valley. On January 10, 1862, Gen. Humphrey Marshall leading CSA forces was defeated here by USA forces under Col. James A. Garfield, who was later to become President of the U. S.

Courthouse in Prestonburg.

Boone Salt Springs — David. KY-404. Discovered by Daniel Boone and companions while exploring eastern Kentucky in the winter of 1767-1768. Later called Young's Salt Works. These springs provided salt for pioneers in the valley and for troops on both sides during the Civil War.

Stratton Settlement — Jct. US-23 and Mare Creek Rd. Founded in 1796 by Solomon Stratton, a veteran of George Rogers Clark's expedition to Illinois in 1778. In the Virginia militia in 1783. In 1788 he explored this region. Eight years later, he and his kinsmen from Virginia settled here. In 1797 Matthias Harman, Andrew Hood and Stratton laid out Prestonsburg for Col. John Preston. Stratton died in 1819 and is in an unmarked grave, 500 ft. east of this spot.

OLD BUILDINGS

Garfield House (Leete Home) — Prestonsburg, Arnold Avenue. Built between 1853-1857. Former headquarters of Gen. James A. Garfield following the Battle of Middle Creek during the Civil War.

Jenny Wiley State Resort Park at Prestonburg.

OTHER POINTS OF INTEREST

Prestonsburg Community College — Prestonsburg, Bert Combs Drive. Founded 1964. Part of University of Kentucky system.

Scenic view of Dewey Lake at Jenny Wiley State Resort Park.

Greenup County

Greenup County, established in 1803 as the forty-fifth county created in Kentucky, was taken from part of Mason County. It was named in honor of Christopher Greenup, an Indian fighter and Revolutionary War Colonel. He was prominent in the origination of the District of Kentucky, was a member of the first Congress, Clerk of the Senate, and became the third Governor of Kentucky in 1804.

After the establishment of Greenup County, part of its territory was given to the formation of Lawrence, Carter and Boyd Counties. The county is rich in mineral resources. Its iron is of supreme quality. Coal is found in great abundance.

Greenup, located on US-23, is the county seat. It was incorporated February 4, 1818 as Greenupsburg. The name was changed to Greenup in 1872. Greenup lies near the Ohio River and the Little Sandy River. Records show the first County Court was held at the home of Andy Hood on February 20, 1804.

Jesse Boone, active in county affairs, aided in organizing the courts and planning roads. He owned much land north of Greenup. He is buried in the Shuff Cemetery, near Eastfork in Greenup County.

Many historic landmarks, especially old ironworks furnaces, still stand in the county.

FAIRS

Greenup County Fair — Greenup. Sponsored by Greenup County Fair Association and Greenup County Extension Service. Second week in September.

Old Fashioned Day — Greenup. Greenup merchants, as well as business and professional people organize the program.

PARKS, RECREATION

Greenbo Lake State Resort Park — Greenup. KY-1, off US-23. Located at the site of early ironworks. Park has 3,300 acres of land and the 225-acre Greenbo Lake. A primitive iron ore smelter, Buffalo Furnace, is located in the park. Iron production ended around 1875. Plans are underway to reproduce blast furnaces and buildings to simulate the 19th century appearance of the area. Park has recreation area, as well as camping and fishing.

MARKERS

Bellefonte Furnace — Greenup-Boyd County line, KY-5. Built in 1826 by Archibald Paull, George Poague and others. The most successful of pioneer Kentucky charcoal furnaces in the Hanging Rock Region. Operated until 1893, leaving an accumulated slag heap of 300,000 tons.

Chanoah Marker (Ancient Indian Old Fields) — South Portsmouth. KY-10. First village in Kentucky built by Shawnee Indians and French traders was visited by Christopher Gist, George Croghan, Andrew Montour, Robert Kallender and a servant in January, 1751. Located on site of an earlier Fort Ancient Settlement, it stood 500 yards northwest of these Adena earthworks.

Eastern Kentucky Railroad — Jct. US-23 and KY-1. A major factor in development of this area, the Eastern Kentucky Railway operated from the Ohio River to Argillite in 1867. Reached Webbville in Lawrence County in 1889. Total trackage is 38 miles. It hauled timber, iron ore, locally made pig iron, coal, but never became part of a Lake Erie to Virginia route planned by its Bostonian builder. Abandoned 1926-33.

Hopewell Furnace — Hopewell. KY-1. In 1824 William Ward built a bloomery forge, converting it to a blast furnace, also known as Camp Branch Furnace in 1832-33. Air-blast was water-powered. Operation ceased in 1944.

Laurel Furnace — Oldtown. KY-1 and Laurel Creek Rd. Built in 1849 by George and Samuel Wurts. Bottom half of the stack, originally 39-ft. high, is carved from one block of stone cliff. Last blast in 1874.

A First in Steel — Boyd-Greenup County line. US-23. World's first continuous steel sheet rolling mill; put into operation in 1923. Conceived by John B. Titus and built by Armco, this process rated as one of the greatest inventions in human history. In 1953 hot-strip mill replaced first continuous mill.

Old Steam Furnace — Wurtland. US-23 at KY-503. Built in 1824 by the Shreve Brothers. First blast furnace in Hanging Rock region to operate blowing engines by steam power rather than water. Abandoned after 1860.

MEMORIALS

Jesse Stuart Monument — Greenup Courthouse lawn. Inscription reads, "Kentucky is my land."

CEMETERIES

Agling Cemetery — Greenup. Graves of early settlers and slaves.

Grave of Lucy Virgin Downs (1769-1847) — Oldtown. KY-1. Oldtown Christian Church. The first white child born of American parents west of the Allegheny Mountains.

Old Cemeteries — South Shore, East Tygart Road. US-23. Mt. Zion Methodist Church and Cemetery. Burial place of Nina Mitchell Biggs, county historian.

Plum Grove Cemetery and Community Church — Greenup. KY-1. Burial place of Jesse Stuart's parents and spot where he began to write poetry.

Riverview Cemetery — Greenup, Morton addition. Some outstanding features of cemetery are tombstones, pioneer burial plots of early settlers, etc.

OLD BUILDINGS

Buffalo-Clay Lick (schoolhouse) — Greenup. Located in Greenbo Lake State Resort Park. One-room school. Plans for a souvenir shop, which will be open to public.

Jesse Stuart Home — Greenup, West Hollow. Off KY-1. Born in 1907, Jesse Stuart is known as the Kentucky plowman who used to scratch sonnets on leaves when he came to the end of a furrow. Stuart is considered one of the few originals among American writers. First book of 700 sonnets, *Man With A Bull-Tongue Plow*, was included in Henry S. Canby's list of "100 Best Books in America."

OTHER POINTS OF INTEREST

Bennett's Mill Covered Bridge — 8 mi. S. of South Shore, over Tygart's Creek. KY-7. One of Kentucky's longest wooden covered bridges, 195-ft. in length. Built circa 1855 by B. F. Bennett and his brother Pramley to accommodate customers at their mill.

Cane Creek Schoolhouse — Argillite. KY-207. One-room school where Jesse Stuart first taught.

Oldtown Covered Bridge — Little Sandy River. Off KY-1. Built 1875. Sandstone abutments support the 170-ft. bridge. Faint traces of posters recommending Gibson Girls show and circuses can still be seen inside the covered bridge.

Scott Farm — Greenup, Oldtown. KY-1. Log salon and old slave cabins.

Jesse Stuart Home in West Hollow.

Jesse Stuart Lodge at Greenbo Lake State Park.

Raccoon Furnace built in 1833.

Johnson County

Johnson County was created in 1843 and named for Colonel Richard M. Johnson, a Kentuckian who had just completed a term as Vice President of the United States. Johnson County, the ninety-seventh to be formed in Kentucky was partitioned from parts of Lawrence, Floyd and Morgan Counties.

The first settlement in Eastern Kentucky was in Johnson County at Harman Station in 1787. Harman Station was a stockade east of Paintsville and was settled by Matthias Harman and a party of hunters from Virginia.

Paintsville, the county seat, was originally called Paint Station. It was founded in 1790 by Colonel John Preston, and is located in a region of Indian habitation which dates back to prehistoric times. Burial mounds and peculiar paintings were discovered on the cliffs, causing the early explorers to call the stream Paint Creek. These paintings were created with dyes made from trees, berries, leaves and roots. Heavy rains would wash these dyes into the creek, coloring it. When families from Harman Station settlement founded the town, they called it Paintsville after the name of the stream.

The legend of Jenny Wiley originated in Johnson County. She was captured by Indians and taken downstream and across the Ohio River. She later escaped her abductors near Chillicothe, Ohio and returned, on foot, to her home. She died here and her grave is about seven miles from Paintsville at River, Kentucky. A monument in her honor is standing in the cemetery.

FESTIVALS

Johnson County Apple Festival — Paintsville. Apple King and Princess Parade, arts and crafts and apple butter making. Apples available in all forms. Dancing; Apple Ball. Mule derby, band festival, antique car show. Big Sandy Bowl football game. October.

MARKERS

American Historian — Paintsville. US-23. Bypass. William Elsey Connelley was born on Middle Fork at Jenney's Creek in 1855. He wrote the *Founding of Harman's Station, The Wiley Captivity, History of Kansas* and 13 other major works. He collaborated with Coulter on *History of Kentucky,* edited by Kerr. Died 1930.

Harman Station — 5 mi. S. of Paintsville. US-23, US-460. The first settlement in Eastern Kentucky. Matthias Harman's party of hunters from Virginia built a stockade near the river bank in 1787. In 1788 Indians forced evacuation and burned the blockhouse. In 1759 Harman and others returned and rebuilt a more durable fort. These men at Blockhouse Bottom broke the Indian hold on the Big Sandy Valley and opened Eastern Kentucky for settlement.

Paintsville — Paintsville-Bypass. Jct. Jefferson Ave. and US-23. The second oldest settlement in Eastern Kentucky, it was first named Paint Lick Station, and was established in 1790 by Colonel John Preston. Dr. Thomas Walker probably camped at the mouth of Paint Creek near abandoned log cabins in 1750. Rev. Henry Dixon laid out the town and built the first house in 1826.

The Walker Expedition — Paintsville. KY-40 at KY-581. Dr. Thomas Walker led the first recorded expedition from Virginia into eastern Kentucky. He camped at the present site of Paintsville in 1750. On June 7, 1750 he discovered French cabins at the mouth of Paint Creek. He named the river Louisa, honoring

Johnson Central High School.

the daughter of King George II and sister of Duke of Cumberland.

World War I Memorial — Paintsville. A granite and copper monument sitting in the corner of the county courthouse yard. The names of the 25 Johnson County war casualties are engraved on the marker.

CEMETERIES

Jenny Wiley Marker and Grave — River, 12 mi. N.E. of Paintsville. KY-581. Jenny's capture by Indians and escape after many months are one of Eastern Kentucky's most famous historical events. Jenny was captured by the Shawnee Indians in October, 1787 during a mistaken attack on Thomas and Jenny Wiley's cabin. Thinking it was the cabin of Capt. Matthias Harman, Sr., they killed three of her children and her fifteen-year-old brother. She remained an Indian captive until the end of October 1788 when an escape passage was revealed to her in a dream. During a heavy wind and rain storm, water blew into the rockhouse where she was imprisoned, enabling her to free herself from the rawhide thongs which bound her. She climbed down a large hemlock tree beside the high rockhouse, waded down Mudlick Creek, Paint Creek, and several other creeks and rivers in the area. She saw the Harman Station blockhouse where Henry Scaggs, the only man at the fort, saw her on the far side of the Louisa River. He made a raft of three logs tied together with grapevines, crossed the river, and rescued Jenny just before the Indians arrived. She was reunited with her husband in Virginia and settled in Johnson County in 1800.

OLD BUILDINGS

Cassius Cooper House — Paintsville, 3rd St. Large home, always well painted and landscaped. He was the first druggist in Paintsville.

Daniel Davis Home — Paintsville. US-460. Located on ground where the Battle of Jenny's Creek was fought in 1862, also a widely-travelled route to and from Paintsville. Served as a community center from 1889-1919. Daniel Davis was a leading banker and merchant.

General D. Hager Home — Paintsville, 5th and Court Sts. Two story, 8-room frame house. Bay area in front and porched on both levels.

Mayo Mansion — Paintsville, 3rd St. Built in 1905-1912 by John C. C. Mayo. This three-story, forty-room brick home is the most outstanding residence in Big Sandy area. Mansion now used as a convent and elementary school called "Our Lady of the Mountain."

Stafford Home — Paintsville. Elegant old frame home located so Paint Creek is in view from three sides, as well as much of the town.

G. James Turner, Judge Home — Paintsville, 3rd St. Brick structure with beautiful landscaping.

Mayo Mansion in Paintsville.

Lawrence County

Lawrence County, the sixty-ninth county in order of formation in Kentucky, was created in 1821. It was named to honor Civil War Captain James Lawrence, whose dying words, "Don't give up the Ship" has become a watchword in Naval traditions of this country.

The county's history dates back to the earliest Kentucky explorations, when Gabriel Arthur passed the forks of the Big Sandy River in 1674 as an Indian captive.

George Washington was familiar with the Lawrence County area as he drove the first claim stakes on the Big Sandy River in 1770. This is one of two places in Kentucky visited by Washington, who surveyed 2,084 acres on a tract of land that now includes Louisa, the county seat. Louisa was named after Levisa Fork, a corruption of Louisa, the name of the Duke of Cumberland's wife. A settlement was made in 1789 by Englishman Charles Vancouver. Indians caused abandonment of the settlement until 1815 when Frederic Moore laid out the present town of Louisa.

The county now has 425 square miles to make it the twenty-ninth largest county. It stretches for many miles along the Big Sandy Valley on the eastern border of Kentucky. The first county commissioner was William Waters. It was his duty to choose the site for the courthouse and any other necessary buildings. He appointed five constables and laid off the county into constabled districts. Many accomplished people come from this area, but none as well-known as the late Supreme Court Chief Justice Fred M. Vinson.

MARKERS

Giant Cooling Tower — 1 mi. N. of Louisa. US-23. Completion of this tower in 1962 was an historic event. It was the first of its kind in the Western Hemisphere and had the largest capacity of any single tower in the world when it was built. It is 320-ft. high and its diameter is 245 ft. at the base, 130 ft. at the neck and 139 ft. at the top.

Louisa In Civil War — Louisa, Courthouse yard. US-23. River traffic caused Union forces under Gen. James A. Garfield, later 20th U. S. President, to occupy Louisa in December, 1861. CSA troops attempted capture March 12 and then 25-26, 1863. Southern partisans raided the area November 5, 1864 burning houses, 2 steamers, and looting stores. USA Fort Bishop was completed here just as the war ended in 1865. Also called Fort Gallup and Fort Hill.

Frederick M. Vinson — Louisa, Public Library. US-23. "A great jurist, a distinguished Secretary of the Treasury and a noted Congressman." Born in Louisa, Kentucky on Jan. 22, 1890. City attorney, Commonwealth attorney, Congressman, D. C. Court of Appeals 1938-43. Director of Economic Stabilization, Federal Loan Administrator, Director of War Mobilization, Secretary of Treasury 1945. U. S. Chief Justice, 1946 until death Sept. 8, 1953.

Giant Cooling Tower near Louisa.

236

MEMORIALS

Vancouver's Fort Marker – Louisa. Commemorates 1789 settlement of Louisa area by Englishman Charles Vancouver.

CEMETERIES

Pine Hills Cemetery – Grave of and monument to Supreme Court Chief Justice Fred Vinson. Magnificent view from knob overlooking Louisa.

OLD BUILDINGS

Fred M. Vinson Birthplace (Old Jail) – Louisa, Main and Cross Sts. Historical marker reads "Chief Justice of the United States. A great jurist, a distinguished Secretary of the Treasury, and a noted Congressman." Vinson served as Chief Justice of U. S. Supreme Court from 1946 until his death in 1953. Vinson's father was county jailer at time of his birth. Vinson was the only Chief Justice born in a jail.

OTHER POINTS OF INTEREST

Big Sandy Bridge – This bridge crosses both the Levisa and Tug Forks of the Big Sandy River at Louisa. It connects West Virginia and Kentucky. It is a one-lane bridge and was a toll bridge until recently. It has Fort Gay, West Virginia, on one side and Louisa on the

Big Sandy Bridge near Louisa.

other and was once billed as the only bridge in the world that spans 2 rivers, connects 3 bodies of land, 2 states, 2 cities, and 2 counties.

Fallsburg Covered Bridge – Louisa. Off KY-3. Crosses Little Sandy Creek on farm road. Built in 1924 it is Kentucky's newest and shortest (40 feet) covered bridge.

Yatesville Covered Bridge – Louisa, Yatesville. KY-3. Built in 1879 and is 132 ft. long and spans Blain Creek. Tourist attraction only, not in use.

Magoffin County

Magoffin was the one hundred eighth county to be formed in Kentucky. In 1860 it was established with territory from Morgan, Johnson and Floyd Counties. It is named in honor of Governor Beriah Magoffin from Mercer County, who was the chief officer of the Commonwealth at that time.

There is much evidence that Magoffin County was traversed by white men in the early 1700's, but these explorers left no records. The first settlement was established in 1794 by Archibald Prater, John Williams, Ebenezer Hanna, Clayton Cook and others, but they were driven out by Indians. Six years later, when the area was safer, settlers returned and built their cabins and fort one mile below present-day Salyersville.

Salyersville, the county seat, derives its name from Judge Samuel Salyers, a member of the legislature. Salyersville is surrounded by rich farm land, asphalt rock, and oil wells. The first oil well in Magoffin County was completed September 4, 1919. This brought many oil men and scouts to the section.

In 1912, the Big Sandy and Kentucky River Railroad began operation. Opening up an isolated territory. As a result, many millions of board feet of lumber have been shipped to market from Magoffin County.

FESTIVALS

Annual Homecoming – Connelley Park. Horse show, street dance, "coon-on-the-log" trials. July 4.

Salyersville Art Activities — Salyersville, Downtown. Arts and crafts. July.

MARKERS

First Settlement — Salyersville, Courthouse yard. US-460. Archibald Prater, John Williams, Ebenezer Hanna, Clayton Cook and others attempted to settle here in 1794, but were driven out by Indians. They returned in 1800 and settled Licking Station, on a hill in a horseshoe bend of the river, a good defense against Indians.

Ivy Point Skirmishes — Salyersville. US-460. During the Civil War, the Union Army's 14th Kentucky Inf. operated in this area to scout and protect Eastern Kentucky. On Oct. 30, 1863, 160 of these troops under Lt. Col. Orlando Brown, Jr. repulsed Confederates here and captured 50 prisoners. Another skirmish occurred on Nov. 30, 1863 when Capt. Peter Everett, in command of 200 Confederates, led a surprise attack and captured 25 USA soldiers.

Reuben Patrick Grave — 1 mi. W. of Ivyton. KY-114. He was a Detachment leader, 14th Vol. Inf. USA force, engaged largely in this area. The CSA camped near Ivyton in March 1863. As the posted guard slept on the night of the 20th, Patrick boldly detached their gun from its carriage and hid it in the woods. CSA moved on and left the carriage. Gun was displayed for many

Courthouse at Salyersville.

years but is now lost. Patrick was also a Kentucky legislator 1863-1867.

CEMETERIES

Puncheon Cemetery — Fritz. KY-114. First burial, 1884.

OLD BUILDINGS

Gardner Home — Salyersville. US-460. Built 1830. Early log house.

Prater House — E. of Salyersville, off Mountain Parkway. Built 1820. Early log house.

Martin County

Martin County was the last region of Kentucky to be given up by the Indians. Being a rugged mountain area, it drew only the hardiest of pioneers. The first settler, James Ward, came here in 1779, a veteran of the Revolutionary War and a hunting companion of Boone. Boone.
Around 1812, George R. C. Floyd established the town of Warfield and started a saltworks. It was the first county seat. Floyd and his associates later opened the first coal mines, which were used during the Civil War as hiding places from marauding enemies. Inez, the present county seat, was established in 1873. Eden was the first name given to Inez, but the name was changed because there is another town in Kentucky named Eden.

Martin County was the one hundred sixteenth county formed in Kentucky and was formed from portions of Pike, Johnson, Floyd and Lawrence counties. It was named for Colonel John P. Martin, who came to the county in 1828, became a state Representative, Congressman, and then, in 1848 Lieutenant Governor.

Coal is the largest industry in Martin County, and the coal boom has hit twice there since 1920, when Martin Himler and several other Hungarian families settled at what is now known as Beauty, Kentucky. The Depression hit very hard in Himlerville, and most of the people left, although there are still a few Hungarian families in Martin County. In 1970, the coal boom came again to the county, where there are now several large mines being worked. Most of the people are employed by the mines or in some related industry.

The beautiful, scenic Appalachian mountains in the area are a fascinating attraction during the seasonal changes.

MARKERS

Educator Ward — Inez, Courthouse yard. KY-3, KY-40. William Ward was born in 1877 and buried in Saltwell Cemetery in 1952. He was a well-known author and leader in the field of education for 50 years. Principal in schools of eastern and northern Kentucky; head of the old Sandy Valley Seminary at Paintsville. Author, *Outline of U. S. History;* publisher, *The Mountain Journal* and *The New Day.* Descendant of Pioneer Ward.

Pioneer Ward — Inez, County Courthouse yard. KY-3, KY-40. Born in Virginia in 1758, James Ward settled on Rockcastle Creek, 3 mi. south, where he lived for 50 years and died in 1848. He came to Kentucky in 1779 with the Clark expedition against Indians in Chillicothe and Piqua, Ohio 1780. He fought in battles of Bryan Station and Blue Licks in 1782.

Moses Stepp — 10 mi. S. of Lovely, Pigeon Roost Valley Rd. Colorful frontiersman. Ancient headstone shows he was born in 1735 and died in 1855. Enlisted for three short periods in the Revolution and fought Indians and Tories in west Carolinas and east Tennessee. Legend tells that he was captured by the Cherokees and tortured by nailing his ears to a tree. He tore loose and escaped. In 1826, he settled in Martin County.

A Warfield Skirmish — Warfield. KY-40. A Confederate force under the command of Col. V. A. Witcher plundered and burned eastern Kentucky and ginia during most of Civil War. In the fall of 186 took horses and cattle in this area from friend and While Witcher's men made barbecue, Home Guard from Louisa attacked from a hill to the west. After exchanging fire, both withdrew.

CEMETERIES

Old Mucy Cemetery — Warfield, Roost Branch off Emiley Creek. Graves of Civil War veterans.

Warfield Cemetery — Warfield. KY-40., Graves of early pioneer settlers.

OLD BUILDINGS

W. W. Barrett Home — Warfield. KY-40. Built late 1800's; one of the oldest homes in the county that retains original design. W. W. Barrett was said to have known Abe Lincoln. Not open to the public; tours available.

Martin County Courthouse — Erected 1939.

Presbyterian Church — Inez. Built 1904. First Presbyterian church in county. Oldest church in Inez. Became Wilson Memorial Academy in 1904.

OTHER POINTS OF INTEREST

Coal Mine — Warfield. KY-40. Worked before Civil War. Soldiers hid there during Civil War.

Old Saltworks — Warfield. KY-40.

Courthouse at Inez.

The W. W. Barnett Home in Warfield.

239

Pike County

Pike County, Kentucky's largest county in size and eighth largest in population, was formed from Floyd County in 1821 to become the seventieth county established in Kentucky.

The county was named for Zebulon Montgomery Pike of New Jersey who was one of the greatest explorers of the west, discovered Pike's Peak, and was killed at York in Upper Canada in 1813.

Before his term in the presidency, Colonel James A. Garfield was promoted to General in Pikeville. Pikeville, located on Levisa Fork of the Big Sandy River, is the county seat. Established in 1824, it is the largest producer of underground coal in the world. It also has been selected as an All-American, and an All-Kentucky City.

Located squarely in the Big Sandy Valley, Pike County was the scene of the Hatfield-McCoy feud, beginning about 1880. The bloody vendetta centered around the ownership of a lean razorback hog which led to court proceedings. The Hatfields won the decision which shortly afterwards led to a bushwhacking, allegedly perpetrated by the McCoys. Before the feud ended, some fifty members of the Hatfields and McCoys families had perished in a bloody battle at Grapevine Creek.

The County's banking community is the third largest in Kentucky, after Louisville and Lexington. In 1974 the three local banks more than doubled their assets and deposits.

FESTIVALS

Community Concert Series — Pikeville College, Sycamore St.

Tri-State Singing — Breaks Interstate Park, Potter's Knoll. KY-80 off US-460. Gospel singing. September.

PARKS

Breaks Interstate Park, "Breaks of the Big Sandy" — Elkhorn City. KY-80 off US-460. The park occupies 1,880 acres on the Russell Fork of the Big Sandy River at the Kentucky-Virginia border. A unique undertaking by the two states, the park is set on the rim of the largest river canyon east of the Mississippi River, known as the "Grand Canyon of the South." Through the five-mile cut, the palisades rise 1000 ft. above the river bed. Midway is "the Towers," a pyramid-shaped rock formation half a mile long and almost as wide rising above the river. Twelve-acre Laurel Lake, caves, hidden springs, and the lodge are other features of the park. The visitors' center houses exhibits of Breaks fauna, flora, and geology.

Fish Trap Dam and Reservoir — S.E. of Pikeville, on the Levisa Fork of the Big Sandy River. KY-1789, off KY-80. Dedicated in 1968 by President Johnson, the dam is 1,100 ft. long and 195 ft. high. It impounds the waters in the Fish Trap Reservoir, which at its highest level, will extend for over 25 miles into southeastern Pike County.

Jefferson National Forest — Southeastern Pike and Letcher Counties. US-23, US-119, KY-15. Most of this 550,626-acre forest lies in Virginia. The Kentucky portion is undeveloped. A part of Pine Mountain Wildlife Management Area is in Letcher County. Hunting and fishing are permitted according to state regulations. Although no facilities are provided, camping is also permitted.

Laurel Lake — Breaks Interstate Park. KY-80 off US-460, 12-acre lake. In the vicinity of the lake are caves, springs, wild flowers and variety of plant life.

MARKERS

James A. Garfield — Pikeville City Park. US-23, US-119, US-460. Here Col. Garfield was commissioned a Brigadier General in the Union Army. The man who later became President was sworn in as a General by Squire Charles of Pike County in January 1862.

Known But To God — Breaks Interstate Park. KY-80. Here rests the body of a soldier of the Confederacy, struck down by an unknown assassin in May 1865, apparently on his way to his home in the South. He was buried in a coffin made by 4 men of the community. After the turn of the century, a rose bush marked this final resting place of a soldier who is "Known but to God."

OTHER POINTS OF INTEREST

Duty's Knob — Pikeville. Morgan's Raiders ammunition hideout.

Initial Rock Overlook — Pikeville. US-23. Breathtaking view of Pikeville.

Lookout Rock Overlook — Pikeville. Off US-23. On a cliff overlooking the city, with the still visible signs of an Indian lookout.

Lovers' Leap — Pikeville. Off US-23. Hiking adventure leading to a cliff bearing a legend of two young Indian lovers.

Pikeville College — Pikeville, Sycamore St. US-23. Founded 1889 as a Presbyterian-related secondary school. Now a 4-year coeducational institution. The college serves as the main educational component of Pikeville's Model City Program, adjusting curriculum to meet the needs of the area.

Pikeville College at Pikeville.

Pikeville Cut-through Project.

Swinging Bridge across Levisa Fork of the Big Sandy River.

Quicksand Area

Breathitt County

The eighty-ninth county in order of formation in Kentucky, Breathitt County was formed in 1839 from parts of Estill, Clay and Perry Counties. The county was named for Governor John Breathitt, who died in office in 1834.

Once remote, today's accessibility to the county has changed its economic and living conditions. Located in the heart of the Eastern Coal Field, only thirty percent of the area is devoted to farming while the rest of the land is rich in coal and iron ore.

The county seat, first named Breathitt, was changed in 1845 to Jackson, honoring Andrew Jackson, the hero of New Orleans and the seventh President of the United States. Formerly known as the "Queen City of the Mountains" due to its booming coal period, Jackson is still considered a center for trade and industry.

A famous legend of the county is the "silver cache" reportedly buried somewhere by Jackie Clemons. Before Clemons' death he could not dig it up because his relatives kept watch. Since his death, hordes of people have searched this area for the cache, but have not been successful in finding it.

EXHIBITS

Ceramics and Pottery Exhibition — Jackson. Ernest Shouse Library.

Oil Paintings and Prints — Jackson, 1024 College Ave. Ernest Shouse Library.

RECREATION, LAKES

Middle Fork and North Fork of Kentucky River — Excellent canoeing through virtually uninhabited wilderness, and exciting white water in the spring.

Pan Bowl Lake — Jackson. KY-15. Unique 70-acre body of water. Fishing, camping, recreation.

MARKERS

Breathitt Volunteers — Jackson, Courthouse yard. KY-15, KY-30. During World War I, this county attained national prominence by filling its quota of servicemen by volunteers. No men had to be drafted from Breathitt, the only county in U. S. with this record. During the war 3,912 men registered, 405 volunteered, 324 were called, 281 inducted and 43 rejected. Kentuckians ranked among the highest in the nation in physical fitness.

Quicksand – 1864 – KY-15, KY-30. Part of Co. 1, 14th Kentucky Infantry, USA forces attacked Confederates camped here on April 5, 1864. CSA loses were light, with few killed or wounded and only 3 prisoners and 24 horses taken. Gen. John H. Morgan's CSA Raiders, on tragic last raid into Kentucky, moved here. After two battles at Mt. Sterling, they met defeat in Cynthiana on June 12, 1864 and retreated to Virginia.

Sam and Nola VanderMeer of Morris Fork — Morris Fork, at Morris Fork Presbyterian Church, KY-28. Samuel VanderMeer came here from New Jersey in 1923. "Uncle Sam" to generations of Kentucky youngsters, he became pastor of the Morris Fork Presbyterian Church in 1927, the year he married nurse Nola Pease. Missionaries and community builders, they gave a total of 98 years of service and love to this area, until retirement in 1969.

Lee Junior College in Jackson.

OLD BUILDINGS

"Uncle Buddy" Spicer House — Near Sebastian Branch. House dates to 1822. Still owned by the original family.

Jefferson Hotel — Jackson, 1119 Main St. Built 1912. Four-story brick hotel, owner of first car in Jackson.

Preacher Jim Hudson's House — Quicksand. Near University of Kentucky Experiment Station. Built 1860. Log cabin originally located at Noble, Kentucky.

OTHER POINTS OF INTEREST

Lees Junior College — Jackson. 601 Jefferson. Established 1883. Presbyterian church affiliate.

University of Kentucky Experimental Farm and Substation — for Quicksand. KY-15, KY-30.

Knott County

Knott County was formed in 1884 from parts of Perry, Floyd, Letcher and Breathitt Counties. The one hundred eighteenth county in order of formation in Kentucky, it was named for Governor J. Proctor Knott of Marion County.

Hindman, the county seat, is nestled in a narrow valley 1000 feet above sea level. It was named for James Hindman, who was Lieutenant Governor at the time of its establishment.

Knott County is referred to as "The Cradle of Education" in Kentucky, because it was here that the new world-famous mountain mission schools had their beginning. The three unique schools are Alice Lloyd College, Hindman Settlement School, and Carr Creek School.

Although twenty percent of the land is used for farming, the rugged mountain terrain also produces much coal, oil and lumber.

New and improved highways, as well as the scenic mountains, are attracting more and more tourists to this region of Eastern Kentucky.

MARKERS

Pioneer Educator — Hindman. KY-80. In 1889 George Clarke came to Hindman, licensed to practice law. Seeing the need for education in the area, he established a subscription school with the help of the students and citizens. He died in 1940. His epitaph reads, "Let God be praised and let Eastern Kentucky rejoice that so great a man once graced the soil."

OLD BUILDINGS

Alice Lloyd College — Located 8 mi. E. of Garner. KY-80W. Jct. Renowned mountain school. Alice Lloyd came from Boston in 1916, dedicating her life to the education of youth in this area. Caney Creek Community Center was organized in 1917 and Caney Junior College in 1923. After Alice Lloyd's death in 1962, the college was renamed in her honor because she inspired graduates to serve this region.

Carr Creek Center — 9 mi. S. of Hindman. KY-160. Olive W. Marsh and Ruth E. Watson from Massachusetts, aided by the Daughters of the American Revolution, carved this center of learning out of a wooded hillside overlooking rustic "Singing Carr." When organized Sept. 11, 1920, it was dedicated to the education of mountain youth and is maintained by the contributions of many friends and the Knott County Board of Education.

Founder's Shack — Pippa Passes. KY-80W. Jct. Campus of Alice Lloyd College.

"Old Johnson Place" at Cody.

Hindman Settlement School — Hindman. E. of KY-80, KY-160. Founded in 1902 by Mary Stone and Katherine Pettit to provide an educational opportunity for the youth of the mountains and to keep them mindful of their heritage.

"Old Johnson Place" — Cody. Built 1789. Oldest log cabin standing in Eastern Kentucky.

"Uncle Sol" Cabin — Hindman. E. of KY-80, KY-160. On school grounds of Hindman Settlement School. Cabin was restored to honor the old mountaineer whose vision inspired establishment of school. Furnished with spinning wheel, dulcimer, homemade wooden furniture, rifle and powder horn, iron cooking utensils, coverlets and rugs.

Amburgey Loghouse — Little Carr of Carr's Fork, Knott County. Built 1840. Made of Hand-hewn yellow poplar logs. Author James Still has lived and written in house since 1939.

William Smith, House Site — Smithsboro, near Cody. circa 1820-1830. Site of large log house which became stopping place for travellers.

Well at Johnson's Cabin at Cody.

Wiley Combs House — E. of Emmalena. KY-80. Built 1911. Wood weatherboard house of a style unique in Eastern Kentucky.

Thomas Frances or Old Stamper Place — Little Carr. circa 1794-1800. 2-story log structures originally used as home and slave quarters.

Lee County

Lee County was formed in 1870, as the one hundred fifteenth county to be established in Kentucky. Its history dates back 200 years, when Dr. Thomas Walker became the first white man to visit the area. The county was named in honor of General Robert E. Lee. Its first settlers, former Revolutionary soldiers, began arriving in 1805.

Lee County contains many scenic areas of interest to tourists, amateur naturalists, explorers and archeologists, as well as fishermen and hunters.

PARKS, RECREATION, LAKES, DAMS

Cathedral Domain — 10 mi. W. of Beattyville. KY-52. Approximately 1000 acres operated by the Episcopal Church. Camping, hiking, nature study.

Fincastle — On Walker's Creek. Near KY-2016. Wilderness area. Camping, fishing, hiking by permission. Private land.

Hell Creek — 4 mi. N. of Beattyville, near St. Helen's.

Wilderness area. Fishing, exploring, treasure hunting, nature study. Private land.

Hieronymus Ford — Williba, on North Fork River. KY-2017. Wilderness area. Excellent for fishing and camping. Private land, permission necessary.

Granny Dismal Hollow — Near Heidelberg, Sturgeon Creek Bridge. Off KY-587. Wilderness area. Camping, fishing, hunting, and nature study with permission of owner.

MARKERS

A Masterful Retreat — Beattyville. KY-11, KY-52. Gen. George W. Morgan's 9,000 USA forces occupied Cumberland Gap June 18 to Sept. 17, 1862. Cut off from supplies, Morgan began a 200-mi. retreat. Searching for supplies, the command came this way. Retreat from Gap to Greenup on the Ohio River, was made in 16 days despite harassment by Gen. John Hunt Morgan's CSA Raiders.

OLD BUILDINGS

Chambers House — Fraley's Creek. circa 1850. First house in eastern part of county.

Lee County Courthouse — Beattyville. Built 1873. In use approximately 100 years.

Miller Homestead — Primrose. KY-2017. Ancestral home of the Miller family. Place where Jesse James' gang stopped for lunch after robbing a Danville Bank.

OTHER POINTS OF INTEREST

Fraley's Creek Falls (Church of God) — Williba. KY-2017. Site of first water mill in Lee County. Site of Glen Eden High School.

Pinnacle Rocks — Near Old Landing Community and Post Office. KY-1036. Twin peaks offer magnificent view of the Kentucky River. Daniel Boone's lookout. Site of pioneer powder mill.

Pinnacle Rocks near Old Landing Community.

Leslie County

Leslie County, the one hundred seventeenth county established in Kentucky, was formed from portions of Clay, Harlan and Perry Counties, and was named for Preston H. Leslie of Barren County, Governor of Kentucky from 1871-1875.

The first residents were John Sizemore and his family from North Carolina who settled at the site that is now Hyden. Hyden, the county seat, was incorporated in 1947.

Leslie County is famous for its Frontier Nursing Service which has been copied by the United Nations. The social service activated by Mary Breckinridge has become a part of such present-day agencies as Vista, Peace Corps, Action, and the National Health Service Corporation.

Rugged hills covered with mixed hardwood forests and numerous streams add to the beautiful scenery of Leslie County. Ninety two percent of the land is forested and 2 1/2 million tons of coal are produced in Leslie County annually. Leslie County is noted for its 460,000 acres of the Daniel Boone National Forest, and for the Presbyterian center at Wooton, a mountain mission which originated the first horseback library in

the United States, as well as for Buckhorn Lake State Resort Park.

The surrounding region is watered by "Cut-Shin" and "Hel-fer-Sartain" Creek. Tradition holds that an early pioneer was coming through with his ox train and found one of the creeks swollen from recent rains. The crossing was difficult, and while driving his oxen over the river, he cut his shin on a sharp rock, hence the name "Cut-shin." The following day, he came across the other stream, far more swollen and difficult to cross than the first. As he realized his predicament, he exclaimed, "Well by jiminy, this is 'hell fer sartain.'" and those names have remained with these beautiful mountain brooks.

FESTIVALS

Mary Breckinridge Festival — Hyden. Parade, crafts, beauty pageant, festival held in honor of Mary Breckinridge, founder of Frontier Nursing Service. Last Saturday in September.

PARKS

Daniel Boone National Forest — All of Leslie County. US-421. Hiking trails. Primitive camping allowed.

246

MARKERS

County Named — Hyden, Courthouse yard. US-421. Leslie County was created in 1878 from Clay, Harlan, and Perry Counties. Named for Preston H. Leslie, Governor of Kentucky, 1871-1875, Montana Territorial Governor, 1887-1889, U. S. District Attorney 1894-1898, appointed by President Cleveland. Died 1907, buried in Montana.

OLD BUILDINGS

Will Sandlin's Home — Owl's Nest. Off KY-80. Only Kentuckian to receive the Congressional Medal of Honor in World War I. House was built from a $10,000 appropriation from the State Legislature sometime after his return to Leslie County.

John Shell Home — Laurel Fork of Greasy Creek. 6 mi. N.E. of KY-221. Built 1830. Oldest house standing in Leslie County. Pre-Civil War rough log house with puncheon floors and riven-oak shingle roof.

Woods, Pleasie House — Cutshin Creek, near Dryhill. Built before 1878. Hand hewn log house, now covered with weatherboarding.

Old Lewis Barn — W. of Hyden. KY-80, US-421. Built 1850. Example of mid-19th century barn.

OTHER POINTS OF INTEREST

Frontier Nursing Service — Wendover Headquarters. Off US—421. Founded in 1925 by Mary Breckinridge as first school of midwifery in the U. S. It served all of Leslie County and parts of Clay and Perry counties with horseback-riding nurses. Now jeeps are used.

St. Christopher's Chapel — Hyden, at the old Frontier Nursing Service Hospital. Built of native stone by local craftsman, George Bowling, to house a stained-glass window that was donated to Frontier Nursing Service. Wrought iron work by local craftsman, Eugene Dixon.

Mary Breckinridge Hospital in Hyden.

Frontier Nursing Service Headquarters outside Hyden.

Letcher County

Letcher County was named for Governor Robert P. Letcher of Garrard County, who proclaimed the first Thanksgiving in Kentucky. The county's formation took place in 1842 from parts of Harlan and Perry Counties. The ninety-fifth county to be created in Kentucky, Letcher County is noted for the quiet and beautiful natural surroundings of Pine and Black Mountains. Black Mountain is the highest point in the State of Kentucky, 4150 feet above sea level.

On April 1, 1751, Christopher Gist, in the employ of the Ohio Land Company, came down the Ohio River and left Kentucky by way of Pound Gap.

Whitesburg, Jenkins, and Neon were first settled by hunters and fur traders. Railroads, which opened up the Eastern coal fields, were pushed up the hollows to the headwaters of the Kentucky and Cumberland Rivers in 1910-1912. Crowds hailed the "steam horse" from Jackson to Hazard to Whitesburg and McRoberts. Letcher County experienced a boom which lasted through World War I and after.

Whitesburg, the county seat, is located at the edge of Jefferson National Forest. Whitesburg is known for some of the grandest scenery in the Cumberlands and for being the home of Harry Caudill, lawyer and author of *Night Comes to the Cumberlands*.

Eighty percent of Letcher County's 339-square miles is forested. It is a leading county in oil and coal production with 212 coal mines in operation.

DRAMAS

"Little Shepherd of Kingdom Come" Drama — Van, approximately 5 mi. N. of Whitesburg. KY-1811, off KY-15. Amphitheater. Outdoor drama. July and August.

PARKS, RECREATION

Jefferson National Forest — US-23, KY-15, US-119. Forest extends into Virginia. 550,626 acres.

Kingdom Come State Park — US-119. 1000 beautiful mountain acres named for John Fox, Jr., author of *Little Shepherd of Kingdom Come,* first American novel to sell over 1,000,000 copies (1903). Raven Rock stone formation with large cave opening at top.

Little Shepherd Trail — Whitesburg to Harlan. Off US-119, US-421, KY-160. Trail winds 35 miles along Pine Mountain, and can be travelled by car or on foot.

Pine Mountain Wildlife Area — Whitesburg. Off US-119. Picnicking, hiking, hunting in season.

MARKERS

Inspiration Mountain — S. of Whitesburg. US-119. Little Shepherd Trail part of setting for the *Little Shepherd of Kingdom Come, Hell fer Sartain, Trail of the Lonesome Pine,* which were written by John Fox, Jr., famous for his eleven novels of Kentucky mountains and the Bluegrass written 1893-1919.

Pioneer Ancestor — Near Isom, 4 mi. S. Jct. KY-15 and KY-7. James Caudill, born Virginia in 1753, first came to Big Cowan Creek in 1787. Because of Indians, he took his family back to North Carolina. Returning here in 1792 with his family, he built a cabin and stayed several years then went back to North Carolina again. They settled here permanently in 1811. He was progenitor of large, widespread mountain family. He died in 1840.

Scuttle Hole Gap Road — Near Whitesburg. 7 mi. S. Jct. KY-15 and KY-931. Indians or buffalo probably were the first to follow this gap and make a trail across Pine Mountain. First white settlers came about 1800 and made the trail into a treacherous wagon road, their only route to Virginia for flour, salt and sugar supplies. Called Scuttle Hole Gap, meaning "deep gorge through cliffs." Trail goes 7 miles from here into the Cumberland River Valley.

OLD BUILDINGS

Banks House — Little Cowan Creek. Built 1880. Hand-hewn log cabin.

Solomon Frazier House — Kingdom Come Creek. Built 1850. Visited by John Fox, Jr. and immortalized in *Little Shepherd of Kingdom Come.*

"Moonshiner's Hotel" — Pine Mountain. US-119. Inn used as meeting place for Kentucky and Virginia moonshiners to relate information and escape "revenuers."

Parson's House — Near Eolia. Off US-119. circa 1780-90. Oldest house in Letcher County. Scene of many skirmishes during the Civil War.

OTHER POINTS OF INTEREST

Bad Branch Falls — Pine Mountain. US-119. A narrow 165-ft. 2-stage waterfall in rugged wilderness.

Bull Hole — Pine Mountain. US-119. A mysterious bottomless pit associated with local legends.

Calvary College — Fleming-Neon. KY-7. Four-year liberal arts institution.

Cornetts Woods or Lilley's Woods — Hallie. KY-1103, off KY-7. Over 500 acres of virgin timber. The wooded land was acquired from sons of Lilley Cornett who never allowed anything to be removed from woods. Guided tours.

High Rock — Pine Mountain, Kentucky Ridge State Forest. US-20E, US–119. Scenic panoramic view of vast wilderness.

Hound Dog Hookers — Blackey. KY-7. A variety of

Outdoor drama of "Little Shepherd of Kingdom Come."

hand-hooked wool rugs. Noted for famous Hound Dog Designs.

Pound Gap — Jenkins. US-23, US-119. Natural route from Kentucky to Virginia. Discovered by Christopher Gist on April 1, 1751.

Rainbow Rock — Pine Mountain. US-119. Heads directly to a scenic, 25-ft. arch formation.

Raven Rock — Cumberland, near Kentucky-Virginia border. KY-160, US-119. Prominent peak with an overlook of Jenkins Lake. Used as a lookout post during the Civil War.

Scenic view from Pine Mountain.

Owsley County

Owsley County is in Daniel Boone country. A party headed by Daniel Boone camped near the present site of Boonesville, the county seat, in 1780-1781.

The area retained the name of Boone's Station until Owsley County was created in 1843 from parts of Clay, Estill and Breathitt Counties. Ninety-sixth in order of formation in Kentucky, the county took its name from Governor William Owsley who served as sixteenth Governor of Kentucky from 1844-1848, and was also a prominent judge. One of the landmarks of the county, certified by the Kentucky Heritage Commission, is Boone's Rock on the Kentucky River near the Clay-Owsley line, the "corner rock" of the land surveyed by Boone.

Owsley County is located on the edge of the Daniel Boone National Forest, with Natural Bridge State Resort Park and the new Mountain Parkway only thirty miles to the north.

The County has a small population of 5,200, and has many scenic areas and legends to offer visitors. It is one of Eastern Kentucky's vast unspoiled scenic areas and almost wholly agrarian. About fifty percent of the county's land is in small farms which are well diversified, producing corn, burley tobacco, cattle, and hogs.

FAIRS, FESTIVALS, EXHIBITS

Appalachian Fireside Crafts — Booneville. Off KY-30. Native crafts made by Eastern Kentucky families. Quilts, woodcrafts, children's toys for sale. Monday-Friday, 8:30 a.m. to 4 p.m.

Daniel Boone Festival — Booneville and Owsley County Stock Sale grounds. KY-30. Features craftsmen, flea market, gospel singing, Kentucky Long Riflemen, concert and other family activities. Camping facilities available. July 2,3,4.

Fox Hunters Dog Show — Booneville, Owsley County Stock Sale grounds. KY-30. Fox hunt with prizes and tropies. Different dates each year.

Owsley County Fair — Booneville, Elementary school grounds. Homecoming for people of Owsley County.

One of Eastern Kentucky's oldest remaining county fairs. September.

Owsley County Horse Show — Booneville. KY-30. Horses participating from all over U. S. 18 or more classes, including Tennessee Walkers. Prizes, ribbons and trophies. July 4th weekend.

PARKS, RECREATION, LAKES, DAMS

Begley's Peaceful Valley Lake — 5 mi. W. of Booneville. Off KY-30. Scenic area, fishing and camping.

Daniel Boone National Forest — KY-30. 3000 acres of primitive camp sites and hiking trails with 9000 acres of woodland.

High Rocks — Island City, between the right and left forks of Island Creek. Off KY-11. Approximately 100 acres for camping, hiking and nature study.

Pea Ridge — Between left and right forks of upper Buffalo Creek. Off KY-11. 10,000 acres where early settlers lived. Old house and chimneys still remain. Public land with limited access by fire trails. Camping, hiking, exploring.

South Fork of Kentucky River — Booneville. KY-11. Flows through central portion of county. All-weather road near, access through private land. Fantastic fishing area; large and small-mouth Kentucky rock bass and muskie.

Owsley County Stock Sale — 2 mi. E. of Booneville. KY-30. Features flea market, trading and swapping and stock sales. People from various points in Kentucky attend. Land originally owned by Daniel Boone. Held each Wednesday.

MARKERS

Boone's Station — Booneville, Courthouse yard. KY-11, KY-30. Near this spot in 1780-1781 Daniel Boone and party camped. Camp was called Boone's Station until Owsley County was organized in 1843, then named Booneville. Records in Clay County show that Boone's family owned land here until they moved to Missouri.

Civil War Actions — Booneville, Courthouse yard. KY-11, KY-30. Retreating to Ohio from Cumberland Gap, part of USA Brig. Gen. George W. Morgan's command passed by here obtaining supplies on September 21, 1862. Force of 40 local citizens drove off 75 southern partisan guerrillas on April 14, 1864. Col. C. H. Hanson and 300 USA troops pursuing Morgan's Raiders stopped here to obtain guides and information on June 17, 1864.

MEMORIALS, MUSEUMS

War Memorial — Booneville, Main St, Courthouse lawn. Dedicated to veterans who served their country in World Wars I, II and through Vietnam.

CEMETERIES

Gabbard Cemetery — Ricetown. Off KY-28. Veterans of every war fought by the U. S. buried here, including Revolutionary War veterans. Located on lands that belonged to the Gabbard family before Kentucky became a state.

OLD BUILDINGS

Old Homes — Cow Creek. KY-28. Built 1816-1817. Dudley, Lewis, Reynolds, Gibson. Now privately owned.

Price House — Levi. KY-11. Built during the Civil War for the purpose of selling whiskey. Called a "blind tiger." Now privately owned.

Flannery, Hampton House — Pebworth. Built 1867. Union Army officer.

Ross, Levi House — Levi. Built 1847. Possibly the oldest house in Owsley County.

OTHER POINTS OF INTEREST

Boone's Early Settlement — 2 mi. E. of Booneville. KY-30. Property owned by Daniel Boone until 1820. Now farms, and Owsley County Stockyards.

Boone's Rock — 12 mi. S. of Booneville. On KY-11. Cornerstone of Donelson survey made by Daniel Boone; has now been designated a Kentucky Landmark.

Clay Gap — S. of Island City on Clay County line. KY-11. Old warrior path where Indians crossed Kentucky.

Cortland Falls — Laurel Fork of Upper Buffalo Creek. Off KY-11. Natural falls area with the largest and oldest cemetery in Owsley County. Bob Baker, Jeremiah Smith, Patrick Riley, heroes of War of 1812 buried here. Now privately owned.

Fish Creek Falls — Fish Creek, Northern portion of county. KY-30. Natural falls. Now privately owned.

Kentucky Mountain Baptist College — Sturgeon. KY-30. College of Ministry.

Lincoln Grotto — Island Creek. Off KY-11, right fork. Statue of Abraham Lincoln carved in rock. Now privately owned.

Whoopflarea — Upper Buffalo Creek. Off KY-11, right fork. Approximately 2000 acres. Early hunting camp. Nature study area. Now part of Daniel Boone National Forest.

Price House in Levi.

Farmland scene near Booneville.

Perry County

Settled by pioneers in 1790, Perry County became the sixty-eighth county to be established in Kentucky in 1820. The county was named in honor of Commodore Oliver Hazard Perry, American naval hero of that period. The county seat, Hazard, was also named for him.

No history of Hazard would be complete without the mention of the Combs family. Elijah Combs, his seven brothers, and their parents came to the area in 1790. Elijah was instrumental in forming the county and donated the land on which the city of Hazard stands. Perry County is part of an area remembered for its bloody family feuds, such as the French-Eversole feud which claimed many lives.

Hazard, as well as all of Perry County, has long been a coal mining center, and is one of the largest coal producing areas in the state. After World War I, industry began to boom. The county is now a mining and trade center, and is fast developing its oil, gas and timber resources.

Twenty-five miles southeast of Hazard is the Lilley Cornett Woods, a forest containing 554 acres of virgin woods. It is said to be exactly as it was millions of years ago. Guided tours of the woods are given from April through September.

Perry County is constantly changing to meet modern demands. Yet, the area remains rich in tradition, folklore, beautiful scenery, and state recreational facilities.

PARKS, RECREATION, LAKES, DAMS

Buckhorn Lake State Park — Buckhorn. Off KY-28 on KY-1833. Scenic wooded area, park accommodations and camping. 750 acres of land and a 1200-acre mountain lake. Lodge, dining room, hiking, supervised recreation, swimming, fishing, boating.

Carr Fork Lake and Dam — Hazard. Off KY-15.

Bobby Davis Memorial Park and Library — Hazard, Baker's Hill. Dedicated to World War II soldiers. Library, picnic area, hillside trails and a variety of wild plants. 5 acres.

MUSEUMS

Bill Davis' Sports Car Museum — Hazard, E. Main St. Small admission fee.

MARKERS

Mountain Missionary — Hazard, N. Main St. KY-17, KY-15. Rev. Asbel S. Petrey came here in 1897 and organized First Missionary Baptist Church of Hazard in 1898. In 1902 he founded and was President of Hazard Baptist Institute, a public school since 1941. He organized 12 churches in area. Pastor of Petrey Memorial Baptist Church, 1922-1940. Filled other pulpits until death in 1953.

Murdoch of Buckhorn — Buckhorn. KY-28. Harvey Short Murdoch, 1871-1935, came from Brooklyn, New York and, as field secretary of E. O. Guerrant's Society of Social Winners, founded Witherspoon College in 1902. Became Presbyterian Child Welfare Agency. Log cathedral built 1907. Murdoch was pastor until his death. "To Buckhorn and Eastern Kentucky, he brought a love for baseball, for education and for God."

Saltworks — 17 mi. S. of Hazard. KY-7. Here in 1835, the Brashear's well produced salt from a fine brine for half a century. Wells were drilled by hand, and the salt was sold both here and in Virginia. Transported for $1.00 a bushel over treacherous mountain trails by mule and oxen. The wells were destroyed by flood in 1892.

Uncle Ira — Jeff. KY-7, KY-15. The Ira Combs Memorial Church. Little Zion Church built in 1909 on land settled in 1790 by Mason Combs. Ira, a grandson, was a Civil War veteran. Born in 1844, he began preaching in 1874. For 60 years without pay, he ministered to the Old Regular Baptists in Pine Mountain section. Died in 1934; buried on old homestead. Church dedicated in his honor on Easter Sunday, 1952.

OLD BUILDINGS

Nicholas Combs "Birdseye" — Near Combs. KY-80. circa 1815. Second oldest house in Perry County.

Isaac Eversole Home — Near Krypton. circa 1802. Oldest house in Perry County.

Thomas Johnson House — Chavies. Built 1850. First brick house in Perry County.

OTHER POINTS OF INTEREST

Hazard Community College — Hazard. One of 13 community colleges of University of Kentucky. Confers an associate degree.

Homeplace — Ary. KY-476. Established 1930. Rural community center whose programs included farming, homemaking classes, a travelling library, woodwork shop and medical assistance.

Old Tunnel Mill — Dwarf. Built circa 1770, and operated until 1945. Its power furnished by water flowing from a tunnel dug through a mountain.

Buckhorn Presbyterian Church and Children's Center — Buckhorn. Built 1902. One of the largest rural churches in the U. S.

Courthouse in Hazard.

Tours of Coal Operations — Hazard, 221 Memorial Drive. Mining companies, working with the Hazard-Perry County Chamber of Commerce, give prearranged guided tours of their operations from beginning to end.

 # *Wolfe County*

The one hundred tenth county to be established in Kentucky was Wolfe County, named in honor of Nathaniel Wolfe, a Louisville attorney and the first graduate of the University of Virginia. It was formed from parts of Morgan, Breathitt, Owsley and Powell Counties in 1860.

When the first settlers came to this area, they found it densely covered with forests and watered by the beautiful and wild Red River and the North Fork of the Kentucky River, as well as many creeks and small tributaries. Wild game, including the buffalo, provided the settlers with a plentiful food supply.

Campton, the county seat, has grown slowly over the years from a settlement of seventy-seven people in 1870, to over seven hundred residents today. The early settlers were religious people, for soon after their settlement, they established a place of worship. Records show that the Old Primitive Baptist church on Baptist Fork of Stillwater Creek was erected in 1837. Abe Swango gave two acres of his land for the church site. His son later established a Seminary school on what is

now known as Seminary Creek. Other churches soon followed as the population of Wolfe County increased.

The county is rich in history and legend, and at times it is difficult to determine where history ends and legend begins. One well-known legend relates that, before the end of the French and Indian War, an English sailor named John Swift heard about silver mines in the Kentucky mountains being worked by the Shawnees, Cherokees and the Spaniards. In 1761 he came from Virginia with three friends and found the mine, which they worked for several years.

Swift then returned to London with a small fortune in silver, but was soon jailed for expressing rebellious ideas learned in America. Almost blind when he was released after the American Revolution, he returned to Virginia where he found his partners had been killed by Indians. Using a map he had drawn 15 years earlier of the Red River area in Kentucky, he and a companion headed to Kentucky, but were never able to find the mine again. His dying words were, "It is near a peculiar rock. Boys, don't ever quit looking for it. It is the

253

richest thing I ever saw." According to the legend, the Swift Creek silver mine camp was located on the present site of the Wolfe County courthouse in Campton. Despite the fact that people have searched and searched but never found this elusive silver mine, the area around the Red River continues to be an irresistible challenge to treasure hunters.

The original Wolfe County courthouse was constructed of logs in 1860, but was destroyed by fire in 1887. A large frame building was then erected, but it too was demolished by fire in 1913. The present courthouse of yellow brick was constructed in 1917.

Wolfe Countians learned of a new natural resource in 1903 when the country's first oil well was drilled. By 1905, fifty-eight oil wells were successfully completed. Today the county finds a reawakening of interest in oil wells.

PARKS

Red River Gorge — Off Mountain Parkway in Daniel Boone National Forest. KY-715. A spectacular area of rugged woodlands, wild flowers, streams, limestone cliffs and arches carved by years of wind, rains, and waterfalls. Alleged location of John Swift's legendary silver mines.

Sky Bridge — Off Mountain Parkway. KY-715. 90-ft. long and 30-ft high. Commands a magnificent view of the Red River Gorge area and readily accessible from the lower river road. Recreation area.

MARKERS

Swango Springs Spa — Hazel Green, schoolyard. KY-191. Tradition holds that the healing properties of the mineral spring water here were discovered by owner when treating her pet dog for mange. Its use by humans spread and by 1895 three hotels and many boarding houses were host to people from all over America. Fire destroyed largest hotel in 1910. Visitors to resort dropped off. Mineral water bottled and widely shipped until 1943.

Swift's Silver Camp — Campton. KY-15. John Swift's fabulous journals report silver operations in east Kentucky from 1761-1769, an unsolved mystery. Intrepid searchers have found no trace of his mine, although one Swift camp is reputed to have been on site of Wolfe County courthouse.

CEMETERIES

Carson Cemetery — Hazel Green. KY-191. Early settler John Lacy buried in graveyard. Lacy Creek in Wolfe County was named for him. Unusual notation on tombstone.

Old Graveyard on Hill Back of First Church of God — Campton, Court St. Graves of many early settlers, among them Fielding Hanks who was known for his love of hunting, his reason for coming to Wolfe County.

OLD BUILDINGS

Campton Courthouse and Jail House — Campton, Court St. Constructed 1917. Yellow brick. Present jail house was erected in 1907.

Christian Church — Hazel Green. Established 1841.

Rebecca Timmons Diggins — Campton. Located in the area drained by Swift Camp Creek. Cabin still stands.

Captain James I. Hollon Home — Hazel Green, Main St. In good repair. Two-story wood, original columns.

Hurst Mansion — Campton, Washington St.

The Methodist Church — Campton. Established 1880.

R. L. Miller Home — Hazel Green, Main St. Is well kept as in bygone years. Wood, 2-story, colonial type.

Mize Mansion — Hazel Green. State Senator Mize lived here until his death.

Old Primitive Church — Baptist Fork of Stillwater. Organized in 1837 by two preachers, William Lykins and Daniel Duff.

Swift's Camp Church — Campton. Established 1848.

OTHER POINTS OF INTEREST

Angel Windows — Mountain Parkway, 1/4 mi. off Sky Bridge Rd. Two linked arches that command a spectacular view of the valley below.

Ash Cave — Campton. Near old KY-15. Indian habitat in the cliff country.

Burial Mounds — Burial mounds of Adena people built over 2700 years ago.

Chimney Top — Mountain Parkway to KY-715. Trail from Sky Bridge Road leads to lookout. A high column of stone separated from the cliff can be seen for miles as one travels through the gorge.

Upper and Lower Devils Creek — Mary. 5 mi. from new KY-15. These creeks provided power to operate mills and to float logs to market. Bottomlands abounded in wild game.

Hazel Green Academy — Hazel Green. KY-191, KY-203. Organized in 1880 by J. Taylor Day, William O. Mize and Green Berry Swango. Only college preparatory school serving this area for years. Many of its graduates have gained prominence.

Indian Bathtub — Mary. 5 mi. off new KY-15. This pool caused by a waterfall is a natural wonder.

Red River Gorge Loop Drive — Off Mountain Parkway. KY-715, KY-77. This 30-mile drive passes through an old logging railroad tunnel known as the Nada Tunnel, and along the Red River.

Rock Bridge — 3 mi. from Pine Ridge. Off KY-715, on KY-24. Solid stone bridge over moving stream of water. Largest of its kind. Recreation area.

Tight Hollow — Pine Ridge. Old KY-15. 300 acres of land deep in the Daniel Boone National Forest where virgin forests of hemlock and poplar can be seen. Unchanged since Indian times.

Torrent-Nature's Flower Garden — Leeco. Between KY-11 and KY-715. Flatiron-shaped tract of land.

Winding Stair — Near town of Torrent. Off KY-11. An unusual series of rock formations. Amphitheater-like falls and shelves that cascade down from a high precipice.

Main Street of Campton.

Wolf on facade of courthouse in Campton.

255

Wilderness Trail Area

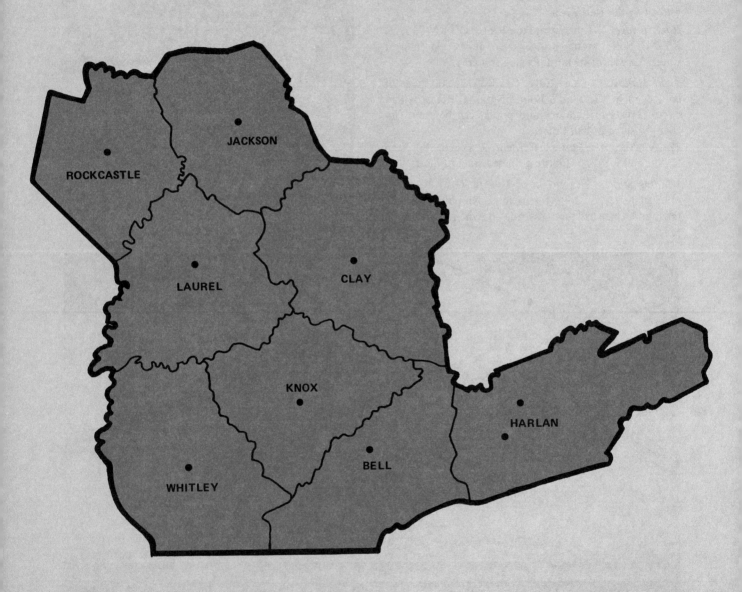

Bell County

Bell County, first known as Josh Bell County, was established by an act of the legislature in 1867 from portions of Knox and Harlan Counties. Josh Bell was a grandson of Thomas Walker, the pioneer who discovered the Cumberland Gap. The county was named in honor of Josh Bell because he fought so valiantly for the birth of this country. It was the one hundred twelfth county in order of formation in the state. Five years later, in 1872, "Josh" was dropped from the name and it became known as Bell County. Pineville, the county seat, is located on the Cumberland River.

The city of Middlesborough in Bell County had an interesting beginning. The outstanding personality in Middlesborough's early days was unquestionably it's founder, Alexander Allen Arthur, who was a native of Montreal, Canada. One summer day in 1886, Mr. Arthur stood on the slope of a hillside in Bell County, about a mile and a half from Cumberland Gap and in the valley below lay Yellow Creek. He is quoted as having said, "the first glimpse of its magnificent amphitheater was bewildering, for I had not imagined or in all my travels ever seen, any place so clearly designed for man's enjoyment and use." Mr. Arthur, pointing to the valley, said, "There is where I will build my city — Middlesborough, I think, would be a good name for it." With financial support from England, Middlesborough developed into a boom town, the largest in the mountains.

FESTIVALS AND DRAMAS

Book of Job — Pineville. Laurel Cove Amphitheater in Pine Mountain State Resort Park. Off US-25E. Outdoor choral drama. Mosaic effect with costumes and makeup worn by actors. Has made three national and two international tours. June-August.

Mountain Laurel Festival — Pineville. Laurel Cove Amphitheater in Pine Mountain State Resort Park. Off US-25E. Coeds compete for Festival Queen and Princess. One of the most popular tourist attractions in the state. Third weekend in May.

PARKS, RECREATION

Cumberland Gap National Historical Park — Middlesborough. US-25E. Located in southeast corner of county, this 20,000-acre park is shared by Kentucky, Virginia and Tennessee. Established in 1959, it is the largest historical park in the United States. Dr. Thomas Walker used this 700-ft. natural break in the Cumberland Mountains to enter Kentucky in 1750. The mountains had held the early settlers back for a long period until this gap, an old Indian trail, was discovered by Walker and his party. Daniel Boone followed this trail years later. One of most famous mountain passes in America. Park features museum of frontier days, old iron furnace, caves, a restored settlement, and a visitors center. Park camping.

Kentucky Ridge State Forest — Near Pineville and Middlesborough. US-25E. and KY-190. Second largest state forest. Hiking, state-regulated hunting in season.

Pine Mountain State Resort Park — Pineville. US-25E., KY-119. Established in 1926 as the first state park in Kentucky. First called Cumberland Park until the founding of Cumberland Falls State Park, after which the name was changed to Pine Mountain. Park features nature center, Laurel Cove Amphitheater, lodge, recreation area, and camping.

Sugar Run Picnic Area — S. of Pineville, Colmar Rd., towards Middlesborough. Off US-25E. Part of Cumberland Gap National Historical Park.

Woodward Park — Walnut St. Pineville. Off US-25E. Located a few feet upstream from the site of Cumberland Ford where Daniel Boone's Wilderness Road crossed to the north side of the Cumberland River.

MARKERS

Breastworks Hill — Pineville. KY-66. Played major role in Civil War since it overlooked Cumberland Ford, gateway to the West.

Cumberland Ford — Pineville. KY-66. Where the Wilderness Road crosses the Cumberland River. Crossing for pioneer settlers coming through Cumberland Gap enroute to the West. From 1775-1797, over 75,000 people crossed the river here.

Middlesborough — Middlesborough, Tourist Information Center. US-25E. English colony founded in 1886 by Alexander Arthur. The project was financed by an English company, the American Association, because of timber and rich mineral deposits here. Almost 100,000 mountainous acres in Virginia, Tennessee and Kentucky were purchased for the settlement, which was named for Middlesborough, England. The railroad to Knoxville and the Cumberland Gap tunnel were built by this company.

Middlesborough Golf Club — Middlesborough, at Golf Club. US-25. Founded 1889. One of the oldest in U. S. The present nine-hole course is located on site where the original one was laid out by English developers who came in 1886 and brought the golf game to this mountain region. In 1899 a financial crash in England took most of the immigrants home, leaving the club with only sporadic golf until 1916, when it was reorganized by local citizens.

Mountain Vision — Middlesborough, W. Cumberland Ave. US-25E. Alexander Arthur (1846-1912) was an outstanding figure in history of Middlesborough. He came here in 1885 to prospect, discovering coal and iron ore deposits. He was president of American Asso-ciation, which was formed to carry out his plans for a mining and manufacturing city.

Oldest House — Middlesborough, N. 19th St. US-25E. Built about 1800 in Yellow Creek Valley, it is the second oldest brick house in the county, and the oldest one still standing. The bricks were made from clay by slave labor. Home of the Rev. John Calvin Colson, "Patriarch of Yellow Creek Valley." A gifted preacher, teacher, lawyer, doctor, farmer, miller, merchant, although uneducated.

Wallsend Mine — Pineville. US-25E. The first to begin operations in Bell County, starting in 1889, with 1500 acres of coal land. Extension of the Louisville and Nashville Railroad to this area in 1888 marked the beginning of a new industrial era. This mine was not a financial success until it was purchased by Wallsend Coal and Coke Co. in 1904, a Kentucky corporation, but the stock was held mostly in England.

The Wilderness Road — Pineville, South. US-25E. Opened Kentucky and the West to rapid settlement and major development. First wagon road built in 1796 in Kentucky from Crab Orchard to Cumberland Gap. A principal highway, maintained as a turnpike for 80 years.

OTHER POINTS OF INTEREST

Chained Rock — Pineville, Pine Mountain State Resort Park. US-25E., KY-119. This chained rock overlooks

Courthouse in Pineville.

Mountain Laurel Festival in Pineville.

Pineville. The huge chain that holds a giant boulder was said to have been placed there to protect the town in early times.

Clear Creek Baptist Seminary — Pineville. US-25E., KY-190. Established by Dr. L. D. Kelley when he saw the need for training ministers who would remain in the eastern Kentucky mountains.

The Coal House — Middlesborough, N. 20th St. Built in 1926 from 40 tons of coal. At present it is the Middlesborough Chamber of Commerce Building.

Between-the-Parks Craft Shop — Between Pineville and Middlesborough. US-25E. Crafts, clothing, articles made by local mountain craftsmen.

Environmental Center — Middlesborough. Cumberland Gap National Historical Park. Facilities and classes for ecological education sponsored by Union College.

Henderson Settlement — Frakes. KY-190. Established in 1925 by Rev. Hiram Frakes. Supported by the United Methodist Church. Purpose is to provide for the economical, medical, educational and spiritual needs of eastern Kentucky children, ages three through high school.

Hensley Settlement — Brush Mountain, Cumberland Gap National Historical Park. US-25E. At its height over 150 people lived here in almost total isolation on this mountain during the 20th century. They lived as settlers did 200 years ago.

Pinnacle Overlook — Middlesborough, Cumberland Gap National Historical Park. Constructed 1921. Travel

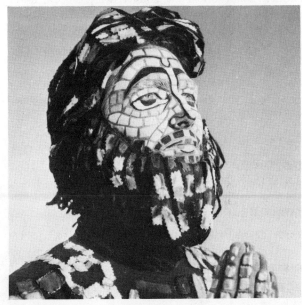

Book of Job Drama near Pineville.

pinnacle loop 2 miles to an altitude of 3000 feet to view three states — Kentucky, Tennessee, and Virginia.

Red Bird Craft Center — Beverly, approximately 20 mi. from Pineville. KY-66. Mountain crafts made by students and families of Red Bird Mission School.

Red Bird Mission — Beverly, approximately 20 mi. from Pineville. KY-66. Founded in 1921. Supported by the United Methodist Church. Purpose to provide for the economical, medical, educational, and spiritual needs of eastern Kentucky children, ages three through high school.

Clay County

When Kentucky was still part of Virginia, General Green Clay, father of Cassius Marcellus Clay, migrated to Kentucky. In 1806, Clay County was formed from portions of Floyd, Knox, and Madison Counties and was named Clay County in honor of this same General who helped write Kentucky's second constitution. It was the forty-seventh county in order of formation in the state. There are 474 square miles of land in the county. Tradition says that Cherokee Chief Red Bird gave the names to the rivers and forests in Clay County. Manchester, the county seat, is located on Daniel Boone Parkway and is situated near Goose Creek. It was named after the great manufacturing town in England where General Green Clay's wife lived.

While Clay County is known for its coal-producing mountains, the mountains themselves are known for the natural wild beauty of the Wilderness Trail.

FAIRS

Clay County Fair — Manchester. Ball park and High School Cafeteria. US-421. July.

PARKS, RECREATION, LAKES, DAMS

Beech Creek Wildlife Area — Manchester. Off Beech Creek Rd. 1200 acres for state-regulated hunting in season.

Big Double Creek — Peabody. KY-66. National forestry park.

Daniel Boone National Forest — Located throughout Clay County. Provides mountain beauty and a perfect scenic backdrop for the county seat of Manchester and the other Clay county communities.

Lee Hacker Park — Near Manchester, off Lyttleton Road. Scenic area. Where Bar Creek and Paces Creek begin. Includes 10 acres of Beech Creek Park. Picnicking.

Virgin Forest Natural Area — Daniel Boone National Forest. KY-66. Near headwaters of Red Bird River. Virgin stand of timber.

Narrows Natural Area — 10 mi. from Oneida. Off KY-11. Covers 2 acres. Rapids in the South Fork of the Kentucky River. Fishing.

MARKERS

Chief Red Bird — 7 mi. S. of Oneida. KY-66. Legendary Cherokee Indian for whom this fork of the Kentucky River is named. He and another Indian, Jack, were friendly with early settlers and were permitted to hunt in area. Allegedly, they were killed protecting their furs and their bodies thrown into water here. The ledges bear markings attributed to Red Bird.

Masterful Retreat — 2 1/2 mi. S. of Manchester. KY-11. USA Gen. George W. Morgan's forces occupied Cumberland Gap June 18 to September 17, 1862. Cut off from supplies and surrounded, Morgan withdrew with his 9,000 men. They camped here, September 19-21 to organize march to Ohio River.

OLD BUILDINGS

Dillion Asher Home — Beverly, near Red Bird Mission. KY-66. Built before 1800. Restored log house of one of the earliest settlers in Clay County. One of the oldest houses in the mountains.

Old Joe Clark Ballad.

Old Joe Clark's home in Sexton's Creek.

Big Double Creek Park.

Old Joe Clark's Home — Sexton's Creek. KY-1350. Subject of folk ballad sung during World War I and later wars by soldiers from eastern Kentucky. Joe Clark, born in 1839, was a shiftless and rough mountaineer. Ballad had about 90 stanzas.

OTHER POINTS OF INTEREST

Burning Springs Natural Gas Area — Burning Springs. US-421. For many years this 50-acre field seeped gas naturally above the ground surface.

Chief Red Bird's Camp — Small community of Big Creek. 6 mi. from KY-66. Historical marker where Chief Red Bird and tribe camped. A nearby cliff features Indian writing. Now privately owned.

Goose Creek Salt Works — Garrard. KY-11. Historical area. Old abandoned salt mines where the Federals and Confederates fought in 1862 to control valuable salt mines.

Newfoundland Scenic Area — Oneida. 4 mi. N. of KY-11. Scenic 2000 acres of wooded area.

Threshing Rock — Hector. Historical and scenic area located at head of Bar Creek and Paces Creek and in one acre of Beech Creek. Large rock formation where Indians and early settlers threshed their grain.

Harlan County

In 1819, Harlan County became the sixteenth county to be established in Kentucky. It was formed from parts of Knox and Floyd Counties. It was named in honor of Major Silas Harlan, a young Virginian who came to Kentucky in 1774 and built Harlan Station near Harrodsburg on the Salt River in 1778. He served under General George Rogers Clark in the fight against the Indians. General Clark said, "He was one of the bravest soldiers that ever fought by my side." Major Harlan was killed in the Battle of Blue Licks while commanding his detachment in 1782.

Mount Pleasant, the early name for the county seat, was settled as early as 1819, and for a century remained little more than the usual frontier or back-woods town. Because there was another Mount Pleasant in Kentucky, Harlan County changed the town's name to Harlan in 1912.

Nestled among the friendly Cumberland Mountains, the county is known as the Coal Capital of Kentucky. The serene beauty of the mountains, a quaint swinging bridge, scenic trails and crystal clear creeks are only part of what Harlan County has to offer.

An indigenous mountain plant called "pokeweed" has played an important role in the growth of Harlan County. It was the mountain man's continuous search for pokeweed that led to the fabulous thirty-eight mile Little Shepherd Trail along the crest of Pine Mountain.

The "pokeweed pickers" were also responsible for the location of Harlan County's modern airport on top of a ridge near Loyall. The continuous search for pokeweed also led to the creation of a modern highway, US-119 into Harlan County, after engineers had tried and failed for years to find a suitable route.

FAIRS, FESTIVALS, EXHIBITS

Annual Hobby and Craft Show — Harlan Christian Church. Sponsored by the Harlan County Extension Homemakers Association. Exhibits, demonstrations and sale of crafts and home-baked goods. June, during Harlan Homecoming.

Harlan Sidewalk Art Show — Harlan, Courthouse Square. Artists display art work. June, during Harlan Homecoming.

Harlan County Homecoming — Throughout Harlan County. Events include a pet show (Harlan Courthouse); Horse Show (US-119 Putney); Square Dancing (Harlan); Pokeweed Sallet Festival (Cranks); Art Show (Harlan Courthouse); Man-of-the-Year Dinner (Harlan); Old-Fashioned Ice Cream Social (Harlan Courthouse); Exhibits and Mountain History and Heritage (Harlan); and Homecoming Services in local churches.

Kingdom Come Swappin Meeting Festival — Cumberland. US-119. Southeast Community College. Dancing, singing, craft exhibits, pickle contest, bean supper, flea market, etc. October.

Harlan County Poke Sallet Festival — Cranks, Stone Mountain Park. US-421. Pokeweed eating, music, entertainment. June.

PARKS

Cranks Creek Park — Cranks. US-421. Shelter house, game area, nature trails.

Gene Goss Park — On Little Shepherd Trail. Water, overnight camping.

Little Shepherd Trail — Winds along Pine Mountain for 38 miles, skirting through Kentenia State Forest and crossing Harlan and Letcher Counties. It derives its name from the writings of John Fox, Jr. There are 7 overlooks along the trail, and 14 picnic stops. The Little Shepherd Trail, memorializing Fox's young hero, was originally a fire trail built in part to give foresters quick access to the untouched interior of the mountainlands.

Kingdom Come State Park — Cumberland, on the Little Shepherd Trail. Off US-119. State Park named in honor of John Fox, Jr.'s *The Little Shepherd of Kingdom Come*, first U.S. novel to sell over a million copies. Lakes, fishing area, picnicking, hiking, camping,

playground. Famous stone formation, Raven Rock, is a huge cavern with opening wide enough to shelter an army.

MARKERS

County Named, 1819 — Harlan, Courthouse yard. US-119, US-421. For Maj. Silas Harlan, born in Virginia, 1752. Came to Kentucky in 1774. Built Harlan Station, 7 miles south of Harrodsburg on the Salt River in 1778. Killed in 1782 at the Battle of Blue Licks.

Courthouse Burned — Harlan, Courthouse yard. US-119, US-421. The courthouse at Harlan was burned in reprisal for the burning of the courthouse of Lee County, Virginia in Oct. 1863. County records in clerk's office nearby were saved.

OTHER POINTS OF INTEREST

Big Black Mountain — Lynch. KY-160. Kentucky's highest point in elevation, 4125 ft. above sea level.

Castle Rock — Cranks, on Stone Mountain. Named because of its castle-like formation.

Coal Mines — Harlan. Major industry of county. 179 licensed coal mines, 118 underground and 61 surface-augerstrip or combination.

Pine Mountain Settlement School — Pine Mountain. KY-221. Unique chapel, educational buildings, Laurel House, Mountain Craft Shop.

Rebel Rock — On Laden Trail, near Little Shepherd Trail. KY-2010, off US-119 to Cumberland. So named because the rebels used it as a lookout during the Civil War.

Sand Cave — Located on the north slope of Cumberland Mountain. Bachelor's quarters for Hensley Settlement. The cave lies beneath White Rocks, the highest point on the mountain. The men used the natural geological formation as a hunting lodge and retreat. During the spring and summer, a mountain waterfall to left of cave opening, provided shower facilities.

Coal miners in Harlan.

Jackson County

Jackson County, one hundred fifth in the creation of Kentucky counties, was carved from Madison, Estill, Owsley, Clay, Laurel and Rockcastle Counties on April 15, 1858. It was named after the "Old War Hero" and seventh President, Andrew Jackson. The county seat, McKee, took its name from John R. McKee, one of the first citizens of the county, who did much to secure the passage of the act establishing the county. McKee is located on Indian Creek near the center of the county.

The county, for the most part, lies in the "Eastern Coal Field" area. The old Boone Trail crosses the southwestern edge of Jackson county. In some places, the worn banks of the road are approximately 15 ft. high, evidence that it is a very old trail.

Most of Jackson County is federally-owned forest land, and is known as superb country for hiking, back packing, and exploring.

PARKS

Bond Park — McKee.

Fish and Game Club — Gray Hawk. 4 acres. Fishing.

S-Tree Camp Site — 7 mi. S.W. of McKee. Recreation facility provided by U. S. Forest Service. Scenic, forested area. Camping.

Turkey Foot Park — 5 mi. W.N.W. of McKee. Recreational site built by U. S. Forest Service. The Warriors Trail passed this way from Cumberland Gap to the Ohio River. Camping, scenic area, swimming.

Tyner Reservoir — Tyner. US-421. 92 acres in Daniel Boone National Forest. Fishing, boat docks, picnicking.

MARKERS

County Named, 1858 — McKee, Courthouse yard. US-421. Named for Andrew Jackson, 7th U. S. President, 1829-37, and the first president to be elected from west of the Appalachians.

Warrior's Path — Gray Hawk. US-421. A primeval trail that ran 2 mi. E. of and along War Fork Creek, between the Shawnees of Ohio and Cherokees of east Tennessee. The Indians called it Athiamiowee, "path of the armed ones." This path was followed by Gabriel Arthur when he was released from the Indians in 1674; as well as Thomas Walker in 1750, Christopher Gist in 1751 and Daniel Boone and John Finley in 1779.

CEMETERIES

Elkhanan Clark Cemetery — N. of Gray Hawk. 19th century tombstones. One old tombstone inscription reads, "Susan M. Engle, daughter of T. J. Engle, Born Jan. 27, 1852 – Died Oct. 16, 1856."

Pictured Rocks in the Wasioto Pass.

Courthouse in McKee.

OLD BUILDINGS

Abner Holcomb House — Union. Pre-Civil War. Large log house also used as church and school. First normal school in Eastern Kentucky.

Courthouse — McKee. US-421. Original courthouse was log structure built across Main Street in front of present courthouse and served until the second courthouse was built about 1873. The third courthouse, built of brick was completed in 1923 and burned in 1959. The present courthouse was built within the brick walls of the old one. All courthouse records were saved during the fire.

W. R. Reynolds House — Tyner. US-421, near Jct. N. of KY-30. Erected 1919. First Jackson County Agriculture Agent, 1914-1947, as well as County Judge, 1949-1953, State Agriculture Committeeman 1953-1954.

OTHER POINTS OF INTEREST

Annville Institute — Annville. A boarding school since 1909. Has a work program in addition to academic program.

Pictured Rocks — War Fork of Station Camp. Indian camping site on Warrior's Path south of the Indian Village of Eskippakithik. The Pictured Rocks were located in the Wasioto Pass. On the afternoon of Jan. 29, 1753 and expedition of Ottawas and Caghnawagas (French-praying Indians) going south to fight the Cherokees and Catawbas in North Carolina, attacked a group of Pennsylvania traders. Eight prisoners and 300-400 pounds of merchandise were captured.

The Bond Foley Lumber Co. in Bond.

Knox County

In 1799, Knox County was formed from part of Lincoln County to become the forty-first county created in Kentucky. This early county was named after General Henry Knox, a native of Boston who distinguished himself at the Battle of Bunker Hill in 1775 and later became the nation's first Secretary of War.

The first known pioneers who came to this county were Dr. Thomas Walker, a physician and surveyor, and a small company of men who together explored the rim of the Cumberland Mountains and found a pass for the Loyal Land Company. The "gap" through this solid mass of rock was found on April 13, 1750. Walker's party of men built the first log cabin in Kentucky, and stayed the winter about six miles from the present site of Barbourville. It was Dr. Thomas Walker who named the Cumberland Mountains and Cumberland River for the Duke of Cumberland, son of George II, King of England. Later, Knox County was crossed by the Wilderness Road, east of Barbourville. Many pioneers and hunters used this trail on their way to settle the rich, wild land west of the Allegheny Mountains.

Barbourville, the county seat, was founded in 1800 and named for James Barbour, who provided the site for the town. Although there is no evidence of it, Barbourville is said to have had a horsedrawn sheet railway system in the early 1900's. Barbourville was the site of the first Civil War battle in Kentucky, which took place at the intersection of Cumberland Avenue and Daniel Boone Drive.

FAIRS, FESTIVALS

Daniel Boone Festival — Barbourville, Court Square. Celebration commemorates Cherokee Treaty. Long-rifle shooting contest between Kentucky Team and another state. Beauty contest. Long-rifle Queen crowned. Barbecue, parade, music and entertainment. October.

Knox County Fair — Barbourville. Fairgrounds. July.

PARKS, RECREATION

Dr. Thomas Walker State Shrine — Barbourville. KY-459. Replica of first log cabin built in Kentucky. Park recreation area, amphitheater. Dr. Walker discovered Cumberland Gap in 1750. 12-acre park has picnic area and playground. Admission free. Open year round.

OLD BUILDINGS

First Cabin in Kentucky — Barbourville. US-25 and Knox St. Near here is site of first structure built in Kentucky by a white man in April, 1750. Erected by Dr. Thomas Walker's party while exploring in the interest of the Loyal Land Co.

OTHER POINTS OF INTEREST

Civil War Actions — 1 1/2 mi. N. of Barbourville. US-25E. First Civil War skirmish in eastern Kentucky, Sept. 19, 1861.

Union College — Barbourville, College St. Established 1879. United Methodist Church affiliate since 1888. The classroom building, a landmark on the Union College campus, has been listed on the National Register of Historic Places. Many Lincoln momentos on display at Speed Hill. A Civil War Home Guard flag sewn by local people is also on display. Legend relates the flag was hidden in a featherbed mattress when Confederates entered the town in 1861.

Courthouse in Barbourville.

Laurel County

In 1825 Laurel County was the eightieth created in the formation of Kentucky Counties and was formed from parts of Rockcastle, Clay, Knox and Whitley Counties. It was named for the growth of mountain laurel along the banks of its many rivers and streams.

London, the county seat of Laurel County, was, for one day, the capital of Kentucky, after the assassination of Governor Goebel on January 31, 1900.

Bernstadt, a thriving community located west of London, is known as Kentucky's first site of mass immigration. It was settled by Swiss immigrants in 1881, and it is still known for its exceptional homemade cheeses.

FESTIVALS

Laurel County Homecoming — London. Levi Jackson Park. Full moon weekend in August.

PARKS, RECREATION, LAKES

Bittersweet Trail — Berea to London. US-25.

Indian Trail — Daniel Boone National Forest. London. KY-80. Scenic lookout.

Levi Jackson Wilderness Road State Park — London. KY-229, off US-25-I-75. Wilderness Road and Boone's pioneer trails both start here.

Wood Creek Lake — Bernstadt. Off I-75. Reservoir, fishing.

MARKERS

Defeated Camp-McNitt's Defeat — 2 mi. S. of London. US-25. In 1786 pioneers camped here for the night and were attacked by Indians. Nearly all were slain or captured.

The Hazel Patch — 7 mi. N. of London. Off US-25S. At the foot of Wildcat Mountain, site of a Civil War battle located on Skaggs Trace and Boone Trace on the Wilderness Trail. Site of Wood's blockhouse, built in 1793. This was the earliest permanent building in the wilderness.

Swiss Colony — Bernstadt. KY-80. Founded 1881. Kentucky's first mass immigration site. Colonized by 336 farmers, mostly from Bern, Switzerland. Colonists credited with improved farming methods, as well as with cheese and wine production.

The Wilderness Road — London. US-25. Opened Kentucky and the west to rapid settlement and major development. First wagon road built in Kentucky in 1796 from Crab Orchard to Cumberland Gap. Became principal highway which served as a turnpike "toll road" for 80 years.

Wilderness Road Inn — 1/2 mi. S. of Levi Jackson Wilderness Road State Park entrance. KY-229. Site of the home-tavern built in 1804 by John Freeman on a Revolutionary War land grant. The tavern stood beside historic Wilderness Road. Tavern burned 1962. Freeman (1761-1841) grave nearby.

MUSEUMS

McHargue's Mill — London, Levi Jackson Wilderness Road State Park. KY-229, off US-25 and I-75. Mill still in working order. Contains one of the world's largest millstone collections.

Mountain Life Museum — London, Levi Jackson Wilderness Road State Park. KY-229, off US-25 and I-75. Reproduction of pioneer settlement, complete with log buildings.

Laurel Lake Spillway.

CEMETERIES

Wildcat Mountain Burial Ground — 7 mi. N. of London, on top of Wildcat Mountain. Off US-25S. Battleground and burial ground of Civil War skirmish.

OTHER POINTS OF INTEREST

Sue Bennett College — London. KY-192. Established 1897. Methodist affiliate.

Mountain Life Museum.

McHargue's Mill at Levi Jackson State Park.

Tobacco in Kentucky.

Rockcastle County

Rockcastle County lies in the foothills of the Cumberland Mountains. It was formed in 1810 as the fifty-second county to be established in Kentucky, from portions of Lincoln, Pulaski, Madison and Knox Counties.

In 1767, Isaac Lindsey, a pioneer hunter, came upon a rock which, on close observance, resembled an ancient castle. The river flowing nearby was then named Rockcastle, and in later years the new county was also given the same name.

Mount Vernon, the county seat, was incorporated in 1817 and originally called "The Mount". Later, the name was lengthened to Mount Vernon in honor of George Washington's home on the Potomac.

Mount Vernon and other small communities in Rockcastle County played an important role during the Civil War. The county was the center of main trails for the armies of both the North and South. After the Battle of Perryville, Confederates, led by General Braxton Bragg, retreated through Mount Vernon eastward through the Cumberland Gap in order to escape the pursuing Union detachments.

Rockcastle County is rich in natural resources. Coal, limestone, clay and timber, farming and livestock are the leading factors in the county's economy. Country music has played an important role in the county's history, as a settlement north of Mount Vernon pioneered this American music style. John Lair, the "father" of Renfro Valley, originated the Renfro Valley Barn Dance so that the traditions and customs of country and folk music could be preserved throughout the years.

FAIRS, FESTIVALS

Bluegrass Festival — Renfro Valley. Off I-75 on US-25. Three continuous days of Bluegrass music by professional and amateur musicians. July.

Annual John Lair Day and Annual Renfro Valley Homecoming — Renfro Valley. US-25. Renfro Valley country music shows, amateur talent contest. First weekend in July.

Little World's Fair — Brodhead. US-150. Horse and cattle shows, exhibits, midway and entertainment. August.

Old Time Fiddler's Convention — Renfro Valley. Off I-75 on US-25. Professional and amateur fiddlers. June.

Renfro Valley Barn Dance and Renfro Valley Jamboree — Renfro Valley. Off I-75 on US-25. Features country music; Sunday morning gatherings for gospel singing. Nationally known center for broadcasting country and bluegrass music. Each Saturday night during summer months.

Renfro Valley Rodeo — Renfro valley. Off I-75, on US-25. August.

Rockcastle County Saddle Club Horse Show — Renfro Valley. Off I-75, on US-25. Sponsored by largest saddle club in Kentucky. July.

LAKES

Lake Linville — Renfro Valley, off US-25 and I-75. Provides water supply for majority of Rockcastle County. Camping, fishing, boating.

Rockcastle River Narrows — 7 mi. from London. KY-192, onto country road for 10 mi. There are signs on KY-192. One of Kentucky's wild rivers. Canoeing, fishing and hiking.

Fort Sequoyah — Livingston. US- 25. Riverboat tour. Train rides, Indian dances, jewelry. Open daily during summer months and on weekends.

MARKERS

CSA Returns to Tennessee — Mt. Vernon. US-25, US-150. After Battle of Perryville, Oct. 8, 1862, Confederate forces retired to Bryantsville. Gen. Braxton Bragg began retreat Oct. 13 and moved through here with USA in pursuit.

MUSEUMS

Renfro Valley Museum — Renfro Valley. Off I-75, on

River Boat at Livingston.

Saltpetre Cave at Mount Vernon.

US-25. Displays of pioneer furniture, clothing, tools, firearms, and early American folk music.

CEMETERIES

Renfro Valley Cemetery — Renfro Valley. US-25. Many early pioneers buried are here: Col. William Fish, owner of original Renfro Valley home; Ann Logan, wife of Col. Fish and daughter of Nathanial Logan; William Hayes, Indian fighter, ancestor of Capt. Jack Hayes and Peasley Hiatt.

OLD BUILDINGS

Chasteen House — Renfro Valley. Off US-25. Oldest house in Rockcastle County. House erected without nails.

OTHER POINTS OF INTEREST

Castle Rock — 3 mi. N. of Livingston. KY-490. Named in 1767 by Isaac Lindsey. Rock resembling castle was source of the name for Rockcastle River and Rockcastle County.

Saltpetre Cave — Mount Vernon. KY-104. Cave extends through a mountain with openings at each end. Cave was a source for gunpowder production from 1797 through Civil War. Large rooms inside cave with streams of water flowing through permitted war operations inside of cave. Museum gives history of cave. Open for tours.

Wildcat Mountain — Livingston. Off US-25. Site of historic Civil War battle.

Whitley County

Whitley County was the fifty-ninth county created in Kentucky and was formed from part of Knox County in 1818. The newly formed county was named in honor of Colonel William Whitley, an early Kentucky settler and Indian fighter who led a body of troops to protect travellers along the Wilderness Road, and also served under Isaac Shelby in the War of 1812. The founders of Whitley County included John F. Sharp and Brinton Litton, who served as representatives from the county in the State Assembly during its formative years.

The county's northern boundary is formed by the Laurel River, while the southern boundary is formed by the Tennessee state line. A major portion of the area is included in The Daniel Boone National Forest, and there are large deposits of coal.

Williamsburg, the county seat, established in 1818, lies near the center of the county and has a population of approximately 5,000.

Corbin, the largest population center in the area, is considered unique due to its location at the point where two other counties, Knox and Laurel, join; therefore, the city has sections in all three counties.

An area noted for its unusual natural attractions, Whitley County is the site of the beautiful Cumberland Falls, known as the "Niagara of the South." Here the waters of the Cumberland River fall sixty-two feet over a precipice of solid rock, just below a fifty-foot stretch of rapids. The falls have gained world renown for a remarkable "moonbow," one of two in the world. The other is at Victoria Falls in Africa. The moonbow is visible during the phase of the full moon.

FAIRS, FESTIVALS

Nibroc Festival — Corbin. Presentation of distinguished citizens awards; crowning of Queen Nibroc. Nibroc is Corbin spelled backwards. Parades, square dancing, horse show, entertainment. August.

Whitley County Fair — Williamsburg. September.

PARKS

Daniel Boone National Forest — Corbin. 460,000 acres of timberland, as well as, native plants and wildlife protect easily eroded soils on hills and mountainsides of Kentucky.

Cumberland Falls State Resort Park — S.W. of Corbin. US-25W. Famous for the most impressive waterfall east of the Rockies. Lodge and cottages, swimming, fishing, horseback riding, hiking, picnicking, square dancing.

MARKERS

"Aunt Julia Marcum" — Williamsburg, Courthouse yard. US-25W. Marker commemorates her patriotism, reciting that she was the only woman fighter to receive a U. S. pension by special act of Congress. She lost an eye and was badly wounded defending home against marauders in Civil War.

Pioneer Hero-Heroine — Williamsburg. KY-92. Graves of Capt. Charles Gatliff and wife. During Revolution he fought against Indians on Virginia frontier and came to Kentucky in 1779. Wife and 4 children were among 250 captives taken in 1780 at Martin's Station in Bourbon County and taken to Detroit by British and Indians. In 13 years his wife made her way back to Virginia while Gatliff fought in many Indian campaigns. When reunited, they settled here on land grant in 1793.

Scott's Raid — Williamsburg, Courthouse yard. US-25W. Commemorates raids of CSA Col. John S. Scott out of Tennessee.

Dr. Thomas Walker — Williamsburg, near Three Point. KY-26. Marker commemorates the arrival of the first white men, Dr. Thomas Walker and his party, to the area and their stop at Blakes Fork on April 26-27, 1759.

OTHER POINTS OF INTEREST

Cumberland College — Williamsburg. Established 1889. It is one of the largest private colleges in Kentucky. Fully accredited Baptist senior college.

Niagra of the South.

Travel Notes

Travel Notes